SHREDDERS!

JAW BONE

SHREDDERS!
The Oral History Of Speed
Guitar (And More)
GREG PRATO

'During that time, it was
guitar players galore. Every
band had a virtuoso guitar
player.' **MARK WOOD**

A Jawbone book
First edition 2017
Published in the UK and the USA
by Jawbone Press
3.1D Union Court,
20–22 Union Road,
London SW4 6JP,
England
www.jawbonepress.com

ISBN 978-1-911036-21-0

The photographs in this book are
from the following sources: front
and back covers, foreword, and
all player portraits in the first plate
section © Richard Galbraith. All
player portraits in the second
plate section © Steven J.
Messina, except: Curt Kirkwood
© Greg Prato; Mark Wood ©
Maryanne Bilham. Uli Roth photo
courtesy of UDR Music.

EDITOR Tom Seabrook
JACKET DESIGN Mark Case

Printed in China

1 2 3 4 5 21 20 19 18 17

CONTENTS

FOREWORD
by alex lifeson

On these pages, Greg Prato has delivered a fascinating presentation of not only the history but the personal observations of all things rock guitar from many of the great guitarists of the past half-century, in their own words.

A clear, in-depth chronicle told honestly from the perspective of the players who have learned and showcased their skills from a long line of talented predecessors and providing an insight that frankly could not come from a casual observer.

In these chapters, the reader will glean a bounty of information regarding individual players and their impact on the music scene of the time—opinions on technique and gear, the value and differing forms of practice, support from the industry, and many other points of interest.

For anyone with a deep interest in the role rock guitar and its diverse myriad of players have played, *Shredders!* will satisfy completely.

ALEX LIFESON
NOVEMBER 2016

INTRODUCTION
by greg prato

'How fast can you play?'
'What make/model guitar do you have?'
'Who is better, Van Halen or Vai?'

All common and seemingly important questions if you were a guitar-playing teenager living on Long Island, New York, in the mid-to-late 80s—as yours truly was.

For much of the decade, if you were to tune into MTV, flip through the pages of a publication aimed at guitarists, or stroll through your local store that sold musical instruments, you were exposed to what is now called 'shred'— guitarists who spent many an hour in their bedroom, perfecting their playing … and poses. In fact, for some, being able to show off your skills on the six-string was the most crucial component of their musical expression.

And as a result, it was very necessary for grunge and alternative rock to 'cleanse the pallet' in the early 90s, and get the focus back to the importance of songwriting and quality of lyrical content. But throughout my changing music listening tastes, I never parted ways with my trusty recordings of Van Halen/DLR, Rush, Thin Lizzy, Queen, King's X, King Crimson, Jimi Hendrix, Jeff Beck, and Steve Vai's *Flex-Able*—and continued to listen/inspect them throughout the years.

In fact, if you were to ask me, post-grunge, what one of my favorite rock concerts I've ever witnessed in my life was, I would most definitely have said the David Lee Roth/*Eat 'Em And Smile* tour stop at Nassau Coliseum (on Saturday,

THE AUTHOR HARD AT WORK, 1986.

January 23 1987, to be exact)—which of course spotlighted the exceptional talents of both Steve Vai and Billy Sheehan.

But over the years, I have always wondered what a lot of the guitarists that I spent so much time reading about and listening to way back when were currently up to. And after going on a serious 80s-guitar listening spree (*Not Of This Earth*, *Surfing With The Alien*, *Eat 'Em And Smile*, *Disturbing The Peace*, *Master Of Puppets*, etc.), I was determined to do what was right, and tell the story of the shred movement that thrived throughout the 80s, hit hard times in the 90s, and then was seemingly reborn—as nimble-fingered as ever—in the early twenty-first century.

After conducting nearly seventy all-new interviews with shredders past and present (as well as a few 'anti-shredders,' to get both sides of the story), I believe for the first time ever, we now have the full story of speed guitar.

Prepare for blast off!

GREG PRATO

QUESTIONS? COMMENTS? FEEL FREE TO EMAIL ME: GREGPRATO@YAHOO.COM

CAST OF CHARACTERS

pre-
shred

A study of the guitarists who helped pave the way for the shredders of the 80s and beyond.

JOE SATRIANI [Chickenfoot guitarist; solo artist] Y'know, the funny thing about decades is sometimes they don't start until a few years into them. It's sort of like the 60s didn't really start until the mid 60s. It's funny how we think in terms of the beginning of the decade, but sometimes, it takes a while to get over the previous one. So, when I think about those 80s guitar players, I guess I'm still reeling from what happened in the 70s. Van Halen came along really late in the 70s.

TREY AZAGTHOTH [Morbid Angel guitarist] For me, we must include the late 70s, because back then, there were many amazing bands and guitarists that I grew up on, and of course, Eddie Van Halen was one of them. Many continued into the 80s and after, but I think the late 70s is a better timeline to start with when discussing epic guitarists and innovation. I also really got into people such as Frank Marino, Uli Roth, Robin Trower, and Tony Iommi, to name a few. The late 70s had some pretty amazing 'feeling' bands that we just can't leave out—Foghat, Blue Öyster Cult, UFO, Scorpions, Judas Priest, Rush, Blackfoot, and the list goes on.

WOLF MARSHALL [magazine columnist, editor, tablature transcriber] Although the 80s was an explosion—that came almost out of nowhere—if you look back at the roots, you started to see the underground. Uli Roth, that's one guy. He was definitely a precursor of Yngwie. Allan Holdsworth. Although he was in jazz-rock, Van Halen was listening to him. So they were there, but they were just underneath the surface. The Scorpions weren't as popular back in 1977 as they were when they were doing 'No One Like You,' but if you were into rock guitar, you knew about them and you knew they had a great guitar player. And before that, Michael Schenker. And I loved the Michael Schenker Group and I loved him with UFO. So all those things were the beginning of that 80s movement.

CRAIG GOLDY [Rough Cutt, Giuffria, Dio guitarist; solo artist] Always, in my book, it is going to be Ritchie Blackmore—he set his foundation before, in the 70s.

TREY AZAGTHOTH Guitarists such as Frank Marino were presenting guitar playing and tones from a more psychedelic realm of imagination, applied to the use of musical theory and other tools.

FRANK GAMBALE [Chick Corea Elektric Band, Vital Information guitarist; solo artist] All those great fusion bands of the 70s—Return To Forever, Frank Zappa to some degree, Jean-Luc Ponty, Weather Report—really inspired us. And people like myself were just following in the great tradition of what we knew and loved, in terms of that kind of music.

TY TABOR [King's X guitarist; solo artist] I'll be honest with you—the 80s were a depressing time for me musically, and for guitar. I recognized there were some legendary players to come out of the 80s, that I loved listening to and that I still listen to. I still put on Satch [Joe Satriani] records from then. I still listen to the great guitarists of the 80s. But when you take those three or four guitarists out of the picture, music in general was somewhat a sad state of affairs for guitar—as far as I was concerned—in the 80s, coming out of the 70s.

The 70s was all about guitar. Every huge band up until disco … and even during disco, there were huge rock bands out there, playing big gigs. But the early-to-mid 70s was just 'guitar extravaganza.' It was two guitars, bass, and drums in pretty much every rock band. Unless it was Led Zeppelin, with one guitar. But it was just in your face, unbelievable, God-like guitar playing throughout the 70s. Whether it be Humble Pie, Peter Frampton himself, all of the British rock bands from that time that we all were listening to.

For me, that was a really healthy, amazing time in music for rock guitar. And there were still a lot of independent FM stations all over the countries. It changed during the 70s, but at the start of the 70s, they were still there, and regions played different music from other regions. There wasn't a national playlist yet. There was no 'company' that was going to buy out all of America's music at that time. That happened in the 80s. And that was an incredibly, horribly depressing time, where I felt rock music was crushed by industry. Crushed by the machine, by conformity, by making it 'You must sound *this way*, look *this way* to get a deal anymore.' And it was now all calculated. That was how I feel about the 80s, to be honest with you. Van Halen wasn't that—they were the real deal that everybody copied.

MICHAEL SCHENKER [Scorpions, UFO, Michael Schenker Group, Temple Of Rock guitarist] I feel what original people created in the 70s, it was something used later in the 80s. But it was simplified. If you listen to drums—the drums went, one bass drum, one snare drum. Keeping it very simple. The snare became very loud and took up a lot of space. Lead guitar playing wasn't necessarily simplified, but it lost a lot of feel. It became technical. Drums became very primitive and guitar playing became very technical. It was more commercial.

The Scorpions, they basically copied everything UFO did. So whenever UFO would release an album, one year later, the Scorpions would release an album with similar stuff on it. They used to come to my home and listen to my latest compositions, and I didn't think much of it. But I guess in the 70s, my contribution was important for the 80s. Bands like the Scorpions simplified it and made it more acceptable for the wide mass—the people who really cannot get that deep, but with a good packaging for the eye and playing it in a simple way that makes the people who watch them [think], 'Oh … maybe I can do this, too!' It made it more accessible.

BRUCE KULICK [Kiss, Union, Grand Funk Railroad guitarist; solo artist] The guitar is an extremely personal instrument that has every element of how you finger the chords or notes, and the vibrato and the intention that you play it how well next to the fret, and how you pick the guitar, where you choose to pick it—is it an up-stroke, down-stroke, pull-off, hammer-on. The amount of techniques is why I think it's such a popular instrument. You go back enough years in history, it was a different instrument—with Benny Goodman, it was with wind instruments. The guitar wasn't huge—it was just becoming popular once they could amplify it and strings got lighter. And then, by the 60s, it took over. And it's continued to take over … especially in the 80s.

STEVE LYNCH [Autograph guitarist] Our predecessors in the 60s and the 70s—without them, the 80s players would have never happened.

eddie

The man who ushered in the shredder
craze of the 80s … Eddie Van Halen.

STEVE VAI [Frank Zappa, Alcatrazz, David Lee Roth, Whitesnake guitarist; solo artist] When I look back at it, there's really a few guitar players that just came and created a paradigm shift on the instrument. And in my life, it was Jimi Hendrix and Edward Van Halen. I was in college when I heard Edward, and it was a revelation. He had definitely raised the bar with innovation and sound and tone—that was unprecedented at the time. And it was a form of 'shredding,' so to speak.

JOE SATRIANI The first time I heard him, I thought, 'That's *exactly* what I want to be doing. And that sounds like what I've been doing with my friends for a couple of years, but no one let us do it.' [*Laughs*] I was so happy when the world accepted Van Halen's guitar sound as a new paradigm.

ADRIAN BELEW [Frank Zappa, David Bowie, Talking Heads, King Crimson guitarist; solo artist] I saw Eddie Van Halen right before Van Halen made it big. I was still rehearsing with Frank [Zappa] in LA, and one night, I went to the Whisky A Go-Go, and Van Halen was playing there. And I was already doing what they call right-handed fretting, where you put your finger on the neck with your right hand and do trills and things. I was already doing that, and I didn't know that anyone else in the world was doing it. So when I saw him do it, it kind of astounded me—that he was doing it better than I was.

DAVE MENIKETTI [Y&T singer-guitarist] I remember when they opened for us in LA a couple of times, I sat out there in the audience and watched them each time, and thought, 'This is completely different. I have not seen anybody else do stuff like this before.' And that's how it was for everybody—it was a shock.

STEVE STEVENS [Billy Idol, Michael Jackson, Vince Neil, Bozzio Levin Stevens guitarist; solo artist] I was at a raging party the first time someone put on the first Van Halen record. And it got to 'Eruption,' and I literally ran across the room—this is the days of turntables—lifted up the needle and put it back on, and asked the person whose party it was, 'Who the fuck is this?!'

Eddie was a total, complete assault. Not only technically, but the sound of his guitar was astounding at that point. It's funny, because the band that I was in before Billy Idol, we were called The Fine Malibus, and I was in a loft on 30th Street in Manhattan with them, and I had access to all the best 'amp tweakers' at that time, and I had kind of run a parallel path of wanting to use original, old Plexi Marshalls and doctoring the amps. I had an 'amp guru' named Henry Yee, and we came upon very similar thoughts about guitar sounds. And as I learned what Ed was doing, there was a lot of similarities. I just thought, 'This guy really nailed it—exactly what I thought rock guitar should sound like.'

K.K. DOWNING [Judas Priest guitarist] Extremely influential. Guitar players come along every now and again and set the benchmark—and I think Eddie did that. Actually, I'm in my office now, and I've got a really great picture of me and Eddie— just the two of us—drinking a bottle of beer. I think it's in Seattle, somewhere. We look like just a couple of young, snot-face kids! We got to hang out quite a bit—in their early days, they would come to Priest shows. But I think the first time I saw Eddie play live was supporting Black Sabbath in my hometown, Birmingham, with their first album. And they certainly packed a punch—that's for sure. But the thing that I liked about Eddie's playing more than anything else was how absolutely precise he is as a guitar player. A very clean and precise player. Really tight. And he certainly had his own style and technique. And that's what all the great players have.

JEFF WATSON [Night Ranger guitarist; solo artist] Eddie was out early. I heard that right as I was leaving my band to start Ranger.* And we were just blown away by Ed.

---

* Night Ranger's early name.

He really changed the landscape for guitar players—with his tone and approach to rhythm guitar I think was really monumentally different than everybody else's approach. Y'know, sliding notes in between and not just doing barre chords and strumming—he was really using it as a rhythmic/melodic instrument at the same time. Which was really counterpoint to the vocals, and I thought really made the band fly.

JAS OBRECHT [Guitar Player editor, 1978–99] When I first saw Eddie Van Halen play in 1978, I thought that if musicians were rated like light bulbs, this guy would be 160 watts. His playing was incandescent. Onstage and [on] record, he was uninhibited and absolutely fearless. He not only played brilliant rhythm parts and wonderfully melodic solos, he expanded the boundaries of rock guitar in a way no one had done since Jimi Hendrix. His playing, especially on the instrumental, 'Eruption,' upped the game for everyone.

The technique of tapping the fingerboard had been around for decades, but it was sparsely practiced, and almost always as a novelty. Eddie brought finger tapping into mainstream rock'n'roll. He spread the gospel of tapping even further with his solo on Michael Jackson's 'Beat It,' which was heard by millions of people around the world. And credit where credit is due: the distinctive rhythm guitar on that song was played by Steve Lukather.

Eddie did all this with a Strat-style guitar that he'd 'slapped together' himself from various parts, and decorated with black electrician's tape and Schwinn bicycle paint. His outfitting the guitar with a single humbucking P-90 pickup helped him create a unique sound on his early albums.

His impact was enormous. Within six months of the release of the first Van Halen album, young guitarists all across the country and in Europe—and especially Japan—were sporting copycat guitars and playing pale versions of 'Eruption.' But no one surpassed the original, because the real genius of Eddie Van Halen has always been in his hands and his imagination. I saw this myself one day in 1980, when Eddie showed me how he plays 'Eruption.' He did this with an unplugged Strat, and you know what? The whole song was there.

TONY MACALPINE [solo artist] I remember the first Van Halen record when it came out, I was eighteen years old and I was really way into that—that whole thing, that whole energy, and Eddie with the hand-built guitars and everything. I was really into the whole persona. It was really influential for me.

GREG HOWE [Howe II, Michael Jackson, Enrique Iglesias, 'N Sync, Justin Timberlake guitarist; solo artist] He was probably my biggest influence, because prior to that, I had played guitar, but really never took official lessons. I took three guitar lessons in my life. Didn't learn anything, so I kind of learned on my own, and eventually discovered pentatonic scales and found as a teenager that it was pretty easy for me to play along with Led Zeppelin records, and play along with Jimmy Page. I figured, 'Well, this isn't very difficult, so I guess there's not much to this.'

And then I heard Van Halen, and it was a completely different level of guitar playing—in terms of technique, at least. And there were so many things that I heard him doing that I had just not heard prior to that. It really inspired me and got me really interested. I was the young kid who wanted to 'crack the code.' In a certain way, even though there probably wasn't as much a musical quest with my trying to transcribe his licks at first, it eventually led down that path. So I got very interested in guitar for probably the wrong reasons at first—because of wanting to figure out what Van Halen was doing. And then through that, I became a much better player, and became much more interested in music. He was probably my biggest influence.

PAUL GILBERT [Racer X, Mr. Big guitarist; solo artist] I was lucky enough to hear Eddie Van Halen after I played guitar for a couple of years—with Jimmy Page as my idol, and with The Beatles as some of my musical foundation. Eddie Van Halen is 100 percent great, and he unintentionally really messed up a lot of guitar players—because everybody was so enamored with the flashy parts that it knocked a lot of people off balance. It's funny to see the repercussions of it. The 'Eddie Van Halen bomb' went off and it destroyed a lot of people's rhythm. [*Laughs*] Which is funny, because he has such good rhythm. But it's not his fault—it's the listener's fault for just listening to 'Eruption' and nothing else.

At that guitar stage of my life, to me, the thing that made a guitar player a professional/listenable/awesome guitar player was their vibrato. And all those guys had stunning vibrato—in the same way that you would listen to Mick Ralphs, early Ace Frehley solos on Kiss records, Gary Moore, Michael Schenker, and Brian May. Their vibrato was 'the signature.' And to this day, Yngwie, man, his vibrato is one of the most beautiful things. My impression is it just gets completely ignored, because of the flashy parts. So like everybody else, I was drawn to the flash, but hopefully, in my own playing, I managed to not be seduced by only that. And I think so much of the guitar community just forgot about rhythm and vibrato and a lot of essential, beautiful, musical things, that again, was all there in Eddie,

Yngwie, and Randy's playing. For some reason, they were so exciting 'athletically,' that it just knocked everybody off their feet. And when they picked themselves up, all they could see with that was the athleticism.

DAVE MENIKETTI He was one of a kind—especially how he was using his picking hand, as well. I won't say that no one else was doing it, but with his tone, he was doing a lot of semi-muting picking stuff, that was really distinctive for the style of songs that they were doing—such as 'Ain't Takin' 'Bout Love,' where it's obvious he's not just picking the strings in a standard way. He is, but he's using his palm to 'mute pick' a lot, as well. That's part of what he was doing, as well. Again, not unusual, but given with that and all the other things he was doing, it made for a distinctive sound for him.

MARTY FRIEDMAN [Cacophony, Megadeth guitarist; solo artist] I fell in love with Eddie Van Halen's guitar tone, and believe it or not, I think the best thing about his playing is the stuff that he does when he's not doing that finger tapping stuff. That never appealed to me, although it probably influenced more young guitarists than any other thing in the history of guitar. I would suggest listening to what he does between all that finger tapping and you'll find some fantastic, juicy-ass phrasing. Man, that guy is a natural. Love it.

ALEX SKOLNICK [Testament, Alex Skolnick Trio guitarist] Van Halen the group, the music crossed over to the mainstream in a way that Yngwie's didn't, and even Ozzy, for as popular as his music was. Van Halen had mainstream hits, guest appearances with Michael Jackson. Across the board inspired guitar playing—way beyond the hard rock genre. I think he got unfairly overshadowed by his own innovations. His two-handed technique and speed just became so identified with him, yet, there were many great musical innovations that he did, that I think were not appreciated enough. Such as his sense of rhythm, his timing, his personality in his playing, his innovations with certain unique phrases … I could go on and on. So I think Eddie Van Halen is just in another whole category by himself.

TY TABOR When I heard Eddie Van Halen, my jaw hit the ground. I just thought, 'I might as well quit. This is the most amazing thing I've ever heard.' And different from what other people were playing at the time. The same thing happened when I heard Satriani and several really great players in the 80s. But it was a different kind of thing. It was like, technical excellence with heart. And I had not heard those two put together in a long time. In the 70s, you had guys that played from the heart, but weren't necessarily technically awesome. And then you had technical players who were from the other side of the brain, and just left me totally cold. Well, the 80s brought the first group of guitarists I remember that put those two together. Eddie Van Halen is a good example of it—he was technically amazing, and yet he played from the heart. Yngwie, as much as I totally recognize his impact and influence, I personally wasn't really listening to him at all back then. But Eddie Van Halen, for sure. I mean, you couldn't get away from it.

EDDIE VAN HALEN WOULD HAVE A BIG IMPACT ON
METAL GUITARISTS IN BRITAIN, TOO ...

BRIAN TATLER [Diamond Head guitarist] I guess it was similar—everyone was blown away by 'Eruption,' we all had to have a go at that. I was amazed at how he could get such a great sound with one guitar. There is very little or no double tracking on the first six Van Halen albums—he could perform in the studio, which I found really difficult to do. He would throw little licks in as he went through the track. I could not do that—I would have to concentrate on getting a rhythm track down, then add a solo. But Eddie seemed to be able to do it all in one, giving it a very loose feel. Incredible stuff. How did he manage to get such a brilliant riff out of just an A-minor chord in 'Ain't Talkin' 'Bout Love'? I probably picked up on the speed of 'I'm The One' and 'Atomic Punk' for early Diamond Head. One of my favorite middle eights of all time is 'Panama.'

BILLY SHEEHAN [Talas, David Lee Roth, Mr. Big, The Winery Dogs bassist; solo artist] We had sat down a couple of times and he showed me some cool stuff. He's a wonderful guy and very generous with his knowledge. Touring with them in 1980 [when Billy was in Talas] was a great revelation—in many ways. Our first meeting with Eddie, Talas was in a dressing room—on the first night of the first show. The room was an L-shaped room, so I was sitting at one part where I could see the door. No one else in the room could see the door. The door opened and Ed walked in. I remember later on, the guys said, 'You should have seen the look on your face,' because here comes Ed, he walks in, and goes, 'Which one of you guys is Billy Sheehan?'

I gathered where he had heard of me from—from Denny Carmassi, because I did a thing with Denny Carmassi and Michael Schenker. So we shook hands and talked a little bit, and we watched the band from the side of the stage a few times.

They were really nice to us—they let us do encores and all that stuff. And at the end of the tour, Ed gave me his phone number, and said, 'I'm going to give you my phone number … but don't tell Michael I gave it to you.' And I thought, 'Oh. That's intriguing.'

So time went on, and sure enough, I saw him on the next tour. They played a show in Buffalo and he said, 'Come up to the hotel room, I've got some music to play you.' The guys in Talas were actually sitting downstairs at a table with David Lee Roth, and I went upstairs to Ed's room, and we're talking. He says, 'What would you do if I asked you to join Van Halen?' And I said, 'I'd say, What plane do you want me on?' And we shook hands, and I thought, 'Did I just get asked to join Van Halen?' Sure enough, I went to another show of theirs, and Dave was there walking past, and he said, 'Hey, I heard that you had a little talk with Ed. I guess we'll see you when the tour is done and we'll see what happens.' I said, 'Wow. Great!' And that was that.

Unfortunately, it fell through at the time. They said, 'We didn't want to make a change,' and I'm glad they did, because I like Michael, and as much as I wanted to be in Van Halen, I felt terrible about popping him out of his gig. And as a fan, I hate to see when bands change. But yeah, they did ask me. And then another time it came again—it was before Dave got back in the band just recently.* I went up to Ed and Al's studio—it's not far from my house. We jammed for a while and thought about doing something again. It's been an ongoing thing, and like I said, it was a great honor that they even thought of me. It didn't work out, but that's OK.

BRUCE KULICK The first time I heard Eddie Van Halen, I was absolutely floored. I was also petrified. Here's a guy who clearly understood very, very passionate lyrical lead playing. I didn't know immediately that he was a fan of Eric Clapton—who is one of my biggest influences. But I guess that's kind of why I responded to his playing, and it didn't really matter if he was going to play very fast—which he could, and that was the intimidating part of his talent. And of course, some of the tricks—between the divebombs or the Floyd Rose whammy bar things and then all the finger tapping. So he really turbocharged the kind of rock lead guitar playing that I loved, and he made me have to 'up my game.'

But I was really, really freaked out when I heard it, because it was so good, and yet so different and unique to me. Certainly, by the time I got the opportunity to

---

* Roth left Van Halen in 1985, before rejoining in 2007.

work with Kiss [in 1984], and especially, I remember the conversation when Paul Stanley said, 'We're sending Mark St. John home. You're the new lead guitarist.' Which I kind of felt was headed in that direction, after about eight weeks on the road with them. He said, 'I want you to be competitive with all the guitar players, and do all the things that are popular now with guitar.' Which is great. It was a good thing from the time that I heard Eddie and from the time I actually had the opportunity to work with Kiss, I did bravely move into that territory. In other words, find a guitar that could have a Floyd Rose on it, see what it would be like to finger tap something, try to play flashy but still with a good melody and emotion— which is something that I always felt people like Eric Clapton, Jeff Beck, and Jimi Hendrix did.

Out of those three guitarists that you mentioned,* for me, Eddie absolutely came from the kind of style of guitar playing that really resonated for me. Once I got over the fear and I started to embrace some of the stuff, and I was actually really influenced by the trickery that I would do with Kiss, when I had a solo on *Crazy Nights* [at the beginning of the song 'No No No'] and I'm doing a whole little hammer-on piece. And no, it wasn't 'Eruption,' but it had elements of Eddie's fancy guitar playing, that took lead playing to another level. I'm still a huge fan, and everything I said about the Eric Clapton connection, I was kind of aware of, but recently in one of the guitar magazines, they shared some audio of Eddie being interviewed and playing note-for-note 'Crossroads.' And it was unbelievable to hear it, because you could still hear that fiery kind of guitar player Eddie is, but he's still playing it 'Eddie-style' but he had all the phrasing of Clapton and all the vibrato down, and that's why he's still at the top of the game.

He was one of the guys that all the lead guitar and approach that I want to use came from—guys like Clapton, Beck, and Hendrix. I always need to mention those guys, because they were such a big influence for me growing up. And of course, there's Leslie West, and the solo that Paul Kossoff does in 'All Right Now'—these are all things that are so important for lead guitar playing. But when it came to going further in time, Eddie Van Halen was the one to take it to the next level, and turbo-charged it.

RONNI LE TEKRØ [TNT guitarist; solo artist] He influenced everybody. For me, it was about his sound—that crunch and definition, that transparent guitar sound of his I've been trying to get through the years. So he was a big inspiration sound-wise,

---

* Eddie Van Halen, Randy Rhoads, and Yngwie Malmsteen.

and his way of playing rhythm guitar and his soloing. He reinvented soloing, you could say.

HANK SHERMANN [Mercyful Fate guitarist] We were used to more old school type of playing from 70s guitar players at that time. Certainly, this guy—bursting with energy, totally in control with all the notes he's playing—to this day, I'm still amazed by the first album, which is still my favorite. It's really amazing what they created on that album. The impact is he changed the way that you could play on the guitar. His solos are pretty harmonic and bluesy, but the way he performed it, is exceptionally fantastic. I started to play guitar in 1977, but I was highly into Ace Frehley of Kiss, who had a much old school approach to the guitar playing. I didn't get into Eddie Van Halen and the first album until much later, though. But I was blown away.

TREY AZAGTHOTH Eddie Van Halen was the one who did the most for helping create the kind of music and guitar playing that mostly had the big impact for me, out of those three guitarists you mention. Eddie was absolutely brilliant and a real visionary. Not just his soloing, but also just how he would pick up a guitar and play. He was one that even if you played on his rig, you can't sound like him, unless you actually play like him—meaning using a similar picking and fretting attack. His playing was so full of dynamics and his flow with the solos, and his rhythms were quite unique and unusual for that time in my opinion.

RICHIE KOTZEN [Poison, Mr. Big guitarist; The Winery Dogs singer-guitarist; solo artist] Back then, I was very young and I was learning a lot, and the first guitar player that I really became obsessed with trying to figure out what he was doing was Eddie Van Halen. Because up until that point, I was playing and I never really thought about guitar players. I thought about playing guitar to play a song—to play a Rolling Stones song or a Beatles song or whatever it was—but I never really got into guitar players for guitar playing sake. And it wasn't until I heard the 'Beat It' solo that I discovered Eddie Van Halen. So it was pretty late in the game—I had been playing for quite a few years, and then suddenly, I discovered Eddie. And that changed everything.

GEORGE LYNCH [Dokken, Lynch Mob guitarist; solo artist] Eddie was just ... I think when a person like that big of a talent and you have the responsibility and having that giant 'voice,' I think sometimes it can do bad things to the rest of your life.

You're going to be a slave to the weight of this gift you have. He never seemed to be particularly happy for some reason … I think now he's probably happier. Difficult to talk to, but probably had things on his mind—like being the world's most famous guitar player!

AUTOGRAPH WERE THE OPENING ACT ON VAN HALEN'S
1984 TOUR, BUT THE BAND'S MEMBERS FOUND FEW
OPPORTUNITIES TO HANG OUT WITH THE HEADLINERS …

STEVE LYNCH [Eddie] was actually very private. He knew who I was, and he wasn't happy about me being on the tour.* He kind of just avoided me, actually. I hung out a little bit with David Lee Roth—we went to the Cheetah in Atlanta, the strip club. That was kind of fun! But the main person that really hung out with us was Michael Anthony. He would come backstage and hang out with us right after the show—almost every show. Just the nicest, down-to-earth guy. He liked hanging out with us—he thought the vibe was really good back in our dressing room. He even hung out on our tour bus. That's the main person I hung out with. Eddie stayed to himself—I didn't bother him and he didn't bother me. I maybe talked to him three times the whole tour.

BRUCE KULICK For me, the Sammy Hagar version of Van Halen really gave the band an opportunity to stretch out in ways I don't think they ever could have done with David Lee Roth. I'm actually a fan of both versions of the band, but where I'll hear many people just want to know about the David Lee Roth era, I don't agree with that. In fact, in some ways, I think some of the stuff they accomplished with Sammy gave more facets of styles of music and let them explore more musical territory. I don't think Eddie's playing changed, it just put him now in another landscape, that was even bigger and broader. But again, I don't want to take away from what they did initially, because his guitar was huge, the songs were amazing—I still get off on hearing 'Panama.'

But when I think of some of the material that I love from the Hagar version of Van Halen, you had a singer who could really reach high notes—and powerfully. Sammy is just an incredible singer. I had a chance to jam with him at the Fantasy Camp, and I've got so much respect for him. But I thought that the songwriting was able then to be more mature. It wasn't always tongue-in-cheek, even though they'd

---

* Supposedly because Steve was utilizing a similar tapping technique.

have fun with some songs. The element of keyboards—which I had no problem with, even though some people may have thought it was crazy—obviously, they experimented with 'Jump' already, but I think they developed incorporating that in their sound much more so during the Sammy Hagar time.

But Eddie's guitar was huge, the playing was great, the songwriting was terrific, there's so many amazing songs. I thought they sounded incredible. There was no downside. Some bands, you change the singer, the whole dynamic gets ruined. And here, it became a whole other animal, that was pretty incredible. I remember seeing them live—going with Eric Carr to see them—and backstage after the show, they're sitting there eating lobster and steak. [*Laughs*] They were always very cool with us. I have a lot of respect for those guys.

BILLY CORGAN [Smashing Pumpkins singer-guitarist; solo artist] Van Halen ushered in this virtuosity—that the virtuosity on the guitar can be 'pop.'

JENNIFER BATTEN [Michael Jackson, Jeff Beck guitarist; solo artist] Number one was Van Halen. He was one of the most inventive, innovative guys out there. He's personally responsible for selling half a million guitars for guys that wanted to play like him.

JAS OBRECHT Eddie showed that you could spend fifty bucks on a guitar body, eighty bucks on a neck, and as he put it, 'Slap it together'—rout the body, stick in a pickup, paint it, and have a beautiful, unique-sounding instrument. Eddie Van Halen opened the door to that whole industry. And all of a sudden, it wasn't that essential to have a '59 Les Paul, pre-CBS Fender Stratocaster, or some other spectacular vintage guitar—you could play something you made yourself and sound good. That's an extraordinary leap, and I think Eddie was largely responsible for the success of those companies. He brought in a whole new spirit of inventiveness.

randy

Ozzy Osbourne guitarist Randy Rhoads shows that classical and metal can coexist.

RUDY SARZO [Quiet Riot, Ozzy Osbourne, Whitesnake, Dio bassist] I first met Randy when I auditioned for Quiet Riot in 1978 and joined the band. I had actually watched him play before, but I did not meet him—so I was aware of his unique style of playing. Especially in Los Angeles, where a lot of guitar players were a little derivative. Randy—because of his musical education that he had, because his family had been musically educated—had a whole different musical background than most of the guys that were playing around town.[*] And it really showed. Not only in his articulation, but also his choice of notes. Quiet Riot was influenced by the sound of the day—glam/British pop, with a little bit of British R&B, like Humble Pie—Randy did stay within the boundaries of that style of music, even though he had a larger musical vocabulary than what was being displayed onstage.

When I started teaching at Musonia, I'd hear him not only going through his lessons, but he would be practicing on his own—in between students—going into the classical territory, that he did not go to when we were rehearsing with Quiet Riot. He started to display more of his musical vocabulary than what I was actually aware of. The only time that I ever heard any reference to Van Halen coming from Randy was when he was teaching, and a student might request to learn a Van Halen song—then he would go and learn it and show the student

---

[*] Randy's mother, Delores, founded the Musonia School of Music, where Randy taught guitar.

how it's played. But I never heard it in his own music, outside of a teaching role. What Randy would do—which is something that I learned from him when I taught at Musonia—was when you're teaching a student, to split your lesson in two halves. One half, teach the student what they want, and the other half, teach the student what they need.

I heard about [Randy's Ozzy tryout] when he went to audition, because he didn't know if he was going to get the gig. He basically went to audition because Dana Strum—who recommended Randy to Ozzy—had been calling him multiple times, and he just wanted Dana to stop calling him. [*Laughs*] So he went to just get it over with. And he got the gig basically when he was just tuning up and noodling on his guitar. Then for a few days, Randy did not really know what it meant to actually *get* the Ozzy gig, because there was really no band. There was no master plan—it was just kind of like, 'Well … now that I've got a guitar player, I've got to put together the rest of the band.' So Ozzy flew back to England, he had Randy join him, and then they put the band together there. Randy was just taking it a day at a time. Quiet Riot was actually breaking up, anyways, because we had just hit a wall—about trying to get a record deal. The bands of our genre— Dokken; there was another incarnation of Mötley Crüe called London, Ratt— nobody was getting signed. Nobody really cared in the music industry for that type of music. They were focusing on new wave and punk. So everybody was really disappointed, and that was the reason why Mrs. Rhoads told Randy, 'Listen, if you want to make something of yourself musically, you're going to have to leave and go to where what you do is actually acceptable.'

Before *Blizzard Of Ozz* was released in the United States, during a break that he had come back from England to visit his family, I got together with him, he played me the record, and I said, 'Wow. This is not he guy I've been playing with in Quiet Riot—this is a whole new level here.' I knew that even before I got to play with him in Ozzy. When we were in Quiet Riot, there were certain musical parameters. He was in a box. We were doing a certain style of music. And Ozzy gave him the opportunity to invent a new style. Something that he had never had the creative freedom to do. Quiet Riot was trying to get a record deal—so we were trying to not only follow a trend, but be in a mold. But with Ozzy, he already had a record deal, and Ozzy told him, 'Listen … *just be yourself.* Write what you want to write.' And that's what came out. There's a unique progression—I say 'unique' because very few artists can make records back-to-back within months of each other. Because remember, *Blizzard* and *Diary* were recorded within months. But if you listen to the first batch of songs—which are very diatonic-based in composition—by the time you go to *Diary Of A Madman*, he had shifted his gear in composition to expand it. Incredible. He was playing songs with multiple key changes and going into a more mature songwriting style—while keeping it 'metal' and heavy. It was like opening up a huge funnel of creativity.

ALEX SKOLNICK Randy was very much a pioneer of the classical feel in hard rock. Taking a classical melodicism and combining that with virtuosity. I guess you could say Ritchie Blackmore had done it, but Randy Rhoads did it in a sort of 'post–Van Halen' way. And he was admittedly inspired by Van Halen—as far as tone and some of the two-handed technique. But he definitely did his own thing with it. I think he had a big impact for a lot of us at that time.

CRAIG GOLDY Randy Rhoads was just so special. It was also more creative than it was dynamically with the tone. He re-revolutionized guitar in a different way—it was more in the songwriting and more of his contribution as a team player and as an individual. Randy's creativity is what stood out the most to me, because it wasn't like he was playing something that was way over my head and way over my skillset. I was able to learn most of what Eddie played, I was able to learn most of what Yngwie played, and I was able to learn everything that Randy did. But what Randy did was unique—as far as how it was created and how it was presented.

JEFF WATSON Randy was such a nice writer. Most of his strength—to me—are within his writing skills. Writing lines and licks and really working solos out beforehand—which is something I do. When I was developing, I stopped listening to guitar players altogether. So I wasn't as aware of Randy until Brad went off to do the Ozzy thing.* And I'd heard a couple of things on the radio, but I didn't buy albums at that point. Randy would incorporate really neat note choices in his rhythms to the songs and would use them as intros.

RUDY SARZO I can give you my point of view as somebody who actually got to play those songs with the band† and my point of view as a fan, because I was not involved in the recording process of the albums. *Blizzard* was a perfect end of the 70s/beginning of the 80s record. To me, that record really segues from one era into the other, because it kind of nudges it forward—not as much as *Diary*. *Diary* was much more of a statement of the new generation. And I've been

---

* Brad Gillis, Jeff's bandmate in Night Ranger.
† Rudy joined the Ozzy band in 1981.

misunderstood in what I'm about to tell you—I was sitting in the bus next to Ozzy when they brought in the final mastering of *Diary*, and he hated the mix! The mix has nothing to do with the songwriting or the performance—it just has to do with the way one person, a mixer or mastering person, envisions what the record sounds like. And 99.9 percent of the time, it's not related to any of the members of the band—it's an engineer. It was such a departure sonically from *Blizzard*—he was expecting *Blizzard Part Two*, as far as the sound goes—not the composition or the performance or the arrangements, but the way it sounded. And it took him a while to really embrace it and actually realize that is the seminal record of what 80s metal was going to sound like.

There's not a bad Randy solo, because he would always compose sections that were different. His solos stood alone. For example, when you're going into 'Believer,' it's a whole different section of the song—it's not like he's soloing over the chorus or a verse or anything like that. Every song, it's something different. 'Steal Away,' the section is a solo section. Even in 'Mr. Crowley,' there is the middle one, where it is kind of like the verse itself, and then it goes into the outro—and that to me is the big solo section. And then he starts doing the circle of fifths, diatonically, to F major. That in itself was another piece, that I think made the song climax. I love 'Tonight,' because it is not your typical metal song—it's very melodic, but it's heavy as hell. 'Little Dolls' is very different, 'Flying High Again,' that's another one that followed the tritone changes during the solo, but it doesn't sound like anything else in the rest of the song. It's related to, but it's very different.

PAUL GILBERT Randy's tone had so much distortion that it was always over the edge. You can hear it if you listen to 'Flying High Again,' he uses all these extra noises, that he's constantly 'battling the fire-breathing dragon,' and the fire is leaking out the edges. That's something you had to deal with then, because everybody used *gobs* of distortion. And to this day, when I teach, the thing that I have to spend so much time with—that anybody who plays with distortion does—if you play one note, you've got to somehow control those other five strings. And it's not really that much of an issue if you play with a clean sound or play an acoustic guitar, because it's just not as sensitive—the guitar is not taking off on its own.

But with a distorted rock guitar—like everybody was playing back then—you really had to alter your technique to deal with that. You had to learn to mute all the other strings and be quick with your volume knob on your guitar, and your pedals. It was not easy to stop. It was fun to hear when all didn't go well and you would get that little feedback. One of my favorite moments is the very first thing you hear on the live Ramones album,* and you just hear this shriek come out of the Marshall stacks—before they even start to play. And you go, 'Man, this is going to be good!' All he did was like, *look* at the guitar, and it went, 'WAAAAAAH!' It was screaming already before he even starts playing.

GEORGE LYNCH Randy was very, very quiet. He was an impressive player—listening to him play classical guitar and electric guitar, he evolved very quickly in the context of playing with Ozzy. I didn't particularly care for him that much when he was in Quiet Riot. Like a lot of us, he dug Eddie a lot, which is pretty hard not to do when you're living in LA at that time, when Eddie was on the rise.

RON 'BUMBLEFOOT' THAL [Guns N' Roses guitarist; solo artist] A person that was a huge impact in the 80s for me was Randy Rhoads. He would put a lot of classical pieces right into the songs.

RONNI LE TEKRØ His classical approach, I think he was definitely 'in there,' like Ritchie Blackmore, in a sense. You could tell he came from some European kind of inspiration. But for being an American guitar player, he wasn't bad at all. [*Laughs*]

RON JARZOMBEK [Watchtower guitarist] What I really like most about Randy is his phrasing. While other guitarists did bring a classical influence into their own music, Randy seemed to incorporate it into a metal framework. He also brought harmonic minor to the forefront—with songs like 'Revelation' and 'Mr. Crowley.'

RUDY SARZO It wasn't like we discussed [classical guitar]—he just did it. All of a sudden, he's gravitating more toward playing classical guitar right before the show, and after soundcheck. And Randy was solely—toward the end—playing classical guitar. So there wasn't much discussion as to 'why you're doing that' or not. I could hear the shift from *Blizzard Of Ozz* to *Diary Of A Madman*—where he wanted to go musically. And there was no question about it—it was just like, 'Oh OK, so I guess the next record is going to be even more in that direction.'

His personality was very laid back. He never really fit the mold of what people would think a rock star would be, because I think he had such a strong foundation in education. I think he behaved more like a teacher than an actual rock star. Although when he got up onstage, he kicked butt, and it shows in

---

* *It's Alive* (1979).

every single photo. But then if you look at every picture of Randy performing live, there is a clarity to what he's doing. It's almost like he's facing the guitar's fretboard toward the camera and the audience—so they can watch what he's playing and learn from that.

PAUL GILBERT I lived in a really small, almost rural town. And of all the places for Randy Rhoads to do a clinic, to have him do it there* … if you wait long enough, weird coincidences will happen. And that's one of them. But I was a huge Randy fan at the time, so of course, I went. My impression of it was he was a super nice, down-to-earth guy, and really willing to share anything that he knew, and just really generous, friendly, and cool. And of course, seeing him live a couple of times, the 'ferocious guitar god/axe-wielding giant' was also apparent and very inspiring.

If anything, remember, this was early 80s, so the gear that was available back then was really different than what you'd find if you walk into a music store now. And the main thing in guitar being that back then, having a Marshall with a master volume wasn't that common. So the only way you could get distortion was by actually cranking it up to stadium rock volume. So when Randy did this clinic, he had a 100-watt Marshall stack—one of the white stacks was there—and he couldn't really play it, because he knew he would *kill* everybody with the volume! So the only disappointing thing was that I really wish he played more in the clinic—he mostly talked.

And I completely understand why, because if he had played, we would have all suffered severe hearing loss right then and there. And his rock style really relied a lot on that sound—that was a big part of it—and it was impossible for him to play with that sound in that situation, of a little music store with that 100-watt amp. It looked great, but everything he played … it might as well have been an acoustic guitar, because it was so clean, because there was just no way he could crank up. It was amazing to see him, but the whole time, I'm going, 'Man, I wish he could play!' And then that night, I went to the Ozzy show, and he blew my socks off—because he could crank it up, and played amazing.

MARTY FRIEDMAN I saw Randy Rhoads when he was on tour with Ozzy—his enthusiasm was absolutely fantastic. Just a 'guitar star,' y'know?

TREY AZAGTHOTH I actually saw Ozzy live with Randy on the *Blizzard Of Ozz*

---

* At the store Music City, in Greensburg, Pennsylvania, on February 2 1982.

tour, and Randy was excellent. One of my fav songs by Randy was 'Believer,' which they actually played at this concert.

KARL SANDERS [Nile guitarist; solo artist] I was in high school when I got the *Blizzard Of Ozz* record. I remember bringing it home, putting it on, and going, 'Holy fucking shit! Listen to that tone ... listen to what that guy's playing ... listen to the fire contained in these tracks!' And I was lucky enough to get to see Randy Rhoads play. I remember me and a schoolmate, we went down to Atlanta on a school night—it was a Wednesday night. It was during the *Diary Of A Madman* tour. And then two or three days later, Randy was killed.*

RUDY SARZO I've had passings in my life, but they had been expected—everything has been expected as 'the circle of life.' But I've never had anything like Randy. Like, he's there one moment, and then I wake up, and he's gone. That is something else. Once I wrote the book,† it gave me closure, because I was able to talk about it. And it also gave me the hope that I didn't have to talk about it again. Every time I talk about it, in my mind, I go there, and it's not a good place to go.

PAUL GILBERT My dad heard it on the radio, and he knew that I was a big fan. So he just came in, and said, 'Hey Paul, I heard some bad news on the radio. That guitar player you're into, Randy Rhoads, just died in a plane crash.' Everything that Randy did was otherworldly. It was great to see him in that clinic—coming down to earth for a moment. But his life and his passing were really beyond my experiences as a fourteen-year-old kid going to high school and playing in garage bands. So it was shocking and it was sad, but it was also real. I think that kind of thing is hard for anybody to take, but especially being that young, there's not much you can do to deal with it—other than learning the music and being inspired by it.

MARK WOOD [solo artist, violinist] Randy Rhoads and I were going to be doing a project—believe it or not—because as you know, Randy was leaving Ozzy at some point. He was not pleased with that. And my producer was good friends with Randy Rhoads, and he was like, 'I just played your stuff for Randy—he loves it. He wants to collaborate.' But unfortunately, he died. So that was a really fascinating moment for my career looking back.

---

* Rhoads died in a plane crash in Leesburg, Florida, on March 19 1982.
† *Off The Rails: Aboard The Crazy Train In The Blizzard Of Ozz* (2008).

BRUCE KULICK Randy Rhoads, I was first turned on to him with Ozzy, and then of course, his tragic passing. I even thought, 'Maybe I can get an audition to be in Ozzy?' I was also kind of freaked out by that, because I knew what Randy did on the guitar, and again, here is a guy … as much as Yngwie had the violin/classical/ Paganini influence, I'm not sure who Randy's influence was. But clearly, here is a guy who played with classical chops, and he was able to supercharge it. And there is no mystery to me how he influenced so many players. But again, being younger than me, I don't know if he was ever a Clapton fan or something like that. But his triple tracking of solos was also a bit alien to me, and not something that is my 'go-to comfort zone.'

So I didn't feel bad not getting the audition with Ozzy, because I didn't think that I was the right guy for it. I mean, fate had something else in store for me that I was absolutely the right guy for. I was never under-qualified, over-qualified … Steve Vai would not fit in Kiss, OK? Yeah, he fit in David Lee Roth because how are you going to top an Eddie Van Halen? And that made sense, even though you knew that wasn't going to last. Steve Vai is an alien on the guitar, and working with David Lee Roth is probably … well, it's kind of like working with some sort of alien kind of person! David Lee Roth is all over the map, from what I read. But getting back to those three guitar players who certainly changed the course of lead guitar, Eddie resounded the closest to me, Randy probably being second, and Yngwie third.

AT ONE POINT, THERE WERE PLANS AFOOT FOR THE OZZY/RANDY/ RUDY/TOMMY ALDRIDGE LINEUP TO RECORD A STUDIO ALBUM …

RUDY SARZO It was going to follow the release of *Speak Of The Devil*. *Speak Of The Devil* was going to be the Black Sabbath re-recordings, with Randy playing guitar—even though he was against it. He sat down with Ozzy and Sharon and they came to terms about it. *Speak Of The Devil* was supposed to be done while we were still touring. It was a hefty touring schedule that actually got cut down because of Randy's passing. So basically, what we actually got to perform were the dates that were booked prior to March 19.

He had a very clear vision, and everybody within our circle knew about it—he wanted to go back to school and get his degree. He had already made connections with some of the people in the New York studio scene. But that doesn't mean that he was not going to continue with Ozzy—he just wanted to expand his musical vocabulary. Which was not the norm thirty-five years ago, but it is the norm today—for musicians to be in multiple projects. I won't go as far as saying he was going to all of a sudden solely become a classical guitar player. I think classical music—even before he started to play with Ozzy—was part of his musical vocabulary, because he grew up playing classical guitar. It's just that now, he could actually find a place to put the classical guitar skills that he had into this own music. He couldn't really do that in Quiet Riot when we were playing on the Strip. But I would go as far as saying I don't think he would solely become a classical guitar player, because he loved playing electric too much.

In two years—or less than two years—he recorded two albums, extensive touring … he was exhausted. Not only exhausted from the traveling and performing—he was exhausted mentally of playing the same songs every night. He found himself in a rut. He just needed to take a break, expand, do something else, and come back to it. Because that was as much a part of him as anything else—he wrote those songs. He just needed to take a break musically, creatively stretch out, and then come back to it. The reason why he wanted to get into the New York studio scene was basically so he could just show up and play different styles of music—get that out of the way, and then go back to what he was doing. The easiest way for anybody to be creative with their instrument—not as a composer, but as a musician, to be able to approach different musical styles—is to do a session. You just show up and play. They give you the music, you perform it, you get some creative fulfillment from doing it and the challenge of it all, and then you go back to your band, and keep doing what you were doing. But boy, that's refreshing. It's a brand new challenge—you do it and you have fun. And then you might even pick up something from a session that you can bring back to what you've been doing all along, and approach it from a different direction. And getting a degree in music was definitely at the top of his list.

BILLY CORGAN Rhoads is interesting that he's coming in after Van Halen, and we don't know where he would have gone. So it's a tragic story in the sense that we only have that one flash of time to really gauge him, where he's at his best. As much as I love Randy Rhoads, I still see him as following Eddie Van Halen.

GEORGE LYNCH I know Randy was influential, but I don't think he had the magnitude that Eddie and Yngwie had. That's just from my perspective, I'm not sure if I'm reading it wrong or not, but I don't hear his influence across the board in the guitar lexicon, as much as I do Yngwie or Eddie—especially Eddie. But yeah, he's one of the big, top-of-the-pile guys, for sure.

DAVE MENIKETTI Any one of these guys—the way that they pick and the way that they have their tone that comes off of their fingers and everything else, it's distinctive enough to where you go, 'That sounds like … ' and that's certainly what Randy had going for him in his short period of time on this earth as a guitar player.

ALEXI LAIHO [Children Of Bodom singer-guitarist] Randy Rhoads, it's funny—I had already heard Steve Vai and Yngwie Malmsteen and all those crazy fuckers, before I ever heard any of the Ozzy stuff, really. When I heard the *Tribute* live album with Randy Rhoads, that was the first Ozzy thing I ever heard. And he really did change … I wouldn't say everything, but he really made a huge difference in my playing, because just the way he carried himself playing live—all the riffs, fills, and solos.

RUDY SARZO Randy, at his worst, was outstanding. At his best, *he was Randy Rhoads.*

Yngwie

**Swedish guitarist Yngwie J. Malmsteen
takes the classical-meets-metal
merger into the stratosphere.**

ALEX SKOLNICK Yngwie also had the classical feel, but he upped the technique level significantly. With Randy Rhoads, you could hear the Bach influence, as well as hard rock, he listened to a lot of the standard hard rock—somebody growing up in the 60s and 70s. But Yngwie Malmsteen brought this mystique, as well as a Paganini or Liszt—one of these classical virtuosos that is rumored to have 'sold their soul.' [*Laughs*] He brought that to guitar, which was very different at the time.

RONNI LE TEKRØ He came out the same time as me. I was playing fast in Scandinavia—at the same time he was around. I like Yngwie, I've met him a few times. We just come from a different approach—I come from Queen and songwriting, he comes from Paganini and Bach.

BILLY CORGAN Malmsteen is different in that he came from the Ritchie Blackmore School of Diminished Minor. [*Laughs*] Even Malmsteen, he benefitted from a generation that had already grown up on … for me, it's hard, because if you're starting from the point of the 80s, Van Halen is already three, four, five years in. To me, I don't put those guys [Eddie, Randy, and Yngwie] as equals in the sense that I think it's always easier to come after somebody.

I'm sure Yngwie Malmsteen would say he didn't give a shit about Eddie Van Halen. And maybe he did and maybe he didn't. And you can make an argument that he lived in a bubble and only listened to the guys that he listened to, starting with Blackmore, and obviously Uli Jon Roth, and maybe some Michael Schenker. That's tough for me, because when somebody follows five or seven years later, the game of figuring it out is infinitely easier.

CRAIG GOLDY Yngwie Malmsteen re-revolutionized guitar as far as that whole melodic minor thing—it sounded like a violin player on rock guitar, if you didn't know any better. Which I didn't at the time. I didn't know what he was doing and how he was doing it. I was just like, 'What the hell is that? And how is he doing that?'

KIRK HAMMETT [Metallica guitarist] You have to understand, with Yngwie, it was a very unique situation. I don't think a lot of people know this, but I first heard Yngwie on the same tape-trading circuit as *No Life 'Til Leather** and the Exodus demo and all these different types of tapes that were being traded on. I heard Yngwie's first demo—before he was signed—and I couldn't believe it. I thought, 'Oh my God … this guy sounds like Ulrich Roth!' I remember bringing that very tape to Joe Satriani, and playing it for Joe, and he said, 'Wow! This guy's really something. He has a lot of technique and he really knows what he's doing.'†

And then there was also a guy in the store—someone's who kind of infamous— his name is Gary Brawer, who used to work at the same store. He sets up all my guitars and a lot of guitars for a lot of musicians—he works in San Francisco. Anyway, Gary piped in with, 'Is he speeding up the tape?' And Joe said, 'No, no, he's not speeding up the tape. He's playing that in real time.' The only other person I knew who could play like Yngwie at the time … was Joe! And I think Joe prided himself on being one of the only people who could play that way. But when Joe heard Yngwie, I think awareness came of there was this guy named Yngwie and it was like, 'We're going to be hearing a lot from this guy in the future.'

Also, Yngwie's influence on me was that he sounded like Ulrich Roth. And I loved the fact that he sounded like Ulrich Roth. He also sounded like Ritchie Blackmore to a certain extent. And what blew me away is it was public knowledge that he was only nineteen years old at the time. So for me, to hear someone my age playing that way—completely influenced by the same people I was influenced by—really blew me away. Again, just really inspired me to play much more. I was always very, very careful—like I was with a lot of other influences—not to

---

* Metallica demo tape from 1982.

† Kirk was taking lessons from Joe at the time.

consciously play like him. Not to start playing tons of arpeggios and thirty-second notes—a neoclassical style. I mean, a lot of guys just jumped on that and sponged off his style. But I consciously did not go there.

It's like the conscious decision I made when I first heard Van Halen. I knew that it was only going to be a matter of time before everyone was going to be using their right hands to be hammering a note—just like Eddie Van Halen—all over the fretboard. And while I can appreciate the technique, I wasn't going to sponge it off and use it all the time. It was a very conscious effort. It's difficult for me to not sound too much like … Michael Schenker. It's difficult for me not to play a bunch of Hendrix licks all over the place. I can certainly do it. And when I played with Michael Schenker,[*] I was basically throwing a bunch of his licks back at him, trying to just sound like I could keep up with him. [*Laughs*]

HANK SHERMANN Me and Michael were in Mercyful Fate, driving around, and there was this guy who had a demo tape [of Yngwie], and put the cassette on in the car. We heard it and … *what?!* We couldn't believe it.

MICHAEL ANGELO BATIO [Nitro guitarist; solo artist] I was at Yngwie's very first show in the United States—with Mike Varney. I'm a little older than Yngwie, and I didn't move to LA until '83. But I was on Shrapnel Records in 1982, with an album called *US Metal*. He did three *US Metal* albums—I was on the second one.[†] So I was completely unknown then. But I had a really good promo shot—I was cool looking for the time! So when I moved to LA, Varney and I were friends, and he had actually set up some auditions for me. He got me to audition for Kiss. I didn't obviously get the gig, but I got to be friends with Gene Simmons. And I learned very early on not to be starstruck. Because I was totally starstruck with Kiss, and that's one of the main reasons why I think I didn't get it. I was a fan—I wasn't coming in as being a possible bandmate.

But when I went to see Yngwie, I had already had my style down. I have a degree in music, so I studied orchestral music and when they called him 'neoclassical,' I always used to think that term was wrong. He's more of a Baroque-styled guitarist—in the style of Bach and Vivaldi. Whereas classical music is more in the style of Mozart. The classical era is Mozart and Haydn. So I always thought that term was incorrect. But seeing Yngwie for the first time was really incredible. I saw him with Steeler, I was backstage, and it was great. There was such a huge

---

* On a 2015 episode of *That Metal Show*.
† He contributed the track 'The Haunted House.'

buzz, because he took that Randy Rhoads kind of classical influence and put this technique to it that I was playing—the kind of really serious violin style technique. I always had great technique on guitar, and I studied jazz and fusion and things like that. So it was a fantastic time.

JAS OBRECHT I was an editor for *Guitar Player* magazine when one of Yngwie's friends sent us a demo tape he'd made while still living at home in Malmö, Sweden. To this day, it's the most exciting Yngwie recording I've heard. It had 'Black Star' and several other songs on it, just a brilliant demo tape. It was immediately clear that Yngwie had tremendous chops and a mind-boggling facility with what soon became known as 'neoclassical' music. He really stood out.

The first time I saw Yngwie play, he had just been brought over to the United States by Mike Varney, owner of Shrapnel Records. Yngwie was making his debut with either Steeler or Alcatrazz. As I watched, I thought it was a clear case of a ten-dollar band with a million-dollar guitarist. After the show, Yngwie, who was all of about eighteen years old, came right up to me backstage and said, 'I know you. You're Jas Obrecht. Back in Sweden, I learned English by reading your magazine.' I kind of gave him a 'yeah, sure' look. Yngwie continued, adamant. 'No bullshit, man. In the September 1980 B.B. King issue, you're the guy in the T-shirt on page 71.' The magazine's photographer, Jon Sievert, and I stood there with our mouths agape when Yngwie said this. When we went back to the office, we checked. Sure enough, he was right, right down to the page number.

JOE STUMP [solo artist] I remember reading about him in the 'Spotlight' column in *Guitar Player*. I was reading his influences—he loved Blackmore, Uli Jon Roth, Bach, and Al Di Meola. And I'm like, 'This guy sounds like he'd be right up my alley, because I like all the same stuff!' And then sure enough, I heard him—I had the early Steeler and Alcatrazz records, and then I started to learn a lot of the stuff, because it was a lot of those sensibilities that Blackmore and Uli had that I loved, combined with Al Di Meola's pick hand, and an even more extreme classical influence. I started to learn lots of solos off those early records, and I had the *Rising Force* record as an import—before Yngwie became much more popular. And some of the stuff on the debut *Rising Force* record—granted, the production of the record maybe doesn't hold up as well—Yngwie's tone and playing is still a benchmark.

MIKE VARNEY [founder of Shrapnel Records; magazine columnist] My friend, Bill Burhard, owned the Record Exchange, which was one of the top distribution centers for heavy metal imports in the United States. And some exchange student from Sweden was a metal-head, and he went into Bill's store, bought some records, and said, 'Here is a cassette of some local guy that I think is great.' Bill listened to it, and said, 'Man, this guy is exactly what you're looking for!' I went over to Walnut Creek and listened to this thing, and I said, 'Yeah, this guy Yngwie is great.' Or 'Ing-wee'—I don't think we knew how to pronounce it for quite a while. [*Laughs*] So anyway, I had that in my mind for a few months, but I thought, 'I'm in my early/mid twenties. Am I really ready to bring a guy over from Sweden and go through all that?' It just seemed like an arduous process, and I was a little new in the game at that point in time—I had only released six albums or something.

Anyway, Yngwie himself sent me his own material, and a nice recording that had him talking to me about his influences and what style he was playing and his music. It was pretty cool. I wrote about him in *Guitar Player*, and I think before I wrote about him, Ron Keel and the band Steeler—later on, the band Keel—came up to me, and said, 'I'm looking for a guitar player for Steeler.' So Ron Keel flew up to San Francisco, sat down, and went through my stuff, and Yngwie's music seemed like the most compatible with what they were doing. So I invited Yngwie out to join Steeler. At the time, he was extremely excited. But I think it was more a vehicle for him in his mind to get out of Sweden and make a name for himself. He wasn't in the band very long. And because I was so young, the thought of signing somebody to a long contract didn't seem right, because I was new in the game. So anyway, I was happy to be a conduit, and produce his first record with Steeler.*

I've maintained a pretty good relationship with him through the years. A very nice guy, and misunderstood in many ways. A lot of the things that Yngwie would say that people would get all up in arms about … he's very smart, it was just deliberate—he was having fun, being as outrageous as he could be, and enjoying it with a sense of humor. One time, he called me, and said, 'Man, I just did a *Guitar World* interview. They asked what I thought of Jeff Beck, and I said, I never really listened to him!' [*Laughs*] Something like that—he said it just for fun. He loved to create controversy, and thought it was funny. I've always enjoyed him and he is quite a talent.

And what he told me years ago was, 'When you buy a Malmsteen album, you're going to know what to expect. I'm not going to follow a fad and become something else—I'm going to do *my music*.' And he's been consistent at that, and still has a really good following. I think that's a lesson for a lot of people who try

* *Steeler* (1983).

to change with the times, and then they lose whatever they've built up. I think his fan base is still strong because he has always been true to what he does.

Ron had written the material—Yngwie's main contribution was he'd create these amazing guitar solos. He was very confident in the studio, and he laid down some incredible stuff. He played like a guy that had an incredible amount of intention—he didn't just plug in and meander around. He went out there to kick ass and take names. You could feel the power coming off the tracks. He played with such aggression, and he was there to make a statement. I think that's what really set him apart, too—he really knew what he wanted and had a good idea of his concept and what he wanted to present, and he could go out there and materialize it. It didn't take very long for people like Ronnie Dio and other people to come sniffing around, looking to add Yngwie to their group. When Steeler would play, there would be a lot of celebrities down there, checking them out— other players and people looking for guitar players.

He made a huge splash. And part of it is because kind of the way Metallica broke—I was in touch with a lot of metal magazines and a lot of guitar fans around the world. The word got out on Yngwie pretty quickly, when we started spreading it out there through the underground. It was kind of funny, but the word of mouth thing … like Metallica had a huge tape-trading fan base, that they kind of built up. And there's a magazine called *Metal Mania* in San Francisco, that was one of the first to really help get Metallica solidified in the underground. And they also put Yngwie on the cover of their magazine I think, before he even got going, when I'd just started working with him. They jumped on it right away, and said, 'This is the new guy.'

JEFF WATSON Regarding Yngwie, he came on like a fucking lightning thunderstorm. He really hit hard. I remember Alcatrazz opened a show for us right when Yngwie came to America. It was '83, maybe. We played a Sacramento show and I remember talking to Yngwie after soundcheck—he was pretty aloof at the time. He was pretty cocky. But I didn't get a chance to hear him soundcheck, because I went out to dinner and came back after their show. Night Ranger went on, we did our silly pop songs, and I think Brad and I each took a standalone solo in the middle of the show, and I wasn't getting the reaction I normally got when I did my stuff. I don't even know if I was tapping then—it was before the eight-finger stuff I came up with for 'Rock In America.'

But afterward, a friend of mine who had been at the show in the crowd had recorded on a cassette player Yngwie's solo in the middle of Alcatrazz's set. He gave me the cassette tape, and I was on a tour bus with Steve Morse—he rode with us, because he's one of my best friends. We stick it in the cassette player, and we just looked at each other, and went, 'Fuck. What the hell is this?!' That was just jaw-dropping for us. If you read his book,* you get kind of an idea of where that came from—his practice regimen. He was never without his guitar—even as a little kid at school, he would miss classes, in between classes, at lunch, no matter what, he was at it. So many hours a day it's incalculable now to add that up.

JAS OBRECHT After paying his dues in Alcatrazz, Yngwie made his enduring mark on music with his brilliant debut album, *Rising Force*. His shows in support of the album, at least in San Francisco, were sheer pandemonium—guys were stage diving, the mosh pit was as intense as any I'd seen, and his manager had a semi-automatic pistol strapped on underneath his sports jacket. The vibe was intense. It didn't take long for Yngwie to fall prey to some of the excesses of big-time rock'n'roll, though. Ultimately, he injured himself in a car crash [in 1987], which slowed his career for a year or two.

BRUCE KULICK Yngwie is a guy who is clearly influenced by violin and classical guys. It was a little overwhelming for me, the way he played. Yet, I thought the guy had the most incredible vibrato and a very, very powerful tone came out of his Strats with the Marshalls. So I had a huge respect for the guy. I remember Eric Carr and I one time going to see him in the city, and I remember hearing a lot of things about him being pretty 'rough around the edges' and rude with people. And he was really a total gentleman with Eric and me. That meant a lot to me. But I could never play in his style. I could never pull that off. And he does it so intensely and so perfectly—it's pretty remarkable. But I always tend to favor the guitarists that were influenced by my influences. In other words, I can relate to an Ace Frehley—even though I think he plays different from me—much more than I can relate to an Yngwie Malmsteen. Because you know that Ace listened to Jimmy Page.

TONY MACALPINE As far as Yngwie goes, I think we touched on the same influences—I was really way into Al Di Meola, as he was too. So it wasn't really new to me. The differences were I think that I was really concentrating on instrumental music, and he was doing stuff with a band.

---

* *Relentless: The Memoir* (2013).

MARTY FRIEDMAN Yngwie is the guy I know the least about, believe it or not. I just never was a big Bach/mixing classical with rock type of guy. I never was a Deep Purple/Jimi Hendrix guy. But I was blown away by Yngwie's enthusiasm on the instrument and the aggression on the instrument—it was just super appealing to me. And his unapologetic, sticking to his guns style, I really think is a fantastic thing. So nothing but good things to say, although I haven't heard a whole lot of his work.

TREY AZAGTHOTH I didn't listen much to Yngwie Malmsteen. It wasn't really the style I was so into, even though he certainly was amazing at it. For me, his blues playing was more of my taste compared to what most people associate to him and his work.

KARL SANDERS Some of the Malmsteen stuff is still valid today—as guitar exercises to build technique. Like one of the things in my regular practice routine is the solo to 'I'll See The Light Tonight.' It's a really challenging pattern it starts off with, and it works its way around—it's quite an exercise.

RON 'BUMBLEFOOT' THAL He was the one that just turned up the 'intensity knob' physically. You had guys like Eddie that had fantastic technique, but as far as someone that turned it into shred—which is not a dirty word. Shred really was something that all the guitar players of the 80s aspired to be. We measured our skill level on, 'How fast can you play, and how clean?' Yngwie really upped the bar. He raised it. He made it where everyone really started to practice. It was like, 'Holy shit. There is a new level to the game we have to try and beat, or at least meet.' A huge impact—it made everybody feel like they needed to get their hands in shape even more. And it also made a lot of people pay attention to classical music, and how to implement it in rock and metal.

BACK IN THE DAY, IT WAS RUMORED THAT YNGWIE HAD DECLARED
VIVIAN CAMPBELL THE FASTEST SOLOIST ON THE SCENE …

VIVIAN CAMPBELL [Dio, Whitesnake, Def Leppard guitarist] I don't think he ever told me that directly, but I have heard other people mention it. He might have said it at some stage to someone. But I don't get how. Sometimes, you can't see the forest from the trees—maybe I am, or maybe I was. But that's not what I was meaning. I think when Yngwie plays fast, he's in control—he knows where the brake pedal is.

I usually drive off the edge of a cliff! It's entirely impulsive and I've never really felt that when I'm playing like that, that I have much control. I really feel like you're riding a motorcycle and one of those chambers goes around and around, and if I stop moving, I'm going to fall off.

STEVE VAI It wasn't until Yngwie hit the scene that shredding—the concept of deep, masterful, virtuosic control on the instrument—reached a new level. As far as electric guitar playing goes, it was Yngwie. Like the music or not, you have to pay honor to what he did, because he showed us what was capable. So I think as far as 'shredding guitars' go, [Eddie and Yngwie] are very different players, but they both made a major contribution to the virtuosic bar, in guitar playing. That's my feeling. Randy had an impact, but I think as far as sheer, terrorizing speed … Yngwie.

shrapnel records

THE record label for all your shredder needs.

MIKE VARNEY I was sitting around at the end of the 70s, and I was getting frustrated, because I was a big guitar fan, and disco music and punk rock and all this stuff was kind of 'dummying down' the virtuoso guitar stuff—people like Al Di Meola, Uli Roth, Michael Schenker, and Eddie Van Halen. There just was like a lull around 1980 or so. So in 1980, I decided to start Shrapnel, and I went state by state to the various music magazines, and said, 'I'm putting together a compilation of the ten best unknown guitar players in America, in the heavy metal style. And I'm looking for anybody in your neck of the woods that might be a candidate. Do you have anybody that can be one of the ten best?' There was really no territory that I approached that didn't think they had somebody that could be a contender. So a lot of these magazines ran articles on my search for the ten best unknown guitar players in America, in that hard rock/heavy metal style.

And Jas Obrecht at *Guitar Player* magazine was reading about it in *BAM* magazine—a San Francisco publication—and Jas got ahold of me, and said, 'Hey man, if you find these guys, I want to hear them. I'm the editor at *Guitar Player* magazine.' I wrote back to him and we got in conversation. I said, 'I just made a record for EMI.' I wrote a musical with Marty Balin called *Rock Justice*, and we had Jeff Pilson involved in it—singing and playing.* And various other people— the rhythm section from Y&T and a guy from The Tubes. It was a big kind of revue show in San Francisco, and I co-wrote it, and there was a soundtrack out on

---

* Pilson eventually became the bassist in Dokken.

EMI. Jas asked to hear it, and somehow, that led to an invitation to come down to the *Guitar Player* magazine Halloween party, and I brought a couple of young shredders with me.

And these guys participated in their jam, and I saw the publisher [Jim Crockett] hanging out, and this guy Tom Wheeler hanging out, who was I think senior editor at the time. I looked at *Guitar Player*, and I said, 'Y'know, you've got this guy with his Ferrari, and this guy with his mansion, and this guy with his 5,000 guitars. But what about the guy who just goes to work at a regular blue-collar job, and always wanted to be a guitar player, and hasn't given up on his dreams—he's still playing and practicing and buying gear—what about *those* kind of guys? These kind of guys need to be in *Guitar Player*, and people reading *Guitar Player* magazine would have somebody to read about in their peer group, and it would be an obtainable thing for most people that were good. Maybe it would be something for them to look forward to, and look for themselves in there, and create a nice groundswell and grassroots kind of thing. I have this idea; I want to write this column.'

At the time, I had just maybe turned twenty-three, and they said, 'Well, write something. Let's see what you've got.' So I turned in a column, and they said, 'Yeah. We'll do it.' We created this column, and that's how it all started.* Billy Sheehan's first piece of national press—as far as I know—was in that column. Scott Henderson, Paul Gilbert, Yngwie Malmsteen, Tony MacAlpine, Vinnie Moore, Jason Becker, Greg Howe, Richie Kotzen, I think Michael Lee Firkins, maybe Joey Tafolla … at least most of those ones. A lot of guitar players made their debuts—it was their first piece of press on a national or international level.

Basically, I'm a huge record collector, and I still buy tons of records. I know it's not fashionable now, but now I'm actually into CDs instead of vinyl, but at the time, I had tons and tons of vinyl, and really loved to collect. Like I was alluding to earlier, there just wasn't a whole lot happening in 1980. I had just got out of college and had a degree in business administration with an emphasis on marketing, and I thought, 'I don't think I'm alone here. I think there's some guys out there that really want to hear some ripping guitar playing. And there are guys out there that are ripping, and the focus is on disco, punk rock, and new wave.'

We really didn't have a focus on heavy metal in that early part of 1980, which I kind of just caught a wave or helped create a wave, and Shrapnel was started to become the first dedicated heavy metal label in America, but also, to find the

---

* Varney's column, 'Spotlight,' in which he wrote about three up-and-coming guitarists each month, first appeared in the magazine in 1982.

greatest guitar players. It was kind of a niche market, but that's what I studied in school, and that's what I was trying to create. I never wanted to be a huge record company—I know that seems crazy—but I was never really that anxious to be huge. I just wanted to do stuff that I liked and work with artists that I thought were cool, and do stuff that I would want to listen to and buy myself, for the most part.

MARTY FRIEDMAN I lived in Hawaii and I was teaching some guitar students, and one of the kids told me that Varney had a column in *Guitar Player* magazine, looking for new guitar players. So my student told me to send him my stuff, and I did. Although Varney didn't put me in his column—which frustrated me at the time—he gave me a record contract, and I was one of his first albums. So I was happy about that.

JASON BECKER [Cacophony, David Lee Roth guitarist; solo artist] When I was sixteen years old, I sent [Varney] a cassette demo with about ten songs, hoping to get in the magazine. He called me and said that I was really good, but my recordings were sloppy, and I should re-record them. He also suggested that I go meet Marty Friedman. After Marty and I spent a few months hanging and jamming together, Marty asked me to join him on his Shrapnel album. We had become close friends, and really played guitar well together. We had become a creative team.

TONY MACALPINE I was sending tapes out in the very beginning, and I sent tapes to a bunch of different people and labels. I sent a tape to Mike Varney at *Guitar Player* magazine, and he featured me in a 'Spotlight' column, and that was the start of it. He called me, and said, 'What would you think about coming out to California and doing a record?' He approached it that way, and I came out to San Francisco, and ended up staying there for about ten years and making a bunch of records.

PAUL GILBERT Mike lived in Northern California, and I was from a small town in Pennsylvania. And I had no idea how to get any contact with the music business—this is before YouTube, before the internet. You had the mail, with an envelope and a stamp—*that's* how you contacted people! And Mike had a small feature in *Guitar Player* magazine—which was really the only magazine at the time—and at the end of it, he said, 'Anybody who sends me a cassette, I promise I'll send a reply.' And that was exciting to me. Randy had just passed away, and I had this harebrained idea that since I already knew a lot of the tunes, that maybe some kind of strange miracle would occur, and Ozzy would hire me for his band. It was so farfetched that I didn't really have my expectations very high, but I thought, 'If I don't try, I'm always going to regret not trying.' But of course, the only thing I could think of was this Mike Varney guy, who had put his address in a magazine.

So I made a cassette of some solos and a couple of tunes, and sent them to Mike. It took three days for the cassette to get out there—I think it might have even been before there was FedEx! [*Laughs*] So you had to wait three days. And Mike called me up right when he got the cassette, and really encouraged me. He was really complimentary about my playing. And I don't know if he knew Ozzy or anything, but he seemed like he had some connections. When he found out I was fourteen years old, then he sort of told me the reality of that. But he was still very encouraging and wanted me to record for some of the compilations he was doing at the time. Part of the deal was he would advance the money for the recording studio and I'd bring my band in to record it. Just that … again, nobody could do home recordings then—there just wasn't the gear. And even if there was, I couldn't afford it. But the idea of going into the studio was just a dream.

So I began to send Mike demos of songs and I was really trying hard … this was the most exciting thing that had ever happened to me, so I was really trying my best. And he would call me up usually three days later, and he would say, 'This is horrible. Are you joking? This is extremely bad.' He would just cut me apart. And he'd say, 'The guitar playing is fine, but your songwriting is so bad I can't believe it.' So, I sent him another song, and I thought, 'Oh, he's going to love this.' And again, he calls me up and goes, 'This is even worse!' Fortunately, I had the optimism and the energy to keep going, and just go, 'OK. Let me keep trying.' So that's what I did, and it got to the point where he said, 'You just sent me a bunch of songs … I like them all. Instead of doing a compilation appearance, let's form a band around you when you get to LA, and we'll do a whole album.' So he wasn't just 'beating me up'—he was telling me the truth, and it was nice to hear that. And to be able to be inspired by it. It's kind of a rough way to be inspired, but again, I was fifteen, sixteen years old at that point, and had tough enough skin to deal with it and just work hard enough to get my writing together.

MIKE VARNEY They had to be way better than I was on guitar—that was the first thing! [*Laughs*] I guess a lot of it had to do with their style and proficiency, but a lot of it was their drive. Yngwie was ready at nineteen to come to America. That takes some drive—to leave your family and come out there and go for it. Guys like Richie Kotzen sent me a zillion tapes. I think I got two demos a week from Richie at one point. And other guys like Tony MacAlpine were extremely driven.

It was one thing to be great and have great vibrato, phrasing, and technique, but the other thing was that drive. If you want to invest in this guy, are they going to be getting up every morning, and go, 'I've got to push myself further. How am I going to get better? How am I going to get out there?' And the guys that I bet on for the most part, are the guys that had that drive and dedication, and really, if they got as good they were for me to sign them, they had to give up a lot of 'pleasures' of their youth to focus on their guitar playing. [*Laughs*]

And oddly enough, most of the artists I signed never drank or did any drugs. They were kids from good homes that were really focusing—everything was riding on their guitar playing. That's what I really looked for—all those techniques, stylistic things, and originality. But a lot if was, 'Can this guy be a guy that people will look up to, and say, 'This guy is a serious force to be reckoned with,' and will this guy have a career? Will this guy be around twenty years from now, or will he just fade out?' Most of the guys that I've worked with—at least the guys I've had success with—are still active, doing their thing. You can go to a lot of other labels and look at artists that they've signed, and no one's ever heard anything about them ever again.

So, there is something about that feeling that I had about various people, that they were really committed. And if somebody was too arrogant or too distracted, or not committed, I wasn't that interested in them. They had to also present themselves in an image basis, to where somebody could come along and say, 'Man, I need a guitar player to play with David Lee Roth, I need a guy to play with such and such.'

GREG HOWE I graduated in '82, and immediately, almost the day after I graduated, put a band together.[*] We started playing out in clubs, and our goal was to try and get signed and become rock stars. My brother was two years younger than me—he was playing in my band with me, so we had to get fake IDs to be able to play in clubs. He was still in high school. We pounded the club circuit on the east coast for a good six/seven years, and showcased for record labels. We did a bunch of recordings—we did everything we could to try and get discovered. We actually did get a development deal with CBS for a while, and then that eventually fell through.

Finally, it was like, 'Maybe I'll submit a tape to Mike Varney'—mostly because he was a record label. I was almost positive I was not going to get selected, because

---

[*] The band was initially called Duke, then Howe II.

he had the 'Spotlight' column in *Guitar Player* magazine. So I figured my chances of being selected are so slim, and my chances of being selected, and also asked to record on his label, was almost nothing. But I figured, 'Look, I've got to do everything I can. So I'll throw a tape together and send it to his PO Box, and see if he selects me.'

The one thing I did do is I sent the tape directly to *Guitar Player* magazine via Federal Express, because I knew somebody would have to sign for it. So I sent two versions of my demo to Mike Varney—one to his PO Box and one to *Guitar Player*, in the hopes that because someone would have to physically sign for it and physically carry the package, maybe it would increase my chances of being heard. And that is exactly what happened. I sent the demo to him and the very next day, I got a phone call from him, and he said, 'I really like your playing. I want to feature you in my "Spotlight" column, and also, would you be interested in doing a record?'

I was pumped. We had been trying for years to get discovered and get somebody to listen to what we were doing, and here was a guy that was finally interested—in me, at least. And I figured if he was interested in me, then I can use that as the vehicle to get some notoriety for the band. That's really how it happened. And the deal that I signed with Mike Varney was a four album record deal, and we negotiated it so I could have two of those albums be recorded with my band, and two of the albums be recorded as solo albums.

MIKE VARNEY We were the first label to really do guitar instrumental kind of records. My distributor was Important Records, and the owner told me, 'Man, you guys are doing really good with this instrumental stuff,' so he told his staff, 'We've got to make our own records!' And he tried to capitalize on some of the stuff that Shrapnel got going. So that kind of opened up the door for Joe Satriani and for Steve Vai. Obviously, their talent is immense and would have got there anyway, but that label at that point in time that signed them, the owner of the label credited Shrapnel a number of times as being the reason why he set out to find—in his mind—the next great guitar players. And he really did a great job by finding Joe and Steve.

RICHIE KOTZEN I will tell you it became a personal obsession of mine. I remember when I thought that I was doing something that was worth a look by Shrapnel Records, I became obsessed with trying to get into the column. So I would send my demo tape every week, and I would change the order of the songs—I only had four songs. I thought, 'If he puts the tape in and doesn't hear something that grabs him in the first couple of seconds, he's going to take it out. He has a lot of tapes to listen to.' So I was flipping the order, and then I somehow was able to find his phone number, that had an answering service attached to it, and I left messages. I remember I was playing live with my cover band all over Pennsylvania, Delaware, and New Jersey, and I would come home late at night—three in the morning—and I would look at the answering machine, and if the light was flashing, I would get excited and think maybe he called and left a message. And of course, I would be disappointed, because he didn't call. And if it wasn't flashing, I would curse him. I would say the most horrible things about him—not knowing him, never having met him, but just pissed that he didn't call and he didn't acknowledge my demo tape.

And then finally, one day, I was having dinner, and my phone rang, and it was my friend from Boston, who had gone to Berklee. He called me and said, 'You're such a jerk, Richie. I can't believe you didn't tell me.' And I'm like, 'Tell you what?' 'You're in *Guitar Player* magazine this month.' He read it to me, and I said, 'Well, who are my influences?' Because I knew then, if he knew who the influences were that I stated, then I'd know it was true. I listed Eddie Van Halen as an influence, and then I listed Carlos Montoya in there—even though I didn't know any of his songs, I wanted to sound like I was 'deep.' So he read me the article, and I ran to the newsstand, and there I was! I was seventeen, and I was featured in the 'Spotlight' column.

And then my obsession shifted—I wanted to get signed to the label, I wanted to make a record, because I found out Greg Howe made a record, and Greg lived less than an hour from my parents' house. So I started hanging out with Greg and going to his house and talking to Shrapnel Records and talking about Mike Varney. And then, suddenly, Mike called and wanted to make a record with me.

MIKE VARNEY I would say the first real 'guitaristic' thing would have probably been Steeler—the one that really had the incredible guitar playing. And then two records later, came Hawaii with Marty Friedman, and then we had a bunch of cool metal albums. Vinnie Moore was this young guy, and I said, 'Hey, I've got a band out there called Vicious Rumors'—they've made probably twenty records by now. But he came out and joined them, and did their first record with them,[*] and I offered Vinnie a solo deal and he told me he didn't want to be away from his girlfriend and family out here in California, so he quit, and went back home. I was

---

[*] *Soldiers Of The Night* (1985).

getting so many tapes in the mail—I'd open up my mail, and … Corpse Killer. Wretched Beast. Blood Of Satan. All these bands sending me this stuff. I'm like, 'Man, I don't want to be involved with this kind of stuff, really.'

So I started thinking about it, and I thought, 'Y'know, maybe I'll make an instrumental record with somebody. Kind of forge a different kind of genre. I don't have to deal with all these lyrics and dark stuff.' I thought, 'The path of least resistance is to try some instrumental stuff.' So I put Billy Sheehan and Steve Smith from Journey together with Tony MacAlpine, and recorded *Edge Of Insanity*. And that thing did really, really well. Then I stuck Andy West, from The Dregs, with Tommy Aldridge, who has played with everybody from Whitesnake to Ozzy, and had those guys make a record with Tony MacAlpine on keyboards.* I started making these little supergroups of instrumental guitar records. That kind of became my focus—to bring these different guys together and create these kind of 'super sessions.'

MacAlpine was #21, he went from being more heavy metal with good guitar playing to focusing on some of the really amazing guitar players and putting instrumental projects around them with guys who were known at the time as being the standout instrumentalists of bass, drums, etcetera. So we started doing all that stuff. Paul Gilbert/Racer X—that was the twenty-third record we did, and that was the case of Paul had hooked up with a bass player from my town in Novato, California, and they needed a singer, and I knew this guy, Jeff Martin, and hooked him up. I hooked him up with Mark Slaughter first—he did some demos with him, but they liked Jeff Martin better. Slaughter didn't have a problem having a career, so good for him.

JASON BECKER Mike is very energetic and extremely funny! He absolutely loves music, and loves being with creative people. He is definitely a businessman, but wants to be a good person.

TONY MACALPINE Mike Varney is a man of a lot of energy and a big vision. Great guitar producer. He really has his idea in how and the way the records should come together. He's a real person that's in the center of the pulse for knowing a lot of different musicians, and putting them in contact. It was through him that I met Deen Castronovo—that went on to Journey fame—and it's through him that I worked with Steve and Billy, and so many other great players. And I was able

---

* Vinnie Moore's *Mind's Eye* (1986).

to work with other up-and-coming musicians—like Joey Tafolla. Mike Varney has been a great thing for the whole guitar movement. And that's something that everybody remembers.

NOT EVERYBODY APPRECIATED SHRAPNEL'S ROSTER OF ARTISTS.

MARTY FRIEDMAN I really didn't like it, to be honest with you. I thought they all had loads of technique, but I could care less about technique—everybody in the music business has technique, y'know? It's a given. It should be taken for granted. All that I care about is how I feel when I listen to the music, and a lot of that just sounded like guys showing their abilities—and I couldn't care less about that.

DAVID T. CHASTAIN [Chastain CJSS guitarist; solo artist] Since he did have that column, he was able to sign a lot of the shredders and produced albums for them. It was a good and bad thing. In the end, too many of the recordings sounded alike in production and style, so people got bored with them. Many of the players have stood the test of time and are still active today. I would like to think my record label, Leviathan Records, also did the same thing ... except we concentrated as much on songs as to how many notes could be played.

Leviathan Records was the first to sign Gus G.* I recognized that he not only was an excellent guitarist but he also knew how to write a great song with melody. Leviathan Records was bombarded with tons of technically proficient guitarists but I needed to hear some melody besides just a torrent of arpeggios, hammer-ons, sweeps, and ungodly speed. After awhile that all sounds the same to me ... *and I am a guitarist*. While I understand the practice and hard work it takes to do all of that, I prefer music that says something other than just 'I practice a lot!'

JASON BECKER I thought Shrapnel was awesome! I didn't really listen to most of the artists, because I was doing my own thing. I had a lot of respect for them, though. But to have a label dedicated to wild guitar was perfect for this sixteen-year-old boy.

NUMEROUS BANDS CAME TO VARNEY IN SEARCH OF GUITARISTS ...

MIKE VARNEY All kinds of them. Dokken—as early as 1982—asked me if I knew

---

* Gus went on to play with Ozzy Osbourne.

a bass player, and I said, 'Yeah, Jeff Pilson.' It was drummers, it was bass players, it was everything—it wasn't just guitar players. Even Third Eye Blind—as outside as that reference may be—came to me looking for a guitar player, and I recommended Tony Fredianelli, who was in a band called Apocrypha, on Shrapnel. And Tony got the gig. He was with them for about a year before they signed, and then he joined back for about ten years after they broke—because he couldn't hang in there anymore with a wife and kid, with promises of stardom. He had to go back home and tend to business, but then when they broke, they came back and got him.

But when David Lee Roth's people wanted a guitar player, I recommended Jason. He was the only guy that I recommended. I had a lot of other people, but I thought that he made the most sense to me. He seemed like the guy that would be the best at it. It's too bad that he got sick—there's no telling what amazing things he could have accomplished. But Mr. Big … when Paul Gilbert finished his agreement with me, I had this friend, Eric Martin, who was a soul singer, but he could sing rock great. He was ready to make another soul record, and I said, 'Man, you've got to make a rock record. Billy Sheehan's free, Paul Gilbert's free, let me introduce you guys.'

So I hooked them all up and talked to the manager of Eric Martin, who was working with Journey, and I just said, 'I've put these three guys together. Get a drummer, and it's turnkey. And I don't want anything for it—I'm just trying to help three friends that are looking for something to do.' I did a lot of that kind of stuff—put bands together, get people gigs. And it was hardly for anything in return. It seemed like the thing to do. And things always came back, people appreciate when you do that kind of stuff, and helps create a good relationship.

MICHAEL ANGELO BATIO I like Mike Varney and I respect him—think about how many people he's discovered, and are still here. Yngwie Malmsteen, myself, Tony MacAlpine, Greg Howe, Paul Gilbert, Vinnie Moore, John5, Richie Kotzen … we're all still rockin'. And we're all still relevant. I think it's a testament to him. When I got signed to Shrapnel, for me, it was like being in the Special Forces, because he was very critical of guitarists he signed. He only signed the best of the best. And I think time has proven he was correct. And I'm not trying to brag about myself, but I was up there with those artists, and I was good enough to be signed to Shrapnel.

The only reason I didn't do more Shrapnel albums is because once I moved to California, a year later, I was signed to Atlantic Records. So I was signed to two major labels, and then by that time, it's the 90s and I've got my own thing—I'm already established. So I took a different path. But Mike and I are still really good friends. I respect his eyes and ears for talent. He was uncanny at picking just amazing people, and they're still here. *He was the man.* Shrapnel Records was THE label in the 80s. It was like a badge of honor to be on that label. I thought of him like that back in the day, and nothing's changed my opinion of him, thirty years later.

RON 'BUMBLEFOOT' THAL Just for fun, I was making these weird little guitar songs, and I was always focused on my band. My dream was to have a band that everybody knew the members on a first name basis, and every one of those names defined a sound in the band, and they all had their strong identities musically. Like The Beatles and Kiss. When you say 'John, Paul, George, Ringo,' each name means something musically to you. A musical personality that you can hear and pick out, and it's a major contribution to every one of them of the music. The same with 'Gene, Paul, Peter, Ace.' That was what I always wanted.

And while I was trying to work toward that—and having bands and writing songs and doing everything a band does—on the side, just for fun, I was influenced and inspired by guys like Vai, and I would make these fun little guitar songs. I was reading the 'Spotlight' column, and I was like, 'Y'know, just for the hell of it, let me submit this.' I did and he gave me a great review.

We stayed in touch for years and he would recommend different situations for me. I remember one time, he recommended a possible band with Jeff Pilson and I forget who else, as a possible band we could put together. But at the time, I just wanted to stick with my own game plan that I had. In hindsight, I think I should have done both—it would have been good to listen to those who knew a lot more than me. Anyway, we stayed in touch, and he told me he was looking to expand and do vocal music, as well, on a subsidiary label. So I signed, and we did two albums together.* And through that first thing that got submitted, it felt good, like, 'All right, I'm starting to get on the map. I'm starting to get legitimized. I'm leaving the basement and I'm getting national recognition by somebody.'

In fact, one of the first letters I got from somebody that wrote to me from that column—who I'm still very good friends with—is Guthrie Govan. He wrote me a letter, introduced himself, and we were just teenaged kids. For years, we'd send each other cassettes, handwritten transcriptions, and demos of songs we just made. We've been good friends for twenty-six years. So being in that article was

---

* *The Adventures Of Bumblefoot* (1995) and *Hermit* (1997).

the first feeling of, 'OK.' Not that I didn't feel it couldn't happen, it was more like, 'The work is starting to show results. All this ass-busting, this is the first step of it. I've finally got some recognition.' And then it continued from there with other magazines and getting on different comp CDs.

MIKE VARNEY Every artist made records that at their time were considered by somebody as being groundbreaking or their favorite record. I wish I had more nerve and I could take a stand and say [which Shrapnel albums are his top three favorites], but honestly, I've got so many that I really do believe are great for what they are. And to try and pick three is just too hard. But in the early days, some of the more popular ones were the Marty and Jason solo records, the Racer X records, MacAlpine, Vinnie Moore, Greg Howe—all that stuff. I'm too much of a music fan—it's hard for me to say three things.

MARK WOOD He was 'the guy.' *He discovered Yngwie Malmsteen.* Of course, Yngwie probably would have been discovered at some point, but I'll never forget, some of the guitar players turned into really big careers—including mine—because of Mike.

HERMAN LI [DragonForce guitarist] I really liked a lot of the albums on that label. Michael Lee Firkins, Jason Becker, Marty Friedman … they played a part in my guitar development. Even though when I got into it, the 80s were gone and it was the 'grunge time' and Korn. I just went back and bought all those albums and listened to it.

RICHIE KOTZEN I owe a lot to Mike Varney—if it wasn't for him, I might be working at a tile floor covering store somewhere … or maybe I would have taken a different route … and maybe I would have gotten signed with my band. But none of that happened. And Mike Varney opened a lot of doors for me, so I'm really thankful that he acknowledged my tape back then.

racer x & cacophony

Two 80s bands helped launch the careers of three shredders: Racer X (Paul Gilbert) and Cacophony (Jason Becker and Marty Friedman).

PAUL GILBERT Mike Varney had given me the opportunity to do an album. The next goal was to find a band. Nobody knew who I was or anything—I remember calling up musicians and they'd never call me back, because I wasn't offering a proper gig where there's a salary. So I was just hoping that people would play with me out of the goodness of their hearts … and it wasn't happening. So I ended up just finding a couple of students at school* that were willing to jam for the fun of it. And they weren't really the players that I wanted for the record, but it allowed me to make demos and at least have something tangible that I could show to any better musicians in the event that I found them.

So eventually, I found Juan Alderete—who plays with Mars Volta and has had a pretty successful post–Racer X career. But he was the first guy that we really became a sort of 'duo'—we jammed together all the time and hung out all the time. And our original drummer, Harry Gschoesser, he was always trying to interview me—he was actually from Austria, and I think he had an extra gig on the side, of interviewing Los Angeles musicians. He was really a go-getter—just always trying to jam.

And the funny thing is he had short hair, and that was a really big issue—I wouldn't even jam with him because he had short hair! [*Laughs*] Finally, he

---

* Paul was attending the Guitar Institute of Technology (GIT) at the time.

cornered me and said, 'Just come in this room for a second.' And he was great. A really good drummer. He kept promising—with his Austrian accent—'*I vill vear a vig! Vhen ve do ze photos, I vill vear a vig!*' And when we did the photos … he didn't wear the wig. It's funny looking at it now, I see it with different eyes now—to me, it's like, 'Hey, he's got long hair.' But it wasn't 'big' hair. It was funny how much of an issue that kind of thing was in the day. Then it was a search for the singer, and Mike actually hooked us up with a lot of people. And when I heard the demo of Jeff Martin, I really liked his vibrato and his compositional sense. So Jeff came out, and that was the core of the band.

MICHAEL ANGELO BATIO I love Paul Gilbert on guitar, and I loved Racer X. I had a rhythm guitarist in my band at the time, and I remember Gene Simmons saw me play, and I sent him a demo of four songs. And the one song that I did not write, it was my rhythm guitar player that wrote it. Gene calls me from I think he was recording at Cherokee Studios. He calls me at my apartment in Hollywood, and he's like, 'Michael, I want you to get down to the studio right now. I want to talk to you.' So I go down there, and I'd known Gene Simmons from auditioning for Kiss. He always loved my guitar playing.

And I learned not to be starstruck. By this time, I was just, 'Hey Gene, how are you doing?' Not that I'm trying to be condescending, but I really understood the distinction between a fellow musician and a fellow artist, versus a fan. How you relate. He goes, 'Michael, your guitar playing is light years ahead of other guitarists. What the fuck do you need another guitarist for? You play two guitars as the same time!' And then he starts bugging me about this one song. He goes, 'What is this song? *This song sucks!*' And on the four-song demo tape, it was the song that wasn't mine.

But the thing I loved about Racer X—here's how I'm seguing to Racer X— Paul Gilbert was able to shine with Bruce Bouillet as another guitarist with him. I was not able to do that. Once I got rid of my rhythm guitarist and we became a four-piece—a power trio with a singer—the clubs were so packed. And I found for myself, I have never really been able to be successful in a twin guitar band, whereas I thought Racer X was highly successful. I thought they did really cool music and they were doing records on Shrapnel.

What happened with me was I was in a band called Holland. We weren't that well known, but we were on Atlantic Records and we had toured with Aerosmith. So I had released my major label album. And then, I had left the band and started a band called the Michael Angelo Band, playing around LA. So for about that year, year and a half, where Racer X released a few records, I didn't. I was writing songs, we were working on an album, and then I got signed in the band Nitro. I was playing a lot around Los Angeles. But I loved Racer X, I thought they were great. *Street Lethal.* They did a lot of great things.

PAUL GILBERT Our goal was, of course, we wanted to get the big record deal. And we tried and tried and tried. We were really successful in LA as a local band—we'd do shows at the biggest clubs in LA and sell them out. We'd do two nights in a row. Really doing great locally. All the record labels had come out to see us … and everybody didn't like us.

So we just didn't know what to do. And right around that time, Billy Sheehan called me to form a band.* And Billy was a huge hero of mine—I used to go see him play all the time when he played in Talas. It was a rough decision for me, because not only did I really like Racer X's music—even though the labels didn't like us, I really liked it—but the guys were my best friends in the world. We really hung out just about every day.

So to sort of turn my back on my friends and also leave some music that I was really into, that was hard to do. But at the same time, suddenly, there was this hero of mine, asking to form a band. And then I knew that Eric Martin was the singer, and I thought he was great, and I knew the management was big management. I thought, 'This has all the ingredients of being a giant band.'

Racer X just seemed stalled. We tried everything, and it didn't seem to be going anywhere. Either way, I knew that if I left, it would be painful and I'd be leaving something that I loved. But at the same time, if I didn't take the opportunity, I'd be wondering, 'What would have happened?' So I just had to make a choice, and obviously, I went with Mr. Big. Fortunately, I've been able to reform Racer X years later, and still rekindle my friendship and musical relationship with those guys. So it all turned out really well in the end.

BILLY SHEEHAN Paul used to come see Talas when we'd play Pittsburgh. I remember a tall, skinny kid standing in front of the stage in front of me while we played. Eventually, he got in a band and ended up opening up for Talas.

I'm usually getting ready when the opening act is going on, so I don't get to see them, but I heard them from the back, and said, 'Who's that guitar player?' And I remembered Paul, because he attended my very first bass clinic I ever did—

---

* Mr. Big.

which was in Pittsburgh. So I remembered him as a fan and then an opening act.

And when I moved out to LA, Paul was already there, going to Musicians Institute as a student, and they had a guitar contest one night at Gazzarri's, and I was one of the judges—and Paul was in the contest. I remember telling the other judges, '*Wait until you see this kid play.*' Paul got up there—I was already in David Lee Roth's band—and was just great. Everyone agreed he was the winner. I think he won a Marshall amp or a thousand bucks at Guitar Center. And when me, Steve, Dave, and Greg would go out to the bars, at the Troubadour, the room was separated by glass, so you could talk at the bar. And I remember seeing Paul's band play there—Racer X. And we would watch them and say, 'Pretty awesome. Pretty cool stuff.'

So I knew him from the early days, and when it came time when I left Dave's band to put a band together, I thought, 'Paul would probably be the perfect guy.' Because Racer X I think had just broken up, because they just could not get signed by anyone. And it kind of discouraged them and it fell apart. So Paul was looking for something else, and I called him. I told him, 'I've got a singer in San Francisco and I found a drummer. Let's see what happens.' So we got together and started Mr. Big.

He's got a great song sense, and he's just a fearless slave laborer to perfection and musical excellence. He'll sit down and learn a piece of music by some obscure artist or a famous one, or sit down and learn every Beatles song ever, every Hendrix song ever, and really is a great, great student. Therefore, he's always coming up with fantastic new stuff, because he's always learning something new. And a wonderful guy to work with. Great, creative person to write songs with. He's one of my dear friends.

MARTY FRIEDMAN I was going to do a solo album. I was just about done, and Mike Varney says, 'You've got to hear this kid!' I'm like, 'I don't care about hearing any kid.' He's like, 'Well … just hear this guy.'

I met him [Jason]—I had him come to my apartment, and he was like, sixteen. I just fell in love with him immediately. Not only because he was so good on guitar, but I've never really met a guy who was that naturally friendly and cool, and also, good at guitar.

Back in those days, most of the flashy guitar players were kind of jerk offs, y'know? And to some extent, myself included—I probably cleaned up my act pretty much by then, but I had been an egotistical … not quite a douchebag, but when you're young and you get adulation, it tends to get to some people's heads.

And I will admit that when I was in my late teens and early twenties, I probably thought I was a lot better than I actually was.

But then, when you get into real life, certain things put you in your place, and you realize that in the real world, there's people that are way, way, way better, and you eventually get humble. So I got humble. And then I met Jason. And this guy had so much talent, but he was so humble and so cool. I'm like, 'I'm never going to find another guy who can play like this, so it would be great to have a band with this guy, because nobody else can harmonize my stuff.' And my music had a lot of harmonies in it—very difficult things—and he could play them with ease. I was like, 'This is the only way I'm going to get Cacophony music or my solo music done live—to have this guy play with me.'

JASON BECKER Mike Varney introduced us. We became best friends really quickly. We got along great. I instantly loved his guitar playing. I wanted to learn from him. I hadn't heard anything like his style. If I remember correctly, it was Mike Varney [who came up with the name Cacophony].*

MARTY FRIEDMAN [Jason was] just an abnormally cool dude. You wouldn't even know the guy was a guitarist. I think the thing is he got really, really good at his instrument before he had any kind of band experience. He had no 'band life.' Where I was just the opposite—I was already playing in bands and banging groupies before I could even really play. So I had already been there and done that way before I even met Jason.

So by the time I met Jason, I really developed as a guitarist and as a recording artist, and he had developed as a really, really sick guitarist. So he was very green in the terms of 'putting on a show,' and what goes into making a show, rehearsing, playing live, looking cool, appealing to the people in the audience. He had none of that. But he had everything that none of the other guitar players had—*abilities that were jaw dropping*. So that left him with a very unique and very pleasant, likable character.

JASON BECKER Touring with Cacophony was a blast. We were playing at a club in Southern California, and some Carvin reps came to see the show. At one point, Marty and I were having trouble getting in tune. Peter Marino, our singer, proceeded to tell the audience how terrible Carvin was. Marty and I

---

* Cacophony then issued two albums on Shrapnel: *Speed Metal Symphony* (1987) and *Go Off!* (1988).

looked at each other and shook our heads. At that same show I met a kid who was too young to get in. That club even said I was too young, so I couldn't go in until we were actually onstage. Of course, I snuck in anyway. This kid was really sad, so I spent time with him outside the club before and after the gig. I gave him some picks, too.

After a gig on a hot muggy night in Jacksonville, we all went to a fan's house to hang out. I grabbed an acoustic guitar and started playing and singing really loud a song I was writing on the spot about our day, the gig, and us hanging out with the fans. There were lots of people there so it seemed appropriate. A guy came out of his room and said, 'Do you know what time it is?' People were whispering, 'That is Jason Becker!' He said, 'I don't care who it is, I have to go to work in the morning!' I cracked up and played quietly.

MARTY FRIEDMAN We toured Japan and America—absolutely some of the best memories of my life. Loved every second. But our music was just too eclectic to really make use of Jason or my abilities in the mainstream. At the time, Cacophony was very, very abstract. Even though we were abstract, we did have our fans, but they were not enough to 'make a living off,' so to speak. Even though we loved each other and we loved the band we were in, we both knew that if we separated, we'd probably get into a much more mainstream and popular situation. And as soon as we did, Jason joined David Lee Roth's band, and I joined Megadeth. So we knew what we were doing. But it was very amicable.

JASON BECKER Gregg Bissonette* asked Mike Varney for some great guitarists, and Mike suggested me. I sent tapes of my stuff. Dave asked me to record some versions of his songs. He loved what I did and flew me down to LA. I really liked Dave. We hung out and talked quite a bit. I learned a lot from his experience and stories. He was good to me and he seemed to appreciate my youth, talent, and humility.

MARTY FRIEDMAN I had a mutual friend with the management of Megadeth, and they'd gone through like sixty guys—to no avail. My friend said, 'Why don't you audition?' Actually, I had an audition for Madonna the same week, and I got Megadeth, so I wound up not going to Madonna. But at the time, I was very borderline homeless, so I was really happy to have *any* gig, but even more happy

---

* Drummer, best known for his work with David Lee Roth.

to join Megadeth, because it was very similar to what I was already doing in the 80s—not so much Cacophony, but my previous band, Hawaii, was like a New Wave of British Heavy Metal/thrash band, but with way more intense guitar. So that fit right in with Megadeth, and it was a very lucky time, because I was eating lollipops for lunch and shit like that. It was lucky timing.

JAS OBRECHT In 1990, when I interviewed him, Jason had just completed the sessions for David Lee Roth's *A Little Ain't Enough*. Fans were anxiously anticipating Roth's new album and upcoming tour—after all, Dave had previously performed alongside Eddie Van Halen and Steve Vai.

In early 1991, *A Little Ain't Enough* was released and went gold, but a tour with Jason Becker on guitar was not to be. At the time of our interview, Jason had just learned that he'd been diagnosed with amyotrophic lateral sclerosis, better known as Lou Gehrig's disease.

JASON BECKER I had been feeling a lazy limp in my left calf for a few months. I even toured with Cacophony with that feeling. When I moved to Southern California, I finally went to the hospital to see what it was. After a bunch of tests, they said it was probably ALS. I didn't know what ALS was and I didn't care. I just went about playing guitar for Roth. Luckily, I was able to finish the album, but during rehearsals for the tour, my legs would shake and my hands would fall off the guitar. Dave and I sadly decided I couldn't tour. He was sadder than I was.

MARTY FRIEDMAN We both had our gigs and we were both on top of the world. I had an arm problem and he had a leg problem—at the same time. His leg was kind of numb, and my arm was giving me problems. The doctor told me I should give up guitar. I had just joined Megadeth and was about to record *Rust In Peace*, and Jason was limping on one of his legs. He'd just joined Roth's band and was rehearsing to record an album with them. So we were still hanging out a lot in LA, and we were commiserating with each other. It's like, 'What the fuck? We both got these dream gigs, and now, we're both not going to be able to play anymore and have to give this up.' I was very fortunate that mine did heal. But his didn't. Just a big waste at the time, but as a result, he's probably inspired more people in a much, much bigger way, and, as a bonus, continued to create great music—so I can't feel negative about his situation.

BECKER WAS LEFT TO WATCH FROM THE SIDELINES AS
ROTH TOURED IN SUPPORT OF *A LITTLE AIN'T ENOUGH* WITH
ANOTHER GUITARIST, AND MARTY JOINED MEGADETH.

JASON BECKER It was sort of difficult, but not as bad as you might expect. I remember when Marty called me and told me he got the Megadeth gig. I was happier than when I got with Dave. He was my best friend and mentor, and to watch him succeed was a huge thrill for me. It was only hard with Dave when he did a national radio show and he was asked why the album band wasn't touring. He said something like, 'Some people are better smoking cigarettes in the studio, and some people are better live.' I was so pissed and hurt. I would have been awesome live. I never smoked in my life, either. He could have told my story, but it was all about him.

JAS OBRECHT The Becker family was initially told Jason's life expectancy was three to five years. By 1996, he'd lost the ability to speak, so his father developed a method of communicating via eye movement similar to that used by Noirtier de Villefort, a character in Alexandre Dumas's *The Count Of Monte Cristo*. From his wheelchair, Jason continued to compose music with a computer that responds to eye movement.

On his 1996 album *Perspective*, he wrote that ALS has 'crippled my body and speech, but not my mind.' He followed up with 1999's *The Raspberry Jams* and 2003's *The Blackberry Jams*. *The Jason Becker Collection* came out around 2008. In his autobiography, *Crazy From The Heat*, David Lee Roth praised Jason as 'the kindest, gentlest, most flexible, absorbing, want-to-learn spirit that I've ever really worked with.' This parallels my observations of the man. As with Randy Rhoads, I don't think we have enough of Jason's music on record to really figure out where he would have fit in the grand scheme of things. We're very lucky to have the recordings he was able to complete.

JASON BECKER I am doing pretty well. My health is pretty stable. I communicate pretty quickly with a system my dad invented. It isn't a computer thing. Each letter consists of two specific eye movements that my caregivers and I have memorized. It is way faster than any computer system I have tried. I can say anything I want. I use this for composing music using Logic Pro. I give detailed instructions for what notes to put where and what instruments to use. You would be surprised at how fast it can go if I am extra inspired. I wrote a three-minute orchestral piece in the last three weeks. At first, it can be a one note at a time thing, but as I go along, there is copying and pasting chords and counterpoint stuff. I can often hear something in my head first, so it isn't like I am stabbing around in the dark.

MARTY FRIEDMAN Had Jason not gotten sick, we would have probably done a lot more together. It was such an eclectic band that I couldn't really see it happen any time back then, but actually now, if Jason could play now, I'd do it in such a heartbeat, because there's so much more interest and so much more acceptability to intense music now than there was back then. So people listen to Cacophony, and their ears can accept it now, whereas ten years ago or twenty years ago, it was just like, 'What the fuck is this noise?' But now, it's completely acceptable. I'm praying that Jason gets better and can play guitar again. Then you'll see a reunion.

practice
makes perfect

**Does practice make perfect?
And, if so ... how much?**

JOE SATRIANI In the beginning, your fingers hurt, and you're just trying to get your fingers to move around and remember how to get from one chord to the next. And then that goes quickly.

The first three years of guitar playing is when the most amount of change occurs. You go from not being able to play an F to suddenly knowing where every minor scale is in every key. If you're really working hard, you cover that ground within three years. But it does take I think a lot of hard work. If you're starting to learn how to play, and you're a young teenager, that means you're still in school; you may not have to work at a job when school's done, which means you can sit down, and spend hours playing guitar. It gets harder when you're an adult. This is a big part of the answer. I know this because I was a teacher, and I used to teach eight-year-olds and eighteen-year-olds and twenty-eight-year-olds and fifty-eight-year-olds! It's different—those stages in life and how they allow you to practice.

I was no different. When I was in high school, I made sure that I had *hours* to practice. And when I became a young professional, I really practiced like crazy—like ten hours a day—because I could arrange my schedule that way. But then as I became more successful, I realized I had to put more time into writing. What coincided with that was the fact that I actually didn't have to practice so much, because most of that practice is memorization. So by the time I was eighteen, I actually did know where everything was. I knew how to play all the modes of the harmonic minor scale in every key, in every position of every string. It's like, 'I've just done this ridiculous amount of practicing.'

So, when I get to practice now, I'm thinking about the tour, the session, and new things that I haven't done. But when I look at the guitar, it's totally familiar to me. When I was fifteen, it was very unfamiliar. I was always wondering, 'Wow. What the hell is Jeff Beck doing? I don't know how to do that!' I think the nature of practicing between an accomplished player and a beginner is basically that. There's so much finessing that has to go on when you're a pro and you play for many hours. And you're not even close to finessing when you're a beginner.

KIRK HAMMETT Before I joined the band, I discovered the New Wave of British Heavy Metal. And I discovered bands like Def Leppard and Iron Maiden, that had musicians in the band that were only two or three years older than myself. That hit me like a lightning bolt of inspiration. I was seventeen, eighteen at the time, so I had deduced that the only way that these people were able to get songs together, get their playing together, and get their band situation together, was to practice. That hit me in 1980. Literally, what I would do is I would get up, I would play guitar, I would take a food break—which was breakfast—and then I would play guitar again, play until the afternoon, take a short break, run some errands, maybe grab a snack, come back, and play some more.

Throughout this time, I had this whole thing—it's not the greatest thing—but what I would do is I would work only long enough to buy a piece of equipment, or only enough to get a credit to go on unemployment. So I worked it out that if you worked for four-to-six months, you can get unemployment for like, the next three months. I did that, so that I would have lots of time to practice!

At that point, I was hanging out in Berkeley with my guitar teacher, Joe Satriani. And he would give me on graph paper—y'know, the paper that had all the little squares on it—he would write out chord diagrams, scale diagrams, three-octave scales, modes, how to practice the modes, three-octave modes. And what I would do is I would divide up my practice time with going over scales, getting that embedded into my head, playing all those scales, and then I would use a part of my practice time to come up with riffs—songwriting riffs—and maybe a cool lead guitar lick.

And a part of it, I used to 'record copy,' because back then, we didn't have guitar magazines that had all the music laid out to all the popular songs. Back then, the only way to learn songs from Black Sabbath, Led Zeppelin, or UFO was to sit down and learn by ear. I would put aside a certain amount of time, just to record copy—that's what me and John Marshall[*] used to call it. Which means we would copy stuff off of records—that could be anything from UFO to Jeff Beck to Al Di Meola to Van Halen to Judas Priest to Dixie Dregs. I was listening to all sorts of stuff back then—as I still do, now. And all the more difficult stuff that I could not figure out—like a lot of the Ulrich Roth stuff from his solo albums—I would bring it to Joe! I'd say, 'Joe, what scales is Ulrich Roth using? What arpeggios and what chords is he outlining in his solo?' And Joe would break it down to me, and we would deconstruct a solo, and I would learn so much from that.

So Joe taught me how to deconstruct solos and figure out what scales and what chords were being suggested over the course of the guitar solo. I would take that knowledge of how to deconstruct solos, and I did a lot of deconstructing on my own. So, basically, it would be theory, record copying, and songwriting. That is pretty much how I still divide up my time right now. The only difference now is I like certain jazz grips—sometimes I call chords 'grips.' So I'm trying to expand my knowledge of jazz chords, so I have a whole slew of jazz progressions that I'll go through, and that in itself just helps my playing overall. That's the only difference between the 80s and now—I have a lot more jazz stuff incorporating into it. Jazz and bossa nova. And I have different warm-up exercises now—that are customized to what I need to work on.

STEVE VAI Back when I was a teenager, I was honing my chops and 'preparing the vessel,' so to speak. But when the time came to actually create music and record—or should I say, cast the mold of the performing entity that I was at the time—that took as much time during the day. But, the focus was different—it was on playing. Like, I remember when I did the *Eat 'Em And Smile* record,[†] I played as much as I ever played every day, but I wasn't sitting there doing scales and exercises and studying and stuff like that. I was just running 'Shyboy' until I could do it in my sleep—standing on one foot, with half a whammy bar and a blown amp! Whatever it took.

ACE FREHLEY [Kiss guitarist; solo artist] Before Kiss, when I was starting out, yeah, I used to practice for hours. But once I was in Kiss, the set was the set. We did the same set every night. It was like a Broadway show. I had to be careful about where I was standing, because a bomb was going to go off! So in essence, the whole show

---

[*] Metallica roadie/Metal Church guitarist.
[†] David Lee Roth's full-length solo debut from 1986.

was almost choreographed—every song—because of all the pyrotechnics. There was very little rehearsal or practice involved once we got rolling.

K.K. DOWNING It's kind of an interesting one, the 'practicing regime.' As you grow up being a guitar player, with scales and stuff, I was a big fan of the natural minor scale, really—I used to practice that like an idiot. [*Laughs*] I thought I was quite advanced, because through the 70s and the early days, everything was pretty much pentatonic stuff. But I thought that I was being pretty smart by adding the extra couple of notes, so I used to practice that scale more than anything else. Utilizing three notes per string, and I used to pick up speed. And that was pretty much it, sadly. But around '83, '84, like a lot of other guitar players, I started to go on to harmonic minor and whole tone/half tone and diminished—just broadened the repertoire a little bit. But up until then, my practicing was that, really—rather than just normal string exercises.

RIK EMMETT [Triumph singer-guitarist; solo artist] I'm not really much of a 'practicing guy.' My time of practicing was in my teenage years, and maybe in my really early twenties. But by the time you're in a rock band and you're touring, and then you're trying to write material for records—and then I was also a columnist for *Guitar Player* magazine, so there was that monthly duty—you just don't really have the time. And maybe I wasn't cut from that cloth anyway—I think there's a certain kind of player that develops that discipline and tries to follow a regimen of that. But not for me. When I would find time, I would invariably use the time to be writing and fiddling around and playing.

The other part of it is for me, I don't necessarily approach the playing of guitar from the point of view of always trying to improve and develop my technique. In that regard, maybe I'm more like a slightly older generation of guitar players— maybe the Pete Townshend kind of guys of the world. It's like, you've developed a certain level of facility, and now, it's more a question of you play for pleasure and recreation, and you get into that creative mode, and you're doing it based on the skillset that you've already got. You're not necessarily trying to push yourself to the next level all the time.

And I don't say that to be sounding negative or to be putting down the guys that do approach it that way. Steve Morse is a guy that I know, and I know Steve does have a level of discipline to this physical technique, and he really does need to keep it at a certain level in order to be able to accomplish the things he hears inside his head. For me, I'm kind of happy playing over a set of changes that I'm pretty comfortable with, and blowing in blues-based kinds of ways that I know and my hands know and those are the patterns that I like.

I teach at a college level, and see students all the time that are in a jazz program, and they are built from that stuff—where to them, it's really a marriage of technique to intellect. And they're trying to push themselves to the next level. And the side that I try to show them is, 'Y'know, music can also just be a real pleasure, where you're connecting with an audience. That's a big part of it.' So having said all that, I tend to be a 'song guy.' Songs kind of function on a different level than monster technique.

STEVE MORSE [Dixie Dregs, Kansas, Deep Purple guitarist; solo artist] Certainly, every day. And certainly, in the two-hour range—and longer, if I was on the road. On the road, I would try to review everything that I screwed up or could have done cleaner, and make little exercises that would accentuate the one movement or difficult shift that I felt that I needed to improve. And then I had a regimen of an hour of just skills and calisthenics, that I did daily. Plus, a warm-up before the show, plus the show. So, when you're doing gigs, you get more of a boost. But, you can also overdo it and pull muscles and tendons and over-stress parts—which I did, occasionally, when we were playing two shows in a row, and a lot of the songs were difficult.

STEVE LYNCH I used to practice three or four hours a day, until I went to the Guitar Institute. That was in March of 1978, and that's when I started getting into it probably ten to twelve hours a day, seven days a week. And I even played sometimes as much as sixteen hours. I was kind of obsessed with it. It was like an addiction. I did that seven days a week for a whole year, and then I started to slow down a little bit, because my hands were kind of falling apart. [*Laughs*] I actually wore down cartilage in my fingers, and I went to a hand specialist, and he said, 'You've got to cool it, or you're really going to be feeling this later on in life.' And sure enough, I did. I've gone through a couple of operations on each one of my hands—for carpal tunnel and everything. It always comes back to that I can play again—that's the main thing. But during the 80s, I would go back to my regular schedule of two to three, sometimes four hours a day, because we were always writing and playing and performing a lot. Pretty much from '83 to '89, it was nonstop.

MICHAEL ANGELO BATIO Back in the early 80s, I was a session guitarist in Chicago. When you think about, 'Where was Oprah Winfrey?' Chicago. 'Where was Phil

Donahue?' Chicago. There were all these daytime talk shows, like Jenny Jones and really big ones, that were based in Chicago. Chicago during that time was the TV and radio-jingle market of the United States—not LA. And I was a top, first-call session guitar. You name it—Taco Bell, Pizza Hut, Kentucky Fried Chicken, United Airlines, United Way. And I used to teach guitar. So I had a guitar in my hands … I would literally be in the recording studio at eight in the morning until sometimes two or three, sometimes four. And I would teach lessons four days a week, and then on the weekends, I'd play in bands. So my practice schedule was just constantly a guitar.

Once I moved to LA, I've had a practice regimen that I've used since the old days, and it's served me well—I've never had a hand injury. So I have two kinds of practice schedules—for shows where it's about fifteen minutes, and it can go for as long as an hour. But I can do it really in about ten, fifteen minutes—that's the first part of it. If I get longer, then I start doing more and go about an hour. No more than about an hour and a half for a show, because then I'm *too* warmed up—I want to play great during the show, not during the practice. And then when I do records, I will practice ten, twelve … my record is fourteen hours in a day. And I'll go two to three weeks before I put one note down for a keeper, because I just want to be so dialed in. So it's really two practice regimes.

In the 80s, it was the same way. I didn't get to practice much when I was doing that much work—teaching, studio work, playing. Because that was the practice—I just had a guitar in my hands. But once I moved to California, once I stopped the sessions, stopped the teaching, and just slowly went to play in bands and music, in that regard, to be a major little recording artist, the short practice regimen, fifteen minutes to an hour, and the long one for doing records. And I've never changed that.

ALEX SKOLNICK I was still in high school until the mid 80s. My first year out of high school was 1987. I joined the band with guys that were older, and I was associated with that generation, although I'm more of a 'next generation' musician. So, at that time, I was really young and I was committed to the instrument. I tried to do at least a couple hours a day. I had occasional days where I would play all day. But I think it increased more once I joined an established band in high school—which was Testament.

Having gigs and having that incentive—playing in front of a live audience, that increased my practice a lot. So, by 1986, when I was about to finish high school, I was doing the first Testament gigs, I think I was playing hours every day. But there's some that say they would play all day/every day. I needed to get outside, I needed to read books, I needed to stimulate my imagination. There were moments, but I wasn't like the quintessential 'lock yourself in a room and not living' practicer. But I did practice a lot.

HANK SHERMANN I was playing the guitar every day. First of all, getting to know the instrument, and I had a few friends who could decipher some of Ted Nugent's cool licks and Angus Young's cool licks, and some rhythm things. I took a few shortcuts there, and then Ace Frehley's stuff, and figured out, 'OK, so *this* is how they're doing it.' And then I started to build up my style—trying to imitate Ace Frehley. So that is probably usually how everyone starts.

Then suddenly, when I had a little more experience and a little more drive and felt good about it, then I started to develop my own kind of notes and how I play them. But a lot of practicing and also at the same time, composing. Very early on, I was into composing songs, and did that that from the get-go. So I'm constantly figuring out new riffs and things like that. I started when I was seventeen years old—which is kind of late. But at least I got started and kept going, kept going, kept going, and suddenly, we were into having this punk band called the Brats, and shortly thereafter, Mercyful Fate came about in 1981.

BILLY CORGAN Four hours a day, every day. A mixture of both [practicing scales and playing along to records]. I played along to records, and I never tried to imitate, per se. I just tried to understand that technology—how people were able to play so fast was just beyond my mind.

JENNIFER BATTEN That was my 'disciplined era.' I took a test to get into GIT in '78, and I flunked. I had been taking lessons since I was eight years old—I was taught tunes and techniques, but never really the tools that I needed to be a pro. I went to a weekend symposium that GIT advertised in *Guitar Player* magazine, and it was just full of all these monster jazz players giving seminars. I'm sure most of which went over my head, but I was so intrigued and absorbed in it, that I decided to sign up for the school that weekend … and I flunked. So I was sent back to San Diego where I was living, and studied with a monster jazz player named Peter Sprague for six months.

My discipline at that time, I probably put in three or four hours a day, just to keep up with what he was showing me. And six months later, I was able to get into the school, and then, my discipline went up about ten times, and that's all I did for a solid year. Sleep, eat, and play guitar. For a couple of years after that, I had the discipline, as well—I would set an egg timer for one hour, and do one hour of arpeggios, one hour of sight reading, and then on to maybe chord scales and all these different things I needed to get together. And as I got more and more gigs, I didn't have time to keep up that kind of practice schedule. But back then, it was a discipline I do not have now.

PAUL GILBERT In the 80s, it was a lot—I loved playing guitar. And the athleticism was really rewarded at that time. Everybody around me would get excited about it. I liked it too—as much as I loved the vibrato and the songwriting and the beauty of music, I liked the athleticism, as well. It was exciting and people were doing it really well. And I found out the more I practiced, the more I could have success within myself. Everything around me was encouraging me to go in that direction.

The more I worked at it, the better I got, so I just went along with it. And I had nothing but fun doing it, but at a certain point—I was probably about twenty-two, around 1989—I started to get sick of listening to myself. [*Laughs*] In terms of all the sequences and different ways to play sixteenth notes. And as a listener, I started getting tired of it—having been immersed in that kind of thing for such a long time, I really started to crave a contrast. So I started listening to old Beach Boys records and stuff that was really vocal-driven and chord-driven and composition-driven.

It's nice to have spent that time on the athletic side of things, because now when I pick up a guitar to write a song, I'm rarely stopped by any technical problems with the fingers—if I've got an idea, I can get it out. But at the same time, I've got this doubled-edged-sword reputation as a shredder, that doesn't necessarily reflect where I'm at as a music fan or performer for the rest of my life.

JASON BECKER I didn't really have a practice schedule. Whenever I was at home, I just had the guitar on. I never set aside time for certain exercises, or whatever. I did whatever I wanted. I would work on something I sucked at until I was good. I know that some people stress about practicing, and they ask me how long it takes to get good. My advice is to just enjoy it, and to remember that it is all about making soulful music.

MARTY FRIEDMAN I've never been a big 'practicer'—ever—believe it or not. I was fortunate that when I started, I put together a band right away, and even before

I could barely play, I was playing in a band. So getting into the routine of band life—like rehearsing, writing songs, playing shows, recording—that all started at the beginning. And I can't stress this enough, how lucky I was to do that, because you learn so much more and so much faster, and you improve so much faster.

When you're playing shows—even if they're small shows and even if they're for your friends—*they're still shows.* So it's still the same thing you're doing when you're playing at the Tokyo Dome—it's a show. It's not practicing to a metronome and it's not practicing in your bedroom. So, you're already doing the exact same thing that you're planning to do.

Getting started doing that will cut out a lot of the bullshit of … y'know, I don't know what people do when they practice. People say they practice eight or nine hours a day—I have no idea what they would do with that time. The first thing I did was always writing songs, and if I was playing a cover, I would learn that song, and try to play it. But the main thing was about the songs that I had written and my friends had written, and how to make them cooler, and how to actually perform those. And you get in a habit of doing that, the next thing you know, you've built up quite a repertoire of things that you can do on the guitar and you learn how to branch out. Rather than practicing, I was always playing live or working on music, so I was never really like, 'God, I've got to learn this scale or this mode.' As a result, I'm not the most typically educated guitarist, but I think I skipped a lot of the 'boring stuff,' so to speak.

GEORGE LYNCH Very sporadic. Obviously, I was working a lot, so I was either touring or in the studio and playing a lot. But outside of that, I found myself battling laziness. So I would tend to not be as disciplined as I probably should have been in different periods in my career. In the early 80s, I was actually very disciplined until I'd say about probably '85. And then as we became more successful, I probably became less disciplined—up until the very late 80s, and then from '89, I rededicated myself to advancing my abilities. Actually, I answered an ad for a guitar teacher in the back of the paper, and showed up at some guy's apartment with my guitar in my hand, and took guitar lessons. I was very much disciplined from '89 through the early 90s.

RICHIE KOTZEN I didn't have what you would call a 'structured schedule' of any kind. When I started playing guitar, it was something that I just did—literally, I always had it on. I would walk around the house with it, noodling around. I'd lay in bed, and I had a television in my bedroom, and I'd have the sound off—there would be something happening on TV, and I'd kind of stare aimlessly and sit in bed and play the guitar until I fell asleep. I'd wake up, and the guitar would be laying on the bed. Actually, I still do that when my girlfriend is out of town—I'm sleeping with my guitar!

But it was never really a 'practice thing.' I'm not really a guy who liked to practice. It would kind of be a situation where obviously when I was very young, I had to practice, because I had to learn the instrument—I had to practice in order to know where to put my fingers. But now, I don't really practice—I just kind of play and I pick up the instrument when I have an idea for a song, and then I record the song, and I put it back down until I have another idea. And occasionally, I'll pick it up and noodle around. But the thing that really did more for me than anything was playing with other people—that was the key. That was how I really developed, and I think that's important for any young players—to play with other people.

RON JARZOMBEK I don't remember any regular routine of running over scales or anything like that. But I've always been real conscious with a metronome. But back then, I really just played a lot of Rush and Kiss solos, and did a lot of transcribing with a turntable that had 'speed 16'* on it. I did a lot of that ear training kind of stuff. I wasn't focused on the overall speed of everything—just getting everything musically overall.

I wanted to cover all aspects of being a guitar player/musician, rather than just working on the 'guitar playing' part of it. Working on a lot of writing and stuff like that, learning some theory. So, as far as the physical aspect of it, I don't even remember if I had a set routine of playing this kind of a scale, doing this kind of a thing—it was just playing along to songs, keeping good time. Of course, my brother,† we always had little bands together when we were younger, so we were just writing and doing all of that at the same time.

STEVE STEVENS I've never been one of those guys. Maybe when I was much younger. Of course, you had to practice in order to get better. I always felt that technique was useful in a way that as a guitar player, you want to be able to execute any idea that's in your head, and not be limited by your technical ability. And that said, I've never been a fan of guys who just play for the sake of 'Look how fast I can play.' What's the point of that? At that point, it's almost a gymnastic exercise—it's not music.

---

* 16rpm, allowing the user to play twelve-inch LPs at half-speed.

† Drummer Bobby Jarzombek.

I wanted to have enough technique to follow through on any ideas, but also, I was already working with Billy Idol, so the main thing was to write songs. So any ideas, if I sat down for two or three hours, it was usually with a cassette player to record a riff or an idea, so I could present it to Billy as a song idea. So I guess that's more my practice schedule. I've never been one of those guys—I'm still not—who sits down and goes, 'I'm going to work on *this*.' For some reason, I'm just not that kind of guy.

ADRIAN BELEW I've never had a practice schedule. I don't practice, I'm afraid to say. I know that breaks all the rules, but I play a lot and I experiment a lot. I just constantly play, really. I've already played for about an hour this morning on my acoustic guitar, sitting here in the bedroom! My passion for guitar just allows me to always be playing it, and I'm totally self-taught, so I don't know any regiment sort of scales or things like that to practice in the first place.

Sometimes, I write pieces that are very different for me, and then I practice those. But those are usually my own pieces. When I was younger, when I was first learning guitar, I listened to records and worked out everything I could, and that required a lot of time and practice there. But throughout my life, really, I've just created and kind of played at the same time, and never had a schedule.

BILLY SHEEHAN People would come over to my house and knock on the door, and I'd answer the door with the bass on. They'd say, 'Don't you ever put that thing down?' And I'd say, 'No. As a matter of fact, I don't!' Even when I played pretty much every night of the week all through the 70s and up to the mid 80s, I worked a lot on learning whatever there was to learn. It's just an unlimited ocean of things to understand and learn about music and bass and playing. I would just dive in at any particular spot and swim as far as I could, and spend many, many hours at it.

JEFF WATERS [Annihilator guitarist] I started a little on an acoustic folk guitar, when I was really young—I was about eight or something. But I didn't start and do all these lessons that were intense. It was more like I was learning how to play a C chord for about a year. I was part-time. But I started taking lessons around twelve or thirteen—two years of classical. And again, it was once a week, and I would only practice half an hour a night, and simple stuff. And then the third year was a year of jazz, and that was over my head at fifteen. It was just too much. My attention span wasn't there—it was just too complicated and crazy.

So I was right into Kiss, Sweet, and AC/DC. Practicing started with the

1980s stuff, when you had the *Back In Black* album coming out, and the amazing Scorpions stuff, and Akira Takasaki from Loudness, and you had Rhoads with Ozzy, Tony Iommi with *Mob Rules*. That album, one of the most underrated albums of all time—*Mob Rules*—with Dio. Everybody thinks 'Ozzy/Sabbath,' but oh my God, I was just blown away with *Mob Rules* and the guitar stuff, and the overall evilness of the album. You had *The Number Of The Beast* and all the Maiden stuff, the Priest stuff at the time. That's pretty well 1980, when I said, 'This is going to be my life! I don't care about anyone!' [*Laughs*]

And that's when it became not work—you were just sitting there, jamming along to all these players, songs, and records that you loved, and you'd try to figure it out for fun. And then the real big change in me was when the first albums from bands like Razor, Anvil, and Exciter came out—some really important Canadian bands, very important on the 'big four'* and the stuff to come. And then of course, the big four's first couple of records, and Venom and stuff like that.

As soon as I heard Venom, Slayer, and 'Metal Militia,'† *that was it.* I dropped the practice regimen of practicing the diminished scales and classical vibe of Randy Rhoads. As soon as I heard the early thrash stuff, I was like, 'That's what I want to play.' That's when the practicing got really intense, and I started learning this picking from Hanneman and King and Hetfield and Holt and Mustaine. And that was it. I was just full on trying to be a good player, thanks to that thrash era.

RON 'BUMBLEFOOT' THAL In the early 80s, I was just a young teenager, and had all the time in the world, so I would spend every possible waking minute playing—in all different ways. I had an interesting schedule of what I would do. Because by that point, I had been playing for a handful of years—I had started when I was about six or seven years old. I would be practicing for my guitar lessons. I was taking jazz lessons and music theory, and also in school, some classical. Every day I would try and learn an entire album. I would take any album, and by the time I had the last song down, I would forget the first one, but I would go through the practice of learning an entire album.

I would take the Scorpions' *Blackout*, and then I would take Van Halen *Diver Down*, and would start with the first song, drop the needle for a few seconds, retain the sound in my head, play it on the guitar, and then drop the needle again, and just keep on going, and try to learn the entire song, and then do it for every song and learn a whole album. So I would spend a couple of hours learning an

---

* Metallica, Slayer, Anthrax, and Megadeth.
† The closing track on Metallica's debut album, *Kill 'Em All* (1983).

album every day. Some were easy, like AC/DC, some were tougher, like UK, or something that had Adrian Belew or someone like that on it—Allan Holdsworth.

I would be writing songs and recording them, and I also had a band that did some originals, but a whole lot of covers—we did tons of Rush, Ozzy, and Maiden. So I'd be going out, doing gigs. And making demos and doing everything that original bands would be doing. And getting creative with the guitar—just experimenting with modifying the guitar and coming up with bodies and putting an extended neck piece or double neck piece—just all kinds of crazy, strange things I would do, just to see what kind of sounds would come out of it.

So I was really living music and living the guitar throughout the 80s and 90s. I started working when I was twelve, and it was all just to raise money to support the music habit. When I was twelve, I would paint Iron Maiden albums on the backs of dungaree jackets, and that's how I would save up money to get guitars and stomp boxes and whatever I'd need.

Then when I was about sixteen, I got my working papers, and started working as a stock boy at a local deli. I remember at Toys R Us, I was a stock boy there—diapers, ass-wipes, and baby food. Me and all the other longhaired kids, we would just sit in the back, and we would eat little jars of pear juice and strained food. There would be a big pile of baby food jars in the back. From there, it reached a point where I was able to use what I had learned and any skills I had developed, to share them with the rest of the world and be compensated for it. So I started teaching. By the time I was thirteen, I was teaching in mom's basement. Six dollars for an hour lesson.

From there, it became working at a local music store. From there, started working at the Sam Ash Music Institute as a band director and guitar teacher. From there, I set up a whole music department for a private school in New Jersey, that had a jazz band, a choir, music for kids, music history, private lessons—everything. Then I started teaching at SUNY Purchase College, and teaching music production and also on top of just the teaching thing, with all the recording I had done, I started recording other bands, and started producing, collaborating, co-writing, engineering, and every aspect of that. Everything I was doing that I learned how to do, I was sharing with others.

I reached a point where, by my early twenties, I could make a living just from music—between doing gigs four or five nights a week, teaching, and I was also starting to work as a transcriber for instructional cassettes back then. In the 80s into the 90s, that's pretty much how I was living and what my schedule was.

LITA FORD [Runaways guitarist; solo artist] I lived with that guitar attached to my body. Whenever I would go to visit my mother and father, I would sit and talk to them, watch television or whatever we would do, and I would have a guitar on my lap, and I would just be plucking away at the strings—even during conversation. Or if I would go out with a guy, after we had dinner or a movie or a party, we would end up back at his place, and I would always say to him, 'Have you got any guitars laying around?' I was never really interested in the guys as much as the instruments! I would sit around and just pluck the guitar, everywhere I went.

VIVIAN CAMPBELL The only thing I can think of is nervous energy. I drank a lot of coffee, and back then, I used to smoke. So between nicotine and caffeine … as a kid, you're always attracted to the technical players—players who play fast. It was only in my later years that I could start to appreciate guitar players like Peter Green and David Gilmour—people who are not necessarily 'flash' guitar players, but just have so much great style. Although even as a kid, I was a Paul Kossoff fan, as well as being a Gary Moore fan. I really honestly think it's nervous energy, because to be honest, I never even thought of myself as a fast guitar player.

And back in the 80s, when I was doing the early Dio records, I was constantly spinning my wheels at the fact that I couldn't play like Yngwie Malmsteen—that I didn't have that kind of control. I guess I have a good left hand and a not-so-good right hand, because I can't do the alternate picking thing at all. My right hand is good in other ways—I'm good at palm-muting; that has become very much a part of my sound. I've noticed I used my pinky a lot more than most. But I think it's our little idiosyncrasies that make us unique. As a young man, I didn't appreciate it—like I said, I was frustrated that I couldn't play like so-and-so, but it's actually your limitations that helped define your style. And that's the advice that I give to any young musician—it's more important to be unique than to be proficient. You want to have your voice and you want to find your unique voice. And it's your limitations and my limitations that help us to get our voice.

stevie
ray

With hyper-speed shred all the rage in rock, Stevie Ray Vaughan singlehandedly keeps blues guitar alive in the 80s.

ALEX SKOLNICK Many people picked up a guitar because of Stevie Ray Vaughan, in the 80s.

JAS OBRECHT Stevie Ray Vaughan had sparks flying off of him. He was like an unstoppable force of nature. At a time when other artists would spend months perfecting an album in the studio, Stevie recorded his debut album, *Texas Flood*, in two weeks. Two takes of each song, choose the best, mix it, master it, done.

When I met Stevie, two qualities jumped right out: He had a vice-like handshake, unlike people like Chet Atkins and Muddy Waters, who were very careful with their hands. And he was very quick to praise his influences. Onstage, he'd tap into the spirits of people like Jimi Hendrix, Albert King, and Larry Davis, who recorded the original version of 'Texas Flood' and was clearly the main influence on Stevie's singing style. And, in interviews, he was very gracious about acknowledging the influence other musicians had had on him. I always admired that about him.

In the mid 1980s, Stevie Ray Vaughan almost singlehandedly brought the blues roaring back to life. This is not only my observation, but that of Buddy Guy, B.B. King, and John Lee Hooker, all of whom told me in interviews that Stevie deserves the credit for the upswing in their fortunes during this era. He brought hard blues into stadium-size venues. And it was really clear that these venerable bluesmen—the guys who'd helped create postwar blues in America—were really appreciative for what Stevie did for them.

KIRK HAMMETT What blew me away about Stevie Ray Vaughan's playing was, every note, you could hear his conviction. *His fucking conviction.* And his commitment and his dedication. He was *in* every single note. You know when he hit one note he had been striving to hit that note, to make it the best he possibly could, ever since he was a young person. And his tone, his phrasing, his approach, his attitude, everything about Stevie Ray Vaughan I loved. And he was a big Hendrix disciple, as well as I was. I figured out how Hendrix did a lot of stuff by just watching Stevie Ray Vaughan pull out a Hendrix-ism—out of nowhere. Like the sound before 'Foxy Lady,' the sound before Jimi Hendrix actually gets the feedback, I learned how to get that 'fret sound' by watching Stevie Ray Vaughan. So, Stevie Ray Vaughan was a huge teacher for me. And to this day, I'm chasing a tone like his. Listen to his tone: it's sub-harmonic. A really good sub-harmonic tone is very, very difficult. And his bending, his vibrato, his phrasing; I'm still in awe of Stevie Ray Vaughan.

GREG HOWE Prior to him, I wasn't that interested in blues, because blues always sounded boring to me. It always sounded like the same song. Not that it is, it's just to an immature young guitarist right out of high school who wants to shred, blues is not that interesting. And so Stevie Ray Vaughan was a guy who brought that whole genre into a place that was more appealing to guitarists who wanted to still display some technical prowess. And it also really introduced me to blues, because once I started to realize where he got a lot of his stuff from—like Albert King and Hendrix—it was actually probably through Stevie Ray Vaughan that I got much more interested in Hendrix.

Because once I got to really understand the premise of blues, I suddenly had a different perspective entirely. And then, suddenly, Hendrix became this great player. Prior to Stevie Ray Vaughan, I didn't understand what the big deal about Hendrix was. I never understood it. Because again, it's a typical immature, young-guitarist mindset, where it's like, 'This guy's faster, so he's better. Eddie Van Halen is faster than this guy, so he's better. George Lynch is faster than this guy.' So if I listened to Hendrix back then, it was like, 'I don't see what's so big about him. He's not doing anything difficult, so he's not that great.'

But after I started to understand Stevie Ray Vaughan and understand the blues more, I went back and listened to Hendrix, and I was like, 'How the hell did

I miss all this? This is some of the most amazing guitar playing I've ever heard!' It's amazing to me that I didn't recognize that before. But I could feel myself starting to evolve and grow up as a musician. So Stevie Ray Vaughan, he was just one of many influences that really contributed to my development.

RICHIE KOTZEN The phrasing and the way the guitar sounded when he played it. It was the way the guitar sounded. And I knew it was because of how he was playing the instrument. I knew it wasn't because of what he was playing through—really because of how he was playing the notes. And that really resonated with me. I remember I lived in Pennsylvania and we had a barn on the property that was converted into a business upstairs, and then downstairs, I had a huge area that I was able to use as a studio. And my friend and I would sit in my studio in the wee hours, and just play 'Lenny' over and over, and jam on that. And then we used to go around to bars in Philadelphia and sit in on jam sessions, and we'd always play that song. We'd play it for twenty minutes!

He was just so expressive and so understated—he didn't have to play that much in order to engage you on an emotional level. That's what I think is very important. And unfortunately, so many rock and metal players don't understand that and it's very frustrating—it's very hard for me to listen to a lot of metal guitar players, because they learn how to move their fingers really well, but then when a lot of these guys slow down and play slow, they sound like beginners. It's bizarre. I mean, these are guys who I heard play that have amazing technique, play blindingly fast—way faster than I could, way cleaner—and they play slow, and it sounds like they're a two-year student. It's mind-boggling how people miss that stuff. So, I think Stevie Ray Vaughan, when I heard him when I was a teenager, really opened my eyes to, 'OK, there is really way more to this instrument than just playing a harmonic minor scale and burning it up and down the neck.'

CHRIS CAFFERY [Savatage, Trans-Siberian Orchestra guitarist] Even though somebody like Vai or Satriani—they're great players, [but] I think Stevie Ray Vaughan is one of those in the history of music, is going to go down more of like a Hendrix than those guys. And that is because he was the singer, as well. That particular guitar player was very special as a player, but he was also really special as a personality and as a vocalist. He had a fire to his playing, and he had kind of ... I don't know if it's 'perfection,' because he was a blues player, but you never really heard Stevie Ray Vaughan hit a bad note. It would always make whatever he was doing sound like it was exactly what he wanted to do. And he just was so fluent in every kind of style of blues and *Texas Flood* rock. He was so natural at it. It sounded like it was born into his soul.

TY TABOR He's a brick in the foundation of rock that will always be there. *Undeniable.* He was an extension of pure blues and Hendrix. And it was certainly missing at the time. Not saying that he sounded like Hendrix, or that he was totally traditional blues, but he was aggressively 'bluesed out,' with a Hendrix vibe. It's undeniable what he did—to this day. There is no Joe Bonamassa or any of the string of guitarists that have come along since, that all kind of come from his vibe. He standardized blues-rock at a different level than anybody's been able to do before.

ALEX SKOLNICK Van Halen, I think he has the biggest influence, because the music crossed over into the mainstream. They had bona-fide hits. The same thing with Stevie Ray Vaughan. You suddenly were hearing his tunes on mainstream radio and MTV, and later, VH1. It just became popular, in the way Bonnie Raitt was very popular later—blues that reaches a pop audience. So he had that. And I think because of that mainstream crossover, it got a lot of people to play guitar and inspired a lot of other artists. One that comes to mind is John Mayer. In fact, sometimes, it's so uncanny, if I hear John Mayer do a blues, he also plays a Stratocaster, and there's times when his voice is similar. So yeah, you can really hear the influence there.

But I always thought as great as Stevie Ray Vaughan was, he kept getting compared to Hendrix. People said he was 'the new Hendrix.' I never agreed with that. I don't think *he* agreed with that. And I don't think he would have agreed—especially as he was canonized after he passed way.* I mean, yes, he took some of what Hendrix did, put more blues into it, added the Texas flavor, made it cleaner, and a little less psychedelic. But in context, Hendrix was just such a pioneer—considering the landscape when Hendrix came out versus the landscape [when Vaughan first appeared]. Hendrix already existed when Stevie Ray Vaughan came out. So I think you can't make that comparison.

There's a lot of these hierarchies with guitarists, as far as their stature. Often, they don't make sense to me, but the canonization of Jimi Hendrix totally makes sense to me. I just don't think you can compare anybody to him. But that said,

---

* Stevie Ray died in a helicopter crash on August 27 1990, after playing a show with Eric Clapton.

for the time period, Stevie Ray Vaughan did have a tremendous influence. It's just great music to listen to. You don't have to be a guitar player to like the music. His songs come on, you see people grooving to it and having a good time—it doesn't matter if they're a guitar player or not. Whereas some of the Vai and Satriani stuff comes on, some of it helps to be a guitar nerd, I think. [*Laughs*]

RICHIE KOTZEN I was shocked [by Stevie Ray's death]. I remember where I was—I was in my parents' house and someone called me. I think it was someone from a guitar magazine, because I was doing press already. Just terrible news. One of the greatest, most inspirational guitar players that I've ever listened to.

WOLF MARSHALL I have a great story with Stevie Ray. Back in '85, he had an album out called *Soul To Soul*, and they needed me to meet with Stevie real quick—he had one night in LA to do this performance and a quick interview. And we ended up meeting at the Chateau Marmont—it's a mystical, kind of spooky, Hollywood Hills mansion that they later turned into a big hotel. It's just amazing. You walk in, and there's all these shaded rooms, and the lobby looks like something from old Sunset Boulevard. So Stevie and I met there in the lobby before his performance— in the midafternoon—and we hung out for about three hours, just passing the guitar back and forth. He was showing me his favorite Albert King licks, and then we talked a bit—I had the tape recorder going. We got to be really friendly, just from that one time.

I found most guitar players—no matter how big they are—once they realize that you really love the guitar like they do and you're not just using it as a way to get to know them better or to glom onto them, it comes down to just the love of the music. So as big as Stevie Ray was, and as big as Van Halen was and is, it just comes down to the sense of, if you love the guitar and if they feel you're legit— meaning if you love it, too—then the object of the interview is they know you're not going to misrepresent what they say. Which is a lot of times why people like Van Halen and Slash get very nervous, because they've been so misrepresented in interviews. I remember when I did Slash's interview, a similar thing happened—he was very shy and withdrawn at first, but once we connected on Johnny Winter, he said, 'Come on man, be part of my photo session!' It was like we were buddies, suddenly.

That same thing happened with Stevie. And the funny thing is I have a '64 Strat, and I wanted him to see it. It had been a guitar that all these players had played, because I had taken it to interviews—Van Halen had played it, Steve

Lukather, Allan Holdsworth, Larry Carlton—it became my favorite guitar to take around. And when I took it to that interview with Stevie, we traded it back and forth, because he didn't have his guitar, it was already somewhere where he was going to be performing. And he was showing me his favorite Albert King lick, and he kept breaking the high E string on my guitar, trying to show me this bend. After changing the string twice, he said, 'I'm going to give you something.' He reaches into his pocket, and there's a little tiny wire housing—the sleeve of a wire, like a land cord—he pulled the threads out of it and had the sleeve, and passed the high E string through it. It never broke a string after that!

jeff

One of the few guitarists who first hit in the 60s that managed to keep pace (and remain relevant) alongside the shredders: Jeff Beck.

JOE SATRIANI I grew up learning how to play with Jeff Beck records. We weren't doing anything new—there had been tons of classical and jazz instrumental guitar records. I grew up listening to Wes Montgomery jazz records. There were The Ventures and The Shadows. We weren't doing anything new conceptually—at all, as a matter of fact.

And we grew up listening to those Jeff Beck instrumental records and every time we listened to a record—whether it was instrumental guitar from the 50s, like George Van Eps, or from the 60s, like Wes Montgomery and The Ventures and Shadows, and then Jeff Beck and John McLaughlin and Al Di Meola—those were the things that I think gave us confidence to try our fingers at it, you know what I mean? So yeah, they paved the way. They were the architects of it. We were just newcomers, I think. But for people who are half my age, they don't know who Jeff Beck is, really. They know the name, but they don't know the catalog. But yeah, we built our success on their foundations, as they did with the guitarists that came before them.

JENNIFER BATTEN I don't hear a lot of influence [of Beck on Vai and Satriani], other than it was instrumental. Maybe it opened up a path to give people of that genre a voice, instead of always relying on a singer. Now, *the guitar* can play the melody. And especially because *Blow By Blow* was the most successful and biggest-selling instrumental record up until Kenny G. So it was on the top for decades. I don't think there was any guitar player alive who wasn't super aware of it.

GARY HOEY [solo artist] I think he was, definitely [an influence on 80s instrumental guitar albums]. Because when you look back at *Blow By Blow* and *Wired*, those were albums that if you look at guitar music in decades, if you go to the 50s, there were the Chuck Berrys and all these guys that were playing this style, and it fit in the context of a song with a singer. And then you can go into the 60s, it was like, the 60s was more psychedelic, people were all over the place. And then the 70s, it was kind of like fusion was meeting rock and all this stuff, but Jeff Beck made it commercial.

Like, when he did 'Freeway Jam,' when he did ''Cause We've Ended As Lovers,' he showed that rock guitar could have a very precise melody in a non-vocal song, and still draw people in. And I really think that Satriani, myself, Eric Johnson; we all took from that sound and that approach, to the way you treat a melody when you're writing an instrumental guitar track, and make sure it's like a vocal. And that's what Jeff Beck did, I think.

JAS OBRECHT There are not too many guys who have the technical facility to play like Beck. The closest one I heard back then was Eric Johnson, on that *Seven Worlds* tape that he did in the mid 1970s. There's some beautifully played Beck-ian stuff on there. But Beck, especially during the jazz-rock fusion period that gave us *Blow By Blow* and *Wired*, was really a breed apart from everyone else. He was using Sir George Martin as his producer, and he was exploring jazz veins. And Beck often played without a pick, which was rare during that time. Everybody idolized Beck for his articulate approach to playing notes, his fire, his passion, and the sheer force of his personality. Jeff Beck is a class by himself, and I personally think of him as the best electric guitarist to come out of Great Britain.

ALEX SKOLNICK There was an album of his, *There And Back*, which doesn't get enough credit. All the instrumental music that got popular in the 80s was certainly inspired by Jeff Beck. I never had a desire to do that type of instrumental music— the 80s stuff—because I think it didn't have what I liked about Jeff Beck's music. Which was it wasn't just about the guitar. Some of the later instrumental stuff, it seemed like the other instruments were more 'backing instruments'—just to create platforms for the guitar playing. Whereas with Jeff Beck, the other instruments were really important—without Narada Michael Walden on drums, for example,

Wired would be a completely different record. Without Jan Hammer playing the keyboards, it would be a completely different record.

To me, those records are timeless—not just because of the other musicians, but Jeff Beck, he was one of those 'natural tone' guys. He gets so many different sounds, but there's not a lot of bells and whistles. It's just purely from the guitar and maybe a minimum amount of processing. I'd rather hear that type of expression than these sorts of displays of virtuosity, where you can take the other musicians, insert somebody else, and you wouldn't know the difference. He not only opened the door for the later stuff, I think he also really set the bar so high. A bar that I don't think has ever been reached since—except by him, because he's still going and still sounds fantastic.

STEVE LYNCH I think he probably had quite a bit of an influence. I know he did on me. I was a huge Jeff Beck, Jimi Hendrix, and Jimmy Page fan. Those were the three guys that I mainly learned from. And then later on, I got into listening a lot to Al Di Meola, and then Allan Holdsworth.

JENNIFER BATTEN It was kind of like gigging with God.* It was the *Blow By Blow* record on the radio that opened up my mind to just so many possibilities and genres. He hit everything from jazz to funk rock. I mean, he got in *DownBeat* magazine with that. It was basically a rock record, but it did touch into jazz and funk, and even reggae. So that just blew my mind. At first, I'd listen to it a lot, and then I started to carve into it and learn some of the stuff.

I remember during GIT that year, Steve Lynch was also influenced by Beck. Our assignment was to transcribe a song, and play it live. And his choice was ''Cause We've Ended As Lovers' from *Blow By Blow*. Just to have that in my face and hear it live sent me into another level of getting into Jeff. One of the things I did after school was over was to carve into *Blow By Blow* and *Wired*, and learn all of the solos on both of those records. So all those years later, to get a chance to play with him was completely unexpected, and completely joyful.

PRIOR TO WORKING WITH JEFF BECK, JENNIFER PLAYED
WITH MICHAEL JACKSON FROM 1987 TO 1997.

JENNIFER BATTEN It was 180 degrees different. With Michael, it was more like

---

* Jennifer played in Jeff's band from 1999–2002.

a theater show, where everybody had their parts and costumes. Because of everything involved—from pyro to costume changes—it had to be the same songs every night. And because of the genre of pop music, every song that we played had been a top-ten hit, he wanted the sounds to be exactly like the record. So a lot of rehearsal was spent in dialing that in and playing the same things the same way every night. In fact, I was the only one really that got to improvise on a couple different songs that were opened up for that, like 'Working Day And Night.'

With Jeff, it was the opposite—with Michael, there were seven players onstage, and with Jeff, it was only four. So I was 100 percent responsible for the harmony—whether it was guitar comping or guitar-synthesizer triggering. It was a hell of a lot more pressure, in that regard. But also, Jeff wanted things to be different every night. So he wanted it to have a kick in the pants and have us throw him curves—that would send him in a new direction, improv-wise. So that was super challenging and extremely rewarding.

WOLF MARSHALL He's my favorite rock guitar player. *Period.* When I was fourteen, fifteen years old, I was interested in being like Jeff Beck! I even bought my first Tele after seeing his blonde Tele. I wanted that more than anything—that was my first real guitar that I had. And when he got to the Les Paul period, I wanted a Les Paul. And then later, when the Jeff Beck model Strat came out, I thought it was the greatest thing ever. Jeff was designing that guitar at the same time that I was endorsing Fender, full-time. I had gotten a whole new appreciation of Jeff with each new period. I loved him in the period when he was doing all the stuff like *Rough And Ready*, *Blow By Blow*, and *Wired*. In the 80s he adapted very well— he did that thing with Mick Jagger,* and there was the song with Rod Stewart, 'People Get Ready.'

He kept evolving. He played some things that were very challenging. If you've ever heard his album, *Jeff*, man, that thing is so out there—it's like Steve Vai. He came from The Yardbirds, playing real basic things, and he just kept evolving. Jazz-rock, he fit right in with Al Di Meola and John McLaughlin, and was holding his own with Jan Hammer. And when the pop rock thing came out, he was there with Rod Stewart, with 'People Get Ready,' and worked with Tina Turner and was playing a Jackson for a little while—a pink Jackson. He's one of the people that I never got a chance to work with. He doesn't like to do interviews; he rarely goes outside of England—you have to go to him. So he's one of the few people on my

* Beck played on Jagger's first two solo records, *She's The Boss* (1985) and *Primitive Cool* (1987).

bucket list—I would love to meet him. I know he's very private. But I know the things that we have in common, that would easy to relate to—because he loves all the old rockabilly. You have to reach him where he 'lives,' meaning, what matters to him.

DAVE MENIKETTI If you really want somebody who I thought was unique is Jeff Beck. Beck plays—still, to this day—the kind of stuff that most guitar players would just get down on their knees in front of him. Even a guy like Steve Vai would probably go, 'OK … I may be good, *but Beck is outrageous.* And he's been doing it longer than me!' There's guys that are like that, that you just watch their playing and hear what they're doing, and you go, 'I don't get that.' Or you get it, but you look at their fingers and see how they do it and go, 'Wow. That is just so otherworldly.'

STU HAMM [Joe Satriani, Steve Vai bassist; solo artist] I remember with Joe, we would always try and get Jeff to come down to the shows whenever we'd play in London. Earlier this year, I toured with Jennifer Batten, and it was great to have her tell a lot of stories about Jeff Beck. And he is certainly someone that I have always admired and wanted to play with. But now, apparently he only hires attractive female bass players—I'm sure I'm out of the mix!

JENNIFER BATTEN He's a bit of a Jekyll and Hyde on a show day. I mean, everybody does [it] to a certain degree; where you're working on your 'show head,' you're typically very quiet. If he doesn't want to talk, it's 100 percent impossible to engage him in conversation. But once that pressure's off and the show is over, he's just a party. All his best friends are comedians, and I think only people that know him and have had a chance to hang out with him know what an incredible sense of humor he has. I was with him for three years, and there was a lot of different legs of different tours. One of the things we would do during one leg, after a show, we'd get on the bus and watch the intro to *Austin Powers*. [*Laughs*] Like, every single night—for a month. And another thing would be the Monty Python 'rabbit scene.'* He was just a gas.

---

* From the film *Monty Python And The Holy Grail* (1975).

gary

**Gary Moore showed you can be
both technical and tasteful.**

K.K. DOWNING I had the first two Skid Row albums,* and I think he was like seventeen on the first album, but he had a reputation in the UK as being the 'fastest guitar player,' which was quite an accolade, really. Why I really like Gary Moore is he took the blues and put the blues into really good songs. Like the album *Corridors Of Power*, for example: it's totally listenable, and a lot of people wouldn't identify it as a traditional blues album. But Gary just put together an incredible album of accessible songs. And he had the ability to do that.

We actually played with and supported the Gary Moore Band a couple of times in the early 70s, but it was only later on that I discovered Gary Moore playing Jimi Hendrix, for example. That video out there, if you haven't seen it yet, try and get ahold of it—it's absolutely incredible.† He plays a whole bunch of Hendrix songs. And I've also got another tape which is absolutely stunning—I think it's at a famous club in London, and BB King guests.‡ The tone, his ability to 'get in there,' and some of the stuff he did there is improvised and is totally incredible.

VIVIAN CAMPBELL Aside from the monster technique he had and the variety,

---

* The Irish rock band of the late 60s/early 70s, featuring Moore—not to be
confused with the 'Youth Gone Wild'/hair metal band of the same name.
† *Blues For Jimi*, recorded on October 25 2007 at the Hippodrome in London's Leicester Square.
‡ A tape from 1992, probably recorded at Ronnie Scott's Jazz Club.

when I first heard him, he was playing in Colosseum II with Jon Hiseman. He was playing jazz-rock. And then I had *Back On The Streets*, his solo album, which was more jazz-fusion than hard rock. But to hear him play with Thin Lizzy, he was playing straight-up rock. And then in his later career, he was playing blues—and not just like, when myself or whoever else decides to go play blues. He was *really* fucking playing blues. I mean, he was exceptional as a blues player. So, Gary always had so much versatility and so much technique and so much variety.

PHIL COLLEN [Girl, Def Leppard guitarist] I was a huge fan of Gary Moore. Some of the stuff I do now, I go, 'Oh, I got that from Gary.' I had an amazing opportunity to sit there and jam with him backstage. He opened up for us on the *Pyromania* tour. Literally, we were sitting backstage, we started jamming, and he had that '59 Les Paul that used to belong to Peter Green.* And he said, 'Do you want to play that?' And I said, '*Shit yeah!*' We jammed for about an hour, and I got a blister on my finger, because he was using heavier strings than I was. I got to watch him first hand.

Just an absolute inspiration, his playing—his vibrato, and he could shred. He could do the whole lot. I was really fortunate then. And when he started doing the blues stuff,[†] I thought it was great. Because I think he was still very much underrated as a player. When he started doing that blues stuff, it sounded really authentic, plus he added a different element that other players didn't have—his vibrato was fierce. It was just an amazing thing. I know Stevie Ray Vaughan gets all the accolades, but I think Gary's playing was as good, if not better—in a same kind of realm of music.

KIRK HAMMETT I've always liked Gary Moore—ever since I first heard him on Thin Lizzy's *Black Rose*. He's always been a huge, huge influence—in terms of style, phrasing, tone, attitude. It's huge. And I have the honor of saying I own 'Greeny'—Peter Green's guitar when he was in Fleetwood Mac, and then Gary Moore got it from Peter Green in 1971, and had it until 2005 or 2006. And I bought it just a couple of years ago. So to have one of Gary Moore's main guitars—which was owned by Peter Green before that—is a huge source of inspiration for me, as well.

---

* The legendary Les Paul Standard known as 'Greeny.'
† Specifically on *Still Got The Blues* (1990).

PHIL COLLEN I did hear [that Kirk owns Greeny]. That's pretty cool ... *but did he get to jam with Gary on it?* [*Laughs*]

ALEX SKOLNICK Gary Moore had been the guitarist for Thin Lizzy, and I hadn't been familiar with that work. I didn't have anybody around that had their records or turned me on to their records. So the first Gary Moore I heard was some of his solo records. I remember *Corridors Of Power* was one. What I really liked about him is he definitely was a peer of Van Halen and Rhoads, but he was able to sort of go to those places without any of the bells and whistles.

In the case of both Rhoads and Van Halen, I think the bells and whistles were used very well. I can't say that about all their imitators. But they made sense—they actually fit the music and they were perfect. I wouldn't want to hear it any other way. But Gary Moore, he was just playing a Les Paul through a hotrodded distortion sound. And a clear blues influence—I loved hearing his blues influence. And later, when he started doing blues as an experiment, it was wonderful to hear, and then that took off, and he had so much success with that—it obviously made sense to continue in that direction.

JOE STUMP All of my favorite records—whether it's the early Scorpions records with Uli, or the Rainbow stuff with Blackmore and Dio, or Yngwie's early work with Alcatrazz and Steeler—I remember when I first heard Gary Moore, it was on a specialty metal show on the radio. And I heard *Dirty Fingers* or one of the solos, and I was like, 'Holy fuck! *Who is this?*' And then I found out, and obsessively got everything he ever did, and went to specialty import places to get things that were hard to find. Just his guitar sounds on those records—it sounds like your head's right up against the Marshall cabinet as he's playing.

And that's another reason why I'm a Strat guy. The early Yngwie records and Blackmore, it's amazing how they're all Strat players but amazing how different those records sound. But *Corridors Of Power* is quintessential Strat through a hundred-watt Marshall—like you're right in the room with him. Out of all the guys, when Gary Moore plays, it really touches me on a whole other emotional level than a lot of my other heroes. But everything that is great about guitar—whether it's a combination of great emotional playing and badass technique and just unbelievable tone, and the intense sound of his hands.

VIVIAN CAMPBELL It didn't matter what style of music Gary was playing, he always played like he meant it. Like, sometimes I pick up a guitar, and I kind of run through the motions. But Gary Moore, I never ever heard him do that. He always *killed* the guitar. He wanted to murder it. He played with such physical intensity, and he was so committed to every single note. And I don't hear that in many guitar players. In fact, in very, very few guitar players do I hear that. And I chastise myself when I pick up the guitar and go through the motions. I think, 'Gary wouldn't be pleased with this!' It really reminds me to bring intensity and my A game.

TY TABOR I knew absolutely that he had a huge influence on a lot of my friends. A lot of people were constantly talking about him to me, and always putting CDs—or cassettes probably, back then—in front of me, making sure I'd listen to it. I do recognize that he kicked butt, and in rock history, is one of those unsung heroes. I mean, he got this due—everybody knows who he is. But I think most guitarists believe he's not as big as his impact was.

K.K. DOWNING A sad loss, obviously. A huge loss to the guitar world.*

---

* Moore passed away on February 6 2011 after suffering a heart attack.

11 the ozzy gig

During the 1960s, The Yardbirds were the launching pad for some of rock's all-time great guitarists (Eric Clapton, Jeff Beck, and Jimmy Page). Were Ozzy Osbourne's 80s-era bands (which launched the careers of Randy Rhoads, Brad Gillis, Jake E. Lee, and Zakk Wylde) the heavy metal answer to the 'birds?

WOLF MARSHALL Ozzy always had such good taste in how he picked those guys. That shines in all his different albums.

GEORGE LYNCH There's Randy, who became iconic and well renowned, and went out early in a blaze of glory. And then there's Jake E., who I think was hurt by the whole experience and process, and I would imagine regrets it to a large extent. And then there's Zakk, who is somewhere in the middle—he wasn't what Randy was, which was a game changer in the way that people looked at guitar.

I think it's a double-edged sword—it can be wonderful for any guitar player career-wise to have a gig like that. At the same time, it could be like the child-actor syndrome, where it defines you and it's hard to get out of that definition— you'll be forever known as that, and most likely, playing other people's songs and other people's solos. I mean, for Gus G., that's the case—I don't think when people think of Ozzy, they think of anything that Gus G. may have written or composed solo-wise. He's playing Zakk and Randy parts. So I don't think that's very gratifying at all.

DAVE MENIKETTI I was asked by Ozzy to join the band too, at that time. And I turned it down for other reasons—I didn't want to get into something like that when Y&T was just starting to kick butt. But it was [a high-profile gig], because you're front and center. Ozzy's band—because of Randy—ended up being a catalyst for an amazing guitar-player scenario there. And anybody that took over after that had to come up to the standard that Randy Rhoads had. You know you're not going to be crap if you're going to get that gig, and it's going to give you more notoriety as a guitar player—no matter how long you're in that band. So it was certainly a good position as a guitar player that wanted to get his name out there for his chops.

For me, I didn't want to do it because Ozzy asked me at the end of the *Black Tiger* tour, and *Black Tiger* was taking off in Europe and the UK, and we were starting to become fairly popular. And I just thought, 'I would much rather do my own thing in my own band than be a substitute for somebody amazing like Randy.' That just didn't give me something I really wanted out of being a musician—I would rather be creative and do my own thing. It was right after Brad Gillis was in the band. We were doing the *For Those About To Rock* tour with AC/DC, and we did the UK tour with them, and the very last show was in Dublin, in Ireland, and Ozzy and Sharon came backstage afterward, and he asked me to join his band.

I guess he just liked the idea that I was real energetic as well—that I was always running around onstage, jumping around, and doing all kinds of crazy stuff. That was what he wanted, and he felt at that time—as he explained to me—that Brad was 'boring' to him. [*Laughs*] He goes, 'He doesn't know how to dress like a rock star! I have to grab him and move him around the stage—he just stands there! *I want a guy like you!*' And I heard the live record with him [*Speak Of The Devil*], and I thought he was brilliant on it. I thought, 'You don't need anybody else.' But obviously, he's looking for a showmanship kind of thing, as well as a player. I guess at that point, he was frustrated. But it wasn't interesting to me. So I respectfully said, 'Thank you … but no thanks.'

GARY HOEY I did an audition for Ozzy, which was the reason why I ended up going out to California, because he came out to Boston which was where I was living, and he was on WBCN radio, doing his big tour—'I'm looking for a guitarist. Come down and give me your demo.' So I got him a demo, I got a call from a guy, and they flew me to California. I tried out for the band and played with Ozzy in the room, and he sang. In my early career, Sabbath was one of my big influences.

So this was like going to meet the Pope, for me. I didn't get the gig, but Ozzy told me I should move to LA. I moved to LA and ended up signing to Warner Bros Records within four or five years.

It was pretty insane, man—I was studying jazz, living in Boston, and I get this call to play with Ozzy, and they give you four or five songs that you have to play. I learned the songs, I knew a bunch of songs anyway. From what I remember from it is they had the Marshall stacks set up and were set super, super loud. I remember thinking, 'These amps are so friggin' loud. Can I just turn them down a little bit?' And they didn't want me to turn it down. They wanted to see how you could handle 'arena rock.'

And then the other thing I remember is doing a five-minute guitar solo. That was part of the audition—everybody sat down, and you had to stand there and play your 'rock star guitar solo.' That was a cool part of the audition—you had to shred and do that whole kind of Randy Rhoads thing, quiet down and do some chords, and make it something. That was a challenge—doing it in front of one of your idols. And I got a call back to play again with everybody, and Randy Castillo was on drums and Phil Soussan on bass. They were amazing. That was an experience I'll never forget.*

WOLF MARSHALL There was a period—just before I did my contract with Hal Leonard—that I got a chance to play [with Soussan and Castillo], between Jake E. Lee and Zakk Wylde, to go and play with the band. They were having open auditions ... they were auditions that you were called for, but they were 'open,' meaning it wasn't just one guy at a time—they may pick two or three guys, and during the week, they would have them come play with the band. So I thought it would just be a kick to do that. And it was a lot of fun—I did my shtick, I did my Randy licks, and they took my picture. [*Laughs*]

But ultimately, they wanted somebody unknown. I had been in guitar magazines for nearly ten years by that point and done videos. So I think (a) he wanted somebody completely unknown, and (b) somebody that was completely different—like Zakk Wylde is completely different from Jake E. Lee, and Jake E. Lee is completely different from Brad Gillis, and, of course, Randy Rhoads. So I think some of that comes into it. And I think they wanted somebody in their early twenties—I was probably eight years older. But I didn't really want to be in the band ... I would if they asked me, but I just wanted the experience of playing

---

* The tryout took place circa 1987, after Jake E. Lee's exit, and the songs Hoey recalls playing included 'Crazy Train,' 'I Don't Know,' and 'Bark At The Moon,' plus some jamming.

those tunes with that band. Y'know, play 'Suicide Solution' and put in my solo, and play 'Crazy Train,' 'I Don't Know,' and 'Goodbye To Romance,' that I'd grown up hearing and teaching kids for years.

GEORGE LYNCH I had a recent opportunity to discuss with a very well-known singer—he is a 'legacy guy'—the possibility of working together, and it came down to, I'm not interested in going back and just being the guitar player playing another well-known guitar player's parts and songs that I didn't write. I mean, I understand that's part of the gig, but in addition to that, I wanted to be the guy that came in and wrote a new chapter. And that's really gratifying about being in a band—is expressing yourself through composition and creativity, and having that live on in musical history. And that would be the advantage of playing with Ozzy, if you were able to do that. I don't see anybody doing that at this point in Ozzy's band. But at the time, it was absolutely a great opportunity to do that—for very few guitar players.

WOLF MARSHALL They had a great way of turning out beautiful guitar players. It contributed a lot to the music that was happening in the 80s. Those Ozzy Osbourne bands were a big deal all throughout the 80s.

tapping

A style that Eddie Van Halen popularized immediately gets utilized—and, soon, over-utilized—by many other guitarists. But was Eddie the first to two-hand tap?

DAVE MENIKETTI For most of the world of rock'n'roll, Eddie Van Halen was the guy that made it popular. Most fans of rock music were just blown away by his 'Eruption' solo. They'd never heard anything like it before. They thought it was the most amazing thing, and it catapulted Eddie to the status of 'greatest guitar player in rock'n'roll.' That's the kind of stuff that something like that does for a guitar player. It makes enough of an impact where people start giving out amazing platitudes. Obviously, it worked really well for him.

ROSS THE BOSS [The Dictators, Manowar, Death Dealer guitarist] It was another thing that Spanish guitar players started, and Mr. Van Halen obviously took it and modernized it and brought it out to the public, which was a great thing—when used properly. I think I used it in one song or two songs, and that was it. It wasn't my whole repertoire. A lot of these guys, that's all they did. Every time you looked at them, their hands were on the neck, and still some of those guys are like that—it's kind of boring. To me, it's a great thing, I love to hear it, and some guys do some real intricate stuff with it—but it's not for me. But I do respect it—I respected it when Mr. Van Halen did it for the first time. But then it was run into the ground.

TY TABOR When I first heard it, I was absolutely amazed by it. The first person I heard do some tapping was actually Allan Holdsworth, who I think maybe is who Van Halen got it from. But not used in a way that Van Halen did—Holdsworth would just do an occasional note, and it would have a weird sound of its own when you tap, and then shake the string. It just has a weird vibe, compared to picking a string. So I recognized right away the hand-tapping stuff was unique-sounding, just by doing it that way. But I had never heard anybody even *think* of doing what Van Halen did with it. And when I heard that, that's one of the things that made me think, 'Man, I might as well just quit playing!' I knew that it was phenomenal.

It affected all of us—even I went through some hand-tapping. Believe it or not, there is a lick in 'Over My Head' that is hand-tapping—and I took it straight from Holdsworth and Van Halen. And I almost got into it too, myself. Everybody did, because it sounded so cool—everybody wanted to know how to do it. It's just like when a pedal or an amp becomes real popular, and then everybody has the sound. It's just the way of things.

TREY AZAGTHOTH Brilliant—that's my thoughts about it. Especially when used in two or three octave scales. Growing up on Eddie Van Halen taught me that. Sure, it became popular in the 80s, but was first debuted in the 70s. Even back then, other guitarists used it here and there. But for me, Eddie is responsible for taking it to the level, that then others would start using it more in their own music, and in their own way. Also, including multiple finger and string tapping. It is a really cool tool or technique, I think.

TONY MACALPINE I thought it was pretty amazing, I really did. I just didn't get an opportunity to see that up close. I remember the first time that I heard the two-hand tapping was 'Eruption,' but I didn't know how he was playing it. I was playing it with one hand! And then I went to a music store, and the guy was like, 'This is not how you play it. You've got to play it *this way*.' Charlie Christian was into that, too, and a lot of jazz guys were into it. It's an amazing thing and it's really kind of cool.

GREG HOWE I think Van Halen probably single-handedly popularized that. I know that it had been done before him, I even heard some stuff with Uli Jon Roth in the early 70s, experimenting with some of those techniques. But Eddie was by far the guy responsible for featuring that—putting a spotlight on that approach. I took to that immediately. I didn't know what he was doing—at the end of 'Eruption,' I didn't know what that was. Until I actually went to see him live. And at this point, I was probably in tenth grade, and the only reason why I wanted to go see him was to see how he was doing that. Within the first five minutes, I saw what it was, and I couldn't wait to get home to play 'Eruption.'

I was really the first kid on the block—from my small town in New Jersey— that could do that. And it was such a brilliant idea, because it was relatively easy to do, and it yielded so many big results. Like, *my mom* can probably even do that! But brilliance is always seeing what's obviously right in front of you, and the fact that no one had really done that before him is further testament to his innovative way of thinking. So everybody jumped on it. And everybody just scratched their head and thought, 'God, why didn't I think of that? This is so easy, this is so powerful, this is so musical.'

But even though I got way into the two-handed tapping thing, I would say around the time that I got signed—which was '88—I was already kind of over it, because it had been overdone so much. Everybody was doing it. So I had at least stopped doing it in that manner and kind of returned to it when I got my record deal, and wrote a song in which I couldn't play the melody that I had written! [*Laughs*] I heard the chorus of a song called 'Kick It All Over,' and I knew what I wanted to play in that chorus, but I tried all these conventional approaches to getting the notes to come out right, and I just couldn't do it. Because I tend to write in my head—I don't write with my fingers. So suddenly, I'm trying all these different techniques, to figure out, 'How can I play this melody that I'm hearing?' And that's when I returned to tapping.

But I returned to it in a different way, because I found that I could approach it from the perspective that the left hand—or the fretboard hand—initiates the note, as opposed to the other way around. Everything that Van Halen had been doing— and most of the people that copied him—was always initiating the sequence with the tapping finger. And what I did was came up with a way to initiate notes with the left hand, and create lines that didn't really resemble that sort of fast, arpeggiated sound that at that time had been popularized by Van Halen. So I returned to tapping, but from a completely different perspective.

STEVE STEVENS Yeah, it got really overused. [*Laughs*] In the 80s, I lived in New York, so we kind of looked at it from a distance as guitar players, because we loved Van Halen, and for me, Eddie Van Halen is a great rhythm guitar player—not just a soloist. But then I started to hear all the other guitar players that were kind of trying to get his sound and that tapping thing. And on 'Top Gun Anthem,' I did some tapping—a very rudimentary version.

But whenever anyone makes a huge splash, you have guitar players that emulate them. I mean, look at how many guitar players tried to play like Jimi Hendrix after Hendrix. So I was never interested in guys who were just doing it to sound like Eddie. To me, Vai did it in a way that was different. It was the same technique, but used in a different way. And that's why I respect Steve in that respect. But all the other guys in metal bands doing it kind of … I don't know, 'Where are they now?' kind of thing.

DAVE MENIKETTI I thought it was overdone later on by too many other guitar players. But how can you keep yourself away from that if that becomes the popular thing at the time? For me, I made a conscious decision not to do it. In fact, about two albums after Van Halen became very popular, the guys in my band actually asked me to start doing that on certain solos, and I said, 'I'm not going to do it. That's not my style of playing. I want to be my own person. Eddie does it, he does it amazingly well, and he's "the guy"—let him do it. That's *his* style.'

So I think that a lot of people got into the habit of using it a bit more than they would have if he had not come up with that, and maybe it was slightly overused for a couple of years there. But it's a popular thing to listen to and it's relatively easy to do once you get the coordination down. So for a lot of guitar players that are just starting out, it's like, 'Wow! Look what I can do and what I can sound like right off the bat … and I don't even know what I'm doing!' When we all started playing solos, there was always one little trick that was easy to do that sounded like you were a lot better than you really were, and that's one of them. It's going to get used and there's a place for it.

PERHAPS THE FIRST ROCK GUITARIST TO USE THE TAPPING
TECHNIQUE WAS STEVE HACKETT OF GENESIS.

STEVE HACKETT [Genesis, GTR guitarist; solo artist] I believe so. I used that technique back in 1971, and Eddie Van Halen credits me with being the originator of that. You'll find that on the very first Genesis album I did, [on] 'The Musical Box.'* He credits me with the influence for that—I don't want that to go amiss, this is very, very important as far as I'm concerned. I was trying to play a piece of Bach,

---

* From the album *Nursery Cryme* (1971).

'Toccata And Fugue,' and I realized to be able to play some of those phrases, it was better to be played all on one string, so that you were constantly hammering on and off on the same string. It enables better speed, distribution, fluidity. It's one of the techniques that I employ up to the present day.

BILLY SHEEHAN I saw Billy Gibbons bend a note with his left hand and then bring his right hand over and touch the fretboard, when I saw ZZ Top open for Alice Cooper—in I think 1973. And I'd never seen that. If you go back and watch any video footage of anyone pre-Van Halen, of course, there are a couple of guys that had done it—Paganini did it, and there was an Italian guy from the 50s that did it.[*] It's nothing new under the sun. But prior to Ed Van Halen, you never saw a guitarist's right hand go over to the neck for anything … or rarely. Of course, there was no Van Halen yet, and I saw Billy Gibbons do that, and I just went home and started experimenting with it and started doing it on the neck of my bass, and got a reputation for doing that all through the mid-to-late 70s.

And when Ed Van Halen came out, he approached it in his way, which is different than mine—choice of notes, anyway—in what he was doing with it. I was excited and happy to hear it—because it was amazing and awesome. But I was also broken-hearted too, because I thought it was *my* shtick! It was one of my trademark things, but it's a great lesson to learn—you can't necessarily patent or trademark the things you do on an instrument. It's open to everyone.

Ed really was the man to popularize the technique by very, very far. And it did inspire me to look further into more possibilities of tapping. And he showed me some things either backstage or in hotel rooms or dressing rooms—that I use to this day, as a way to play an arpeggiated chord across the neck, tapping-wise. I still use that a lot. So I'm still further developing a lot more things with it. Every day, there's a whole bunch of new things I'm working on. It really never stops, as far as what the possibilities are and exploring them.

ANOTHER OF THE FIRST HARD ROCK GUITARISTS TO UTILIZE A FORM OF TWO-HANDED TAPPING WAS ACE FREHLEY, AS EVIDENCED IN CONCERT FOOTAGE FROM A KISS PERFORMANCE AT THE WINTERLAND BALLROOM, SAN FRANCISCO, IN 1975, DURING HIS UNACCOMPANIED SOLO.

ACE FREHLEY I remember playing the Garden, and I remember Eddie Van Halen

---

[*] Probably Vittorio Camardese.

being in the pit, watching me play. Who gets credit for what, I mean, everybody in rock'n'roll steals from everybody else. I don't care if I get credit or not. It's something I was doing early on though, yes.

STEVE LYNCH I saw Harvey Mandel do it back in the early 70s. There was an old jazz player named Johnny Smith, and there was a guy from 1965 on YouTube, this Italian guy—he was actually a doctor and he just picked up guitar as a hobby, and he's a monster at the whole tapping thing. So there were a lot of people doing it. And I used to see it during the 70s a bit more and more. I started to get more and more involved with it, and then, when I saw Emmett Chapman do the clinic with the Stick at [GIT], that's what really set me off on it. Then I started writing down everything that I was learning at the school, but I would write it down for both hands on the guitar neck. Then when I heard the 'Eruption' solo come out, I thought, 'Oh, I know exactly what he's doing there.' And I thought, 'God, he's really good at that. That's cool—somebody got it out there.'

By that time, I had pretty much written my first book on it, because that was released in '79—*The Right Touch*. Then I wrote two other books after that—on the same subject.* But everybody was saying, 'That's Eddie's thing'—as far as when we went out on tour with them in January of '84. His manager said, 'That's Eddie's thing. You can't do it.' I remember hearing the story about him turning his back to the audience and not letting anybody see what he was doing.† I thought that was kind of odd—I was writing a book to show people how do that! [*Laughs*]

But they told me that I couldn't do it on the tour. I was very, very disappointed with that, because I thought, 'Well, wait a minute ... am I not supposed to use a pick, either? Is that Eddie's thing, too?' I thought the whole thing was just completely ridiculous, telling somebody that they can't play their own style, because I didn't get it from him—I didn't hear him until I already had a book written on it! That was disappointing. Not to take anything away from him being a great guitar player and an innovator—which he is—but it was disappointing to have somebody tell me I can't do something that I thought I pretty much mastered on my own.

JENNIFER BATTEN That technique turned my world around. When I was at GIT, we used to get a seminar once a month by all these monster players that were in town—Lee Ritenour, Larry Carlton, Lenny Breau, Ted Greene. And one seminar

---

* *The Right Touch: Book II* (1983) and *The Right Touch: Book III* (1987).
† He was said to do this during Van Halen's club days.

that we got was by Emmett Chapman, who invented the Chapman Stick, and that instrument is ten strings—five melody/five bass—and tuned completely differently. And out of the class of sixty, fifty-nine of us—including myself—thought, 'Oh geez, that's a whole new instrument. We're just trying to get these six strings down in this one tuning.' But Steve Lynch—who was in my class—a seed was planted in his head, to experiment with tapping. And I would check in every once in a while, to see what he was doing with it, and it just blew my mind. I knew I really wanted to get into it, but during the school year, it was way too intense to even think of doing something outside of the curriculum.

But as soon as I graduated, I connected with Steve, and he sent me a cassette—in 1979—of solos he had worked out. I tried to learn them with just one finger of the right hand—not having any idea how he was actually executing the stuff. And I was frustrated—it wasn't sounding that great. So at that time, I drove to his house from San Diego to somewhere in LA, to get a lesson, and see hands-on what he was doing. And he was close to finishing his first book at that point, *The Right Touch*. So from that one lesson, I understood how he was approaching the technique. I just carved through his book and then started experimenting from there, and ended up doing a song called 'Cruzin' The Nile,' that was just an experiment as to what I could do with percussion and using two hands with chords. And I was on my way from there.

STEVE LYNCH Allan Holdsworth was probably the last guitar player I listened to before I stopped listening to guitar players all together, because I would listen to them and would start to sound like them. Like, when I was listening to Allan Holdsworth, I was playing two-handed stuff in '77 and '78, and I started to sound kind of like him. I thought he was doing most of his stuff two-handed, but he was actually doing most everything that he does with just one hand—he's got that real *legato* technique going on. I was trying to figure out all this stuff two-handed.

And that's when going to the Guitar Institute of Technology in the early part there, Emmett Chapman—the guy who created the Stick—did a clinic, right when I started to go there, and that just depressed me so much. Even though I was already doing that two-handed technique, it really brought me in full-throttle, because I was amazed by the sounds that he was getting out of the Stick. I didn't want to have to re-learn another instrument, so I just applied the basic theory that he was using, on the six-string guitar that I had, and tried to combine different arpeggios and triads and pentatonic shapes and all that together, to come up with a sound that was unique.

I started writing down ideas, so that I wouldn't forget them. When I was going to the school, when they were showing me different pentatonic shapes, I would write down one pentatonic shape with my left hand, and then I would write down another one that I could play with my right hand on top of it. The same thing with arpeggios, like a G minor arpeggio would go with a D minor arpeggio or a G major arpeggio, with a C major arpeggio on top of it. I could link different arpeggios together. And the same thing with triads, the same thing with different positions of the major scales. Sequencing things to make it sound almost like a synthesizer sequencer. And playing different chromatic runs.

I just started writing all this stuff down—I kept on writing and writing—and I had this huge stack of papers at the end of it. So I took out some of the simpler things for the first book. And then the second book got a little more complex, and the same thing with the third one. Then I started breaking down some of the solos I did with Autograph, and showing how to do the two-handed stuff in that.

STU HAMM I think the first person I ever saw sort of do a thing where they were playing contrapuntally was maybe Victor Bailey, who was another one of my classmates at Berklee. But playing with Steve Vai, and just seeing and playing all the hammer-on stuff like 'Eruption,' when you slow it down, you see a way to get the note to speak, by tapping down on the fret with one hand, so the other hand is free to do the other. It's a fine line to say that I came up with the stuff myself, but there's a lot of stuff … and I have a really good memory.

It's not like I saw someone play 'The Linus And Lucy Theme' and I stole it from them. I had the idea to learn it, and I worked on it for months and months, until I could get the contrapuntal part, and then I could play it. It certainly helped playing piano, and then transcribing pieces like Bach's 'Prelude In C,' where the fourth finger on my left hand is playing whole notes, while I'm playing the eighth notes with the other fingers, and that sort of trained me to say, 'Oh. I can do something where I can play different rhythms with different fingers on different strings.' It was part of the zeitgeist at the time, and I guess we were all doing it. But I didn't hear anyone else play 'Foggy Mountain Breakdown' before I did, so what can I say?

JOE SATRIANI Tapping is just a tool, though—it's just like anything else. When a guitar player, say, goes to a session and a guy says, 'I need something unusual here. What can you do?' And the guy's thinking, 'Well, I can use my whammy pedal, I can use my wah-wah pedal, I can use a clean sound, distortion, delay, reverb, I can pick, I can strum, I can fingerpick, I can use the whammy bar, I can use slide … would you like me to use slide? How about an open tuning?' Finger tapping is just part of it.

Do you finger tap like Tosin Abasi, or do you finger tap like Eddie Van Halen? When you break it down like that, it's like, you are a guitar player, but somebody gave you a paper that said, 'These are all the things that a guitarist can offer you in this session.' Then you realize that it holds equal weight—it's just as important as any other technique. It's just a question of whether it's appropriate.

It suddenly became inappropriate, because people were using it inappropriately, to show off. Like, you'd have a pop metal band, and then the guitar player would jump in front of the camera to do his two-handed solo. That was really just an attempt to say, 'Look, I'm cool! I can do this, too.' But was it really the right solo? Would Keith Richards or George Harrison have done that? No. They would have selflessly found the right part to play. And that's why their solos live on today, and all those other widdly-widdly ones don't. Important to remember how sometimes it's good to be trendy, and other times—mostly—it's *not* good. [*Laughs*]

13 sweeping

Frank Gambale introduces a unique speed-picking style.

FRANK GAMBALE Really, nobody used the technique before me. There were hints at the technique, but nobody did the work that I did or ever played it like I do and did at the time. When it hit, it was really like a slap in the head for a lot of people, because it was like somebody from outer space. Nobody could figure out where all the notes were coming from—especially looking at it, because it looked so graceful and effortless. Especially on video. I was beavering away at the concept for years and years, but I never put the cart before the horse. I spent my whole life pursuing musical ideas or musical concepts that I wanted to be able to play on guitar. And in many cases, I was trying to play saxophone and keyboard licks on the guitar—with the 'current' techniques, as they were, like alternate picking, but they just didn't cut it for everything. So I had to push the boundaries, really, to create and develop this incredible technique, that is now part of the guitar lexicon.

But I put thousands and thousands of hours into getting it. One of the biggest stumbling blocks was playing it in time. That was really, really challenging. And as far as technique, it works better at medium to fast tempos—I describe it as fifth or sixth gear in a car. It's that extra torque and low-revs at great velocity, it's the best analogy I can make. Where sweep picking lives for the most part is at fast tempos, it's not a slow technique, but if I'm playing slower notes, I'll alternate or hammer-on and pull-off.

But when I need to get to that 'extra pace,' that fifth and sixth gear, and comfortably … I stress the word comfortably, because alternative picking at high velocity was for me like torture of some kind. I just didn't have any energy to do the up and down thing so fast. I thought, 'There's got to be a better way.' And the sweep logic made so much sense, that if I had, for example, three or four notes on successive strings, one on each string, it made sense to make a single stroke for all those, and separate the notes with my left hand. It's just plain logical. But doing it in time and having the control was the biggest stumbling block. It just took thousands and thousands of hours—there were *years* when I was practicing twelve-to-fifteen hours a day.

I was already quite a long way along in my sweep technique, by the time I came to the States in '82, I had already been at it close to ten years, developing the technique. So there were lots of periods in my late teens, when I was working twelve hours a day, living at my parents' house, practicing all day long. I wasn't sitting on my ass doing nothing. This kind of technique and creating a new way to play the guitar doesn't happen by chance—it takes a lot of effort and spark of creativity. By the time I got to GIT in '82, a lot of the players had never seen anything like. The students were going, 'What the heck are you doing?' I'd be in a practice room with a couple of students, and I got asked the question so many times, 'How do you do that?' So that just signaled to me, (a) I was doing something very different, and (b) it was time to write a book on the subject. And I wrote the very first ever sweep picking book, called *Speed Picking*.[*]

Now, the publisher wouldn't allow me to call the book *Sweep Picking*—what it is known as today. At the time, there was no precedent. So the publisher at the time said, 'Nobody would know what "sweep picking" is. How can you sell a book where nobody knows what the heck the subject is?' So they kind of forced me to call it *Speed Picking*. Which is not a bad compromise, because it's obviously about picking and it's obviously about a technique to enable speed. But had it been my choice, it would have been called *Sweep Picking*, because I wasn't overly focused on the concept of speed—I was more focused on describing how the technique works and the displacement of notes and re-fingering shapes to enable the right hand to sweep. But anyway, I did the book, and then when somebody would say, 'What are you doing?' I would say, 'Here.' I'd just give them a free copy! '*This* is what I'm doing.'

But the book is one thing—I think it really took off once I did a video on the subject, which was *Monster Licks & Speed Picking*. DCI were doing videos before Warner Bros bought the whole catalog, so it was a DCI video. And they also

---

[*] Originally published in 1983.

felt the same way, that sweeping was not really in the general knowledge at all at that point. Nobody knew what it was. And so the video I think was a real spark, and I've just released a ten-hour video course at my new online guitar school*— called *The Definitive Sweep Picking Course*, which includes the basics plus the last 30 years of developments since my original book and video. We've got a lot of testimonial videos from all corners of the world, and all guitar players—from death metal to rock to country to jazz guys—talk about the contribution I made with sweep picking. So it's really gratifying to see that that's in the public mind now, even though some of the younger kids might not exactly know the history of it. But I lay claim to this method, I really do.

STEVE MORSE I said in one interview, when I was asked about sweeping, '*The only sweeping I did was in the garage.*' But in reality, it's just like sometimes on guitar, you play with your fingers, sometimes you play with a pick, sometimes you play with a pick and finger combination. In other words, the guitar should be versatile. I really needed to learn every form of expression that I could. Jeff Watson's tapping stuff, I just couldn't do, because I kept long fingernails on my right hand—for playing classic guitar. So because of that, I sort of never got into that tapping technique. Because when I tried it, it felt like I needed to come down more vertically to get the traction on the strings. And plus, when you hear Jeff do it, it's sickening how easily it seems to come to him, and how impossible it is for me. So I said, 'All right … I'm not going to try that.' [*Laughs*]

But the sweeping stuff, I did experiment with that, because with distortion, it makes a pretty interesting sound. It's like a cross between a glissando and a pizzicato—it's got the attack of the strings, but not nearly the same as the definition you get by individually picking the strings. But I've really messed with it lately—on the Flying Colors' second album.† It was the first time that I really put sweeping in any solo that I can think of. And really, in the 80s and 90s, I was dead set that I was going to play every note, alternate picking. It's extremely difficult to do so, but I got a precision and an attack that I didn't think I could get any other way. And I still don't believe you can get that sound any other way.

MICHAEL ANGELO BATIO When you look at that style of sweeping, Frank Gambale was the one who talked about 'economy picking.' But see, for me, I was doing sweep technique before I moved to LA, and we called it 'rakes.' I didn't know what

---

* frankgambaleonlineguitarschool.com
† *Second Nature* (2014).

it was called, but we just called it rake technique, because it was literally like raking leaves—that long, sweeping motion. I know Marty Friedman is kind of down on sweeping. When I heard him say that, that he thinks sweeping sucks, I thought, 'That's a really stupid thing to say.'

Here's my analogy to this—it is *a technique.* It is not a style. If you want to make it your style … if I wrote a piece of music that required sweeping and Friedman couldn't do it, I wouldn't hire him. It's that simple. See, I look at myself as this—would I hire myself to be the first-chair violinist in a symphony orchestra? And if the answer is yes, you have to know these different techniques. It's a technique. You make that your style. I thought to do an arpeggio with the sweep motion, if you can do it well, it gives you the ability to do a technique that can play things like a piano, that you can do things that a classical guitarist can do, and you can do with a pick. That's how I thought about it.

And it got popularized with 80s metal. You hear everybody from Metallica on *Master Of Puppets*, Kirk's doing sweeps, to Paul Gilbert, Yngwie, Vinnie Moore, myself—we're all doing it, but it was such a great technique. And then like any technique, sometimes it falls out of favor. But I look at guitar in two ways— one, here's the technical side of it. You've got alternate picking, economy picking, legato, sweep technique, string skipping—all these things. Then the other side is, 'How do you apply it to the music?' And that's your own tastes. That's subjective.

trademarks &
techniques

**A study of several guitarists'
unmistakable hallmarks.**

ACE FREHLEY'S USE OF A KILLSWITCH, 'DINOSAUR
BENDS,' AND SMOKING GUITAR.

ACE FREHLEY I got [the idea] from Pete Townshend. What I would do is for most of my guitars that I played live is I'd even disconnect the rhythm pickup and the center pickup, because for that killswitch effect to work, you really have to have the volume off the other pickups, and sometimes I'd forget to do it or I'd hit a knob. And since I only used the bridge pickup, to make life easier, I just had my roadie disconnect the other pickups, so that effect would always be available to me.

Just bending the E string—the sixth string—really, really radically. That term ['dinosaur bends'] was originated by Gene. It's funny you bring that up, because I was just talking about that yesterday in an interview that I did at Electric Lady Studios. We were talking about all those crazy terms that guitar players come up with for different riffs you do on the guitar, and I said to him, 'Gene used to call these "dinosaur bends," and I just bent the E string all the way up.'

I was on tour in Canada and I got a hold of some fireworks—some smoke bombs. I took out the back plate of my Les Paul, where all the volume and tone controls are, and I stuck a smoke bomb in there and let the fuse hang out and lit it. And I thought, 'Well, there's only one way for the smoke to go—it's going to come out of the pickups, through the canal where the wires go.' And people were amazed by the effect. But after a couple of shows, I ended up screwing up all the volume and tone controls—the smoke made them crackle. I had to figure out another way to do that, so eventually, I got together with one of my engineers when we were gearing up for a tour, and we modified one of my Les Pauls and put a dummy rhythm pickup in, that snapped back with a high-intensity light that ran off a battery. And boom—you have the 'Ace Frehley smoking guitar.' [*Laughs*]

MICHAEL SCHENKER PLAYING THROUGH A WAH-
WAH PEDAL IN A FIXED POSITION.

MICHAEL SCHENKER I loved in the late 60s—when I started—hearing people using the wah-wah pedal. I was fascinated by it, because it had that soaring sound. Not everybody was capable of doing it—there were a few—where there was something about it. But when I tried the wah-wah pedal, there was a particular position where it sounded very nice to me. And I wanted to have that sound—always. I'm not a very technical person, but I can imagine things. So I thought, 'Maybe I better have a look inside and see why the sound goes from a deep *waaah* to a high treble *ooooh*.'

I saw that little wheel in there, and thought, 'If I find that spot where my pedal is on the button, and that is exactly where the sweet spot is and the tone that I like, then I can always find it, and switch on the wah-wah pedal, and have it go immediately to the sweet spot.' That's what I did, and I used it for quite a while—until wah-wah pedals became very fragile. The good ones were created in the 60s. Eventually, I had like eight wah-wah pedals, and they all started to become monophonic and almost impossible to play, and would make this noise—as if you were in an ocean. The sound became thinner and thinner. I was like, 'Shit … this sounds terrible,' and I gave it up all together. When people start making new things that don't sound like the old things, you have to find other ways of finding your sweet spot—and that's what I did.

RUDY SARZO PLAYING THE BASS WITH HIS HAND
OVER THE NECK AND LICKING HIS FINGERS.

RUDY SARZO Back in the late 60s/early 70s, when I was playing in Florida, we used to do six sets a night—which means you start at ten, and you get off at four in the morning. By the time you hit two, you're trying to entertain yourself—you find five different ways of playing 'Play That Funky Music.' I'm not trying to belittle any music—those are great songs—but you have to look at it from a guy that is playing in a Top 40 band, and by two, everybody is drunk in the place. Nobody really cares. Now, *I do care*—but I want to keep myself from falling asleep. So, sometimes I would play a whole song on one string—just to challenge myself. I would play it upside down, on the floor—just to keep myself amused. And the licking of the fingers, again, going back to Miami. Miami is super-humid. I couldn't afford strings—back then, we only had flat wound. And with the humidity, my strings would rust and mold. I used to lick my fingers so it would not feel like I was playing barbed wire—just to moisten them up a bit. But that became habit.

JEFF WATSON'S 'EIGHT-FINGER TAPPING TECHNIQUE.'

JEFF WATSON My facility has been real good since I was a little kid with both my hands. So I decided, 'I'm going to do some ideas that make my ears happy—that's how I play, I go after what brings me a smile.' So I picked weird notes, and sometimes to get them, I had to use my right hand. I thought, 'Well, what if I actually did that and made it into a style?' So I started the eight-finger tapping thing. I was a bluegrass player when I was a little kid, so I have that facility in my right hand, it comes really easy to me. And that's how that started.

I was in the Night Ranger band house—everybody lived there at one point or another. Down the street from my house now, in Mill Valley. We had a piano in there, and I was trying to get these licks on this guitar for the song 'Rock In America.' It was early on—we were just writing it and figuring stuff out. I said, 'Fitz, where are these notes?', because he [keyboardist Alan Fitzgerald] was living there. We figured out what I was trying to play and I said, 'The only way I can get there is if we go like *this*.' And he goes, 'Why don't you work on that?' So I did.

That's where that started, and then I woodshedded it for a couple of years, and it came out on 'Rock In America.' It hit MTV, and I got recognized as being the creator and inventor of the eight-finger tapping thing—that's my 'pedigree highlight,' I guess. But in all honesty, there had to be many, many other guys sitting in their room, trying to come up with the same thing, and maybe even doing more with it. It was just the MTV exposure that got me recognized for it.

CRAIG GOLDY'S 'ONE-HANDED TECHNIQUE.'

CRAIG GOLDY I was giving lessons and I was writing out in tablature note-for-note lessons. So as I was doing that, I would tap the guitar with my left hand and write it down with my right. I thought to myself, 'I wonder if I could play solos with one hand?' I started playing and because it was a percussive thing, all the other strings would vibrate and it made noise. My first instinct was to use my right hand and mute the strings. I started to learn how to play with one hand.

PAUL GILBERT'S 'DRILL TECHNIQUE.'

PAUL GILBERT Racer X, when we started to gain some notoriety and we started to do some press, everyone, all they would talk about was that we were fast and that we were a speed metal band. And I really disliked the name 'speed metal,' because I heard other speed metal bands, and harmonically, they did a lot of the half-step sort of 'Jaws Theme' stuff. I don't know if anybody would believe me, but my chord progressions were still kind of informed by pop music. Y'know, I was taking Cheap Trick songs and just making them faster and heavier, and using those kind of chord progressions. So I really didn't feel that we were speed metal— harmonically. Having people only hear that element was frustrating to me. And it was also funny to me. I thought, 'This whole athletic thing has gotten out of hand.' So the drill was really me just being ironic. I was sort of poking fun at the whole thing.

I remember the first time I tried to assemble a drill bit with three picks on the end, I just used a pencil and some glue. I was doing a seminar at GIT, and I said, 'Everybody, you're not going to believe this. I came up with a revolutionary new way of picking.' I pull the drill out, and as soon as the picks touched the strings, the glue wasn't strong enough, and they just flew into the air, one by one. And it looked amazing! But after that, I had to go back to the drawing board and figure out how to build a stronger drill bit. It's just ironic and funny, but I always forget that it's something that I do—which is stupid of me, because it's like Angus forgetting his shorts. It's something that I really should take advantage of, because it always gets a great rise out of the crowd. Actually, the last album I did, I finally remembered to bring the drill to the studio. It's always fun—I always have fun with it. But it is silly. It was just inspired by how nonsensical the whole speed thing was becoming.

[When Paul saw Eddie Van Halen using a drill in the video for the Van Halen song 'Poundcake'] I kept thinking that I was going to wake up from a dream! I mean, as guitar heroes go, I will never have a bigger guitar hero than Eddie Van Halen. His influence on me when I was a teenager was just so profound that no matter what musical direction I take, my DNA was modified by those first Van Halen/David Lee Roth albums. The Sammy stuff was fine, but my era was the David Lee Roth era. So to have somebody who was that important to me, by coincidence, do that same gimmick, was just *astounding*. And there wasn't a split second where I thought that he got it from me—I was completely off of his radar. I think he just had a drill laying around and discovered, 'Hey, when I get this close to the pickups, it makes a sound.' But it was really unusual, because obviously, it's a fairly unusual thing to do. So to have that coincidence of my hero discovering the same thing was just weird … and wonderful.

GREG HOWE'S 'HAMMER-ONS FROM NOWHERE TECHNIQUE.'

GREG HOWE I have very loyal fans, so I feel very blessed about that. But there have been things that have happened in the guitar community that I initiated—for instance, back in the day when I was teaching private lessons in Pennsylvania, I would notice a lot I would do on the guitar involved not picking notes that normally would be picked. So, if I was doing a string skipping thing, a lot of times, instead of jumping from say, the G string to the A string, and having to initiate the first note with a pick, I would just literally hammer with my left hand. And when I was writing up tablature for the student afterward, I had to come up with my own sort of language sometimes, because it's like, 'This is a hammer-on, but this is actually a hammer-on to a different string, so it's not coming from that string.'

So I invented this term, 'hammer-ons from nowhere,' which really meant a hammer-on to a string that was not previously fretted. And it's interesting how that's now become a mainstream term in the guitar community. I mean, hammer-ons from nowhere I've seen included in tablature. And a lot of that came from, if you listen to my first album,[*] like the chorus in 'Kick It All Over,' that technique—even though it's a two-handed technique, is entirely different from what anyone had done prior to that. Because like I said, almost everybody had been doing things that involved initiating notes with the right hand, or the tapping hand.

And this was really the first time I had ever heard anybody turn that around backward, and suddenly arrange it … in other words, it didn't even slightly resemble the Van Halen approach to tapping. It was a completely different thing. And also, a lot of the linear tapping ideas that I still do to this day, where I play a

---

[*] *Greg Howe (1988)*

scale as a two-handed lick. In other words, I'm hammering two fingers on the left hand, and then tapping using a finger of the right hand, and literally playing scales with no pick attack whatsoever, which gives it a very fluid, keyboard-like, even sound. The kind of sound that Holdsworth gets playing conventionally, somehow. It was also a new thing I had not seen since then. So there have been ideas that are now very mainstream. I like to sometimes see if anyone is paying attention to those things. [*Laughs*]

RONNI LE TEKRØ'S 'MACHINE GUN TECHNIQUE.'

RONNI LE TEKRØ The machine-gun technique, it's almost like a mandolin technique, where I paraphrase a lot of my left hand. I guess that's my invention! [*Laughs*] Like a lot of those special 'flash' tricks, they just appear. Suddenly, it's there. It's more of an effect than an actual music thing. So I rely a lot on flash, and I like to combine different flash techniques to get my own sound and originality.

JEFF HEALEY PLAYING GUITAR FLAT ON HIS LAP.

ROGER COSTA [Archivist and co-administrator of the Estate of Jeff Healey] What happened was, when he was three, his parents bought him a guitar for Christmas—an acoustic. And his dad had played a Hawaiian style guitar, like a steel guitar with a slide. So he tuned up Jeff's guitar to an open tuning, and set the action high, and gave him a steel slide. That's how Jeff started to play. He was small, so he would set the guitar down on the bed, and just make noise. He did that for a few years, and then eventually, he would start to try and figure out how to duplicate things that he was hearing on records—not realizing that there are overdubs and multiple takes of guitars. So he came to the realization that if he could play with the steel bar on the guitar, then he could also use his fingers to figure out chords and make different individual notes.

I think he was seven or eight, and his dad reset the action on the guitar lower, and Jeff just started learning that way. It was comfortable, because that's the way he had been messing around for a few years. So he continued going in that direction. You hear stuff all over the place for years—'Oh, it's because he was blind, he didn't know any better,' or 'His hands were so small, he couldn't reach around the neck.' It had nothing to do with that. It was because of the way that he started playing like a lap steel sort of thing, and it became a natural extension of that—trying to figure other things out. And that's how it stayed.

MARK WOOD PLAYING VIOLIN WITHIN A HEAVY METAL CONTEXT.

MARK WOOD I grew up on Long Island, but my mom was a concert pianist and my father was a brilliant artist—a painter. My mom had four boys, and she was determined to have a string quartet in her family! So all my brothers and I, we were the 'all-brothers string quartet' in the 70s, and we would tour around, play Mozart and Beethoven, and then I'd run home of course and put headphones on— to listen to Black Sabbath and Led Zeppelin. But never associating my stringed instrument with the music that I loved. I still love classical music and always will, but there was something about Duane Allman, Jimmy Page, and Eddie Van Halen. The second Eddie came out, I was like, 'Oh my God! I want to play like *him.'* Never once did it occur to me to change my instrument. It was complete inspiration from the music, not the instrument.

I started to experiment, and then I went to Juilliard on a full scholarship in the 70s, pursuing a classical career. But once I hit sixteen, seventeen, eighteen years old, I realized there is really just no way that I'll ever have interest in being in a symphony orchestra—sitting in the back of the violin section, slumped over, looking at my watch for the rest of my career. Can't wait for the concert to be over. And of course, you're witnessing now the demise pretty much and the crisis in the symphony/classical/orchestra world. Whereas if I continued that career, there is no way I would have ever had a long career.

So immediately, within two years of Juilliard, I left and moved back to my father's art studio, and I started to build electric violins at that time. And I built the first solid body electric violin in history—never really even thinking about it. But I would listen to Jimi Hendrix and Joe Satriani a lot, and listen to these great instrumentalists, and I was like, 'Wow ... I can do that!' And I of course had to reconfigure my playing, because as a classically trained musician, you're not in any way taught how to improvise or explore your own voice. It's a very interpretive type of art form, and wonderful for some people, but for me, it was way too confining. And once I figured out how to improvise and to play 'rock music' as opposed to ... the sound of a classically trained violin player on top of a rock beat is the worst sound. And unnerving. It's like an opera singer trying to sing the blues next to Aretha Franklin—it just does not work. It's oil and water. So I had to figure out a way to make my violin have that credible rock sound.

When I would listen to Hendrix, it was immediate that he was activating a sensibility that was based on blues singers. And I started listening to blues singers—really immersing myself, while I was building electric violins. And then Mike Varney had this little column in *Guitar Player*—there was no violin magazine back then. There was nothing. And I thought, 'Maybe Mike Varney would be interested in showcasing a violinist. I'll send him a cassette.' I put four songs together of my violin through distortion and a wah-wah pedal—my very first entries into that kind of music. And he immediately wrote back, and said, 'This is it Mark, I'm featuring you!' So all of a sudden, I was featured in *Guitar Player* magazine, which was an incredible honor. That's really how it began.

And then, I started to really grow and infiltrate the instrumental guitar world. *Guitar For The Practicing Musician* was out, and the publisher bumped into me through a project I was working on with Randy Coven—rest his soul—and I said, 'I want to do a rock violin record,' and they were like, 'Absolutely.' I signed to a small record deal [with Guitar Recordings], and once the record came out, we had a great publicist, and I was on the cover of *Time* magazine and on *The Tonight Show* within a month. And I also was composing music for the Olympics at the time. So all the media thought it was really interesting. And then a big highlight for me back then was to play at Randy Rhoads's memorial concert, which I was the only violin player. I'll never forget playing 'Mr. Crowley' and Randy's solo, and the crowd going berserk in the middle of my solo. I'd never had that—where they give you a standing ovation for your solo.

steve

Just when seemingly every new rock guitarist was borrowing heavily from Eddie, Steve Vai offered his own distinctive playing style.

JAS OBRECHT Joe Satriani was one of Steve's first guitar teachers. Satch told me that Steve was about fourteen when he came to his first lesson and that he literally had a guitar in one hand and a package of strings in the other. To progress as far as Steve did in a short period of time is a real sign of genius.

BILLY SHEEHAN Steve comes from kind of a different school—the Frank Zappa school. I was a huge Zappa fan when I first started in music. I think I made it up to *Over-Nite Sensation*, and then I went off into a different path. I was a big, big Zappa fan, so I get where Steve's coming from with the Zappa influence. And I liked that it has influenced him in a way that it has—in a very good way. And Steve and I are close to the same age, so we both went through our 'Hendrix years' and our 'Bowie years' and all these other waves of great music that came through popular music at the time. So we had a common vocabulary between us—the songs that we knew and loved. So it was easy to just get along and it was easy for us to work together in a band.

And Steve also is just a very articulate and intense study of music and guitar—he works hard at it and is an absolute perfectionist. All these things spill out in his playing, and that's why I thought he was such a good match for Dave, because Dave, being the 'entertainer,' would bring that part out of Steve, as opposed to the 'muso' part. And Steve is a great combination of both—he's a great musician guy, but he also wants to be entertaining and funny, which he got from I think primarily from Frank Zappa, as well. Just those combination of traits I think come out of Steve and make him an incredible player and amazing performer, as well.

STU HAMM I met Steve ... we were both freshmen at Berklee College of Music in 1978. And as soon as I got there, I heard people tell stories about Steve, and how incredible he was. My best recollection is I got invited to a party at a friend's house out in Brookline, and Steve was probably playing with Axis—with Randy Coven.* And he did Hendrix's 'Star Spangled Banner,' note for note. And I ended up talking to him at that party. I remember also when he would rehearse at Berklee, there would always be crowds of people around, checking him out.

We met, he heard me play, and we had a band called Axis, with Dave Rosenthal and Eddie Rodgers, and we played the Berklee Performance Center, and I played on Steve's audition tapes for Zappa, and then he moved to California to be Zappa's transcriber and I wound up working with an Elvis Presley impersonator in Virginia. He was in California for a while, and I quit the Elvis impersonator band and went back to Boston. Went back to school for a while, and then was just living in Boston, playing, and then I got a call from Steve, saying that he was no longer in Zappa's band, and he was going to do this record named *Flex-Able*, and if I wanted to, he would send me bus fare and I would go out to California. So I hopped on a bus with my amp and my bass and suitcase full of clothes, and slept on this couch in the studio, while we recorded *Flex-Able*.

JAS OBRECHT Another aspect of Vai's talent [is] his transcriptions, which he used to write for Frank Zappa and *Guitar Player* magazine. I've seen several, and his handwritten transcriptions are a joy to behold. My favorite was a seven-page folio transcription of Van Halen's 'Eruption,' annotated with funny directions, like, 'Balls out' and 'Whammy craziness.' And he misspelled 'Van Halen' on every page as 'Van Hallen'! It was just beautiful to see the work he did. Steve's genius for transcription is what first brought him to the attention of Frank Zappa. He gave Zappa some transcriptions he'd made of Frank's music, and Frank asked him if he could double a speaking voice—Dale Bozzio's, I think it was—on a record. So Steve wrote out the music for the notes of the person's speaking voice, and then played it on guitar.

---

* Actually, according to Vai's site, this band would have been called Morning Thunder, and was his second 'Berklee band.'

MIKE VARNEY Vai had replaced Yngwie in Alcatrazz, but it was a little too late at that point in time. He had been known as this amazing transcriber and technician for Frank Zappa and for putting out his *Flex-Able* series. But the Alcatrazz *Disturbing The Peace* record really showed Steve in a rock context.

STEVE STEVENS Being in Billy Idol's band, the whole punk rock thing, he came from that English School of Punk Rock: 1977. And they were really against virtuoso guitar playing, so I would always have to defend the virtuoso guys! [*Laughs*] And Billy loved Public Image, as well as I did—*Metal Box* and all that stuff. And then when the record *Album** came out, it was almost like validation that you could do virtuoso guitar playing in the context of something really, really different.

And both Idol and I really liked that record. He went, 'That Vai guy, he's good, right?' And I went, 'Yeah! He's about as good as they get.' I loved the fact that you have rock or metal guys who are not just doing rock or metal music. When they're taken out of that, and they really shine, it was really refreshing and it was something that I think a lot of the punk people that followed John Lydon into Public Image couldn't deny. You couldn't deny the fact that being technically gifted as a guitar player was still cool—it wasn't noodling for the sake of noodling.

GUTHRIE GOVAN [Asia, The Aristocrats, Steven Wilson guitarist; solo artist] With Public Image, I think it was just the context—you have this figurehead of naughtiness in John Lydon, and the last thing that you would expect him to do is assemble a band with people who have been to Berklee. So I liked the contradiction in the line-up. The vocal delivery on that album is so sneering and ironic, infused with a certain kind of justifiable hate for something or another. I just thought Steve's quirkiness offset the general mood of that record really well. Because it was the last thing that anyone would expect.

BILLY SHEEHAN In the summer of '85, I got a phone call from Dave's office, that he was going to do a movie, and wanted to know if I wanted to be in it. I thought, 'Gee … I guess.' I was already going out to Los Angeles to play a show, because Talas was playing there on the Yngwie tour. So I said, 'As long as I'm coming out there, I'll have a meeting with you.' Immediately, he said, 'Well, there is a movie, but that really wasn't why I called you. I want to start a band. I want you to go

---

* Public Image Ltd.'s fifth LP, released in 1986.

find a guitar player and drummer, and have a band. I'm going to quit Van Halen.'
And I said, 'OK. I'm in!'

I went to the show we did the next night, at the Palladium I believe it was in
Los Angeles, and Dave was at the show. A couple of people started a few rumors,
but we kept it quiet—he told me not to say anything to anyone, just keep it a safe
secret. And I did. So when I finished that tour, they flew me out to LA, and we
began the *Eat 'Em And Smile* adventure.

Originally, Steve Stevens was Dave's idea for guitar. Steve's great, a wonderful
guy, and a great player, but I think he decided to stick with Billy Idol, because they
were very successful at that time. And so I told Dave, 'I know *another* Steve,' and
Steve at the time was on the label that I was on—Relativity Records. He had just
put out *Flex-Able*, and I was actually going to get in touch with Steve to do some
things with he and I together. So I knew him and had spoken with him one night,
and said, 'There might be something coming up that you might be interested in
… and I can't tell you about it.' He goes, 'I think I know what it is! We'll talk about
it later.' So that's how Steve got in—I brought Steve in. I didn't get him the gig as
much as his talent got him the gig. But I was glad to bring him in, and he's the
perfect guy for the job.

STEVE VAI That was Billy Sheehan—Billy recommended me. I was a huge fan.
There was something very alluring about Dave's 'rock star aura.' So it was a little
bit surreal, because I was just such a big fan of the band, also. And making *Eat
'Em And Smile* was a very private affair. All of this stuff was going on in the outside
world, that I had no idea it had such a momentum—the fact that Dave had left
Van Halen, 'Who is this new guitar player? Oh, it's the guy that did 'The Attitude
Song' and *Crossroads*, and he was with Frank Zappa.'*

It was a mystique building, but I was completely unaware of it, because we
were just going into the basement and practicing and practicing and writing and
practicing. I didn't really know about how international press worked, so there was
all this momentum that I was completely unaware of. Making the record was kind
of surreal—working with Ted Templeman, and just Dave himself was incredibly
educational and inspiring.

STEVE STEVENS I met Steve right before he had recorded the Roth record. I was
finishing up *Whiplash Smile* with Billy Idol, and I had already signed a solo deal

---

* The 1986 film *Crossroads* features a cameo from Vai in a scene in which
he and actor Ralph Macchio duke it out in a 'guitar duel.'

with Warner Bros. I was signed by Ted Templeman, and Ted produced Dave's EP,* and he made the decision to leave Van Halen, so my name got thrown in there, and Dave flew to New York. I was already committed to finishing up the Billy Idol record and to do the tour, and I was just not available. And then I think Billy Sheehan was the first guy decided upon for that band, and Dave asked me about other guitar players, and I think somehow, Steve Vai's name came up. I was aware of him from the Zappa stuff, and I said, 'Absolutely. This guy is a monster.'

But when they started the record, they were at the Power Station, and I got a call from Ted Templeman, asking if they could borrow some of my gear. So I sent over a bunch of my Plexis—I was more than happy to help and assist in that. Steve was just such an innovative guitar player. Really, other than his dexterity and being able to do the whole tapping thing, there were a lot of guitar players after Eddie who jumped on that bandwagon. But Steve, I love the fact that he interpreted it his own way, and obviously working with Frank Zappa gave him the courage to march to his drummer, compositionally. Nobody was anywhere near close to what Vai was doing as a solo artist, as well. I respect any guitar player like that.

BILLY SHEEHAN We felt pretty strongly about it from the beginning. Dave was the biggest rock star in the world in the summer of '85. I mean, he had just come off the *1984* Van Halen record, and it was just as big as could be. *It was overwhelming.* We had a lot of faith in Dave, and his ability to come up with ideas and direct what was going on. He was the kingpin and he did a great job of it—arranging those songs and coming up with parts. He was the 'overseer.' Me, Steve, and Gregg [Bissonette] would be down in the basement, bashing out parts, and he'd come down and say, 'I like that. Let's figure out a chorus.' And we would, and he'd go off and finish off lyrics. Just wonderful—he was super great to all of us. Very generous, very kind, and it was an incredible time. I'm so grateful to have been there with him in that situation. It was really an incredible experience.

IN 1986, ROTH AND CO. SHOT VIDEOS FOR WHAT WOULD BECOME THE TWO BIG HITS FROM *EAT 'EM AND SMILE*, 'YANKEE ROSE' AND 'GOIN' CRAZY,' BOTH OF WHICH WERE CO-WRITTEN BY VAI.

BILLY SHEEHAN Just watching the master at work, it was incredible to see Dave do his thing. He had a great eye for what people find funny. We were there on the set,

---

* *Crazy From The Heat* (1985).

shooting, and we did the live thing, and then some of the other things they shot, like for the 'Goin' Crazy' video, we were there for the whole time, and he was in the fat man suit. A lot of that stuff was originally stuff that was going to be in the movie—all the suits, costumes, and stuff like that—because there originally was a movie. Unfortunately, the plug got pulled on it from CBS Pictures. But who knows what would have happened with that? And the songs were intended to be the songs in the movie. I remember the day it went down, I just said to Dave, 'Well, we're way ahead of the game here—we've got great songs and a great band. Let's go out and have an amazing tour, and to heck with the movie business!'

MIKE VARNEY And then once he got into the *Eat 'Em And Smile* record, he really showed this amazing musicality—he and Billy, to do stuff in unison and harmony, and play all this crazy stuff. And Gregg Bissonette is such an amazing drummer. I think that defined the 'super group' for that era. Nobody really at that point in time had a better line-up than Gregg Bissonette, Billy Sheehan, and Steve Vai. That's crazy firepower as far as musicality goes, and musicianship. I was friends with those guys, and would go see them and it was *a spectacle*. Even if you go watch The Winery Dogs now with Billy Sheehan, Richie Kotzen, and Mike Portnoy, it's a spectacle—nobody plays like that.

JAS OBRECHT Vai displayed a huge imagination. I remember doing what might have been Steve Vai's first cover story.* He was living in a house in a rural part of Sylmar, California, right next door to a horse pasture. Vai had this side building, a garage or some kind of farmer's building, and inside, he'd set up the makeshift studio where he had recently recorded *Flex-Able*. Steve had taped off a square in the middle of the main room, and he told me that that's where he stood when he recorded all of *Flex-Able*. As we stood there soaking in the room's vibe, Steve said that in a dream world, somebody would lock him into that building, board up the windows, and leave him in there for a month, just so he could see what kind of music would come out of him. I thought, 'Wow. This guy has the same kind of dedication that Eddie Van Halen had as a kid, or Eric Johnson—these guys who would come home from school and play until bedtime.' Vai was still that way in his late twenties.

WOLF MARSHALL I remember transcribing, I think, 'Shy Boy.' It was great. Being in LA, I was aware of Steve for a long time. He lived not too far from where I

---

* The October 1986 issue of *Guitar Player*.

lived in Hollywood. He used to go to a place called Performance Guitar, on Yucca Street—right across the street from the Capitol Records Building. I actually saw him performing at a booth at NAMM—doing all these great impressions of Allan Holdsworth and things with Van Halen. Just shredding. This was right before he got with David Lee Roth. And I said, 'Y'know … this guy should be doing *something*.' This was right after Alcatrazz. But when David Lee Roth [began his solo career], you wondered, 'Who's going to be "Van Halen"? Who can possibly be put in that role?'

Steve came, and it just seemed like a natural thing. He was perfect for that group. He didn't need to be a copycat, because his style was already so well-developed by the time he got in there, he didn't need to figure out, 'Well, what am I going to do?' He just stepped into that role and he can really play any of that stuff. And he had his own take on it, because he could bring in things that Eddie didn't do and he was different enough sound-wise—even though he was playing through similar, beefed-up, saturated Marshalls and Soldanos. Everyone was using that gear in those days, so the sound could be similar. But he did different things. He had a great touch that was different than Van Halen's, and it all comes down to his vibe—his vibe was so different from Van Halen, but it was perfect for David Lee Roth. Especially that group, that was really so pyrotechnical. It was David with these great support players.

GUTHRIE GOVAN With *Eat 'Em And Smile*, it was the opposite thing [compared to PiL's *Album*]—it was *exactly* what people were expecting. David Lee Roth was in this unusual position of having to come up with a band that in some way would take things up to eleven, having left Van Halen during a very exciting time in that band's career—the last album they'd done was *1984*, which is one of my favorites. I think that's as close to perfect as any Van Halen album ever got. So how do you top that? How do you assemble a crack team of muso-militia? You can almost hear in the album that Dave's concern was to assemble a terrifying line-up and come up with something that was musically more accomplished than what the rock crowd had ever heard before. So it kind of made sense that somebody like Steve Vai would have ended up on the album. That doesn't mean that anyone was prepared for quite how cool the album was. But I can understand the mindset of recruiting Steve.

RON 'BUMBLEFOOT' THAL When that album came out, a lot of people said, '*This* is the album that Van Halen should have made next.' They pushed their limits.

The team of Vai and Sheehan was untouchable. Each one of them was their own bit of 'hero,' in the sense that they stood on their own, and when you put them together—Bissonette as well—it was just the dream team. Everybody was like, 'Fuck. That is the most badass band you can imagine, right there.' I knew Sheehan from Talas, and I had that album with 'Sink Your Teeth Into That' and 'High Speed On Ice,'* and I played it to death, and was following everything he was doing. And when he joined with Roth and Vai, that was just a dream come true band to listen to and to see.

You can't say he made weirdness cool, because it wasn't even weirdness. He just took avant-garde playing, and new sounds and intellectuality, and creativity with two-handed technique and the vibrato bar. He took Eddie Van Halen to the next intellectual level, and definitely, once he joined forces with David Lee Roth, showed what he can do not just as a guitar hero but in a rock band with a singer. Steve Vai I think was a pioneer for the whole next generation of guitar players, who really studied the shit out of what he was doing, and then, by 1990, had all these experimental guitarists that weren't just doing neoclassical shred and straight-up rock shredding but were really exploring the boundaries musically, and getting into all kinds of cross-genres and just having fun with it. Like, they would play insanely well, but they didn't take themselves too seriously. There was a slight humor and an edge and a fun-ness about it, that I think Steve Vai planted the seed with.

STEVE LYNCH I thought that was a really brilliant album. I thought Steve Vai and Billy Sheehan just did an amazing job on it. I think it even pulled some stuff out of David Lee Roth that we hadn't heard before. There was of course David's humor in there and everything, but they tried different things—they really kind of let themselves go with that. But I thought that as far as the musicianship, it took it up a notch from what Van Halen was doing, because there was a lot more technical stuff going on, and a lot more syncopated things. Just everything about it, it raised the bar a little bit—as far as rock albums.

STEVE STEVENS The track that knocked me over was 'Tobacco Road.' I thought it was just brilliant. It's one of my favorite things that Steve has done—to this day. I guess because it's really blues-based and rootsy, but also when he does the solo on it, it's just great. And because I was aware of the record that they were doing, when

---

* *Sink Your Teeth Into That* (1982).

I got an advance copy from Warner Bros, I thought, 'They got exactly the right guy.' That record is classic, it really is.

STEVE VAI I just remember there were two episodes that happened that kind of brought me into the reality of what was going on. One was I found myself doing photo shoots with Neil Zlozower, and another, I was walking out of a gym, and this guy almost hit me in his car. He started yelling profanities and screaming at me, 'YOU ASSHOLE! YOU DICK!' … *while he's blasting* Eat 'Em And Smile *out of his windows.* And then, finally, when we got to the first gig,* we were walking into the hotel, and it was just festooned with people, and I needed security every place I went. And then being onstage, we blasted through the first three songs, and then there's that moment where Dave stops and holds the mic out to the audience. I never heard anything like that—it was 20,000 people screaming at the top of their lungs. For fifteen minutes. It was a shock—it was like, 'Holy shit.' Billy and I are looking at each other going, 'What is going on?' It was so loud that our ears were crackling. And then the party and escapades that took place just that first night, it was all like, 'OK. *This is really happening.'* [*Laughs*]

BILLY SHEEHAN [It was] wild … but it was never like, disrespectful stuff, that I hear sometimes. The band and crew, we had a lot of fun. But on our bus, we had two busses—there was Dave's bus and the band's bus. And on the band's bus, there was never any drugs, never any shenanigans, nothing was ever done disrespectful to anyone. Anyone participating was a willing adult, making a decision of their own choice.

And it was all cool. I have friends to this day that I met on that tour, and they're married with kids and we still say hello once in a while. It was a great, great thing, and it was a great bonding thing for myself, Steve, Gregg, and Brett Tuggle, who was the keyboard player. We just had a dinner recently—we do it often, we get together, me, Steve, and Gregg, and just tell stories of the old days. It's pretty hilarious. It was an amazing thing. I'm forever grateful that Dave brought us along in that adventure, because it was a life-changing experience.

JOE SATRIANI That was fantastic. And the tour was amazing. I think I almost retired at one point, because I remember going to a show—they were playing at the Cow Palace, out here in the Bay Area. And Steve brought me in for soundcheck, and I

---

* At the Hampton Coliseum in Hampton, Virginia, August 16 1986.

got to walk around the stage, see how they were doing it, meet the guys, and then stay for the show. And I remember looking at those guys up there, and I'm looking at Steve, and I'm thinking, 'This is like a level of rock performance that has never been achieved before.'

They were so extremely talented, it was basic good time rock'n'roll, but they were playing with chops that no one had ever brought to rock'n'roll before. Steve and Billy were just like rock gods up there, and I'm thinking, 'Wow. I don't think this is like my thing at all anymore.' And I looked around the audience, and there's lots of young kids there, and they're thinking, 'Well, if *this* is where you start … ' [*Laughs*] And I'm thinking, 'Wow. That means that the next generation is going to be even more outrageous.'

Ultimately, I ordered it in my brain and my emotions that it was just another version, that I shouldn't let it affect me. But I just remember being so impressed with how Steve had developed and how he played with Billy. And in a way, how Dave had managed it to be this sort of crazy rock'n'roll circus, with the best players ever. It was a huge development; it was a huge statement in rock music and rock guitar playing, certainly. Steve was right at the front. He put that flag further down the field than anybody else did before, and said, 'This is possible.' And there was nobody there with him at the time. He was right there at the front of the race, so to speak.

FOR THEIR NEXT ALBUM, *SKYSCRAPER*, ROTH AND CO. EMBRACED CURRENT TRENDS IN MUSIC—INCLUDING SYNTH POP AND DANCE.

BILLY SHEEHAN Well, *Skyscraper* was a whole different world. I give Dave great credit for trying to mix rock music and dance music, and it was very insightful for him to see the future that dance music was going to be. However, if you're a rock guy, the dance music people hate you. And if you're a dance music guy, the rock people hate you. So, traversing that Berlin Wall … actually, it would make the Berlin Wall seem like a picket fence! It's tough negotiating to bring peace to that war zone.

But Dave gave it a shot and I give him great credit for it. Because if it would have worked, we would all still be bowing down to the genius that *Skyscraper* could have been—*if it would have worked*. But *Eat 'Em And Smile* we did in a room together as a band. *Skyscraper* was done separately—everybody came in one at a time, nobody was there. Something changed in the air and the atmosphere changed. It wasn't like friend/fun/hangout anymore. It just turned into a business situation, and not so much a 'band' anymore. So it wasn't working for me, and I was quite unhappy with it. It was a tough situation for me to be in. I ended up leaving the band, and didn't know what I was going to do.[*]

JOE SATRIANI Things fell apart. Too many strong personalities.

GARY HOEY I knew it wasn't going to last, because it was *too* good. David Lee Roth was surrounded by too many talented people, and it was almost overwhelming for him—that's why, after that, he kind of went in different directions.

BILLY SHEEHAN If it would have stayed on that [original] course, I think we would have ultimately *crushed* Van Halen. But unfortunately—and I'm speculating here—Dave may have looked at *Eat 'Em And Smile* as a failure, because it didn't sell as much as the last Van Halen record that he was on, or as much as the new Van Halen record.[†] Where in fact, a lead singer leaving a band and starting his own band, statistically, is catastrophic. And that we did do platinum sales and we only played the US—we didn't do the rest of the world with that tour—it was actually a huge, giant success. Statistically, it was a rare success.

WOLF MARSHALL In many ways, it was like the Beatles toward the end—those personalities were so powerful, you couldn't contain it within a single band. Steve had to have a solo career; Billy had to be in Mr. Big with Paul Gilbert. They had to have their own bands. To keep them as sidemen, even as in a rarified position that they were and getting so much exposure, it just wouldn't have been enough—they needed their own bands. To me, it was like The Beatles when they broke up—you had John Lennon and his projects, Paul McCartney and Wings, George Harrison with *All Things Must Pass*, and even Ringo with *Sentimental Journey*. You just realized, 'These guys are four personalities, and they ran that band thing as long as they could, but they just developed.' It was almost too much to be in the same band.

SEVERAL ATTEMPTS HAVE BEEN MADE IN THE YEARS SINCE TO REUNITE THE *EAT 'EM AND SMILE* BAND, BUT AS OF THIS BOOK'S COMPLETION THEY HAVE PROVED UNSUCCESSFUL.

BILLY SHEEHAN Through the years, a couple of times things have popped up. But

---

[*] Soon after, Billy would form Mr. Big with Paul Gilbert.
[†] *5150* (1986).

it's usually a timing situation—somebody's already got something booked. The last time we did was when I ended up playing with Steve, because Dave wanted to do it, and I said, 'I'll do it if we get the original band together.' So Dave called Steve, and Steve was already booked—doing a G3 Tour. So he said, 'OK, maybe some other time.' Then Steve found out I was free, and said, 'Hey, why don't you join me on the G3 Tour and play with me?' And I said, 'Sure! Let's do it.' That's how I ended up playing with Steve on that tour, and a few more G3 Tours, and then the *Real Illusions* record and tour.

MIKE VARNEY Then again, for my buddy Jason [Becker], it was really good that he was able to get in there and get some recognition.* It's helped him a lot—to have that platform and fan base to work from. But that was an incredible band and I don't know what really happened there. Steve Vai moved into Whitesnake and did extremely well there, and had an amazing thing with his signature guitar with Ibanez and *Passion And Warfare*, and Billy Sheehan had a Top 10 song with Mr. Big.† So everybody kind of moved forward out of that band, and did really well. Maybe it was time. To keep Sheehan down or to keep Vai down away from his *Passion And Warfare* record, maybe they were all ready to make that next statement. Certainly, Billy and Steve were 'side guys' with David Lee Roth, and moved into situations where they were equal members—Steve had his own solo career and Billy being an equal member of Mr. Big.

GUTHRIE GOVAN *Passion And Warfare* was amazing—it was a fully realized vision of how far you can take an instrumental guitar album. But there was always something missing, because it was just Steve on his own. Around the time that album came out, it was around the time I was doing my final exams at school, and I guess I should have been preparing for the exams, but instead, I was listening to this new Steve Vai album that came out! I was amazed, but there was something about the guitar tone that wasn't quite the guitar tone that I had bonded with. It seemed a little more perfect and a little more precise. With someone with the level of technique that Steve has, I quite like to hear that in conjunction with a slightly rough around the edges, raw guitar tone. And there was something a little filthier about it around the *Eat 'Em And Smile* days. That's just a personal taste thing.

---

* After Steve left the band, Jason appeared on Roth's
third full-length album, *A Little Ain't Enough* (1991).
† The US #1 hit 'To Be With You' (1991).

JAS OBRECHT I have a lot of respect for Steve Vai. His 'Blue Powder' is among the best guitar instrumentals ever recorded.

RUDY SARZO I've got to say, him and Randy were the most influential guitarists that I've ever been on tour with. And I say 'on tour,' because also, Tony MacAlpine had a huge influence on me when I worked with him [in Project: Driver] but we never got to tour. Steve, I learned so much from him: multitasking, a certain discipline to his work ethic about playing.* It was really welcome. I really enjoyed it and I really benefitted from it. I was able to adapt a lot of that into my own musical lifestyle.

MIKE VARNEY Steve Vai really had so much originality in his playing and his compositions. And his sense of marketing himself—everything from his clothing to his guitars to being such a great-looking guy. He was the total package. And here's a guy with some techniques and riffs that are very unique and original, he's got some songs that don't sound like anybody else, he's got artwork that's eye-catching, he looks incredible. I really think that he was kind of the embodiment of the guitar hero in that time. Joe Satriani, I know they were friends forever and they grew up playing together—or at least Joe was his teacher at one point—but Steve had been in Whitesnake, Alcatrazz, and David Lee Roth's band. Joe was Joe, and did Joe's thing.

Steve had been a hired gun and was able to make good business deals and keep moving forward. That's a real lesson and a real talent. But then again, Steve's a brilliant individual—it's not surprising that he was able to do all that. He is extremely smart and like I said, had an originality and a concept—both musically and visually—that was just incredible for the time. Every time you have your own guitar with an extra string† and you figure out an interesting cut out of it and crazy shapes and sizes and inlays, fans love that kind of stuff. And he took that and created a style out of it. He was one of the first guys to really exploit the seven-string guitar, and look how many people came after that. There were all kinds of metal bands that were playing with seven-strings. Both he and Joe both had a huge impact on guitar.

JAS OBRECHT With his imagination, his technical facility, his personality, his fearlessness, his sense of guitar design, Steve Vai is one of these rare guys who is just a musician through and through and through. I got that sense from Stevie Ray Vaughan, as well. These guys just had sparks flying off them as they played.

---

* They toured together with Whitesnake in support of *Slip Of The Tongue* (1989).
† The Ibanez Universe, designed by Vai and first manufactured in 1990.

joe

Not only did Joe Satriani teach Steve Vai how to play guitar, he also taught countless other renowned rock guitarists, and, in the 80s, helped rekindle the popularity of all-instrumental/guitar-led albums.

JOE SATRIANI When I started teaching as a young teenager on Long Island, Steve Vai was the only one of that group that became world famous. I was just teaching for a few years as pretty much a beginner myself. I think I started playing maybe a year ahead of Steve. So it wasn't like I was an 'advanced player' when I met him— we were just young kids going to the same high school,* and had the same dream about being rock stars. [*Laughs*]

But when I moved out to the San Francisco Bay Area, I started teaching at a local guitar store, and that's where I started to teach Kirk Hammett, Larry LaLonde, Alex Skolnick, Kevin Cadogan, Charlie Hunter, David Bryson. These guys were amazing players, in that even though some of them were just downright beginners, they picked up fast, they were motivated, they were excited, they didn't screw around. There were even some guys that I thought sounded like they were pros the minute they walked in the door—like Doug Doppler. He was pretty young when I met him, but I think he had been playing as long as I had—because I think he had started when he was three or something. His finger tone was amazing. And I marveled at that—that somebody so young could have such a professional sound.

---

* Carle Place High School in Nassau County, New York.

And you mentioned in your question, 'What did I learn from these guys?' What I learned was the diversity of talent. Because there were guys like David Bryson—who wound up in Counting Crows—who was so interested in songwriting, and could really care less about soloing. He just wasn't excited about it. He just thought, 'Oh, you get a guy to do that in the band. But there's no point unless you have *a good song.*' So we worked a lot on songwriting and on theory, to show him the endless options that he had available to him in terms of harmony and structure.

Guys like Kirk, he was in Exodus at the time that I started teaching him. And then after a few months of lessons, he got into Metallica. So he had a very serious job, and immediately, he had to have solutions presented to him. And he was already a pretty ripping guitar player. So a lot of the work was theoretical, but he had to be able to solo. As well as Alex Skolnick, and Larry LaLonde, who was in Possessed at the time.* They had demands put upon them, to be sort of 'new metal shredders.' So that was very exciting.

But you learn to see the strengths that everybody has. You have one guy that has a great memory for harmony, but maybe his fingers are a bit slow, and then the other guy, he's got no limit to how fast he can play, but for some reason, he can't tell if he's in tune or out of tune. Or you have one guy who has perfect timing, and has the perfect sense of pitch, but for some reason, he's not interested in soloing at all. It was very illuminating, let's put it that way. And when you turn inward, you realize, 'Wow. I am a collection of separate talents, and they need to be harvested properly. And players should not get down on themselves for what they're missing. They should really try to develop and explore the things that they have.'

ALEX SKOLNICK It's almost like I know of two Satrianis—the one that everybody knows, that's so famous and went on to do these instrumental records, and the one that is this local legend. So I knew the local legend firsthand—he had taught a few of my guitar teachers, and he didn't mince words, he didn't play favorites. Some of the top players were very challenged by him. Joe didn't care if you were the best on the block. When you'd go to him, he's a serious musician, and he had come from the east coast, so he brought this very high level/east coast work ethic with him. Which in Berkeley, California, that was very different. He stood out. So I finally got the courage to go to him, and I was with him for I think a year and a half, two years.

It's very ironic, because I remember him telling me how there's always a 'flavor

---

* He later joined Primus.

of the month' mentality with guitar … or 'flavor of the year.' He had actually mentioned Stevie Ray Vaughan, and everybody was coming to him, wanting to learn Stevie Ray Vaughan stuff. I was going through my Yngwie phase at the time. He said, 'Right now, Yngwie is "that guy." You just don't want to be too caught up playing like the guy of the moment. And in the future, it will be somebody else.' And it turned out *Joe Satriani* was one of those guys!

But yeah, Joe, you can't say enough about him and being able to play along with him and jam with him in a small room. It had a great impact. He was the one teacher I had that you would walk out of the lessons and you're making plans about what you're going to work on and you just can't wait to pick up the guitar again. Just very diverse, too. He listened to everything. Even though he's so identified now with the music he does—which has a very consistent sound—he was all over the place at the time I studied with him. He was listening to Wes Montgomery, and he could really dive into that stuff, but also, Jeff Beck, and the fusion stuff—McLaughlin and Di Meola. He developed the sound that we all know, and stayed there. But it all came from him being such a diverse musician.

JOE SATRIANI I think all of the students hoped that one of us would succeed—not in our wildest dreams *all* of us would succeed, to some degree. We had a pretty good track record, I think. Because when you're a guitar teacher, you teach people for a few years, and you become comrades after a while. Because everybody eventually catches up to everybody else, and you want to help each other out—to see if you can make the dream a reality. We've all been really fortunate, all of us—myself and my students—that we've been able to create a life for ourselves that revolves around playing guitar. That's pretty crazy.

JAS OBRECHT When I was living in the San Francisco area in the 1980s, the buzz among players was that there were two great guitar teachers in the Bay Area, and both of them were named Joe. The 'Joe' in San Francisco was Joe Gore, who later recorded with Tom Waits, P.J. Harvey, and many others. Today, he makes wonderful effects devices.* The 'Joe' in the East Bay was Joe Satriani. I have to hand it to Satch—for a guy giving lessons, he showed a lot of courage and belief in his playing. Some company had sent him an application for a credit card that said, 'You have a $5,000 line of credit.' Joe took a huge gamble. He sent in the application, got the money, and financed his first EP—the one with the white-

---

* The Joe Gore Pedals line, which includes the Duh Remedial Fuzz and Gross Distortion stomp boxes.

and-black cover.* That was amazingly daring at the time—five grand was a lot of money. And Joe just took off from there.

WOLF MARSHALL That was the next phase—that was 'instrumental metal.' Instrumental metal was kind of a more accessible pop expression, so you could hear 'Always With Me, Always With You' on the radio. It was a great song to hear while you were driving down the street—it fit into that. Not just listening for the shred, but it's being part of your lifestyle. In pop music, that's a rare thing. It's like when people remember, 'Where was I when I heard "I Want To Hold Your Hand"?' 'Where was I when I first heard Randy Rhoads?' It had that kind of impact. So I think Joe Satriani, he was the signature of all that.

Now, Yngwie had been doing instrumental rock for a long time, but this was a very precise, high level of virtuosity. Not that Joe isn't high-level virtuosity, but he put a pop edge on it, that made it almost singable—you can sing some of his stuff. You hear 'La Grange' in 'Satch Boogie,' it almost feels like you're listening to Billy Gibbons. And other times, 'Always With Me, Always With You' is just a beautiful melody—you can have that playing on a violin with strings behind it, and it would be equally effective. So he found a way to make all that happen.

He had been around a long time, too—it's just his time was right, then. Because I don't think it would have been right in '83, '84, with all the hair metal bands. It was just not his time yet. He came after Metallica, he came after Steve Vai, but he was really the guy that was before both of them. But those guys got famous before he did. And he set the tone for that—I think of him and then I think of the new instrumental rock, like Eric Johnson, that started to become more tuneful. And then a lot of other guys came out, and I would say still had an effect—on guys like Jeff Golub, who did instrumental stuff that was more smooth jazz, but it's that instrumental rock thing, that he'd given a new side to and made it more accessible. So then it was able to merge and become a little bit broader in its appeal.

JAS OBRECHT Joe's album *Surfing With The Alien*, on Relativity Records, showcased his skills as both guitarist and songwriter. It was a smashing success. It legitimized the guitar instrumental in a way that it hadn't been legitimate or beloved since the days of Lonnie Mack and Link Wray in the 50s, and the surf bands of the early 1960s. There was this long period of time where instrumentals—as opposed to onstage solo extravaganzas, which are a different species—weren't a big deal. And

---

* *Joe Satriani* (1984).

when *Surfing With The Alien* came out, it was like, 'Whoa! This stuff can resonate with a whole new generation of people.'

STU HAMM The first thing [Joe and Stu] did was a summer NAMM show at the Limelight in Chicago. And then the next time we played, was we did a Japanese trade show for Hoshino and Ibanez, and since he played on my record,* we became friends, and we were both signed to Relativity, it made sense for me to be in his band. It was really exciting—we started off playing places like the Palomino and little clubs in San Francisco, and then by the time we got to New York, there was quite a buzz going—*Surfing With The Alien* was really selling and Mick Jagger came and sat in with us in New York. Then he got the Jagger gig, and then everything exploded.

GARY HOEY That album completely created a movement. It was an album that when that came out, every single guitar player wanted to play those songs and wanted to emulate the sound. I think hearing it on the radio and on commercials on TV; it was incredible. It was a continuation of what Jeff Beck did—taking it to the next level. I think that's what Joe Satriani did. His technique is amazing. I've played with Joe; I've opened up for Joe. To watch him do it onstage every night consistently, it's like a religion to him, in the way that he's in good shape physically, mentally, and musically. It's all there.

RON 'BUMBLEFOOT' THAL That album definitely took instrumental guitar out of the underground—it didn't become just something for musicians. It became on the radio, that people acknowledged as real music, just like vocal music. Because most people, to them, if there's not a singer, it's not a song a lot of times. So having songs on rock radio that are instrumental [*sings a bit of Joe Satriani's 'Summer Song'*] … and the thing is, people would hear these on commercials. They would hear instrumental guitar music all the time, but it was always in conjunction with some other media. It was always part of something visual. So whereas when Satch made songs that the guitar had these singable melodies to it, that's all that was needed. He made vocal lines on the guitar that people could sing and they were great songs and they were on the radio. And that even more so made guitar players equal to the singer.

There always was the dual personalities—you had the singer and you had the

---

guitar player. You had Steven Tyler and Joe Perry, David Lee Roth and Eddie Van Halen. It was always there. I guess you could say that the lead guitarist was the second focused voice of the music, where the singer was the first. So those two, it was like Batman and Robin. But this was the first time that it was making a guitarist the first voice. That was like two Batmans happening in a band. It made it that you didn't even need the singer—you could be the guitar player, and that makes you the front man. I think Satriani became one of the first guitarist front men.

MIKE VARNEY I think that was a very important record. Not only did that help establish him, but when that thing came out, he had a very refined sense of melody and was able to write a song and approach the guitar like a voice, and create very singable melodies over—for the most part—some simple grooves, compared to what some of this crazy progressive metal was. I think more people could appreciate a really well written song that has a more hummable melody. He was able to—very musically—come in and be a guitar hero for everybody.

Some of the stuff that was out there before was just too crazy, and getting almost not musical. And I think he brought things back into a very musical realm, by simplifying things musically and by playing less notes in the melody, and creating songs that the average person could listen to. I think he made a huge contribution. And then the next generation got to hear guys that were going berserk on my label, and here's somebody that put it all together with some really strong songs. I mean, I had a lot of artists on my label that had really strong songs, but Joe's songwriting and focus, and the notes in his melodies were just so musical—I think it had a very positive influence on guitar playing everywhere. My relationship with Joe goes back into the 70s, or 1980, maybe. I've known him a long time. I'm happy for his success—he certainly deserves it.

BRUCE KULICK Incredibly talented and lyrical on the guitar, and passionate, and can play anything, and goes fast as you need. But still plays with a lot of emotion. And probably—like Eddie—from some sort of Clapton point of view, which resonates really well with me. I'm also a big fan of Joe.

GUTHRIE GOVAN I have a history of hearing these players in the wrong order. I heard Steve Vai before I heard Van Halen, and before I heard Joe Satriani. And if you try to listen to all those players and put them into some kind of chronological order based on what they were doing technically, you would start with Eddie, and then go through Joe, and then end up with Steve. That's the way my ear was decoding it.

And yet, I heard Steve first, Joe, and *then* Eddie. So by the time I got to Joe, what came across is he's kind of doing the Jeff Beck thing—in the sense that these are real songs. And I've seen Joe play live and he'll play the melody, and the whole audience is singing along—even though it's not a vocal tune. And that's an achievement in itself. I don't think Joe was trying to push the boundaries of what was possible with the instrument—to quite the same extent as some other players were, at that time.

GREG HOWE The interesting thing about Joe Satriani is that the year that my first album came out, in *Guitar Player* magazine, I came in second as 'Best New Guitarist.' And Satriani came in first, for his *Surfing With The Alien* album. It was cool that I was even in it, but it kind of bothered me afterward, because that wasn't really his first album. He wasn't really 'brand new.' So it was like, 'Well, I'm glad that I'm in this … but at the same time, I feel like he should be disqualified. He's a great player, but he's not a new player. So why is he getting voted "Best New Guitarist"?'

I've always liked Joe Satriani a lot, because there is a fundamental blues thing underneath his flashier stuff. You can really hear a very serious blues influence, and a real musician—very musical, very funky. His songs are very hooky and memorable, and easy on the ears. Not difficult, necessarily—you're not sitting there counting and doing math, trying to figure out odd time signatures. His music is a brilliant thing that he did, which was just to take some great guitar playing and put it to very hooky songs.

JOE SATRIANI I struck out to be as different as possible. I had spent a good five years in a club band called The Squares, playing with two Marshall half-stacks and being very conservative. And I walked into the *Not Of This Earth* sessions with some cassette demos and a drum machine, and no amplifiers, and said to my engineer, 'I'm just going to play through whatever you have in that closet over there.' I mean, I was really inviting the idea of ready-made art of the 60s, because I just said, 'I'm not going to be that longhaired guitar player plugging into a set of Marshalls anymore. I'm just leaving that behind. I'm going to do something different and artistic.' I had to turn my back on what I was good at, in essence.

But what that created was a new pallet for me, or a new set of canvases. And it worked out. And by the time *Surfing* came around, I felt a little bit more confident that I could start to include all of those things that I thought I did well, but was sort of avoiding for the *Not Of This Earth* record. I wanted to bring in a little bit more of my roots of Hendrix and Chuck Berry and all the guitar players I liked. So *Surfing* was more a celebration of my roots.

And then I think when *Flying In A Blue Dream* came by, by then, I was already a platinum selling artist, been on tour with Mick Jagger, people knew how to pronounce my last name. [*Laughs*] It was different. Very interesting, to sum it up in a few sentences, but they were very different records, and my life changed so radically over the course of those three records. Which was I think reflected in the compositions. *Flying* was the biggest opus, because it had everything in it—the simplest music, the most complex, me trying to sing in six different characters, it was an eighteen-song record … that's crazy!

JAS OBRECHT From the get-go, Joe had a brilliant ability for putting together instrumentals. And then when he came out with the vocal tracks on 1989's *Flying In A Blue Dream*, it was just another eye-opener. I never suspected that he would go in that direction, but it sounded great.

STU HAMM It was super-exciting. We went from being one of six bands at the Palomino, to being 'the in thing'—when he made *Rolling Stone* and he was playing with Jagger. But the live shows were really exciting. The focal point was the great writing and playing on the record—that sort of defined that era—but I'd also like to think that what we did with the live show, Jonathan Mover and I, was pretty exciting and people were drawn to that. It certainly picked up momentum.

I remember the first time we played after the Jagger gig was the [1988] Montreux Jazz Festival. And he certainly had much more assured status as a rock star and successful musician, and it shone through in his writing. And then we went out and toured *Flying In A Blue Dream* for, like, *a year and a half.* For the time for bass players, I was born in 1960, and I had an older brother that was six years older than me, that was always listening to *Bitches Brew*, early Mahavishnu, Return To Forever, and experimental music. That music was always part of who I am, as well as rock music. So to be along with the rebirth of this sort of 'instrumental rock thing' was really exciting.

WARREN HAYNES [Allman Brothers Band guitarist; Gov't Mule, Warren Haynes Band singer-guitarist] Joe's a great player, and I think he did a lot to bring instrumental music back into the fold—from a guitar standpoint. That's important, because instrumentals are en vogue for a while, and then they're out of vogue for a while. I think it's important for guitar players—and especially composers—to keep the guitar instrumental alive.

eric

**Eric Johnson breaks through—
with a style reminiscent of such
masters as Hendrix and Beck.**

JAS OBRECHT In 1980, I asked Jeff Baxter—studio legend and lead guitarist for
Steely Dan and The Doobie Brothers—if he knew of any guitarists deserving of
more fame. 'Eric Johnson is just amazing!' Jeff responded. 'When I heard a tape
of him, I went ape. This might sound silly, but if Jimi Hendrix had gone on to
study with Howard Roberts for about eight years, you'd have what this kid strikes
me as.'

The next voice to sing his praises to me was Steve Morse, in June 1982: 'Eric
Johnson is one of the best electric guitarists anywhere. He's so good it's ridiculous.
I'm not kidding—he's better than Jeff Beck. Eric destroys people when he plays.
We've played gigs with him, and it put a lot of pressure on me when it came our
turn to play. All I can say is that if he had an album out, he'd be the first one on
my list of required listening.'

Eric had recorded a [self-titled] album in 1975 with the Electromagnets, but
by the early 1980s that regional release had been long out of print. But, I learned
he did have an unreleased cassette called *Seven Worlds*. I called Eric at his home
in Austin, Texas, and asked for a copy. When I played it, my reaction was similar
to Baxter's: I was floored. The tape began with the original versions of 'Zap' and
'Emerald Eyes,' followed by eight other stellar tracks. Eric's playing certainly held
up to the hype, but it would be another sixteen years before *Seven Worlds* would be
issued on CD.

TY TABOR Eric Johnson changed my life when I heard him, too. I had started getting bored with guitar playing again. I was just starting to feel like, 'I wish everybody didn't have the same tone and same kind of vibe and expression.' And then Eric Johnson came out, and it wasn't that—*at all.* It was something else. There was a combo of blues meets jazz in his lead playing. I remember when I heard his first album, *Tones,* I was totally reinvigorated again, like I was when I first heard Holdsworth. Which I think you can hear a lot of Holdsworth in Eric's playing. Eric most definitely borrows from Holdsworth, but he makes it a lot more melodic and does his own thing with it. Which is unbelievable. So I immediately gravitated toward him. He's the one that really had an impact on me—even though I listened to both Satch and Vai with amazement, during that time, also.

GARY HOEY I played onstage with him before, so I know first hand what the guy can do. And I sat backstage with him, and watched him play through a tiny amp with a ten-inch speaker, and he sounds *exactly* like he sounds. The same with Jeff Beck. Eric Johnson, just the range of what he can do in terms of his lead techniques, his tone choices, and then his rhythms, guitar styles, and the way he fingerpicks and does his whole 'clean thing' with delays and reverbs, it's just incredible; he has such a dimension to what he does. He's one of the best.

JAS OBRECHT In 1986, I wrote Eric's first national cover story. It was for *Guitar Player,* and the cover type read, 'Who Is Eric Johnson & Why Is He On Our Cover?'[*] It was the beginning of a friendship that continues to this day. I adore Eric's music, and he's one of the finest guys I've ever known.

ALEX SKOLNICK Eric Johnson had a great combination of influences that I related to. Eric Johnson would do a Wes Montgomery imitation on his Stratocaster. He actually had a tune called 'East Wes,' that was a tribute to Wes, and it sounded great. Eric Johnson was a Hendrix fan, and you could hear that, too. He came from Texas, so you can hear that he'd grown up around Billy Gibbons and Stevie Ray—that whole sound, too. And I thought he had the natural quality that I liked in a player and just this terrific combination of influences. I also felt like he was a little too much of a perfectionist in the studio. And I think he captures some great moments—especially on *Ah Via Musicom.* I learned some of that.

But to me—and I've actually had this conversation with some other

---

* This was the magazine's May 1986 issue.

musicians—his instructional video is some of the best stuff. He's just playing stuff off the cuff, and there's no processing, there's no going back and fixing. So that's how I like to hear him. But also, I know recently, he's done a tour with Mike Stern, and playing with somebody like that, who is such an improviser and so off the cuff, I think that's really good for him and it's more how I want to hear him play.

But I think of the three,* stylistically, I guess I relate to him more, because he brings these different influences and these different time periods. He can evoke the 60s or 70s with certain tones, or he can evoke the 80s with certain tones. Whereas Vai and Satriani, what they've established is incredible, but it's very much a 'one thing.' They've marked their territory, and it's their territory, and they're awesome at it. But just as a musician, I'm more interested in somebody that covers a lot of ground, and I think Eric Johnson covers a lot of ground—just like Jeff Beck did.

GREG HOWE Eric Johnson I loved, because when he came out, it was like a brand new sound. His tone is so beautiful, his technique is so delicate and musical, and just so much emphasis on musicality. And with an amazing, articulate way of maneuvering notes around, and navigating through notes. I still love him—the touch is so artistic. It's not an aggressive approach. Often, with the metal stuff, there's a real aggressive sort of sensibility about it.

It's almost like an assertive/aggressive thing, whereas Eric Johnson's thing was much more polite, but equally as impressive—and in some cases, even more impressive. So I really liked his music. I also liked the fact that it had some of the same qualities as Satriani would have, in the sense that it was very hooky, easy to listen to, not super complicated, but at the same time, very musical and very hooky. Great songs, super technique, and his tone is—even to this day—one of my favorites. His tone is just beautiful. It's perfect.

JAS OBRECHT Eric has an extraordinary sense of pitch. One time he was taking a break from a session and was going out to lunch. A garbage truck crew was nearby, and a worker threw an empty aluminum can on the ground. As it struck, Eric said, 'B flat.' This guy can really hear stuff.

BRUCE KULICK He had that one song, 'Cliffs Of Dover,' that had some really incredibly lyrical guitar playing, that just flowed so well … and I got a chance

---

* Satriani, Vai, and Johnson.

to see him at a club. We were on tour, and I remember I really enjoyed his guitar playing. It got a little too much of the same kind of thing, but again, it was all about him. Y'know, he wasn't part of a band, with songs and all. But Eric Johnson definitely touched a nerve with playing that kind of very 'lyrical' style. It's complex to a certain degree, but he can almost make a Strat sound violin-ish, with the tone. He was another guy showing how unique guitar can be.

JOE SATRIANI It's interesting, Eric is one of my favorite guitar players ever. His impact on the world was minuscule compared to The Edge or Stevie Ray Vaughan. And I point this out because they all play the Fender Stratocaster. [*Laughs*] So what's so different about him? They're so many connections between Eric and Stevie Ray, as well.

But I think you have to be a realist about it—just go out on the street and ask a hundred people, 'Do you know who Stevie Ray Vaughan is?' You'll get, 'Yes.' And then you'll ask, 'Do you know who Eric Johnson is?' And it's like, 'No. Who's that?' You and I know everything about Eric Johnson, and we could probably talk about how much we loved solos, songs, and guitar tones—but he didn't really enter into the world consciousness like The Edge did, y'know? You can go anywhere in any continent, and everybody's like, 'Oh, I love that guy.'

JAS OBRECHT I consider *Ah Via Musicom* to be Eric Johnson's masterwork, with *Tones* coming in a close second. If I could only go through life listening to one of E.J.'s records—God forbid—*Ah Via Musicom* would be the one. For starters, it has fantastic songs. 'Cliffs Of Dover,' which Eric wrote in about as much time as it takes to play it, is a classic instrumental. 'East Wes'—what a beautiful composition! It's like everything you love about Wes Montgomery filtered through modern tones. It's an homage to Wes Montgomery, but it stands on its own.

The sonic effects and production detail going on in 'Desert Rose' and 'High Landrons' are fantastic. The album also showcases Eric's facility with jazz, country, and other styles. 'Steve's Boogie' is reminiscent of Jerry Reed's playing, and 'Forty Mile Town' just has a beautiful ethereal quality. The album also has that rare quality of taking listeners on a journey from start to finish. Today, when consumers typically download favorite singles, the notion of a concept CD is foreign to many people. But with *Ah Via Musicom*, Eric put together a beautiful, visionary journey that holds up to this day.

bass

Turns out it wasn't only six-stringers
that could impress ...

JEFF BERLIN

STU HAMM Jeff was one of my favorites—with Jaco. I was a big Yes fan, and Jeff played on this Patrick Moraz album called *The Story Of I*, that is one of my favorite geeky records of all time. And when I first got to Boston, he was playing I think with Mick Goodrick and I can't remember who else, at Michael's Pub. And I got there at five in the afternoon, with my record of *The Story Of I* for him to sign. And of course, he walked in at five minutes to nine, plugged in, and they played standards all night. I used to just camp out and beg Jeff to give me lessons, and we became friends.

Having him on the BX3 tour was great, because he's such an incredible improviser—his jazz voicings and his phrasing and soloing ideas. And he gave me a couple of lessons, finally, after years of badgering him. He's such a great teacher, that he gave a couple of exercises that I'll be working on for the rest of my life, that have really improved my phrasing.

Another guy that ... I'm just so blessed, I wouldn't say 'lucky,' because it's been a lot of hard work, but I remember just a few years ago, when I was in LA, I was teaching at MI in the bass department there. And on Thursday night, I hired Stanley Clarke to give a master class to my bass students. And then, on Saturday, I gave a speech inducting Chris Squire into the Bass Hall of Fame. Dude, I remember sitting in my dorm in Berklee, and writing in to *Guitar Player* magazine, 'Best Jazz

Bass Player: Stanley Clarke' and 'Best Rock Bass Player: Chris Squire.' It's still sort of freaky that I—that little kid—came to know those guys, and I'll say they're my friends. It's just an amazing journey.

CLIFF BURTON

BILLY SHEEHAN I never really knew him or knew of him at the time. I'd heard of the band Metallica, but that was when Talas was just coming up, and it was a whirlwind of chaos—just trying to keep things going in the same direction within the band. And I didn't really have time to go out and listen to any other musicians. So I never knew of him—other than hearing about him, or people would say, 'You've got to check out Cliff Burton.' I unfortunately never did until many years after his unfortunate passing.*

And going back now and listening to some of the stuff he did—pretty great player. Pretty awesome. Pretty innovative. His use of distortion … I think maybe we were on some parallel universe a little bit; in that way we were kind of doing a similar thing. But he had his own unique approach to it. Upon revisiting all that— because I didn't have time to while he was around—it was quite wonderful. I like a lot of his stuff. Some bootlegger gave me a collection of forty Cliff Burton solos a couple of years ago, and I listened to a lot of them—there's pretty interesting stuff in there!

LES CLAYPOOL

WARREN HAYNES I remember Allen Woody† asking me if I had heard Primus, and I said, 'No.' But I had heard of them. For whatever reason, I had it in my head that they were more of a metal band or something. And he's like, 'Oh man, *Primus is awesome.* You've got to check out this cat, Les Claypool.' And it wasn't too much longer after that, that we were supposed to play Woodstock in '94. And Woody's mission was to be able to hear Les. I don't think they ever even met.

But we had to leave before Primus came on—we watched it on the closed-circuit TV. And he was just really a fan all the way around—which included a sense of humor. Woody had an amazing sense of humor, as well. So I think in addition to the connection between great bassists, also the uniqueness, and the humor injected into music, I think the Frank Zappa influence.

---

* Burton died when Metallica's tour bus crashed in Sweden on September 27 1986.
† The late Allman Brothers/Gov't Mule bassist who passed away on August 26 2000.

The mighty Van Halen on their first ever world tour, circa 1978: David Lee Roth and Eddie Van Halen (playing his 'shark guitar,' later photographed on the *Women And Children First* album cover).

Three 70s guitar kings and the models they became synonymous with. **THIS PAGE**: Judas Priest's K.K. Downing and his Flying V; Kiss's Ace Frehley lifting a smoking Les Paul. **OPPOSITE**: Deep Purple and Rainbow's Ritchie Blackmore posing with a Stratocaster.

THIS PAGE Ozzy Osbourne and the legendary Randy Rhoads, shortly before the latter's tragic passing in 1982. **OPPOSITE** UFO and MSG's Michael Schenker; Rush's Alex Lifeson and Geddy Lee.

Metallica's Cliff Burton and James
Hetfield in mid-headbang on the *Ride
The Lightning* tour, circa 1985.

I remember Les once time telling me that he was very influenced by standup comedy. And Woody was the same way. Somehow, that affecting a bass player's musical personality is very important in these instances. And I feel like once I listened to Primus, I share that admiration, as well. And then Les and I became friends a few years later. It's great to hear someone have that sort of uniqueness—which usually starts with their own personality, and it translates to the music.

RANDY COVEN

MARK WOOD He was a virtuoso bass player with a whammy bar attached to his bass. I don't know if anyone had done it since—for good reason. But to be in a band with him was a musical adventure, because there were so many notes flying around for me, him, the drummer, and the keyboard player, that it was chaos.

STU HAMM Randy was the first guy I ever saw with a whammy bar on a bass—for good or bad. I can't say that we were really the best of friends—[because he was] playing with Axis before I did, I think there was maybe a little bit of rivalry or juvenile jealousy. Probably more on my part than his. But he was certainly a great bass player and one of he guys that had it all going on at that time. He had even cooler hair than I had back then!

JOEY DEMAIO

ROSS THE BOSS Joey didn't sound like anybody. His setup and the way he plays, it's not a traditional bass setup. So the sounds of it, it almost sounds like a guitar. And he plays a piccolo bass, which is one octave up, and it's very, very trebly. I thought Joey was very unique—there's no doubt. His work on the eight-string bass was very good, too. He had a Rickenbacker bass and a modified bridge, so the strings were like an inch and a half apart—four strings. He had super-thin strings and an incredible amount of bass gear.

When we first started, he had 32 15-inch [speakers] and 24 12-inch speakers running through Peavey 800-watt power amps, and the speakers were all in Bag End cabinets. Dawk had made him a custom-made preamp that had twelve tubes in it, and it was incredible. And the bass was cut in stereo, so he had two pickups in the bass and three pickups in the top end, and he had these switches that you could put any combination of bass and treble in. So it was pretty unique. And the eight-string bass was run in stereo, too. Nothing sounded like that. *Nothing.* And

I was just chugging along with my twelve Marshall cabinets and six heads—forty watts each. [*Laughs*]

'Black Arrows' on *Hail To England*, I think that was the piccolo bass—that wasn't his regular bass. So, the piccolo bass, it was trebly, believe me, being there. [*Laughs*] I would have preferred 'Black Arrows' to be some sort of a song, like 'William's Tale' off the first record. I prefer songs and I don't like solos—I really don't. I mean, I don't like solos by themselves just to show off. He had something on his mind to prove, so I think he proved it. It was fast—no one plays bass as fast as that.

FLEA

STU HAMM I meet Flea on a golf course in LA years ago, and every time we meet we bring that up. He's a real student of the instrument, and I can't overemphasize how many rock/alt bassists he turned on to slapping with 'Higher Ground' and 'Give It Away.' I have had so many 'rock' students ask to learn those fairly simple slap bass lines, players who due to the music they listened to and play would never be exposed to Larry Graham, Marcus Miller, or the other bass masters of the technique—so good for him!

STU HAMM

BILLY SHEEHAN Stu is just a rock solid, clean tone player. A lot of guys love to have him in the band because he's got a great sound and a great rhythmic presence. A real inventive guy, as well. A smart person, and it reflects in his playing. I've always got along really well with Stu, and it was a pleasure to play with him on that bass tour we did a few years back.

STEVE HARRIS

BILLY SHEEHAN I love Steve's playing. I love Iron Maiden. I got very much into *The Number Of The Beast* when it came out. I love that he uses flatwound strings. We did a photo shoot together—Steve, myself, and John Entwistle, at the Rotosound Factory, because we're all Rotosound guys.

I love that he kind of bucked tradition and went with the flatwounds—it gives him a unique sound and cool feel. And he's been very generous to me— whenever he's mentioned me or spoke about me. He's a very kind person. I love his playing, love his band, and I'm glad to see that kind of success happen to a person of that caliber and character.

GEDDY LEE

REX BROWN [Pantera, Down, Kill Devil Hill bassist] Vinnie* and I, in tenth grade, we used to have band sectionals, so they would put us in the room—and of course, I got kicked out of the band six times for playing too loud. So Vinnie and I were in sectionals, and we would play '2112' from front to back! Geddy Lee is just one of those kind of guys, he does it all—he wrote the stuff and he arranged it all and put the foot pedals together.

In the late 70s/early 80s, he would write this stuff, and then would have to incorporate in this new Moog, and then put his vocals on at the end of it—after they had done these extremely experimental things, and made 'pop sense' out of it. The way he did it was just huge. Back in the day, before they got into the synthesizers, they were just a three-piece band. In a TV special I saw about Rush, they show that he's also into baseball memorabilia collecting, and he's so meticulous—everything was labeled. The way he goes about things, the guy is so brilliant. And then his bass playing … *oh Lord!* He's a very, very big influence on me, for sure.

JACO PASTORIUS

STU HAMM It's impossible to say a sentence or two about Jaco, when an entire library could not tell how much he influenced every bass player that came after him. I first saw him on November 8 1978, with Weather Report, at the Orpheum Theater in Boston, when I was a freshman at Berklee. He did what Hendrix did for the guitar and more … destroying all boundaries and showing that there were boundless ways to expand the role and voice of electric bass.

BILLY SHEEHAN

RUDY SARZO Billy Sheehan is top of the list [of 80s-era rock bassists]. What was really interesting about the 80s and rock bassists, very few had the flexibility that Billy had, because a lot of the music Billy recorded and performed was tailor-made

---

* Vinnie Paul, Pantera's drummer and brother of the band's late guitarist, Dimebag Darrell.

to suit his style. Whereas most of us, we had to adapt to the song—it was a very song-oriented period in music. Almost cookie-cutter.

MARK WOOD My first band opened up for Talas in Buffalo. And backstage, Billy Sheehan and I would play this crazy Bach meets Van Halen stuff!

GREG HOWE Part of what helped my first album to be as popular as it was, was the fact that Mike Varney had gotten Billy Sheehan to play bass on it—which was huge. Because at that point, Billy was *really* big. He's a legend obviously now, but at that point, he had just come off the David Lee Roth tour, he was on the cover of *Bass Player* magazine all the time. He was the biggest bass player out there. And for him to be on my first album I think was a gigantic help in making it popular.

STU HAMM Billy's a good friend and someone I admire a lot, and I've had a bunch of yucks with. We had this band, BX3, with him, Jeff Berlin, and me, and we toured the States a couple of times, and went to Asia. I only have the best things to say about Billy. Part of the reason why I became involved in BX3 was so I could steal everything I possibly could from him, and learn everything that he has! He's another guy that has a totally unique style and sound. He doesn't get the recognition he deserves for how many guitar players he influenced, as well as bass players. Billy is a hell of a bass player. Besides all the tapping solo stuff, like, you heard the Niacin stuff, man, *he's a groover.* He's a bass player at heart.

RICHIE KOTZEN The facility that Billy has on the instrument … I've never seen anyone in the world of rock and heavy metal with that kind of facility and execution ability on the instrument. I remember seeing David Lee Roth, and of course, I was impressed with Steve Vai, but I didn't know which guy to look at or listen to. Because Steve Vai would play an amazing lick, and then suddenly Billy would come up and double it, and play something else. It was pretty incredible. His approach is not a typical bass player approach—it's something that is unique to him.

So he's very special, and I'm very happy to have the privilege to play with him [in The Winery Dogs]. I've been lucky, I've actually played with a lot of amazing bass players—I was in a band with Stanley Clarke, which was a total education, because what he does is so far different from what I grew up listening to. I played in a band with T.M. Stevens, who is an amazing player in a funk/jazz sort of vibe. And Jeff Berlin played on one of my records. Very lucky to have played with a lot of great musicians, and I think that's really how I grew—playing with all these different kinds of people, I think it's really important.

BRUCE KULICK Billy I've worked with, and you can't have a more intense bass player than that. Who also just knows how to groove and keep it down. But at the same time, can play incredible lead bass.

JAS OBRECHT The best I've ever seen Billy Sheehan play was when Talas opened for Yngwie Malmsteen in the mid 1980s. Talas was one of very few bands built around the bassist, and Sheehan had the chops to pull it off. He was as exciting as most lead guitarists. When you hear him on Dave Lee Roth's *Eat 'Em And Smile*, he's playing more in the pocket, more like a session player rather than somebody who is trying to be in the front. But that's what the music called for. The record wouldn't have worked as well if Billy was trying to outgun Steve Vai during the solos. Just like James Jamerson brought new bass flavors to soul music, and like Jaco Pastorius did for jazz, Billy Sheehan was able to expand the role of the bass in hard rock/heavy metal music. And, unlike these other two, he did it while wearing spandex.

floyd rose

Probably the most groundbreaking piece of electric-guitar gear to emerge in the 80s was the Floyd Rose locking tremolo system.

GEORGE LYNCH It was a godsend, really. Even though the initial one was … as wonderfully as they were built, I'd say overbuilt, were non-fine-tunable. That was something to deal with, because once you locked the strings down, that was it. You couldn't change the pitch at all, because you'd tune it by unlocking it. So it was tricky to get them tuned in and dialed in. But once you got it dialed in, there was nothing like that previously. You could really keep a guitar with a whammy bar in tune. It was phenomenal.

Before that, all we could do was try putting graphite in the nut and try different string arrangements, and balancing the fulcrum and so forth, but nothing ever really, really worked, and it was very frustrating. So it was really a transformational game changer. Of course, they came out with fine tuners—that was pretty phenomenal. And we all continue to use them to this day. I don't think anything's beaten the Floyd. Although a lot of people have tried to evolve an evolution of Floyd designs, I don't think anybody's ever succeeded at bettering the design.

JOE SATRIANI I think the main thing was the intonation. Everybody struggled with Strats. We all know those painful moments of those live Hendrix shows, where the Strat … you can just *see* Hendrix was thinking like he was in the 80s or something—where he could do a dive-bomb and the guitar would come back in tune. But of course, it wouldn't, and he'd struggle trying to keep that Stratocaster in tune. And that's what led a lot of people to just say, 'Screw that guitar.' And plenty of Les Pauls had the same issue with the G strings always getting caught on the nut and going out of tune.

So along comes the Floyd Rose, and its first idea was a good one, which was to make a better sounding and a better performing vibrato bar, that allows you to pull up or pull down. And then two things happened which I thought were really interesting—Van Halen develops a style based on the fact that he never wants to pull up, he just wants the thing to go down and then flat back on the wood. But then there are a whole group of other people—like myself—who say, 'No. We want the thing to float. So we're going to demand that you push this technology further.' And then we get the finetuners.

Then we get companies like Ibanez, who develop it and wind up making a better one. And Kahler falls by the wayside, and probably a few other companies. And what they allowed players to do would be to have this vibrato bar system in line, on board your guitar, affecting the sound of your guitar in a minimal way—compared to just having a regular Fender bridge or through the body or hard tailpiece. And, then, using it in an extreme way. You could go total 'Steve Vai' with that bar, and the thing is pretty much going to come back in tune. That in itself changed the nature of performance for guitar players. Because now, you would be expected to pull up and pull down and dive-bomb and make crazy noises. And it wouldn't be like 1967. It would be '87, and the thing's in tune, and you can keep playing. It had a remarkable effect on what people felt guitar players should be able to do. It's really something.

You really have to think of other parts of life—just imagine, the first toaster only had one setting. That's very different to a toaster where you can set it twenty degrees of cooking, and then walk away from it. That's remarkable. Today, we have a microwave where you just set it and it cooks it exactly the same way, every single time—to the second. Think about when there was no such thing, how it changed your basic life. Or how about automatic transmission on a car? Things like this, we take for granted. But you can imagine how much more work went into daily routines when these things weren't around. So go back to 1967, you want to do a dive-bomb, you know the first thing in your mind is, 'This is going to fuck up my tuning something fierce.' So you don't do it. But if you've got a JS2410,* you go do it. There's no fear. It's going to come back and it's going to be perfectly in tune and it will sound great. So I think that's pretty huge.

---

* The Ibanez JS2410 Joe Satriani Signature Electric Guitar, produced in 'muscle car orange.'

STEVE STEVENS For me, it was a way to keep my guitar stable, because once you locked it in place, you could do all these kind of … certainly, back in the 80s, a Billy Idol show was pretty 'athletic.' We were definitely keeping that punk rock spirit alive—I would be bashing away on my guitars and the Floyd Rose kept me in tune the whole night, as well as executing the dive-bombs and all the things that I loved about Hendrix—but his guitars would go out of tune.

And also, when you combine the Floyd with that clean sound, I wouldn't have been able to record 'Flesh For Fantasy' without a Floyd Rose, because every chord that I'm playing, I'm wiggling the bar and falling off the pitch. It was really useful in all of that. I think that most of the *Rebel Yell* record was done with a Les Paul that Billy Idol bought me when we went to do the first record, and also, a Kramer Pacer guitar—I think I paid 350 bucks for it. But it had a Floyd Rose on it. I didn't really know if I'd take to the Floyd, so I figured, 'Well, 350 bucks, I've got nothing to lose.' I went to Sam Ash in Queens—I was still living in the basement of my parents' house, and Sam Ash was in walking distance. And it ended up all over that record.

DAVE MENIKETTI I have a love/hate relationship with the Floyd Rose. I like it for the fact that it does what it does well—which is keep the guitar in tune, no matter how much you yank on that thing. But as far as just changing strings and the floating thing and how much it stuck up off the guitar, I never really loved it. But I still use it today on my old Kramer Baretta.

So, for what it's worth, it still works great and for the purpose of what it was made. I'm just not a super-fan of that particular thing—just because of the fact that the old Floyd Roses, they were a pain in the ass for guitar techs to have to change the strings sometimes, and also, the fact that it stuck up off of the guitar quite a ways. And for guys like me—that lay their palm against the bridge all the time—I think it just means that you have to get used to something else.

STEVE LYNCH The first guitars that I had made by Wayne Charvel and Grover Jackson—that's when Grover Jackson was still at Charvel, out there in San Dimas, California—they asked me which [tremolo system] I wanted on there. And I said, 'I want the Kahler on there,' because I didn't like them hollowing out the whole back of the body. I just didn't like that idea. So I got used to the Kahlers. It was easier to change the strings—you didn't have to cut the ball off the string and clamp it down. It was a much easier system, as far as I was concerned.

But now, I'm using Floyd. I think they're comparable. Some people prefer one over the other, but I played both and I like them both. But I got into the whole vibrato thing when I had a Strat, back in the 70s, and it wouldn't stay in tune very good. I got more and more into it when I had that Kahler put on my first couple of Charvel-Jacksons. Up until that point, I was mainly playing just Les Pauls and Strats, but I wouldn't use the vibrato arm that much.

K.K. DOWNING I favored Kahler over Floyd Rose because of the feel. Where Floyd Rose had a heavier feel, Kahler was very smooth. And then, later on, I went to the SpeedLoader, which I think is still an incredible piece of kit, and that's my favorite—even though it's heavy like the Floyd Rose was, the benefits of not having to stretch strings and to be able to change strings in about a minute-and-a-half is real good value for money.

RONNI LE TEKRØ I thought it was a brilliant invention. I used that on a lot of my guitars. But if you listen to the signature sound of TNT, it's a German system that's pre-Floyd Rose, called Rockinger. The Rockinger has better sustain than Floyd Rose. The Floyd Rose is more reliable when it comes to tuning.

TONY MACALPINE I had some guitars with a Rockinger, and then Floyd came along and I put them on the early BC Richs. I just thought it was an incredible thing, that never went out of tune. Just really a great feeling bridge—even to this day, it's a classic feeling bridge and classic, tight vibrato. I use that on my eight-string today—I have a Floyd Rose eight-string bridge. It's really nice.

ROSS THE BOSS They were accurate, but I think guys were using it as a crutch. Guitar players were definitely overplaying that thing, with the bomb drops, the harmonic drops. It's good for what you have to do, as long as it's not overused. My '74 Strat, I used the tremolo on that very effectively on songs like 'Hatred' and 'Metal Daze,'* and they kept in tune. That was the complaint about Stratocasters, that they were never in tune. Well, my guy in Manowar, Dawk Stillwell, he had this system, and with proper lubrication, those guitars stayed in tune.

TREY AZAGTHOTH Well, again, Eddie was the one who really helped showcase the Floyd Rose locking tremolo, [an] awesome device that helps keep your guitar in tune when using tremolo in a heavy application. Then, with the later evolvement of the fine tuners, it's a pretty perfect system, I think.

---

* From the Manowar albums *Into Glory Ride* (1983) and *Battle Hymns* (1982), respectively.

GIT

If you were a Hollywood-based shredder in the 80s, the Guitar Institute of Technology was the school for you!

STEVE LYNCH My guitar teacher from up here … I was actually touring at the time. It was 1977. I called him up from Montana, because I was coming off the road for a little while, and I was going to set up some more lessons with him. He was working at a music store in West Seattle. And they said, 'He's down in Los Angeles. He's in Hollywood, teaching at a new guitar school.' I called up information and got the number, and got him on the phone. I was still in a hotel room in Montana. He said, 'Steve, quit your band, sell all your gear … *and get your butt down here.'* And I was there three months later.

The amazing thing about going there were these players like Ron Escheté, Joe Diorio, my old teacher Don Mock, Howard Roberts, Tommy Tedesco—all these jazz legends—were there, hanging out in the hallways, teaching people how to play, and teaching different classes. Just the experience of that was mind-blowing, to be around these perfected jazz musicians that were right off the charts. That experience was really cool. And the visiting faculty that came, as well—it was a really great experience. I'll never forget it. I'm still in touch with Pat Hicks, who actually started it with Howard Roberts. He was the owner, and he was a great guy. Now, he's traveling around in an RV with his wife. I thought, 'That's brilliant!' [*Laughs*] What a great thing to be doing.

JENNIFER BATTEN I feel really blessed that I went when I did, because it was just getting off the ground. It was the third class ever. There were only sixty students that were divided into two classes, and only three teachers at the time—Joe Diorio, Ron Escheté, and Don Mock. Joe and Ron were hardcore beboppers and Don was the crossover jazz-fusion guy. It was just wonderful. I lived in a friend's garage, so I had zero distractions. I would go from school to the garage and back. I had zero social life, and it actually worked out really well for me.

FRANK GAMBALE GIT for me, a kid from Australia, it was like this incredible eye-opener. And Hollywood at the time—1982—looked like a warzone. Hollywood had reached its absolute worst and bottom at that point. It looks like Disneyland now by comparison. But when I got there, half the buildings were squats full of drug addicts and prostitutes, and bums all over the street. I was twenty-three. We were all scared for our lives. All these kids coming from across the world to go to Hollywood to study, and we're going, 'So *this* is Hollywood?' We were horrified! But the school itself, once you're in the environment, was awesome. To be in a place where you're surrounded by people with a like mind and a like intent, wanting to be better musicians, was great. And the teachers were amazing. There were a lot of great people teaching at that time.

It's a lot different now—still good—but then it was still in its heyday, it still had a lot of energy. It's just a different energy now. Then, it was just incredible. I'm always curious as to why I was chosen 'Student of the Year,' because I rarely went to classes! But I was certainly practicing, and I had a lot of energy and putting groups together, playing lots of performances, playing lots of challenging music. I was just completely 100 percent music and guitar for that year as a student. And then I graduated and started teaching for three more years there. So that was four years where I was intensely practicing. It was a good environment for me; it kept me energetic.

The hardest thing to do is to perform in front of guitar players—*a whole room full of them*. That's a challenge. Regular audiences and the public are, 'Oh, you play the guitar? Great!' When you've got a room full of guitar players, they're all with their arms folded, checking you out. It's a different kind of pressure. So it was good for me. You just play the best you can and I was definitely motivated to taking it as far as it could possibly go. My intention was never to be an average guitar player. I can't live with that. I'm either completely crap or I'm the best that I can possibly be—with no in-between. So if I were to be the best that I can be, it just meant a lot of work and a lot of practice.

PAUL GILBERT It was great. The school itself taught me a lot. I had been primarily self-taught up to that point. And there are great things that you get from being self-taught, that you really can get no other way. But also, GIT opened up musical doors for me that would have taken a long time. So it was really nice to learn and just have a basic music education—to know harmony, theory, ear training, how to write out a rhythm, and what it means if you tell a drummer to hit accents on the end of three. The basic language. In a way, I was fluent already, but I didn't know the labels that people used to communicate to each other verbally, and I didn't know how to write stuff down. So it was really wonderful to learn that stuff—especially at that point.

A lot of that stuff would be really counterproductive to learn as a starting point. In the same way when you learn to speak, you don't get a dictionary and an encyclopedia—you just learn by imitating and then eventually you learn grammar. It's very similar to that. And there were great players there—not only the teachers but the students. Jim Herring was a fellow student when I went there and he was always great, and Frank Gambale was a teacher. But it wasn't just the shred guys—I had never really been exposed to jazz before then. There were some fantastic players—Ron Escheté was a guy I'd always go to his class, and he did just beautiful fingerstyle stuff. So it really opened my ears to a lot of stuff that I never heard before. I grew up listening to rock and heavy metal, and some blues and some classical music, but I really had never heard jazz. And there was a lot of it there, and it really opened my ears.

STEVE LYNCH You know, there wasn't any [competition]. Everybody was there to learn. It was an 'international thing'—there were only seventy people when I first started, because the school was so new. There were people from Australia, different parts of Europe, Scandinavia, Japan, New Zealand, even South America. It was cool, because it was just a learning environment, and people were not only learning from the teachers, but they were learning from each one of the students, too. So it wasn't competitive at all. I think it got that way later on, but everybody there was very eager to learn and very eager to learn from other students that were there, because everybody had a different approach to guitar. Especially internationally. That really made it far more interesting, than if everybody was from the same background, going to school.

STU HAMM I think that was the golden age of MI.* I did some counseling and clinics with Steve Vai back in the day there, and it's a much different school when I was there a few years ago, and certainly, people harken back to those days as sort of the 'glory days,' when Steve Bailey was on the faculty, and Jeff Berlin was on the bass faculty, and Paul Gilbert and all those guys—Dino Monoxelos from Ampeg was there. Certainly, those people harken back to a much different school than it is now. My education was being from Berklee just a couple of years back in the late 70s, early 80s. But a lot of good cats came out of there. That's where people of that ilk would flock to LA, to learn that style of music … and trade mousse and hairspray, and put bands together.

---

* In the late 80s, the Guitar Institute of Technology became the Musicians Institute, the name by which it is known today.

NAMM

By the early twenty-first century, the National Association of Music Merchants (NAMM) had become one of the biggest musical instrument trade shows in the world. But it was during the 80s that it truly rose to prominence.

JAS OBRECHT During the 1980s, NAMM was star-studded. You'd walk down an aisle and run into people like Tommy Tedesco, Herb Ellis, Leslie West, Lenny Breau, Mr. and Mrs. Leo Fender, up-and-coming metal guys, country legends, studio giants. Steve Morse would be over at Ernie Ball's booth, Joe Walsh would be playing at Gibson's display, and Vai and Satch would be onstage jamming together after the show. The Anaheim Convention Center was far less crowded back then than it is for today's NAMM shows. During the 1980s, the shows brought a wonderful opportunity to communicate with people throughout the industry and to see new instruments and gear. The musical performances were often stellar. You'd go see Danny Gatton playing slide guitar with a beer bottle at one venue, and then go watch John Entwistle and Leslie West at another. After hours at NAMM was a musicians' party.

WOLF MARSHALL That was when NAMM was at its height. There was a lot of excitement. I guess there's still excitement now, but it's a little bit different, because it's been so much for so long. I started going to NAMM at about 1978, so I saw the change. And when those tablature magazines really took off and they had a booth for *Guitar For The Practicing Musician*, you'd have guys like Steve Morse signing autographs, and there were lines around the booth. Before that, when I went earlier, it was a trade show—they had a lot of equipment, and occasionally, a guy would show up and play something. Y'know, Jeff Baxter or somebody would come and play a guitar at a booth. And that would be the extent of it. There wasn't the whole performance end of NAMM that we now see, that is so standard—all the concerts.

MICHAEL ANGELO BATIO It was huge. Once I moved to California, there was something else, too. See, I'm from Chicago—the big NAMM show, for at least seventy years or more, was in Chicago in the summertime. And what happened was the unions in Chicago at McCormick Place, where they had the convention, ruined the NAMM show. I mean, if you plugged in a lightbulb, you needed a union guy from Chicago, and they'd charge you a hundred bucks. And so what happened by the time of the early 80s, the show started to shift. See, the winter NAMM show in Anaheim, California, was the small show. Chicago was the big one in the summer. All of a sudden, that started to change, because LA became the hotbed of the planet for rock music.

Because back then, I saw this firsthand—when I moved to Los Angeles, in one year, I went from a Midwest-looking kid to the full-on rock star. I didn't even know I had changed. LA was its own world back then. The bands that came out of LA looked and sounded … even if you were from somewhere else, like Poison, you went to LA. If you were Bon Jovi, you went to LA. You were familiar with the LA scene, because you couldn't compete with it. I remember going back to Chicago, watching some local bands, going, 'These guys look like *amateurs*.' One of the first bands I saw in LA, I go to the Troubadour, I see these flames shooting out of a logo, a guy with two members of his band on dog leashes, throwing raw meat into the audience! It was W.A.S.P. That's my first introduction. I mean, you see Blackie Lawless up there, that guy was a sight to behold. And you're seeing Chris Holmes—a guy who is six-foot-five, just looking wild and playing great.

And it all came together with the NAMM shows, too, because all of a sudden, I became really popular at NAMM. Once I released that instructional video—the *Star Licks* video—it was known in those circles, because music stores carried my video. I couldn't walk around the show. I looked like this full-on rock star—everywhere I turn, people go, 'Hey Michael, can we get a photo? Can we get an autograph?' I was very visible at that time, and the NAMM show really perpetuated that, because you could see the interest—especially in LA. Anaheim kind of made itself. The NAMM show, it was like a movement—it was a wave. The Anaheim show became the major show.

Everybody and their brother was there. I remember meeting Joe Pass. I loved his guitar playing—he passed away many years ago.* He was the most fantastic jazz guitarist, and here, I look like 'Mr. Rock'n'roller.' I'm hanging out with Eric Johnson, and he looked like the 'Cliffs Of Dover' era, where he was young with spikey hair. We looked totally out there. And Joe Pass wouldn't take a picture with me. I said, 'Joe, I studied your book.' He's like, 'Yeah? Bullshit you did.' I was by the Star Licks booth, and I picked up a guitar—because I was doing demos for them at that time—and I played some of his riffs. And he goes, 'Wow! You *did* study my book!' And he took a photo with me. I've got a photo of me, him, and my other guitarist, Guy Mann-Dude. But NAMM was very key to the scene, because everything shifted to LA. LA was the center of the rock universe—especially all the way up to the early 90s. And I was right there in the thick of it.

CRAIG GOLDY In a way, that's what also made me think of trying to do my programs, because a lot of guys came from all over the world, because there was a day where everybody came together—the well-known and established rock stars were there, and the guys from the public, the average Joes who were trying to break into the music industry. And they would spend thousands of dollars on plane flights and hotel rooms, just in hopes that they would walk down the halls, bump into somebody, and be able to hand over their demo packet to them, in hopes that that person would go home, listen to it, and try to do something for them.

And the spirit that was with the NAMM show then seems a lot different now, because it seemed more pure. It was just basically what it was—the National Association of Music Merchants. 'This is what's coming out next and this is what we're trying to do for you guys.' And also, networking—'Hey, I got an album coming out and I really need help with some of my equipment or a new guitar,' and develop relationships. We helped one another. It was a real community.

It started out that way. There are still some companies that have that same spirit, but it was beautiful back then, because that's what it was really all about. It was like a community of everybody coming together and people's hopes and dreams could actually come alive, or they might bump into somebody and they hear a demo, and the next thing you know, they're trying to help them get a gig, because somebody they know is looking for a guitar player, or a singer, or a

---

* Pass died in 1994, at the age of sixty-five.

drummer. And the next thing you know, they're flying him in for an audition and he's part of the band. There are actually stories like that. And that was beautiful.

MICHAEL ANGELO BATIO What I found in the 80s was guitar clinics weren't really developed that much. I actually was never even asked to do a clinic—until around '87. Back then, again, by that time, NAMM had taken over and LA was 'the place.' So, it wasn't so much clinics then—clinics were more a product of the 90s. What happened was they took guitarists like myself and we were the endorsements. The 80s, what really happened was NAMM was making metal music so popular. Now we got into the music stores. I remember Gibson Guitars, Henry* coming and talking to me about doing ads. I wasn't even known yet.

What they did is they just looked for these killer players with a really cool image, and I was in Randall ads next to Vivian Campbell or Neal Schon. Really, the 80s were not so much clinics; it was the endorsements. It was where they paired together the artist that could really rock and really play with the companies. Joe Satriani, his music brought instrumental guitar to the forefront, and he brought Ibanez from pretty much an unknown company to the forefront. All of a sudden, artists got associated with products. That—to me—is the 80s. I got associated with Wayne Charvel, with my double guitars and quad guitars. They were built by Charvel, and I was using Randall amps. We all had really big endorsements. I think that was really one of the products of the 80s.

GARY HOEY I thought it was the best time for the NAMM show. That was the best time it ever was—compared to now. Because I think in the 80s, people could go to the NAMM show, people were more excited about music in general—people wanted to own it, people wanted to buy it. And as a guitarist, you could come to the show, play and try out equipment, get loud, and nobody would tell you to turn down. And you could build a little crowd if you did something that people thought was sounding OK. And you could get endorsements. It was a very exciting time. It was a great time to be a guitar player.

---

* Henry Juszkiewicz, chairman and CEO of Gibson Brands Inc.

mags & **tabs**, vids & stores

Several guitar-based publications become extremely important to players worldwide— especially after the popular 'tablature' system was introduced. Around the same time, home videos of guitar lessons and advice from top players began to appear, while stores selling guitars and gear continued to thrive.

JAS OBRECHT *Guitar Player* magazine is older than *Rolling Stone*. *Guitar Player* started in '67—six months before *Rolling Stone*. The timing was perfect. An explosion in guitar music was going on, and *GP* was the only guitar magazine around. From the beginning, the editors were able to run in-depth interviews with not only celebrities like Jimi Hendrix, Yardbirds-era Jeff Beck and Jimmy Page, but also players in all styles of music that featured guitar. This approach attracted a loyal readership that included many of the musicians we interviewed.

By the late 1970s, the guitar had become the dominant instrument in rock and pop. In fact, you could make a compelling argument that it was the dominant instrument in all of American music. Naturally, other publishers took note. In 1980, *Guitar World* was launched, with a different approach than *Guitar Player*, and their formula has worked for thirty-five years—my hat's off to 'em. Around 1983, *Guitar For The Practicing Musician* came along. And *Musician Magazine* covered guitarists, as did *Frets*, *Living Blues*, and many other publications. Lots of instruments were being sold, lots of people were dreaming of being in bands. These were the glory years for guitar, and people were hungry for information.

Two weeks before I interviewed for *Guitar Player*, I interviewed for *Creem*, which was based in my hometown of Detroit. My dad advised me to wear a three-piece suit to the interview, and actually bought me a conservative Brooks Brothers suit. So I wore it to the *Creem* interview. Well, when I came walking in the door there, the editors, who were mostly women, looked at me like I was some kind of a narc. So when I got to the *Guitar Player* interview, I disregarded my dad and wore a regular shirt and jeans. Good call! Don Menn, who became my editor later that day, came in barefoot, his hair tousled, and wearing cutoff jean shorts and a King Tut T-shirt. Mounted on the wall behind his desk was a numbered goldtop Gibson Les Paul that Pete Townsend had destroyed onstage. I thought, 'This is the place for me.' They hired me on the spot. I spent twenty good years there—for the most part, it was a very happy time.

WOLF MARSHALL I wrote for *Guitar World* and *Guitar For The Practicing Musician*, and I was interviewed twice in *Guitar Player*. *Guitar Player* was the first one that was actually dealing with guitarists in-depth. You would see an occasional article in *DownBeat* or something—maybe something about Al Di Meola or Wes Montgomery, but it was amongst a lot of musicians. *Guitar Player* was the first to actually focus on the guitarists and the gear. It got quite big by the late 70s. I used to *devour* that magazine. I think I have all of them from the 70s—I absolutely loved it.

Then *Guitar World* came in 1980, and they were a little more 'street,' they had a little bit rougher vibe, a little more interior rather than the big picture guitar playing. They would get into some other stuff that was a little more cutting-edge or hardcore. And they started doing some transcriptions—I remember *Guitar Player* ran my Pat Martino 'Song Bird.' And then in the 80s, they started seeing them pop up in *Guitar World*, too. Transcriptions. So it was a one-off—every once in a while, they had maybe Ritchie Blackmore, and they'd have the 'Highway Star' solo or something.

When I did an issue with *Guitar Player* in I think 1984, they interviewed me for transcribing, but they also had my transcription of 'You Shook Me All Night Long' and Angus Young's solo. And then the final thing was *Guitar For The Practicing Musician*, where they actually featured the music—much more so. At least six transcriptions per issue of the full song, plus in my articles and a lot of the other articles … Steve Morse wrote a column for them called 'Open Ears,' and they had a lot of other players writing.

But mine was a monthly column called 'Music Appreciation,' and I would pick an album and we would take the key moments. Like, we would take Larry Carlton's *Room 335*, and we would go through the recordings. A lot of times, I had the chance to actually spend time with the player as I did the article—Allan Holdsworth for instance, or Larry Carlton. They lived in town near LA, which is where I was. We would be able to hang out together and we would play stuff together. I think that led to a better exposure of the music of the guitar player—in addition to an interview or story. So that's what I found different about *Guitar For The Practicing Musician*.

STEVE MORSE John Stix made a magazine called *Guitar For The Practicing Musician*. He came up to me and said, 'I'm making a magazine with this title, and I wanted to see if you want to write a column.' I said, 'Well, I love the title.' Because that was one of my things—to be a good guitarist, you have to practice. At guitar clinics, that was a theme I constantly hammered on. People say it's all luck to make it. I said, 'The more you practice, the luckier you get.' So the first column basically started the template—he would interview me and ask leading, open-ended questions. I think he edited from our conversations, the first few columns. And then gradually, we got to the point where he would give me a phone call, and say, 'I want you to talk about *this*.'

And he was, like, the perfect editor. He knew what he wanted me to talk about. He didn't know exactly how I was going to say it, but when I would submit it to him, he would say, 'OK, this part here, I don't think you're explaining well enough what a person could do to be that way.' In other words, he would give me actual constructive criticism. And the end result was all in my words, but it was edited and condensed and directed by him. So I thought it was a really good partnership, because he had the overview that I don't have. That was a wonderful experience, and they made several books from the column, that fans all say they like.

Guitar Player, I did my first interview ever with Jas Obrecht, and it was his first feature interview for the magazine. So we got to be friends—we were both working in the same town. He really liked the humanity of hanging around and seeing the band. He would come to shows and write about it, and then do the interview afterward, and it gave people a chance—this was before the Internet—to be there, with how descriptive it was. It was very important. The magazines would tell you about reality stuff, like, 'Here's this guy on the road. They had to drive nine hours to the next gig.' They would sort of describe the reality of things, but then, 'Here's the "nuts and bolts stuff"'—here's the setup, here's where the pedals were, and here's our interview about practicing and so forth.' And then later in the magazine would be a flexible disc that you could play on a record player, or tablature, or both. So it was multilevel interests for the reader, because you've got some of that human curiosity stuff in interviews, and some nuts and bolts stuff, because you had, 'Here's the lesson that we're concentrating on, and here's the musical example.' Plus, the tablature and musical examples and a lot of technical columns, where the columns were mostly guitar lessons—'Try this, and here's how you do it.'

It was quite a resource for players. And something that I didn't have when I started to play. The closest thing we had was a songbook, and they had the chords that a piano player just said, 'That sounds like B flat 6,' and the chord chart that came with it would be going from 6 to 1 on the strings, it would be 'XXX,' and then one finger laying across three strings on the third fret. And that's not what The Beatles played on that chord! But that was it—that was the songbook. And some of them, for me as a kid, I was going, 'This is stupid. I hate sheet music.' I got fed up with that real quick. The guitar magazines were just a wonderful resource for players—to be able to get actual transcriptions by guitarists.

RIK EMMETT I think I had done an interview with Jas Obrecht, and I'd like to think he went back to the magazine and said, 'This guy's legit. This guy's for real.' And I had always been a subscriber to the magazine, and there had been a couple of times where I had written letters to the editor. And one of the things that I complained about was that it was sort of a San Francisco area-based magazine, and it was very West Coast–centric in its coverage. And they didn't tend to devote as much time to ... like I always thought of it as the guitar player's bible. So I thought, 'Come on, you guys have to have more of an international kind of scope, and you can't be too parochial in the way you think about the world of guitar, because your magazine matters to people *all over the place*.' But my specific— and probably self-serving—point, was, 'There are a lot of good Canadian guitar players, and you don't write about them enough.'

And I think, being Canadian, I tended to have a little bit more of an international kind of view of things—partly because, in Canada, there was a lot more success, and I'm not talking about numbers, I'm talking more about demographics. I'm talking more about per capita. There was a lot more airplay for say, progressive bands. And there was a pretty strong scene in Toronto, where I lived, where progressive rock bands from Italy would become known quantities— they might even be able to come and play a live gig. Gentle Giant would be able to sell out a smaller venue—people knew who they were. And *Guitar Player* tended to be American and pretty mainstream. That would be something that I would write to the editor, and say, 'Hey!'

So I think one thing led to another, and then Tom Wheeler—after I had now become somebody that had been interviewed for the magazine—said, 'We can kill two birds with one stone here. How about you write a column for us?' And I went, 'What?!' The catch was, he said, 'We want somebody to write a back-to-basics column. We want something that's very fundamental.' And then I went to the other guys in the band, and said, 'They've asked me to write a column. It's going to be a back-to-basics kind of thing—this isn't going to be some column where I'm able to talk about crazy, fantastic, esoteric, build-up-my-image-as-a-virtuoso kind of stuff. I'm teaching kindergarten. Should I do it?' And the other guys in the band said, 'Are you kidding? Just having your name in the masthead, that's validation. You should definitely do it.'

So that's how it started, and I did it twelve or thirteen years. I loved it. It had a lot to do with shaping the human being I became—in the sense that the guy who had been my teacher in college level for one semester, he and I remained friends, and I would go over to his place and we'd sit and jam together and talk guitar. And he would say, 'The reason that you're writing there is because you're a great teacher. You're articulate and you can be pedantic when you need to be. These are all good qualities, and now every month, you're reinforcing those things.' And sure enough, here I am later in life, and I teach at a college.* I guess it's just part of my nature, and I enjoy it.

STEVE LYNCH What was cool about them is people that were writing articles, they would show some really interesting things about how they approach different songs, how different artists play different solos, and jazz teachers, blues teachers— whatever they were—they would come in and be guest artists that would do columns. Like I did, for all three of them, actually. And I had a gas doing it, because it's cool when you can just look at somebody's perspective and go, 'Gee, I never thought of it that way.' I would read all these magazines and I would read all of these different columns, because I would always get something out of it, and I think that it helped catapult people to a different level of playing.

MIKE VARNEY I would say that the guitar magazines were really my friends and were responsible in helping me promote some of my artists. After *Guitar Player*,

---

* The Humber Institute of Technology and Advanced Learning, also known as Humber College, in Toronto, Ontario, Canada.

I wrote a column called 'Hometown Heroes' in *Guitar World*. I was offered a column in *Guitar For The Practicing Musician*, but I didn't want to spread myself too thin. But these magazines, the coolest thing that I remember is *Guitar Player*'s sound page. They had a little record that was made of plastic, and you could rip it out of there, put it on your turntable, and play it. All these artists, like Tony MacAlpine, had a sound page, and I think Marty Friedman and Jason Becker may have had a sound page, Michael Lee Firkins had a sound page. So those would go out in 125,000 guitar magazines. And all of a sudden, boom—you got people interested in what you're doing. So that was a big part of *Guitar Player*'s success with my stuff, because of that.

Also, they had 'Best Record,' 'Best Producer,' and we would win various polls back then. And those polls really helped to propel the genre. And I remember some magazine came out, and it had three of my artists on the cover—a couple of times I think I had stuff like that happen. I thought, 'Man, we've really made it and made a good impact here.' *Guitar For The Practicing Musician* was a great magazine—John Stix was the editor. He really did a lot to push the magazine forward. I had the inside front cover—full-page color ad—there for years. I got bumped by some big guitar company, I think. But having that presence there every issue was a big help.

TONY MACALPINE They were as essential as the internet is today, because that was your one way to get a feel on what was going on, and get your hand on the pulse. That was really the only way. People knew what to look for when they really wanted to research something, or find out what kind of gear somebody was using. You went to these various magazines, and you were able to read these in-depth articles, and take in the pictures, and learn about somebody's rig. So it was really amazing, and there was a lot of tablature you could learn. It was really cool. We actually did a little pull out record in *Guitar Player* magazine—a track that wasn't included on the *Edge Of Insanity* record—it was called 'Billy's Boogie,' which Billy Sheehan and I played together with Steve Smith. A lot of that stuff was really amazing.

RICHIE KOTZEN In the 80s, guitar magazines were everything—that's how you found everything out. That's how you found out who was putting a record out, what was happening, and what people were listening to. I remember also that the sound page was a big deal. When my [self-titled] record was recorded and we were releasing my record on Shrapnel, it came out in 1989, and all I cared about was—'Was I going to get an endorsement, was Ibanez going to do a full-page ad to promote my record, and was I going to get a sound page?' Because everybody that went on to do great things had a sound page. I got a sound page, so I was happy!

GUTHRIE GOVAN They were important—in a number of ways. I had a particular fondness for *Guitar Player* in the latter half of the 80s, which for me was a golden age of that magazine. I would read them avidly. It seems to me that the duties of a guitar magazine are to expose the reader to exciting new stuff—not just to give them month after month of stuff that they already knew about. I see this to some extent with guitar magazines now—every year or so, every guitar magazine has to have Jimi Hendrix on the cover, or they have to have Stevie Ray Vaughan on the cover. And pivotal players although they obviously were, they haven't done much lately. I like the idea that I could read about someone in *Guitar Player* and be intrigued by what I read, and then would seek out audio to back up what I'd been reading.

I particularly love the fact that they had sound pages in those days. It's probably not possible for a magazine to have something like a sound page now and have the same impact, because we're spoiled in the Information Age—everything's on a plate, wherever we are on the globe. But back then, to buy a guitar magazine and in the middle there is this free piece of floppy vinyl, and on one side—I remember this vividly—we have 'Blue Powder' by Steve Vai, and on the other side, we have 'Because It's There' by Michael Hedges. I'd never heard of Michael Hedges. That to me is *Guitar Player* doing its job—getting the reader excited about something. It's like, 'We know you haven't heard about this guy yet, but we think you might like him. So, check this out.' I was always very fond of *Guitar Player* for that reason.

There were interesting instructional columns going on around then, and then of course, there was the 'Spotlight' column. I was in a slightly strange place at that point in my life, where I was spending a lot of time playing and a lot of time recording instrumental music on a primitive eight-track home studio that I had put together. Because there was no internet and I lived in a relatively small town, I didn't really have direct access to a lot of musicians who were as committed to what they were doing as to what I was doing.

So, in a sense, I felt kind of insulated or insular—a lonely musician doing things on his own. And doing things like sending tapes to the Spotlight column felt a bit like sending out a message in a bottle to the rest of the world. To say, 'By the way, I'm doing this. I have no idea if it's any good or not. I await your confirmation one way or the other.' Obviously, it was a really exciting thing for me, when Mike Varney listened to the stuff I was doing, and put it in his 'Spotlight' column, and wanted to make an album with me. It did feel like validation, at a point in the twentieth century when it was hard to know where else to find validation.

MARK WOOD *Guitar For The Practicing Musician* had a record label called Guitar Recordings, and John Stix was the producer and the main publisher of the magazine. He and I struck up a really nice relationship with Randy Coven and Al Pitrelli, because I went to high school with Al Pitrelli and knew all of that scene, and would do solos on Randy's record and bump into John Stix. I really tried to get him to sign me. 'But Mark, you're not a guitar player.' 'Well, check out what I'm doing.' 'Oh, this is cool!' They would send out my recordings without telling them that it was a violin player, and these players just could not figure out my riffs, because it was done with a bow and different types of tunings. So it was really fun to shake that industry up a little bit with my work. So Cherry Lane and Guitar Recordings were in a strong enough position in the industry to promote people like Blues Saraceno and Eric Gales.

CHRIS CAFFERY Also, in the 80s, general magazines like *Creem, Circus,* and *Hit Parader*—the regular rock magazines—they were also very important. So it's like, that kind of exposure, that's really all we had. We didn't have YouTube; we didn't have the live concert videos as much. To a point, you had MTV, but a lot of the cult and underground people were only on specialty shows. So these magazines were a lot of where we went to, to be exposed to people. It helped us not only see our favorite players, but it was the first time you were able to get tabs, which are now something that is heavily YouTube'd and broken down to the point where it's very easy for people to learn online.

MIKE VARNEY The tab thing, yeah, a lot of this stuff was too unfamiliar to a lot of guitar players, and the tab thing made it a lot more real and had them break it down, so they didn't have to learn how to read music to actually tackle some of this stuff. People seemed to love that. It all went hand in hand to creating a genre, and people saw it in almost a different way to take a piece of the business and run with it. So between the instructional videos, people like REH and Arlen Roth, and the other companies that did instructional videos, that helped to fuel these artists. Most of my artists had instructional videos.

It was kind of funny—one guy had a magician and somebody else said, 'I can't just make a video … I've got to get a standup comic.' The videos started getting competitive and the production got more outrageous as people thought they had to add something else in there—along with the lessons. All in all, the interest in becoming a better guitar player was really out there. The bar was raised way high, and there were a lot of guys that were willing to take it on, and with the help of the magazine and tab and whatnot. It was a more realistic goal for some of these guys.

KIRK HAMMETT I thought they were great. They contributed a lot to a lot of kids becoming rock guitar players. And it made it extremely convenient to learn other people's music, other bands' music, other bands' songs, other guitar players' solos. Before that, before *Guitar World*, before *Guitar For The Practicing Musician*, you only had one magazine—that was *Guitar Player*. And it was largely slanted to more sophisticated players, more jazzy players. So if the new Thin Lizzy album came out, and you wanted to learn songs, you had to do it yourself.

But when *Guitar World* or *Guitar For The Practicing Musician* came out, all of a sudden you had all this incredible information suddenly accessible, with different information month after month. So that made it really, really easy to be able to become a 'rock musician.' I owe a lot to those guitar magazines myself, because I've learned a lot from them.

There's been certain things I haven't been able to figure out over the course of time—like the chord progression, not the riff, but the chord progression for 'Kashmir' is something I could never figure out. It turns out there is a droning open G string that runs through the four or five chords Jimmy Page is playing. It would have taken me a long time to figure that out. One day, I just happened to pick up the magazine, thumb through it, and see in tablature that chord progression, pick up my guitar, play it, and go, 'Oh, *that's* how it went. Thank you, guitar magazines!' It was fantastic.

TREY AZAGTHOTH Well, the introduction of tab in general is an awesome system— it is I think less complicated than reading staff. Those magazines posting tab monthly of popular songs, it was an extra fun thing that allowed the reader to engage a bit more into the magazine.

WOLF MARSHALL You had players that now, you could understand what they were doing, because it's in slow motion and it's under a magnifying glass. You could understand, phrase-by-phrase, 'Eruption.' Suddenly, it's not as crazy, overwhelming, and over-the-top as when you first heard it, just coming at you like a bombardment.

RON JARZOMBEK I remember buying some Kiss songbooks for full albums, and they were all wrong. Every guitar player knows that Kiss tunes down to E flat, and they would have it actually written that you played an E flat somehow on the guitar. It was just so wrong. I think as the whole popularity of playing guitar grew, they got better transcriptionists, who would come out with articles, and things got a little more accurate. I remember one guy transcribed the solo from 'Flying High Again,' and a bunch of readers wrote into him, and said, 'Hey, you got this wrong.' So he corrected himself in the next issue!

But I think nowadays, there's *too much* tab, and people don't focus on the writing and what goes into the solos. There are so many players nowadays that just do the playing, they think that's all that there is. And there's so much more to just playing guitar—you have a lot of writing, rhythmic things, multitracking, where you have to know about harmonies and stuff. And so much of that is gone. I think just having tab out there contributes to that, because people aren't aware of why those notes are there. In some ways, it's making a lot of really good guitar players, but mentally, I don't think they have much of a grasp on what they're doing.

But tab now is a hell of a lot more accurate than it was when I was kid, let me tell ya. When I was figuring out solos myself, I remember one of the first solos that I did was 'The Sails Of Charon' by the Scorpions, and I had that thing note-for-note. Ever since then, when I was working with that speed-16 record player, I just developed my ears and it gets better and better. Now, with tab, everything is just spoon-fed to all of these guitar players. They don't do anything for themselves, and I think that's a bad thing. Whereas before, you had to be able to cover more aspects of being a musician and a guitar player.

WOLF MARSHALL I did go through a lot of systems of writing down solos. Back in the 70s, I was teaching a lot of students privately, and they wanted to learn the rock of the day—Jimmy Page, and then, later, Randy Rhoads. And I had to figure out ways to write licks down for them, so they could retain it. I dabbled with tablature and created a few other systems that I was using. There was a company, Star Licks, that I worked for, and we developed a different way of doing the notation—using a fraction underneath each note, so it didn't occupy a whole staff. And that way, they could have the little booklets and they were very compact. So that worked really well for a while.

But the tablature itself came out of lute music in the Renaissance period—they were using that for notation back then, in the 1600s. And it was always in the periphery of acoustic guitar music, because it was always within the 'folk-guitar tradition,' where people didn't read. Most folk guitarists are not sight-readers or even know much about music theory—they just want to strum chords or pick licks with fingerpicking. So when they wrote out stuff for like, Leo Kottke, you couldn't just do that in any other form. I don't know how you'd teach that, because there were no videos then.

So tablature started getting aligned with folk, and then some guys started using it in rock. There is a book about Led Zeppelin, their big songbook—*Led Zeppelin Complete*. There was a system in there that was like my fraction system. Some people were using a modification of the string with a circle around it and then the finger above it and the fret number below it ... but that's kind of clunky. So anyway, tablature got really huge by the early 80s, and that's when *Guitar For The Practicing Musician* sprang up, and it really sprang up out of Cherry Lane.

Cherry Lane had Ozzy Osbourne and Michael Schenker, and they had those early recordings—*Blizzard Of Ozz* and stuff. So they were looking for rock guitarists to transcribe them, because so much of it is based on the technique of the player. And you can't just write it out if you're a pianist; there's things inside there—whammy bar, tapping, and stuff—that a pianist wouldn't relate to. Especially in those days.

So I got lined up with them by simply going up to John Stix—I met him at NAMM. He was just starting *Guitar For The Practicing Musician*. I gave him a transcription—I can't remember of what—to say, 'Hey, I like that you guys are writing tablature.' He called me a month or two later, and that's when I started my relationship with Cherry Lane. It's the same time tab exploded, and I was doing books for them—I did Ozzy Osbourne, Michael Schenker, a couple of Van Halen albums. And then Hal Leonard started doing the same thing—I did Ratt, Iron Maiden, and all the other artists they had signed. And, of course, the first three Yngwie albums.

You know what it comes down to? It was like a moment in time where all these things came together. For me, I had been transcribing for about ten years, professionally—having stuff published in *DownBeat*, and in *Guitar Player*. But then, when the tablature industry got huge and actually had a magazine that had monthly, multiple tabs, I was in the right place at the right time with the right skills. But all the unseen work that went on for maybe ten years, that led up to being prepared for that opportunity.

MICHAEL ANGELO BATIO I used tablature before tablature was popular, because I always thought … and again, I credit my music degree—I've studied music since I was a kid. I saw in the 1970s that there's this thing called 'tablature.' We couldn't even get tab paper—I had to actually take staff paper and draw an extra line, because it didn't exist back then. And I was one of the people that looked at this, and said, 'Y'know, this is the perfect way to write guitar notation, because when you see regular musical notation, you don't know what position to play that C note in. You have to interpret it from yourself. Whereas tab leaves nothing to the imagination. If I want a twelfth-fret D on the fourth string, I write '12' on the fourth string. And that's it. So my idea of tab back in the early days—before it was really established—I used it all the time. I taught all my students tab. By the way, I taught Tom Morello—he was one of my students!

WOLF MARSHALL I listen first and I figure out what grooves are in it, what the time is, feel where the rhythm is, feel the song form—big picture. And then you lay that out in your mind. It's got an intro, a verse, a chorus … or is it more free than that? And then there's usually the typical guitar solo in the middle, and then some kind of chorus/verse/outro, and the outro may have another solo—Van Halen used that formula a lot, and so did Bon Jovi. A lot of bands that were in the pop-metal era. It became a formula, so you'd listen, and of course you can hear power chords, and you have to be aware of things like special tunings. Because when you listen to Ratt, they did a lot of drop D—like Van Halen did on 'Unchained.' So you have to be aware that that's happening.

If you've got a background in guitar, though, you realize that's one of the standard things they did. Johnny Smith did that, and he's a jazz guitarist from the 50s. He had a lot of solo guitar pieces where an E string is a D. Chet Atkins did that—a lot of players. So you had to come out of it knowing that, that they specialize in those techniques, and then you see if they're in the tune. Then I get down to the minutiae or the details, and that's when you actually start transcribing—'OK, you've got a four-bar intro'—and you figure out what's happening there. I listen to it a lot, I play it on the guitar, I double-check everything and make sure it's all playable. And I write everything in notation—I didn't use tab for myself; I read music. So I write that out for students and for the publishing business. So the tablature would come last.

JOE SATRIANI It's funny, you mention tablature, and I never bother reading it. I just assumed it was always around, so it's news to me when it was created. I just know that when people started to pay attention to me, and they asked me to write columns, they would say, 'Hey, can you do it in tab?' And I would say, 'I don't know what tab is.' I started out as a drummer, so I learned how to read drums first, and then I learned how to read manuscripts. I never had the need to communicate through tablature. So at that point where *Surfing* took off and *Guitar For The Practicing Musician*, *Guitar Player*, and *Guitar World* were having me as a contributor, I would defer to their guitar department to turn everything into tablature. And to this day, I never look at tablature, so it's not part of my everyday world at all. But I guess it's having a big effect—it's just another language to express music on guitars. So if that's what people need, more power to them.

BILLY CORGAN I never used tabs. I never learned anybody else's solos or songs. I would listen to those records and try to understand, because ultimately for me, what distinguishes guitar players is not so much the technical, because now, you've got eleven-year-old kids who can do 'Eruption' on YouTube. So you can argue it's not that hard once you know how to do it. But in the time that you had the ability to look those things up, to me, the way I would discern the difference in how the people played was in their attack.

And I think that's what I do—I would play along and try to understand the way they attacked the guitar. And in that, I learned a lot from Van Halen and Tony Iommi, and that had probably more of an influence than what I played. Because what I played was always, to me, different, and people always would have a reaction to it—they either liked it or they didn't. People who didn't like it, they didn't understand why I chose this note or played this style. And I was obviously coming a lot from alternative guitar playing, too. Same thing—it took me years to figure out that people actually liked what I did.

ALEX SKOLNICK I also never used the tablature, because I found that the best way to learn music that you want to learn is just to hear it. It takes much longer to do it yourself, but there's many ways of playing an existing piece of music. And not all the tablature is right. And sometimes, there's more than one way, and you can find a way that works for you. It was always the sound that inspired me, so I was more inspired by sound than by paper.

TY TABOR I personally don't read tabs. I like to figure things out like a puzzle, and feel it out when I learn things, so I've got a different side of the brain going than tabs when I play. They've never had any use for me, because I just can't look at black and white on a paper and feel anything from it. But I totally recognize how much it meant to so many other people, because at one point, we put out some tabs for people, and I remember how thankful so many guitarists were that I would see every day on the road, saying, 'Man, I'm so happy to have that, to finally see how you played that part, because I wasn't thinking that way.' I know it opened up doors for a lot of people to discover new things, so it certainly was a huge boost. It raised the bar of the average guitarist once great tabs were out there.

WOLF MARSHALL What happens is, some things are really hard, maybe because they've got a lot of fast, technical guitar playing. You think of Allan Holdsworth, Yngwie, some Van Halen solos where he's really shredding, or Randy Rhoads, like the live stuff,* where it's really intense as far as the velocity. But then, to be able to properly transcribe a B.B. King blues lick—and be able to capture his rhythm—is really challenging. Because those metal guys play pretty metrically—you have a drumbeat, you can hear it, it's falling against the beat. But B.B. was kind of loose and floating.

So I would say it varies—some of the stuff would be Allan Holdsworth and Yngwie for the rock or jazz-rock, and then on the other side of it, to accurately transcribe a slow blues by B.B. King. Because there's so much in the cracks of the time, that you have to decide, 'Are you going to really overwrite it so it can hardly be viewed and understood, that it's just a mathematical formula that's so complicated … or are you going to simplify it and put an expression above it, like, 'the tempo is floating' or 'it speeds up and slows down'? I've used a 'plus' or 'minus' since the 70s, to indicate that the time is a little bit loose—in a good way.

My favorite tablature songbooks that I worked on are the Randy Rhoads books that I did, especially the live album, *Tribute*. And I liked very much doing the first Van Halen album—that has a lot of personal significance. And I think I also did *OU812*. Also the first Yngwie album, I really enjoyed doing that.† After that, believe it or not, there came a point in the late 80s, early 90s, where the publishers had a lot of other folks transcribing, so they would have me check the transcriptions and just put my name on it—'Introduction by' or 'Edited by.' And some of my students transcribed some of those books. They wanted me to do Van Halen, but they had to have somebody else do Faith No More or some of

---

* Notably the material on *Tribute* (1987).
† *Rising Force* (1984).

the other bands they had signed. They wanted those albums out—*Riverdogs,*[*] or something—so they would have me work with the transcribers.

After the mid 80s, there became more people transcribing, because they saw it as a market. So you got more people popping up and doing that. But originally, there were only four of us that I can think of—me, Jesse Gress, Andy Aledort, and Dave Whitehill. We did almost all of it between the four of us. Steve Vai was in it, but he wasn't in that 'pool'—he was already playing out and on tour, so he couldn't do it every month. He did a few transcriptions in the early 80s, but when he got in bands that were really moving—he couldn't participate in that, it was too much work. Not that it was too much work for him to do it—the workload would have been impossible. You have to devote yourself to doing that.

STU HAMM I did these instructional videos—remember back in the days when they had 1-900 numbers to learn tapping licks and stuff like that? It's so funny! But it was certainly important and it still is.

WOLF MARSHALL There was a company, Star Licks. We were doing the 'licks' of players, and it was twenty licks—fast and slow—with a music booklet. And we had done three years of that. It was very successful—a lot of people liked to learn that way and it was easy. You didn't have to read music. And all the popular styles, from Van Halen to Eric Clapton, they were all covered. Then, we had a chance to do audios with some of the star players. So we went over to England, and did the first one with Brian May. And he said, 'Well, why don't we just do a video?' It was *his* idea. So we went to a studio where the video was happening—he had a video apparatus there—and he sat in front of his gear. It was what we had done in terms of the audiotape, but he did it on video. It set the style and template for all the others that followed.

I would say he was the first, and then Tony Iommi right after that; Albert Lee; Larry Carlton; Steve Lukather; myself; Louis Johnson, the bass player; Al McKay, the funk rhythm player of Earth, Wind & Fire; Carlos Cavazo. So we had a good, broad cross-section—country, jazz-rock, fusion, funk. Mine was pure instructional rock—it was what I taught all my students. It was just how to play the common licks that you know—whether it was Eric Clapton from Bluesbreakers, or something inside the shapes of the guitar, so you knew how to get around on the instrument. That was the first batch. And then later, guys

---

[*] The 1989 debut album by the band of the same name, which featured Vivian Campbell on guitar.

signed up who wanted to do it: the Night Ranger guys; Ray Flacke, the country player; Ray Gomez; Jeff Berlin; Michael Angelo; and there were more.

Once I got with Cherry Lane, it was 1987, and I started with Star Licks in '84—it was between '84 and '87. Cherry Lane wanted to do some videos, so they had an exclusive contract—that was in the clause. They didn't want me to do any more Star Licks. So Star Licks went on using that template indefinitely, and then I went on to work with Cherry Lane, and we produced the two Billy Sheehan videos. And later, when I was under contract to Hal Leonard, I would produce videos. Because we were going to go on with my guitar method, and we could never get around to everything in a five-year term. I had to do two years of touring behind my guitar method. I literally had to do a tour of fifty-two cities, doing four performances a week: Guitar Center; Sam Ash; in those days they had a place called Mars Music that was in the southeast; and all the big music stores that went throughout the US. It was literally a national tour … actually international, because we did Canada, too.

The point is, in all that, I couldn't do a video. Much later, I did one for Hal Leonard called *Lead Guitar*, and it came out in the early 2000s. That was a much broader spectrum, because what was nice was the music scene had changed, and I didn't just have to focus on the pop stars of the day—I could have Chuck Berry, B.B. King, Albert King, Stevie Ray Vaughan, Van Halen, Jimi Hendrix. In those days, they would have wanted me to just do the latest metal—the latest shred licks or the latest cool radio licks and MTV licks. There was a time period where if you put out an instructional video and said, 'I want to do something on Scotty Moore and Wes Montgomery,' they'd say, 'No.' It was kind of cool that after that scene had changed after grunge, I came back and did the video I really always wanted to do—that focused on ten or so individual players, and each one of them had a big effect on the music.

FRANK GAMBALE Doing those videos were a lot of fun. I think it really helped me focus and organize my thoughts and put it into a form where others would get it. I've been a teacher as well as a player for many, many years. I remember having roughly forty private students when I was only sixteen. So I've had to organize my thoughts in an accessible way for my entire playing career, really. Instruction is all about the lightbulb going on, on the student. It's the message being received and the comprehended, fundamental reason why a lick exists, or why these notes are played in this order.

To me, I'm all about the 'why.' There are a lot of people who show licks, but there are very few who can actually deliver 'Why?' It's kind of like teaching someone to fish—you can give people fish all day long, but they're going to be hungry tomorrow. My approach is to teach people to fish. So that was the motivation behind a lot of those videos I did. And it also holds true to the courses I'm delivering at my online guitar school.

JEFF WATSON I was a little bit uncomfortable doing instructional videos. I really don't like a lot of attention on myself—I like being in a band, I don't like a lot of spotlight, except for when I step in to do my little thing. So having a film crew set up just to have me sit and jam, I don't play my best. It's not my strength. And that was before I got to my level of playing I currently reside at. Since I've left Night Ranger, I've become a completely different and more effective guitar player in a lot of ways. You have plateaus and climbs, and it's been a really nice slope up, because of my dedication and also because a lot of my friends are just monsters—so I have to qualify to be in the room.

MICHAEL ANGELO BATIO As far as the guitar magazines, I didn't get much coverage in the 80s. I don't even know why. But what I did was I had an impact on guitar— it was profound in a very different way. I did the first instructional shred video ever on Star Licks—before Paul Gilbert, before Yngwie, before anybody. I was already an established teacher, I was already a local LA player, but I wasn't famous yet. But I was drawing really great crowds in Los Angeles. I didn't get the magazine coverage, but I loved *Guitar World*—I'm a columnist with them right now. It wasn't really until later.

My instructional video alone—just my Star Licks—influenced John Petrucci, Michael Romeo … even Ted Nugent saw it! Steve Morse told me he saw it. I talked to Kiko Loureiro from Angra, and now Megadeth; he studied my video. Dimebag studied my video. Whereas Steve Vai had a hit song, I had *a hit video* that was out all over the world. And then I did *Speed Kills* a few years later, in the 90s. Herman Li told me he made a career out of taking my stuff. I showed my 'over under' technique; I showed a way of playing guitar that was a more jazz/ technical oriented way to play, and it wasn't a rock style. It wasn't old-school—it was new-school. Even today, when you listen to a lot of these young death-metal players, listen to the leads—it's very reminiscent of the style that I directed into shred guitar.

And I'm not saying it's me alone, but my teaching was something that has been kind of overlooked, but has impacted a planet of guitarists. I mean, I've toured fifty-eight countries. I can't go anywhere without people telling me about my instructional videos—especially the Star Licks one of the 80s, which was the very first shred one. The first time anybody ever showed even an A-minor sweep was my video. I didn't say I invented it, but I came up with this really great teaching concept, and again, I credit it to my education. I took it based on old classical-guitar manuals, piano manuals, so that's where my notoriety on a global scale started. It wasn't songs—it was this technique, that was just mind-boggling, and it was different. And it was a way to play passages that people couldn't play before on a guitar.

For me, things came later—I'm in all the guitar magazines. But back then, I wasn't. Because people didn't understand the impact of my instructional stuff back then. I was the no. 1 video—I was outselling Tony Iommi, Jeff Watson, Brad Gillis, Steve Lukather. I was the no. 1 seller for their company for two years straight. But the guitar magazines didn't really see that—they were just looking at, 'Who's got the song on the radio?' And the interview wasn't there, so they didn't really realize the impact my stuff had—until later.

CHRIS CAFFERY In the 80s, Sam Ash was smaller at that time. Guitar Center really didn't develop then. New York City had a street—48th Street—that had a lot of different music stores. It was Rudy's Music, Manny's Music, and there was a Sam Ash there, and there was 48th Street Guitars. It's like, you would have a street now that is all Chinese Restaurants—*it was all guitar stores.* Used guitars were very affordable back then. You could find really nice Les Pauls for under a thousand dollars, whereas now, you can't even touch them for less than five.

And you had local music stores—like where I grew up in North Jersey, there was a place called Robbie's Music, and there is a place called Alto Music that is still around, and they actually expanded—they're a pretty large store in Orange County, New York, that does a lot of really good online sales. There were a lot more small stores around. You would go into a town, and you would have like ... Joe's Music or whatever would be the case, and it was something where you could specialize in taking care of one little community, whereas nowadays, people can't afford to keep a small store open, because things like Guitar Center, Amazon, and BestBuy, they destroyed small retail.

STEVE LYNCH Guitar Center was still fairly new at that time, and they had a good variety. I liked the guitar store here, Freemont Music. There were a couple of small ones down in LA that I really liked, too, but I can't think of the names of them—

one was right off of Sunset. Of course, I've been to Manny's in New York City, and Sam Ash. Now, I kind of have a tendency to look at Sweetwater, because just the variety of stuff that they have. I'll go into a guitar store and check out different things that I want, and then I'll go onto Sweetwater.com and I'll buy it through Sweetwater—because there's no tax and there's no shipping charge or anything! I know that's not good for the guitar stores, but it's a really good idea, because they've got a lot more variety—they have warehouses full of all this gear. They don't have just guitars to choose from—everything you can order from them. It's pretty amazing.

RONNI LE TEKRØ I grew up in almost like a communist structure [in Norway]. It would have a local music store and you would have big record stores, but there were no chains—it was all independent. It was a total different youth than growing up in America.

GUTHRIE GOVAN I grew up in the southeast of England. In the town where I grew up, there were no remarkable music stores. There were, however, *understanding* music stores. I remember being a six- or seven-year-old kid, and I'd go in there with my dad, and they would let me try out electric guitars all afternoon. I guess it added a certain cutesy, quaint quality to the atmosphere of the store, and no one seemed to mind. But a lot of my early grounding in how I play electric guitar came from just hanging out in these stores, before I was able to afford an electric of my own. I guess this is a nice opportunity to namedrop Hodges & Johnson— which of course, no longer exists. And Future Music, which again, no longer exists. Those stores were there when I needed them.

But in terms of the whole 80s and 90s thing, where do I go to buy my pointy Ibanez, we have a street in London called Denmark Street, which is the famous guitar-store street. You go there in the same way that you would go to the zoo—to marvel at the whole range of things that are on offer. In the end, I found myself doing all of my shopping in a more boutique place, called Chandler Guitars, which is on the outskirts of London, in a place called Kew Gardens. That was one of those stores where everything in there was worth buying. They have a more stringent selection policy for what gets put up on a stand with a price tag. So I came to trust that place, and also, they had great repair guys who worked in there. So I became dependent on that place, as much as anyone with as little money as I had, needed to be dependent on any guitar store.

JAS OBRECHT When I worked at *Guitar Player* in the 1970s, 80s, and 90s, I could choose who I wanted to interview every month. I often had carte blanche to do whatever I wanted. And so I would just keep my ear to the ground and get reports of who was up-and-coming, and jump on it before anybody else could. Most guitarists back then grew up reading the magazine, so they were happy to hear from us. In those days, people would give you an in-depth interview, and we could run long articles. You seldom see that anymore. The long-length journalism is dying out in print magazines. It used to be, I'd interview U2, and I could use all 2,000 words. Then it became more like, 'You can talk to The Edge, but your article can't be longer than 300 words.' So what do you do with the other 1,700 words?

By the late 1990s, I didn't like the direction that music magazines were going in, how so much of the reporting was becoming truncated, sensationalized, or focused on gear instead of creativity. I've had a lifelong interest in how people write songs, their views on creating solos, who their influences are, and these sorts of things. I always want to walk away from an interview with a strong sense of who the musician is in the grand schemes of music, spirituality, and especially, creativity.

WOLF MARSHALL A lot of music magazines appeared that were in that mold— *Guitar School, Maximum Guitar, Premier Guitar*. A bunch of them came out that featured music transcriptions—as well as the interviews. And I was heavily contracted to *Guitar For The Practicing Musician*. I wrote every month from '85 through '91. I had a contract where I went with Hal Leonard.

So when they offered that chance to be under a five-year contract with Hal Leonard, it came with the exception that I would have to write for *Guitar World*, because at that time, Harris and Hal Leonard were closely involved—Harris of course published *Guitar World* and *Guitar School*. They wanted to do similar things, so when I was with *Guitar For The Practicing Musician*, I interviewed B.B. King, Stevie Ray Vaughan, several other players. And the same thing with *Guitar World*—I became one of the editors, and I wrote an article called 'Rock History' that ran for about three years. And I also did stuff with Eric Johnson, Paul Gilbert, Joe Satriani … and Nigel Tufnel!

And after that, in '95, I had my own magazine for three years—*Wolf Marshall's Guitar One*. That was the first time that had happened, that somebody who came out of the music world—rather than the publishing world—had their magazine. I got Steve Vai involved in it, Alex Lifeson, a whole bunch of guys. That was a joy.

It was nothing but transcriptions and related articles. So if we did an interview, it would have to have music in it. Columns, tips on how to play better, stuff like that. And I left that in '98 and wanted to just take a hiatus for a while.

I ended up in 2000 getting involved with *Vintage Guitar*. A lot of the other magazines, to me, they lost their focus. And I think some of it was the guitar playing and grunge just wasn't as exciting as Randy Rhoads and Van Halen—let's be honest. Steve Morse, Slash, and Van Halen—that was a golden era. And the grunge thing just didn't last like that. There was a lot of other stuff—girl singer-songwriters like Sheryl Crow came out, and Jewel, and the whole scene became different. I feel I was very fortunate to have been involved in that part of the trade, when all of that stuff was so exciting. It was a blessing for me.

KARL SANDERS One glance into my garage—where all my guitar magazines from the 70s and 80s are—would answer that question unequivocally. They were super-important to me. I bought every single one I could get my hands on—and devoured them, cover-to-cover.

the man
who **sang**

Singer Graham Bonnet worked with the likes of
Ritchie Blackmore, Michael Schenker, Yngwie
Malmsteen, Steve Vai, and Chris Impellitteri. Here,
he shares his thoughts and memories of each.

RITCHIE BLACKMORE [RAINBOW]

CROSSING PATHS WITH BLACKMORE That was a pure fluke. Roger Glover just
happened to be working with Whitesnake, and I was managed by the same people
that managed Whitesnake in England. He just happened to be working with them,
and Rainbow was looking for a singer—they had already auditioned seventy-nine
singers or something, and I was number eighty, eventually. Micky Moody—who
was the guitar player in Whitesnake at the time—spoke to Roger Glover* about
me, because Rainbow were playing a game at the studio in Switzerland, like,
'spot the tune.' And they just happened to have one of my old tracks they were
playing, and Ritchie said, 'Where is this guy now?' So Roger Glover said, 'Well,
I'm working with one of his friends, Micky Moody, and I can get in touch with
him through Micky.' And that's how I kind of got the job. I had a record out in
1968, called 'Only One Woman'—my cousin and I, we were called The Marbles.
And the songs were written for us by The Bee Gees. My cousin used to be in The
Bee Gees years ago, when he was a kid. And that's how the job came around—
basically through a spot the tune game.

---

* Glover was also the bassist in Rainbow at the time.

BLACKMORE IN THE STUDIO It was kind of funny, because he was such a 'throwaway' guy—he would come in for an hour or something, and say to Roger, 'OK, what are we doing today? Which songs are we doing?' I was just amazed—he'd play four or five different solos, and Roger would piece them together. I'd never seen it done that way before. It was kind of a different approach for me, because I'd always been used to working with session men, where their parts were all written out. And the whole band was a complete surprise—the way they worked, it was different all together for me. But Ritchie would come in, play something, and say, 'I think that will do it!' It was surprisingly easy for him—it was kind of incredible in the end.

BLACKMORE ONSTAGE He was always different. Every night was different. Some nights, he'd be very out of tune, because I would find it hard to pitch, and I would say, 'What key are we in?' Because he'd be using that whammy bar like crazy, and the guitar would go all over the place. This was in 1980, you must remember—it was a different time to where it is now, technically. And it was sometimes very hard for me to hear where we were at. I've listened to some of the live stuff and we're all out of tune—everybody's in a different damn key. So some nights, I would go over to the keyboard side of the stage to kind of pitch my notes, to see which key I was in. Because he was thinking more about the visual thing sometimes than the playing side of things. But he played incredibly well—don't get my wrong. It's just that some nights, you'd be *so* out of tune, I don't think he really heard it.

FAVORITE BLACKMORE SOLOS ON *DOWN TO EARTH* (1979) I think 'Lost In Hollywood,' probably 'Since You've Been Gone,' because that was kind of funny— he did like a country thing on there, which was kind of cool. Every track, I love that album—I just think it's amazing. He plays so well on everything. He inspired Yngwie Malmsteen, for instance—I know for a fact he was very influenced by Ritchie. But also 'Eyes Of The World,' and 'Bad Girl,' too—which wasn't on the album, it was a B-side.

WHY IT DIDN'T WORK OUT I left. Cozy left the band, and Don Airey was going to leave the band. We were rehearsing in Copenhagen for the next album, and Cozy wasn't there anymore. We were looking for a drummer, and Bobby Rondinelli came in—we started to rehearse and nobody was that enthralled by the whole thing. It was like, 'Who's going to be at rehearsal today—all the band, or just two of us?' And it became a really slow process—trying to write new tunes. And sometimes, it would just be me and Don Airey, looking at each other like, 'Well

… where's the rest of the band?' Everybody else was out sightseeing or whatever. It was a lack of interest. Because Cozy had gone, he was a friend and we missed that atmosphere and the buddy thing. And Don said, 'Well, I'm going to leave the band. I think I'd rather go work on ships than do this, because we're getting nowhere.'

At this point, because we had no songs, I decided, 'I might as well go home and wait until they've got something happening. Some kind of arrangements.' I went home, and they called me up to say, 'Well, we've got all this stuff down. Are you going to come back?' And I said, 'No. I don't want to.' I'd been home for a while, and nothing seemed to be happening. Then they said, 'OK, we'll get another singer in to do the tracks you don't like,' and I said, 'Well, we only have one track that I know,' that was another Russ Ballard song, 'I Surrender.' That was the only song we had. I had put down some backing vocals for that, because that's all there was to do at the time, and it eventually became a hit for Joe Lynn Turner, when he sang for the band.

But there was nothing happening. It just seemed like it was going to go down the shitter, so to speak. It didn't, obviously, but it felt like that at the time. So, Don stayed in the band and I left. Because I thought he was going to leave—for real. I thought, 'Well, that's it—if Don leaves, he's one of the mainstays of the band, and the band will fall to pieces.' But it didn't. He stayed.

BLACKMORE'S PERSONALITY He's very shy. Chooses his friends wisely. He gives the impression of being dark and moody, but he really isn't—he's a very shy and a very sweet guy. We got on very, very well. Every night before a gig, we'd always speak together if we were going to play a joke on someone onstage or whatever, and sort out a new routine for the evening. So we always had a drink before we went onstage—he and I. We became very close, but it's been a very long time since I've seen him. But he had lots of anger for other band members—for ex–band members, for instance. Under it all, I think he was just a little insecure about certain things. But a good guy.

MICHAEL SCHENKER [MICHAEL SCHENKER GROUP]

CROSSING PATHS WITH SCHENKER Because I had left Rainbow, Cozy was in the Michael Schenker Group, and I went to see them play in LA. I saw the show, and Cozy came up to me and said, 'What do you think of the band?' And I said, 'It was fantastic. Great guitar player. You're playing really good, Cozy. I liked some of the tunes—they're not bad. Overall, the band is great.' And he said, 'Well, how do you feel about joining the band?' And I thought, 'What do you mean? Why? You have a singer.' And he said, 'We're going to let him go.' 'Why?' 'Because we want *you*.' 'Oh … OK!' And that was it. I went back home and they went back to England, I seem to remember, and they sent me a tape of three songs they wanted lyrics written to and melodies. On it, it said, 'URGENT.' [*Laughs*] So that's how I joined—it was like, 'Do you want a job? Here you are, have it.'

SCHENKER IN THE STUDIO That was something I was never there for, because I used to work during the daytime—because I was up early. And both of us, being heavy drinkers, had different schedules, unfortunately. So in those days, we were terribly full of any kind of alcohol you wish. So he would work at night—I would never work at night, because by nine, I'd be falling asleep. He would work at night and I would work during the daytime. So I never saw him record anything—at all—during my stay with the band.

SCHENKER ONSTAGE One disastrous night—the infamous night. But it was so cool to play with him earlier this year [2015] in Japan. To actually be onstage and stay onstage for more than two minutes, and do two songs together—and we both laughed, because we were both thinking the same thing. Like, '*All is forgiven*.' Michael is just incredible—he played so great. To be able to sing with him again and have fun—it was water under the bridge. All was forgiven.

FAVORITE SCHENKER SOLOS ON *ASSAULT ATTACK* (1982) It's hard to pick one, because he's such a cool player—he understates everything. He's not like all over the place and everybody's going, 'Where the hell is this solo going?' I like 'Samurai' and 'Assault Attack.'

WHY IT DIDN'T WORK OUT Because a very disastrous thing happening to my pants! I had a pair of jeans made—one of those places where they make your jeans in an hour—because I didn't have any. And what happened was, we were all shit-faced, basically … well, I was more shit-faced then anybody. We were playing with Whitesnake that night, so my friends and I from Whitesnake went to the pub. I came back from the pub, went into the dressing room area at—I think it was a college we were playing in Sheffield, England—and I knocked on Michael's dressing room door, because I had left my jacket in there. And said, 'Could I get my jacket?' Michael said, 'Oh no, go away. I'm sleeping.' 'Come on'—I had money in there or something—'I need it now, please, just hand me the damned jacket and you can go back to sleep!'

Anyway, he didn't, I went back outside again, went to the pub again, came back just before the show, was still drinking, and by the time I got onstage, I wasn't even me anymore—I was somebody else. And I remember every song I'd learned from their old MSG albums, I had written everything out, because I had to sing some of the old stuff and I didn't really know them, and all of the new stuff, I didn't know the words to those, either! So I had thirteen sheets of paper all over the stage, like wallpaper. And what happened is, we went onstage, and as we started to play, the audience pushed forward, and where all my papers were, were where the floor monitors were. And the monitors crunched up all the papers, so I couldn't read anything. And I swore at the audience—'You fucking cunts!' Whatever I said.

At this point, I was using all my force to shout at them, my zipper broke … and out pops my penis! There it is, thank you very much. So I get a hold of it and start waving it around like it's part of the act. [*Laughs*] And it got worse and worse—they started swearing at me, and I told them all to fuck off. There is a recording of this—I've never heard it and don't want to. But that's what happened. I just looked around and said, 'I can't fucking take this,' and ran offstage, and they played the whole set without me, instrumentally—every song.

By this time, I was out of the theater and I was in a cab going back to the hotel, and one of the roadie guys that was with me said, 'You'd better get out of here in the morning—they're going to fucking kill you!' So I was on the earliest morning train back to London, and I got back to London at King's Cross Station, and my manager was waiting for me. He said, 'I heard what happened, Graham.' And I said, 'Well, what's going to happen to Reading?' Because we were supposed to headline the Reading Festival in a day or so or whatever. And I said, 'I know I can do it. I know I got shit-faced, I know I screwed it up, but I can do this.' He said, 'Well, it's too late—you're fired from the band. *They fired you.*' And that was it.

SCHENKER'S PERSONALITY Well, again, he keeps to himself, like a lot of people do—Ritchie and Michael are very similar in that way. They don't go out to clubs and that kind of thing. They don't hang out with other bands. They hang out with their girlfriends or wives. And I'm a little like that, sometimes—I'm not one of those people that likes to go early to clubs and watch the other bands. They're very similar. I never really got to know Michael. He's a very quiet person. As I said, he keeps to himself.

YNGWIE MALMSTEEN [ALCATRAZZ]

CROSSING PATHS WITH MALMSTEEN He was someone we found through a friend of ours who worked in a store. He knew I was looking to put a band together that was kind of similar to Rainbow, and I was looking for someone that played guitar like Ritchie, because the songs I was making up were in that kind of style. This guy told us about this young guy who was playing around LA, and he's really good, and, 'Do you want me to ask him to come down for an audition?' We said yeah, he came along, and we gave him a Russ Ballard song to listen to that I had on one of my albums, and he played it perfectly.* And he looked like Ritchie Blackmore a bit—he wore the same kind of clothes. He walked in wearing his stage clothes, basically. And as soon as he played that one song, we said, 'Fuckin' hell! Yeah, this is the guy!'

YNGWIE IN THE STUDIO It was nuts. It was like we were playing a stadium or something. He had everything turned up to twelve—as opposed to eleven—and Marshall stacks, the whole bit in the studio. It was kind of funny, because we used to watch him doing the solos and he's doing a whole act like he's onstage. He was a kid, but everything he played was just immaculate and genius stuff. Amazing guitar player.

YNGWIE ONSTAGE Very good—he was always on it. Whereas Ritchie sometimes was sloppy—but I blame that on the 'devil drink,' all of us were a bit sloppy in Rainbow once in a while. But Yngwie, even though he probably had a few, was a younger guy and I guess could take it better. He played very well live—he just over-played a little. He'd play through like … *everything*. He saw people looking at him, so he did a bit more. He was taller than me and would stand in front of me and do solos—that was really annoying, when I'm trying to sing a verse or something. That was the only thing that made me get a bit crazy at him, because he wanted everyone to look at him and not listen to the band as such.

FAVORITE YNGWIE SOLOS ON *NO PAROLE FROM ROCK 'N' ROLL* (1983) I like what he plays in a song called 'Suffer Me,' because it's real feel. And probably 'Jet To Jet.' I like the way he plays in 'Suffer Me,' because it's a ballad kind of thing, and he puts a lot of emotion into his solo—it's not just all over the place. It's actually got

---

* 'SOS,' from Bonnet's album *Line-Up* (1981).

some kind of feel—all of his solos have feel, he's just technically a very good player.

WHY IT DIDN'T WORK OUT Because his ego got bigger than the band. [*Laughs*] It was just nuts—he became too much. He had no stage etiquette whatsoever. Like I said, he would play through everything, and it just became a mess. And he became a very obnoxious person as the days went on, for some reason. And then one day, he tried to strangle me. He got annoyed at me for something that had happened, went for my throat, and that was the last straw. *Digging his thumbs into my throat wasn't funny.* One of our roadies attacked him and put him in a headlock, and said, 'You touch Graham again, you're going to die.' And that was the last night he was in the band, because it was just ridiculous.

MALMSTEEN'S PERSONALITY Very varied. Up and down. Strange. It depends on how much chemical intake had happened that day—for all of us, it wasn't just him. Because me too—I was a terrible alcoholic. I still am, but I haven't drank anything for years. About fifteen years. Everybody was a bit messed up. When everybody is messed up and trying to play onstage, it just does not work. And sometimes, one of us—or all of us—were completely confused onstage. But his ego got really big.

STEVE VAI [ALCATRAZZ]

CROSSING PATHS WITH VAI Our drummer, Jan Uvena, was in with some of the guys from Frank Zappa's band, and he got in touch with somebody who knew Steve Vai. He said, 'We know a guy who would be ideal for the band if you're looking to change direction a little.' Because it became too much like Rainbow to me. It didn't have its own personality. And when Steve came along, he said, 'I can't play like Yngwie.' And we said, 'We don't want you to play like Yngwie. We want you to play like *you.*' And he came up with such great ideas. I was so impressed because he was so different. But he was like a friend of a friend that knew him—it was one of those things that just kind of happened.

VAI IN THE STUDIO It was great. He accommodated the vocal, for one thing. And if I did something kind of cool, he would copy what I sang. He was great. We both thought very much alike—as far as songwriting goes. And when he did a solo, it wasn't widdly-widdly, 'Look how fast I can play.' It was with feel and weird, quirky parts in it. That's what I liked about his playing. It was just so different—at that time. It was all new to me—that tapping stuff and funny noises coming out of the guitar. He was just so different. Very inventive.

VAI ONSTAGE Fantastic. Certainly spot on. I don't think I ever heard him mess up. He was a very clean person—he was very awake and aware when he was onstage. Not like the rest of us … well me, anyway. But that was to boost my confidence, I would have a drink—or six—before I went onstage. Steve was very clean—he was very 'hippie.'

FAVORITE VAI SOLOS ON *DISTURBING THE PEACE* **(1985)** I like the 'God Blessed Video' tapping thing. I like what he plays on that. Also, 'Mercy,' and I like how he plays on a song called 'Will You Be Home Tonight.' 'Breaking The Heart Of The City,' too—that was a cool one to do, because what we did with that is he did harmony on the guitar and I did vocal harmonies, and put the harmonies spot on together. We ghosted each other really, really closely. That was a lot of work. We pulled that together on our own in a separate studio, while the band were recording with Eddie Kramer in another room, and he and I recorded that together, because we wanted it to be really personal. It took us all day to put it together. It was tiring, but it worked out really well.

WHY IT DIDN'T WORK OUT Because he got offered a better job. [*Laughs*] You wave money in front of somebody, and no matter how 'hippie trippy' and how much they love the guys in the band and the music, *money talks*. So that's when he went to David Lee Roth.

VAI'S PERSONALITY He's a very relaxed guy. He's a real sweetheart—he really is.

CHRIS IMPELLITTERI [IMPELLITTERI]

CROSSING PATHS WITH IMPELLITTERI That was a pure fluke again. He called me up because he had heard that Alcatrazz had fallen down the shitter, and he called me up to say, 'What are you doing? I've got a band.' And I said, 'What's your name again?' [*Laughs*] Because I didn't hear it—I thought he was talking about spaghetti, I wasn't sure! I remember him repeating it over and over again, '*Impellitteri*.' 'What kind of a damned name is that?' Anyway, he came over and he had some songs and tapes and riffs he'd put down, and he asked me if I'd write the songs. So I did that.

I was paid a little bit of money and it came around that we actually went out and played live—which I didn't think was going to happen. I thought it was just going to be a recording thing and that would be it. But it ended up we did play a couple of gigs live. Not many. But it was another experience … with a guitar player, AHH! [*Laughs*] He was like, 'How fast can you play?' But where is the emotion? OK, you can play ten million notes in two seconds, but where's the feel? Sometimes, he would lose the feel of the song, because there was too much going on.

IMPELLITTERI IN THE STUDIO Fine. He was always very on it, but if he couldn't make those ten billion notes, he would get a little upset. So the day would end if he couldn't play ten notes that sound like one.

IMPELLITTERI ONSTAGE Live he was fine. But I think he would sometimes overplay a little bit. But he overplays anyway. That's his style, that's his thing. But sometimes, he gets a little too much, I think.

FAVORITE IMPELLITTERI SOLOS ON *STAND IN LINE* (1988) I think 'Stand In Line,' that song. It's just interesting. I think it doesn't take away from the song. Some of his things take a left turn, but this one goes straight ahead. But that one just stands out. It's probably the better track on the album, anyway. Better crafted—solo-wise, vocal-wise, and lyrically.

WHY IT DIDN'T WORK OUT At that point, I was living in Australia, so my family was away from me, and it got too much. I was commuting from Australia to LA every so often, and I got totally fucked up—I was never un-jetlagged. I was jetlagged permanently. And it was becoming a little too much, health-wise. So I thought, 'I can't do this any longer. I'm not happy.' So I lived in Australia for three years, and played locally.

IMPELLITTERI'S PERSONALITY He's a little bit precious. [*Laughs*] You can't touch his hair before he goes onstage, if it's been sprayed. I remember he did his hair and was looking in the mirror, had his guitar on, and was all ready to go, and I went over and patted him on the back … and I accidentally pulled on the back of his long hair. He went, 'Oh my God! You touched my hair!' And I was like, '*What?*' He's like, 'Get away from me! Don't touch me! Don't touch me!' 'Oh blimey, what's up with you?' A little strange sometimes.

He's a very clean person—he's not very 'rock'n'roll,' as they say. He's a little precious, but is a great player—no doubt about it. He's a really nice guy.

AND THE WINNER IS …

The only album I think of when I think of Alcatrazz is *Disturbing The Peace*. It's 'thinking man's heavy metal,' basically. It really was an adventure, that album. I remember my mom and dad were over from England, and I took them to Cherokee Studios one afternoon, and they were just amazed at the music that was going down. They loved that album. It was an opportunity to actually sing and write something substantial lyrically. I always have stories in my songs if I can put them in there—some sort of an experience I've had. But this was just so much fun to do, with such a great guitar player. Steve is really one of my favorites.

megadeth's bassist on megadeth's guitarists

David Ellefson has played alongside Dave Mustaine, Marty Friedman, and other exceptionally talented guitarists in Megadeth. Here, he shares his thoughts and memories of working with each.

DAVE MUSTAINE

PLAYING STYLE He is a really intuitive, gutsy, rock'n'roll guitar player. He—to me—is on par with people like Ted Nugent, who are just very visceral and in-the-moment. It's like Dave lets his emotions dictate his music. Dave's music is very much a reflection of his personality. You can't judge a guy's personality strictly by his band's music, because to some degree, we all write things and play things that would be maybe considered a little 'out of our wheelhouse.' But I think with Megadeth, Dave has been able to put a lot of those things into the records. Things like the *Risk* record, even things that were on *Super Collider*—things that have taken some public hits. What it shows is for a man who has really exposed his life through his music, you really get to see the full scope of Dave's life—as it has been printed into the recordings of the Megadeth songs.

FAVORITE SOLO I would say probably the solo in 'The Conjuring.'

CHRIS POLAND

PLAYING STYLE Chris is a guy who has a very affable, likable personality when you're in the room with him. And when he picks up the guitar, he goes to a whole other dimension. He plays so skillfully that you just wonder where this music is coming from. It's like he truly is a channel. He is truly a one-of-a-kind guitar player—certainly when it comes into the rock'n'roll context, because most people in rock'n'roll don't play like that. His roots are very much back into John McLaughlin, Allan Holdsworth, and that school of playing, that to hear him sit in front of you and play like that, it's almost unimaginable. And he's one of the greatest bass players I've ever heard.

FAVORITE SOLO I love the 'Devil's Island' solo, because one of Chris's skills is, when he bends, he doesn't bend up in a typical Chuck Berry, rock'n'roll fashion— when he does a two-string or single-string bend. He bends down, and he usually bends single-string.

When you hear toward the end of the 'Devil's Island' solo, there's his sort of bouncy … [*sings the part*] … most people can't cop that, because he's pulling the string down rather than bending it up across the fingerboard.

JEFF YOUNG

PLAYING STYLE Keep in mind, when Jeff got into the band, he was very newly out of his academic studies at GIT in Hollywood. Jeff is an incredibly disciplined player, and because of his training, had a very diverse scope of music that he listened to. But he was also very mechanically proficient. That helped him fill that void when Megadeth needed a second guitar player or somebody that was very juxtaposed to how Dave played. And that really continued to set the bar very high and also carved into stone the dual-guitar role inside Megadeth.

FAVORITE SOLO I would say the solo in 'Hook In Mouth.' When I heard that, it sounded almost mechanical, because it was played so well. And it was something very different than I had even imagined would fit into that little section where the solo needed to go. It's one of my favorite parts when I listen to the *So Far … So Good … So What!* record.

MARTY FRIEDMAN

PLAYING STYLE Marty has a style that I saw develop over the years that he was in Megadeth. I think from the beginning, he had incredible skill as what we now call a shredder-type of guitar player—coming off of *Dragon's Kiss* and Cacophony. I wasn't a huge fan of those records, because to me, it was just such complete bombast of guitar playing. I really appreciated what Marty did inside of Megadeth, because he brought all of that arsenal of his skill and his musicality into the songs of Megadeth.

I like to hear really shredding guitar players inside of songs. It's the same reason why I like someone like Neal Schon in Journey—because there are these incredible songs, and then all of a sudden, you get these sweltering blasts of guitar shred-dom. [*Laughs*] It's also what I liked about Elliot Easton in The Cars, because the songs are so great, and the guitar playing sounds great, as well. And Marty did that same thing inside of Megadeth. I think he continued the trajectory from Chris Poland to Jeff Young into Mary's era—of having a guitar player that was very diverse against Dave. Which I think made the twin guitar team of Megadeth really a standout.

FAVORITE SOLO 'Tornado Of Souls.'

AL PITRELLI

PLAYING STYLE Al was brought in initially as just a very short-term replacement— upon Marty's departure, which happened in the middle of a tour. I knew of Al's playing inside of Alice Cooper, which was fantastic. Only when he was actually out with us did he then put in front of me the first Trans-Siberian Orchestra record,* which I fell in love with immediately, and became a fan of not only TSO, but certainly, Al's playing. To a degree that I try to see TSO every year when I'm home, largely to watch and see Al play.

I think a defining moment for me with Al was when we were in the studio, cutting the basic tracks for *The World Needs A Hero*. We had initially laid down the drums and then Al put down some rhythm guitar tracks, and Al's timing and his ear are absolutely incredible. I had never worked with a guy—inside of hard rock and metal—who had such impeccable timing and such a great ear.

---

* *Christmas Eve And Other Stories* (1996).

Probably one of my favorite recordings of Al is to watch the *Rude Awakening* live DVD, because you get to see Al as a seasoned showman. Because to me, a lot of the tracks on the record, Al was in the band for a very short time, so he didn't have a chance to really lay out of his wares as a musician inside of Megadeth. That live recording is probably one of my favorites, because you get to see him not only make his own stamp in Megadeth, but you also get to see how well he replicated all of the work that came before him.

FAVORITE SOLO I would say '1,000 Times Goodbye.'

GLEN DROVER

PLAYING STYLE I'm not as familiar, because I didn't actually perform with him.* But as a listener of Megadeth music at that point, he definitely continued the course of being a guitar player that sat opposite of Dave's style—which I commend him for that. He also had a very 80s, legato type of playing, which included a little bit of some whammy bar and an ear that had a propensity toward certain types of bends. And for me, probably likened more back to 80s LA rock—in particular, I hear George Lynch in his playing. He was probably the only guitar player in Megadeth that played like that, so I think it certainly sets him apart on the records that he was able to participate on.

FAVORITE SOLO I think 'Sleepwalker' is probably the tune that I would go to.

CHRIS BRODERICK

PLAYING STYLE The way I view Chris's playing was that he was a very schooled and very capable guitar player, able to play pretty much anything you put in front of him. And that allowed for him at that point in Megadeth's career to be able to replicate everything that came before him. Because that was the bulk of the workload for him—was to replicate a huge catalog of music. At the same time, I think that he was able to bring a lot of other great ideas to the band—on the *Thirteen* record maybe more than anything.

FAVORITE SOLO There was some stuff on *Super Collider* that I was really impressed

---

* Ellefson was not in Megadeth during the time Drover was a member.

with—with Chris's playing on. 'Dance In The Rain' is probably the one, because we played that live a few times when we were on Gigantour—we'd play that and have Dave Draiman come out and sing with us. That's probably the tune that is a standout for me—as far as the solo for Chris. At the same time, probably from a musical contribution to Megadeth, I think probably 'Beginning Of Sorrow' was one that really saw Chris's writing style start to integrate well into Megadeth.

KIKO LOUREIRO

PLAYING STYLE Kiko is I would say—truthfully—one of the best musicians I ever played with. He has got a fantastic ear. He has a very natural, easy way about himself with music. When he picks up the guitar and plays, I'm also in awe of just what a fantastic and seemingly effortless musician he is. I think he got to have a really good contribution on *Dystopia*. Maybe not as much as being listed as a songwriter, but to come into that role at that particular time, he was like a connective tissue inside the band—on a lot of musical levels.

FAVORITE SOLO 'Poisonous Shadows' is a song that is a standout for me with Kiko, just because of his overall musical contribution.

rex talks
dime

Pantera bassist Rex Brown shares his
thoughts and memories of playing alongside
the late/great Dimebag Darrell.

DIME EARLY ON

I'd known Dime since before the kid could even play a barre chord. His dad was teaching him barre chords—his dad played left-handed, and also, had a studio. Dime pretty much put himself into the bedroom after that, and learned the two most influential metal albums at the time—*Blizzard Of Ozz* and *Diary Of A Madman*—and emerged out of the bedroom just a virtuoso at the age of seventeen. And it freaked everybody fucking out.

I was friends with both Vinnie and Dime, and I was playing with another band, and they had the only PA in town. And they'd let me borrow microphones and a board. It was one of those things where he just emerged—it was freaky. I happened to be working at a Fotomat at the time, of all things, and that was when Ozzy had just come into town on that tour, and Motörhead was opening up. We went and saw that at the Coliseum in Fort Worth. So at Fotomat, I would look at everybody's pictures, basically. [*Laughs*] And found some really cool pictures of Randy, in that early stage of what that band was.

But Dime, something extraordinary happened to him after those records. He just kept exploring and exploring, and got into all kinds of things. The Scorpions' *Lovedrive* and early Def Leppard was a big thing—*High 'n' Dry* made a huge impact, because he looked just like Pete Willis! Y'know, real skinny, a real kinky perm in his hair, and tiny guy—with this Dean guitar on. But he also played tasty stuff that just came naturally to him.

About that time, we would go down and see all these blues guys, like Rocky Athas, Bugs Henderson, Rusty Burns … this is about the time that Stevie Ray broke out. But these guys had been playing the circuit *forever.* That helped shape what we were listening to. We would go down to the studio and they were doing four on the floor, and we were just amazed at what they would come up with. Because their dad was an engineer—he wasn't producing, he was engineering records and did that through a country label, and also wrote a bunch of songs.

When you're that young, to have that experience of sitting and watching these cats, I think that definitely bled into what Dime was doing—along with Randy Rhoads. And that's a character that he built, because he could play all that fast stuff and do all the scales. But if you listen to Dime, there was a lot of blues and there was a lot of notes in there where it was just about feel and just about that 'warm heart note.' He had that from a very early age, and it's just uncanny how it went through.

We grew up together learning how to play. You still learn every day until you're put in the ground. He still continued to learn different things and different techniques, but some of the stuff he came up with, man, was just out of this world. He had that gift. It's unmistakable. And that's why I think his tone and everything else carries through. But having that magic in the box of the four of us and playing together for so long, that was important, also. Without a foundation, you can sit and be a guitar player and play in your bedroom the rest of your life. But we set out to make a mark.

DEAN ML GUITAR

Dime was one of those wiz kids, and he was about sixteen when he won a guitar competition.[*] One of the things they were giving away was the Dean ML. And he won one of those things. Before that, he had a Hohner—one of those Ace Frehley/Les Paul rip-off kind of things. He was a big Ace fan. So the first Dean ML he won through a contest, and then a mutual friend—Buddy Blaze—got him that first lightning bolt. But after Dime got good, he started teaching at the age of sixteen or seventeen at a music store—this is around the same time we were doing the first record. He *loved* those guitars. He wanted to find an identity for himself,

---

[*] The Arnold & Morgan Guitar Contest at the Ritz in Dallas, Texas, in 1982.

and found it very quick. I think it was because of the guitar contest, and also he liked the way that they played. The old Deans—the '78s and stuff like that—were smokin' guitars.

DIME PRACTICING GUITAR

He used to use the pentatonic scales, and would go up and down, like start on F or E—to get the stretch—and go all the way up the strings, and then he would come down. That was his warm-up—he did that every night. There was a time before the show and he did that until the time we went onstage—probably for an hour. It was just unbelievable on some nights, after all the shots! Some of the stuff he did was unreal when he just let himself be.

WAS IT A CHALLENGE, AS A BASSIST, TO PLAY
WITH DIME, OR DID IT COME EASY?

The funny part of it is, it came really easy. When the two of us sat down and wrote all this stuff, it just clicked. It was so natural. It was just one of those things where the three of us, we were so tight. Even going into when we first got the major label deal, we had played clubs for six years straight. We were so tight—as the three of us—that it just became the norm. But if Dime had his way, he'd have wanted me to play every damn riff with him and the same scale and everything else—but I just kept that low end down. But we were there for each other and we learned all this. It's one of those things that we prided ourselves in what we were doing.

DIME RECORDING SOLOS IN THE STUDIO

He was very methodical about how he wanted to do it. But of course, you have to start, and it was strong, but he'd always want to go back and redo it. I was like, 'Man, do that, but think about the first time you took a pass at it, because that was a really nice structure. Now build upon it.' His solos, at first he tried to do the flash, and then he progressed into where you can flash all you want, but some of that stuff he did is so tasty.

He could play as good as—I'm going to go out on a limb here—Randy did on some of that stuff. And he was a big Eddie Van Halen fan. It was Van Halen and Rhoads, and throw a little Michael Schenker in there. And I think even Matthias Jabs at a certain point came into the mix for him, because that dude's a very underrated guitar player. So when he would come up with those solos, he just played to the track—and whatever the song needed, he played. But nine times out of ten, that first take was just magic. But he was such a perfectionist with everything that he did, that he would want to go over it and over it. And that's what great musicians do.

DIME'S LIVE PLAYING

Like I said, some of those nights where you probably didn't think he could stand up, he'd put that guitar on and it was just insane. We'd sit in the dressing room, going, '*What the fuck just happened?* Oh my God, please tell me somebody captured that on tape!' Which we did—there's all kinds of footage that's been documented and put out there on home videos. But I've seen some other footage of people who had a camera in there that they weren't supposed to bring, and some of that stuff, the way he played and swung that guitar around and did everything that he did, he was a showman. It's unbelievable.

And for a bass player, playing and trying to keep that low-end down as much as you possibly can, and hitting those riffs when I had to hit them with him … all I can say is, it was magic. There wasn't anything preconceived. I mean, we had it well planned out, but the nights it was really good is when we went off the cuff and made it our own. Or soundchecks—that's where a lot of riffs came from, like 'Walk.' And we would write in the studio on the bigger records. Like, *Cowboys [From Hell]* was well thought out. We recorded that three different times, I believe, and the third one is the one we used for the record.

FAVORITE DIME SOLOS

There's so many to count. My top would be 'Planet Caravan,' 'Floods' … I'm one of those kinds of guys where I don't care about the fast shit—I care about that one note that makes the hair on the back of your neck stand up. And that's what Dime could do. He could do anything. Even with that damn whammy pedal—man, that's why my hearing is so fucking bad. [*Laughs*] That cat had so much talent in his little bitty pinky, and he was such a charismatic, loving, and caring dude. He would do anything for anybody. That legacy is with him. But favorite leads, I love them all, man. As far as technique, there's not another cat out there that can touch his ass.

DIME'S INFLUENCES

Ty Tabor. King's X were a big influence. If we were in town, we never missed a King's X show. We were right there in the front. That was one of our favorite bands, and all kinds of crazy shit you wouldn't think we'd listen to. But then again, there was all kinds of music happening around that time—like Jellyfish and Faith No More. It was just the different sounds of the players. Dime was very focused on the metal aspect of everything and trying to be the hot shot. And he was.

He did everything in context and took it to another level. So, the influence of that thing came from all over. You take that Texas R&B stomp of ZZ Top; he was a big Billy Gibbons fan—but he just wanted to do it his way. And, by God, did he. Dime was fascinated with the way that Blues Saraceno approached the way he played. Blues would just come and hang out on the road with us for two or three weeks—him and Dime. But that guy played some mean licks. And he could play everything—I think that's what Dime caught on. But Dime was influenced by any style of music that crossed his path. Too numerous to mention.

PARTYING

First, those guys were straight-edge when I got in the band. They said, 'Well, you can't smoke, you can't drink.' And of course, I walk into the room with a six-pack and a cigarette in my mouth! It's just one of those things—it's rock'n'roll, shit. They were very straight-edge, and then once I turned Dime on to, 'Do you want to get fucked up? Well, let's drink some beers.' Well fuck, I had created a damned monster! I'm not taking credit for that, I'm just saying …

DIME'S PERSONALITY

A fucking madman! Once he came out of his shell, there was no looking back. There was no second-guessing. His personality was warm, charming … there's so many adjectives I could say. But he cared about each and every individual, and he made sure he went out of his way. When you're sitting out there on the road for sixteen months, you're just bored shitless. And the last thing you want to do is play fuckin' 'Cowboys From Hell.' He would find fun ways to keep us all in check—to have fun and make it work. Dime was always that warm, caring individual—since he was a kid. Always sharing and giving, and one of the most generous people I've ever met in my life. I learned a lot from him. It's one of those things where he didn't have to do that.

But we couldn't get him on the bus! We'd have to leave, and he's still out there signing autographs—that's the kind of guy he was. And if we did go to bed, he'd bring everybody inside the bus and blow up every damn speaker, with whatever he was working on. He had all kinds of side-recordings that he did that didn't fit Pantera, and he'd get on the bus and just blaze that shit. I finally had to get off the bus—I said, 'If I see one more hot dog being thrown down the fucking hallway, *I'm going to lose it.*' So I jumped ship and went over to Philip's to get a little quiet, because as you get a little older, the amount of energy this cat had inside of him was just uncontainable.

And then, of course, you have to come down and burn every once in a while, and he would come off the road and do that—take his time off from drinking and everything else, and try to get a personal life after being on that rollercoaster we were on for twelve or thirteen years. It was a pretty hard job to do. But Dime, he was one of a kind. You ain't never going to see another guitar legend like that again.

WHERE DIME'S PLAYING WAS HEADED

Think of where Randy could have gone. Think of what Eddie has done—he's still around and gone through so many different phases and styles, and re-inventing himself. And Dime just didn't get the chance. That's the sad part about it. Other than that, he could have done anything. That guy could play country. He could play a mean acoustic guitar and everything else. But he approached the guitar from a metal standpoint. And that was all he really cared about. Toward the end, he was just getting into fingerpicking and all that kind of stuff. Dime, when he died,* I lost half of my soul, half my right arm … *everything.* Think of where Dime could have gone—the possibilities are endless.

---

* On December 8 2004, Dimebag was shot onstage while performing with Damageplan.

king of **pop** = king of rock?

Michael Jackson went by the title 'King of Pop.' But if you take a look at the guitarists he worked with during the 80s and 90s, could he also be considered 'King of Rock'?

RICHIE KOTZEN For me, the 'Beat It' solo was extremely important, because I did not know who Van Halen was—until that solo. I remember where I was when I heard it. The car was pulling into the driveway, I was in the backseat, and I begged my parents to not turn the radio off, because I wanted to hear the end of the solo. And I didn't know who it was. Somehow, I found out who it was, and then I was turned on to Van Halen, and that was it for me. He was the only guy that I really tried to copy at one point in my career, as a young boy.

STEVE LYNCH I just think that [Eddie] got the song and probably thought of different things to put on it. But I thought he was very creative on it. He did a brilliant job on it. I don't know if he was particularly thinking of, 'Gee, I'm going to throw some tapping in here and try to win over a different type of audience.' I think it was more like he was just doing his own thing.

TY TABOR I sort of remember it differently. By the time he did that, the reason Michael Jackson had him play on the song was because he was already a superstar/ legend guitarist at that point—without Michael Jackson. Michael Jackson was more Top 40, but even Van Halen had hits all over Top 40 for years before that. It may have introduced him to some Michael Jackson fans who didn't listen to rock'n'roll, but in general, I thought he was already an established legend, and that is why he even did it.

GREG HOWE It's hard for me to have the perspective, because by the time that song came out, I had already learned every Van Halen solo on the first four albums. I had learned everything he had done, because I was *way* into it. So that solo when it came out just seemed like almost a caricature of him. It didn't seem like pushing the envelope to me. But I'm sure from the perspective of people who had not really been in the world of Van Halen, it seemed like a fresh, new sound.

STEVE STEVENS It was huge. Any time you bring the rock guitar thing … once again, it proves my point in bringing it out of the context of rock or metal, it has the ability to make a huge impact. And, also, the sound. To me, what I heard was I think Eddie was in one-way channeling Allan Holdsworth or something. I thought this kind of avant-garde/neo-jazz/metal solo being on a Michael Jackson song was just brilliant. The sound of his guitar, nobody sounded like that.

JENNIFER BATTEN That solo made its way into my brain long before I played it with Michael. It's kind of like … if anybody was alive when Kennedy got shot, everybody remembers where they were. Or 9/11. And I remember the first time I heard the 'Beat It' solo—I was at a rehearsal with my cover band, and it came on the radio as we were setting up our gear. And everybody's jaws hit the ground. We just stopped, because it was so unusual and wicked for a pop solo. At first, somebody thought it was Holdsworth, and we just stood there until we sorted out who it was—it was long before you could Google it. And I went out immediately, got it, tried to learn it, and gave up about three times, because there were so many new techniques—wicked harmonics, tremolo bar techniques, tapping. Back at that time, I had one of those cassette decks where you could slow things down, but it was analog, so it would also change the pitch. I eventually got it.

I'll tell you another thing: when I started playing it with the cover band, it felt great and powerful, and I always looked forward to it every night. But when I played it with Michael, it felt really different, and I was disappointed. And I thought it was maybe just nerves or maybe being in front of so many people that made it feel different. A month or two into it, I got a copy of the live show and I compared it with the original, and realized it was so much faster. It just kind of sucked the balls out of it—which there was nothing I could do about the tempo, because that was where Michael wanted it. But it just never seated properly, live.

And I know if the live tempo we played it at was what Van Halen recorded to, it would be a completely different solo.

STEVE STEVENS In 1987, I was signed to Warner Bros as a solo artist, and I was signed by Ted Templeman. And Ted and Quincy Jones were friends, and I guess Ted had introduced them to Eddie Van Halen for 'Beat It.' So when it came time for the follow-up record, for *Bad*, I guess Quincy called Ted and said, 'Who can you suggest? We need the next guy.' And Ted said, 'By all means, Steve Stevens would be your guy.' And then Quincy called me, and I flew out to LA to record.* Michael Jackson was such a huge star by then, after *Thriller*. I expected to go in the studio and there would be an entourage and all this craziness. When I walked in, it was just Quincy, Michael, and Bruce Swedien the engineer. So that was surprising. And it was very much the way I worked with Billy Idol—it would be me; Billy; our producer, Keith Forsey; and an engineer. So it felt very similar.

The version of the song I worked on was well over ten minutes long. And they had certain melodic ideas, and Michael would sing them a capella, and go, 'This is the riff. So let's tackle those bits.' The bits that he would want to hear on there. And then they let the tape run, and I did two or three passes, and it was an extended solo. From what I can tell, the end result is just an edited version of the couple of those passes. The thing I thought was funny was he wore penny loafers. [*Laughs*] He was dressed immaculately, but penny-loafers were *not* a rock'n'roll thing!

But I love the fact that he'd obviously done his homework and knew what I was about, and just wanted my personality and my signature guitar on his recording. He wasn't trying to change me or make me play like Eddie Van Halen on 'Beat It.' That would have been, 'Just get Eddie Van Halen again.' By then, I was using effects in my rigs—once I showed him that, he was knocked out, because he loved horror and science fiction films. That really seemed to strike a chord with him. He was very musically literate, although he didn't say to me, 'Oh, when you get to bar 35, would you play an F sharp?' He would just say, 'Oh, at some point, can you play la-de-da-da,' and he'd sing the line. I'd sit with my guitar—'What's that? Oh OK, la-de-da-da, you got it.' That's the way with most singers. With the exception of Robert Palmer, who I worked with, who knew all about theory and chords, most of the singers I worked with just hum you something they're hearing in their head.

I pulled up to the soundstage [for the filming of the song's music video], and

---

* Stevens appears on the song 'Dirty Diana.'

there was a tricked out van, with all these toys and swings in it. I'm looking at this van, going, 'Wow! Someone must have something set up for people's kids or something.' What I came to realize, it was for Bubbles the Chimp, who was there! Bubbles had the pimp van. And then the greatest thing was in-between takes, it was just Michael and I up there on the soundstage, so he was asking me, 'Do you know Mötley Crüe?' He knows all about rock bands. He wanted to know about staging, lighting, and production and all this, because he was getting ready to plan his first big tour. And he wanted to bring the spectacle of arena rock into the pop world. He had obviously gone to a number of rock concerts, and was really inquisitive about that.

There were a lot of jokes in-between; he loved to joke around with people. There was one bit that didn't end up on the final version of the video—he came running down across the stage, and literally slid through my legs and popped up behind me, and grabbed me by the neck! At the end of the take, everybody goes into huge applause. I had no idea he was going to do that. And for some reason, they didn't catch it—the cameras weren't on me at that point or something. They didn't get it on film.

JENNIFER BATTEN When I eventually moved back to LA in 1984, the Musicians' Union … in order to switch from San Diego to LA, they wanted to make sure that people were not just taking advantage of the LA Union benefits, and not actually living there. So I had to go into the Union once a week for I think two months— and sign in a book, to prove that I lived there. And every week, I would ask where the cool gigs were. There were books of bar mitzvahs and weddings and this and that—nothing that appealed to me. And Barry Squire was dealing with sorting people out for those kind of gigs at the time, and he just kind of laughed and said, 'You've got to be connected—it's all word of mouth.'

In '87, one of Michael Jackson's people called up GIT, and at that time, they had just started their referral service. So a guy said, 'Send us two people,' and I was one of the lucky people that got a call to go in and audition. I'm told there were about a hundred people that auditioned, and I took several days off—just to really woodshed the tunes and make sure I had them nailed. And when I went in to audition, there was no band—it was just me and a video camera, and I never did play the tunes. The only guidance I was given was to 'play some funk rhythm.' So I improvised something and then I started soloing, then I played the 'Giant Steps' tapping solo, which ended up on my first record. And then I ended with the 'Beat It' solo, because I thought he might find that quite useful—and I had been playing that in a cover band for a couple of years. And a couple of days later, I got the call that he was interested, and it was a matter of coming down to rehearse with the band and seeing how it went. Two months later, I was on a plane to Tokyo.

I remember the first night, I was nervous—only fear of the unknown, because all of a sudden, instead of playing for a couple hundred people, I was playing for *fifty thousand*. So I just didn't know if I would start shaking or what kind of havoc my nerves would create. But because of the intense rehearsals, which was a solid two months, once I got onstage, I was very pleased to know that it was just about performing, and everything about the tunes was completely second nature at that point. So that was definitely memorable.

He shut down the Tokyo Disneyland, so we could hang out without the riff-raff, which was unbelievably spoiled. [*Laughs*] After that, I have always had trouble waiting in line for anything—having that insight on how some people don't have to. [*Laughs*] One of the best sounding gigs of all of the ten years was playing at a place called Irvine Meadows—south of LA. The sound—because of how the amphitheater was shaped—was just incredible. And then the Super Bowl was a huge highlight too,* because that was a one-of-a-kind thing, that was only going to happen once, and it went out to a billion and a half people. So those are the biggest highlights.

GREG HOWE Michael Jackson was an amazing experience. It was probably one of the highlights of my career. Jennifer Batten was gracious enough to recommend me for the gig—she knew she would have to be stepping off for a while. Jennifer and I had met at a NAMM show and had mutual respect for each other. But she did let me know that if she leaves the tour for whatever reason, she was going to recommend me—which is exactly what she did.

The experience was very, very intimidating, because I was kind of unprepared. I was unprepared in the sense that she didn't have an exact time that she would be leaving. And this is like, '96. So she said, 'I am going to send you some demos. I'll even send you some recordings that I did with the recorder right next to my amp, so you can hear specifically what I'm doing in the context of the band. So learn these parts, because you may be getting a call, and you'll have to respond to it immediately.' I thought, 'OK, that's great!'

But then, months went by, and nothing happened. I wasn't getting any phone calls. And this is before cell phones really—I didn't want to leave the country or

---

* Jackson performed a five-song medley for the Super Bowl XXVII halftime show, held at the Rose Bowl in Pasadena on January 31, 1993.

leave my house, even, because I was afraid, 'What if this phone call comes in while I'm out of town or away?' So I was turning down a lot of opportunities to do things, for fear of not getting this phone call. Months went on, and I decided, 'I have to get back to my life. I cannot be at the mercy of this imaginary phone call that may never happen.'

So I just stopped listening to the music and got back on track with what I was doing, and another few months had gone by before I even listened to the stuff. Suddenly, I got a phone call around eight on a Monday night from the music director of Michael Jackson, who said, 'We need you on a plane tomorrow morning at six, for a performance in Amsterdam on Wednesday.'

I was freaking out. You can imagine—I had to relearn all these songs and pack my clothes. I only really had about six hours to prepare, because I had to get to Newark Airport, which was about two hours from where I lived, which meant I had to be there two hours in advance. My flight was at six, so I had to be there at four, I had to leave at two, and it's already eight. It was a frantic mess. But I did somehow get through it. I did a quick rehearsal the day of the show on Wednesday morning with the band. We went through about four songs, and everybody said, 'Yeah, it sounds great. It's going to work.' So I was starting to get that sense of relief, like, 'Oh my God, I think this is really going to happen—I can do it!'

We get done going through these songs, and the production manager walks up to me and says, 'You sound great. *Now let's go over the choreography.*' That was probably the craziest part of the whole thing, the fact that Jennifer's role— which was the same role I had—we probably had to interact with Michael more than anybody else in the band. There was a lot of choreography designed for the guitarist and Michael to interact. And all of this had to be learned within a few hours before the show, because I wasn't even told about it until the day of the show. So, it was a very intimidating thing.

I ended up having this gigantic, poster-sized cheat sheet, that surrounded the pedal board, and I had to learn all of the presets on her DigiTech unit, because a lot of songs would have two or three, sometimes four, different presets in the song. So I had a list in front of me that said 'Song 1: Verse for intro, preset 31. Verse, preset 14. Pre-chorus, preset 31 again. Chorus, preset 70. Second verse, preset 71. Step forward, spin around twice, wait for dancer to pass by, move stage left, wait for drummer's cue, go back in position. New chorus, preset 70.' It was a whole bunch of stuff that you had to remember and understand. So it wasn't just learning guitar parts, it was memorizing which sounds go with what part of the song, and then also memorizing all the choreography. And some of the choreography was crazy.

After I did the second gig, I had to wear a wig that mimicked Jennifer Batten … well, actually, Jennifer wore a wig, too, but when she wore it, it looked like it could have actually been her hair. You put a longhaired blonde wig on me, and it just ends up looking like *The RuPaul Show* or something! [*Laughs*] But they had to do it, because the wig was actually made of fiber optic cables that would light up during the 'Beat It' solo. And it had this humongous … probably a four-inch-diameter-sized cable, hooked up to it, that they'd have to feed every time I would go out there, that would go up the back of my shirt. And then they'd have to kind of 'reel me back in' when I went back to my normal post. So it was a very cumbersome situation.

The other significant thing that stands out about the Michael Jackson experience was for the 'Beat It' solo, *you had to perform*. So I had to walk with Michael and move my body with him and get to almost a dance move—while I'm playing the solo and walking across the stage. That was a little nerve-racking sometimes—having to play a classic solo and having to perform while you're doing it.

JENNIFER BATTEN When I was on the *Bad* tour, we were given carte blanche to get anything that we wanted, and we didn't have to pay for it until the end of the tour. Racks were really big at that time, and I got my first rack, which was the size of a friggin' refrigerator. It was before multi-effects, so I had three separate racks for chorus, reverb, and delay. I added also I think a wah pedal and I also had a Boss Envelope Filter for, I think, 'The Way You Make Me Feel.'

It was pretty simple compared to the effects I use now, but the rack was ridiculous in that I had two Boogie Mark III's—one was set for clean, one was set for dirty—and a Boogie Strategy 400 poweramp. And that rack took like three guys to lift. It was just ridiculous. And I also got a Bob Bradshaw mini-switcher system. So, it was pretty involved, with all the different parts involved. And after the tour, I knew I couldn't deal with that myself to do just a regular gig, and I cut those racks down into two racks, and still had to get a Tommy Lift to take them anywhere! A ridiculous pain in the ass. Thank God technology has made things lighter and smaller over the years.

GREG HOWE It was the highest level of *everything*. The best hotels, private jets just for the band. Everything was the best, highest quality that you could imagine for a tour. It's not a good way to get an introduction into this world, because you get spoiled. Nothing even came close to that, since. So it's like, 'Wow. You get paid all this money and I'm staying at these lavish hotels, where all the hardware on the sinks are gold, and I've got a suite, a private jet, my per diem is a lot of money'— everything was just bigger than life and better than you could imagine. That was really my introduction into that world of the sideman gig.

Michael was amazing. He's more amazing than anybody really knows, because you've got a full band that's got two keyboard players, a drummer, tons of back-up singers, dancers, bass player, all kinds of instrumentation, tons of choreography. I don't know if you ever saw the show, but his show was outrageous, with all kinds of skits and props. Huge. He's performing his ass off on every single song, so you figure, 'If I make a little mistake here, if I'm not in the pocket a whole lot on this one section or for a couple of seconds, he's not going to notice that. He can't be noticing that—there's too much to pay attention to.'

And sure enough, he does notice everything. He came up to me I think after the second show, and there was a song that I had to play a pretty simple part in—it was just a clean funky rhythm—and says, 'Hey man, I just want to say you sounded great. But you're a little bit on top of the beat in the verse section of such and such song, so if you can just pull it back a little bit.' And I'm thinking, 'What?! Are you serious? You can actually hear what I'm playing?' He was on another level, that guy. Completely another level.

JENNIFER BATTEN [Michael was] very kind, very respectful. I would think back sometimes, just trying to guess at the amount of pressure he would be under every night—with 50,000 to … gosh, I think the biggest audience was 125,000 people, that had paid big money to see him. He always had to be 'on.' And he always was. If he wasn't feeling up to it, nobody knew. It was great. He was always very kind to everybody—especially at the *Bad* rehearsals, which was when we had the most contact with him. He was there for twelve hours every single day, so during the breaks, anybody had access to him.

I like to describe him as a creative tornado, because a lot of the acts—especially pop acts that are out there—have a team of people telling them what to do. A lot of people don't even write their own songs. And Michael was just an oddball of nature, where not only did he write—for instance, 'Billie Jean,' he recorded all the parts with his voice, and then hired people to carry out the parts with their own instruments. That was just the beginning—music was just the beginning. Then, he built this show on top of it—whether it was dance numbers or special effects and on and on and on. He just had an ongoing imagination that was always wide open.

big break

Several guitarists interviewed for this book pinpoint the lucky break that launched their careers.

ADRIAN BELEW In the mid 70s, I moved to Nashville, Tennessee—in particular, to play with a really good regional band called Sweetheart. Sweetheart did a lot of club dates and a lot of fraternity parties. And they did quite well—played more interesting cover music, like Steely Dan and Wings and Stevie Wonder. Things of that era. The band dressed—every day, all day long—in authentic 1940s vintage clothing. So the idea was, 'Sweetheart' was supposed to be spoken like Bogart would say it—'Shweetheart,' y'know? So that that was one of the traits of the band—wherever we went, people would know we were the band, because we all wore full-on three-piece suits, fedora hats, ties, tie pins, the whole thing. It was a fun band.

One night, we were playing in a club—a little small club in Nashville. It was a biker bar, really. It was called Fanny's. It was painted all black inside—a pretty dank kind of place. Frank Zappa had played a concert in Nashville that night, at a much larger place. He was looking for somewhere to hang out afterward. Frank always like to go and hear other musicians—this is one of the ways he found people to audition. So he and some of his band and some of his crew arrived at Fanny's, and sat down in front of us. Instantly, I knew who it was, of course, and I just did the best I could—I sang better, I played better. [*Laughs*]

He stayed for forty minutes, and we were playing 'Gimme Shelter' by The Rolling Stones, when he walked up as he was leaving, shook my hand onstage, and said, 'I'm going to get your name and number from the limo driver, and I'm going to audition you.' What had happened is the limo driver was a big fan of our band. He was a young guy named Terry Pugh, and when Frank asked him where should he go, Terry said, 'Well, if you want to hear a good band, I like this band, called Sweetheart.' And that's how that happened.

Months went by, and nothing happened. In fact, Sweetheart even broke up during that time, and I joined a little disco band. I was at the end of my rope—three months behind in rent, had no money, and my Volkswagen had broken down. Everything was going wrong for me. [*Laughs*] And I received a call from Frank, personally. He said, 'I'm ready to audition you now. I'll fly you out here to my place in California, and here are the songs you need to learn from all these different records. And you have one week to learn how to play them and sing them the best you can.' I told him that I wasn't a reader, and he said, 'I never work with people who aren't readers. *But I'll make an exception in your case.*'

So I flew to his home. It was the first time I had ever flown in a plane past the Mississippi River—that's how green and dumb I was. I arrived at his basement, which is where the beginnings of his studio were going to be, and there was just utter chaos going on. They were moving gear around and shifting things, and there were people crossing in front of me—because they were getting ready to start their rehearsals. And I was standing in the middle of the room, with a little Pignose Amp on the floor, and Frank was sitting behind the studio console, and he would say, 'OK, play "Andy,"' and I would start playing it. I'd play it for a little while, and he would stop me. 'OK, now play "Wind Up Workin' In A Gas Station,"' and I'd play that one.

Because of all the chaos, I really didn't do well. And I knew I didn't do well. Kind of cut short, and then I had nowhere to go, because they were going to take me back to the airport at the end of the day and put me on a plane back to Nashville. So I stayed around and I watched other people audition—keyboard players and percussionists. Unbelievable. When I saw the auditions they had to do, I was terrified. I thought, 'Well, no wonder I'm not going to get this job!' [*Laughs*] Because they were reading the music off pieces of paper, and it was very, very complex, difficult stuff.

There was a point at the end of the day when everything had died down, and there was suddenly just me and Frank. And I said, 'Frank, I know I didn't do well in the audition. I thought it would be different.' And he said, 'What do you mean?' I said, 'I thought it would just be you and me sitting quietly somewhere, and I would play the songs and sing them, and show you that I can do that.' And he said, 'Well, all right. Let's do that then.' So we went upstairs to his living room, and he had a purple couch. I turned my Pignose amp all the way up and stuffed it down into the cushion in the couch, so it wouldn't be too loud and still sound like a good guitar, and we started the second audition, and we got about ten minutes into it, and he stopped me, shook my hand, and said, 'Here's what I pay. Here's how much we're going to rehearse.' He laid out his whole plan. We did a handshake, and he said, *'You're in the band.'*

RUDY SARZO I got the call from Ozzy because of Randy—God bless him, I'm grateful every single day that he trusted me, that I was going to be the right guy. They only had like, ten days to find a bass player and go on the road, and not only was there a lot of pressure, but there were a lot of questions of, 'Is this person going to be someone that we can trust and rely on, and bring into our circle?' Because it was a very tight-knit circle. So Randy said, 'I know Rudy. He's not an alcoholic or a drug addict, and he can play this. He'll do a great job.' So that's what they were looking for—they weren't looking for a rock star. They were looking for somebody who could do the job, so they could go on tour and not have any catastrophes or any drama on the road. And Randy told me, 'Listen—they're going to test you.' And I understood. They didn't know me. I had no resume. I had never been anywhere with anybody. I was just a guy sleeping on Kevin DuBrow's spare bedroom floor. So Randy, he put his trust on the line—from Sharon and Ozzy—that I was going to do my job. And I did. It took time for me to really prove myself—that I could be trusted. So I'm incredibly grateful to Randy for that, because not everybody does that.

STEVE STEVENS The band that I was in that Paul Stanley had seen—the Fine Malibus—got signed to Aucoin Management, which was Kiss's management. And when I left that band, they continued to manage me, and I think I placed two weeks of ads of a guitarist looking for a band. And then I got a call from Bill Aucoin, asking me if I knew who Billy Idol was. 'Dancing With Myself' was released, so I said, 'Oh yeah, absolutely!' He said, 'He just moved to New York and we're managing him. You guys seem like you would be a good duo.'

That was the beginning of that whole thing. Pretty much from the moment I met Billy, I just started working on original ideas and things, because a lot of my heroes were the established English rock guitar players, who punk rock was trying to get rid of, to a certain extent. So it was like, 'Well, where do we meet?' And where we met was our love of a lot of the New York things, like Velvet

Underground and Lou Reed, and the very roots rock American stuff, like Elvis, and The Doors.

PHIL COLLEN I was in this band called Girl. We were from London, and we'd tour England—we'd open up for these other bands. We opened up for Kiss, UFO, Pat Travers, Ted Nugent, Ozzy. And Def Leppard would open up for those bands in the States. We came out at the same time, so I'd bump into the guys. They'd come by our shows, and we'd go see them. We were playing the same kind of circuit. Before you know it, we're jamming onstage and we'd become friends. Joe [Elliott] actually asked me if I'd come out and play on tour. He said, 'Can you learn sixteen songs in two days?' I said, 'Yeah! Easy!' Because there were problems with Pete Willis. It wasn't really working out on tour. But that got smoothed over.

And then like a year later, he phoned up again, and said, 'You want to come in the studio and play some solos?' I said, 'Yeah, sure!' I had just thought I'd be helping these guys out. And it ended up being *Pyromania*. I came in and played on 'Photograph,' 'Rock Of Ages,' 'Foolin',' 'Rock! Rock! (Till You Drop)'—all the solos. Mutt Lange had said, 'Just have fun. Just play lead guitar.' And he found out I could sing, and had me sing on all the songs. All the heavy lifting had already been done—I just came in and tore it up a little bit, and had fun on it. Then we released it, and it just went nuclear. 'Photograph' went bonkers. I wasn't even thinking like that—I just thought I was playing solos on these great rock songs, and was trying to fit in with that. We had no idea that was going to do what it did. That was pretty special.

BRUCE KULICK My initial introduction to being [Kiss's] lead guitarist was a temporary basis. I think everyone was aware they weren't really sure who was playing lead guitar. Apparently, it started with me doing some 'ghost' guitar work for the band, when Mark St. John had his illness[*] or Paul wasn't real pleased with what he was doing—I'm a little unclear about that, from that time period. But I do know that before I left the studio that day, he saw that my hair was about shoulder-length, and he said something very interesting without letting the cat out of the bag—'*Don't cut your hair.*'

Technically, if I was a session guy, I could have looked like my brother[†]—I could be bald with a shaved head! I just shrugged that off, until I realized there was something going on—when I got a call to do originally two to six weeks of a

---

[*] Reiter's syndrome, also known as reactive arthritis.
[†] Guitarist and producer Bob Kulick, best known for his work with Kiss, W.A.S.P., and Meat Loaf.

European tour. Because I think they felt that either Mark would be over his illness or sooner, even. To me, I already thought I won the lottery by just being the temporary guitarist of the band. And off I went to Europe.

In fact, I worked so hard at being amazing for them that I over-exercised—I hurt my arm! I had to go to a doctor, and in the end it turned out that it healed in time. I missed some rehearsal because of it, which was very concerning to them, but I'm a pretty good person when it comes to committing to do their homework. So I was prepared by the time I was able to jump into rehearsals. What I wasn't prepared for was how energetic they'd be onstage, when they were performing. Anyway, I fly over to England. The first gig, literally, my knees are shaking. I always thought it was an expression, but I'm going, 'My kneecaps ARE shaking.'

But got through the show, and I got this nickname of 'Bruce Spruce'—I was like a tree up there. But I really wanted to concentrate on playing the right parts, and we used to play very fast in that era of Kiss—for some reason, the tempos were bumped up quite a bit. And Eric Carr used to take it to the races, which is what they wanted. And I wanted to play the right stuff. So it was quite remarkable that I hung in there—still thinking that I won the lottery, even if I only did the European tour. A little band called Bon Jovi opened for us, who weren't huge yet.

But there I was, touring Europe and it was very exciting. Eric already had a few years in Kiss—he was already there four years, so he had his gripes. Of which, I didn't want to hear about, if you can understand that. By the time we got back to America, Mark wasn't quite ready, but he was improving. He would join us on tour, so that he could see if he could fit in—even though I already had enough indications, especially from Gene, that they were very happy with me. So, in other words, now I had—as they like to say in baseball—the home field advantage. I was there, I was used to how to work with them, I certainly did my job and at the same time, never tried to upstage them or complain about much—to make my presence there nothing but a positive.

And the fans were reacting; the shows were doing well. It's very funny, whenever I listen to any of those bootlegs from that first tour, to hear how fast everything was. And they also wanted to capture that excitement sometime in December, when they were making plans to do the *Animalize Live Uncensored* home video—because *Animalize* as an album and the hit single 'Heaven's On Fire' really took off. And no, I wasn't in the 'Heaven's On Fire' video, which was a drag.

But Mark St. John was contractually the guitar player of Kiss. So there's another guy travelling, who they're going to try and see if they can ease him in and see if he deserves the job that he had a contract for—with me being a 'week-to-week' person. I couldn't tell you the year the ice hockey craziness went down with Nancy Kerrigan and 'the other one,'* and I used to think of it like that—'What am I going to do, take a guitar stand and knock him out, so he can fall and hurt himself, so he can't take the gig back?' I just had all these crazy thoughts! I was actually so grateful for the opportunity of the gig and I realized, 'This is *not* going to be a competition. I'll be kind to Mark and even warm up with him and jam backstage, and be respectful. It's not my decision.'

So I was very proud of myself that I took a very kind/gentle approach to a very awkward situation—even though there's a lot of different accounts to what happened during the first week or so of the tour. And my recollection was they were testing him by letting him eventually do the first half of a show, and then I would come in and finish the show, and let him do the other half, and then let him do a whole show. And even if I'm off by one-third of that story, I was always suited up and ready. It wasn't the makeup outfits, but we still wore some makeup and crazy clothes—that was '80s Kiss.' And it would have been in December, because the tour started in late November in America.

What was interesting was I saw Mark implode and the gig be mine. It wasn't that he didn't play well—he seemed to try to overcome what he'd been missing out on, and I think he tried too hard. In some ways, he over-performed—both physically and maybe even musically. And they were pretty turned off to it. There is very little on record about the gig that he actually did. I think it was somewhere in Upstate New York.† I do know that they let him know that he wasn't going to be staying on the road, and maybe the way Kiss and the management did this was to kind of contractually give him a fair shot, and then decide 'no' and send him home. I heard he emptied the minibar that night—which is probably true. The night that they let him know, Paul did call me and explained to me, 'We're sending Mark home, and you're the guitarist now for sure. And we're happy to be working with you.'

CRAIG GOLDY It stemmed with the first audition for Rough Cutt. When Randy Rhoads died, Jake E. Lee left Rough Cutt to join Ozzy. So there was an audition spot to take Jake's place. At the time, I was actually living in a car! I was working with a singer, Perry McCarty, and he got a chance to audition for a band called Warrior. He got the gig and felt bad about leaving me behind, because he and I

---

* 'The other one' being Tonya Harding, whose ex-husband and bodyguard hired an associate to attack Kerrigan in the hope that she would be unable to appear at the 1994 Winter Olympics.
† It was at the Broome County Arena in Binghamton, New York, on November 29 1984.

were in San Diego together and we were starting a band. So he says, 'Give me some copies of your demo tape, and I'll pass them around.'

Warrior was friends with Rough Cutt, so the demo tape that I made—with my last twenty dollars, giving guitar lessons out of my car—ended up with Perry, and then Perry gave it to the drummer from Rough Cutt, who gave it to Ronnie.* And then Ronnie said, 'We've got to get this kid up here.' The only problem is how do you find a kid who is living in his car? I had done a favor for a friend, so that friend let me stay at his other friend's house for a while. And that house had a couch that they only let the dogs sleep on—it had no cushions on it, just dog hair.

But that house had a phone, so they found me, and a friend of mine drove me out to the audition, and Wendy† and Ronnie found out that I only had a guitar. So they rented amplification, cables, and gear, so I could take place in the auditions. I met Ronnie that day of the audition. Because the night before, the guitar player of Warrior, Tommy Asakawa, walks in looking like the President of the United States was on the phone, and he goes, 'Oh my God, Ronnie wants to be there … *he wants to meet you!*'

So he was there, right when I walked in—there was Ronnie and Wendy. I got a chance to tell him how important his music was to me and how much his lyrics meant to me—how he had a way of talking about one subject, but the two opposite ends of that subject simultaneously while on top of it all, coming across as being dark, but having a positive message. He grabs my arm, and he says, 'That's right! That's right!' Little did I know that would start something that would continue on—when he was in Heaven & Hell, he would call me at home, and say, 'Goldy, you've got to hear this … ' and read me his lyrics. He would ask me what I thought it meant. I would 'crack his code,' and he would say, 'That's right!'

That night of the audition, he got inspired, so he actually sat in on the audition, and I found out later that was something that he very rarely does. We did 'Man On The Silver Mountain' and 'Heaven And Hell' together. And during that audition, he came over and whispered, 'What's the lyrics to the second verse?' I knew his lyrics, so that created another portion of our relationship that I didn't think was going to go so deep.

Then we were improvising during the breakdown of 'Heaven And Hell'—I would play something and he would sing something. Then he and I started playing the same exact melody line at the same exact time in the same octave. He looked at me like, 'How did you know how I was going to go there?' Then, afterward,

---

* Ronnie James Dio, who was producing the band.
† Wendy Dio, Ronnie's manager and wife, and the manager of Rough Cutt.

he came over and said to me, 'Man, I haven't had that kind of exchange since the Ritchie days.' Then later on, I was saying, 'I hope I get the gig,' and he said, 'Well, if I have anything to do with it, you've got the gig, kid.' He always called me 'kid.' Then sure enough, I was in the band.

We were doing demos together and from to time, and he would say, 'How are things going?' And I'd go, 'Well … things are OK.' Apparently, I found out just how political rock'n'roll can be—nobody in the band wanted me in the band because they all wanted their own friend/guitar player, so they could have more influence over the songwriting, so they could all have more publishing money. I found out that to be true later, even further down the line. So when Ronnie found out they weren't using my ideas, one day he stormed into rehearsal and said, 'Craig's got great ideas and you should be using them. And if you want me to be your producer, then I think you should start using his ideas—otherwise, you guys have very dry days ahead,' and stormed out!

And then one day we were in the studio together—I'll never forget this—I would sit on the floor in the Indian pose, kind of with my legs crossed, right near his chair, and he and I would 'create' together. Now that I think about it, it's almost kind of cute—here's this little kid sitting on the floor, right by his mentor, right by his chair. He'd say, 'Let's try something like this.' 'Something like this?' 'Yeah, great!' One time, it took the other guitar player [in Rough Cutt] like three hours to do one short solo, because back in those days, they would improvise and then do a 'composite.' And for those who don't know what that means, the guy would play like ten times, and then they would take the best of those ten takes and put it into one, as one solo. So it took about three hours for this twenty second solo, and then Ronnie said, 'OK, you're up.'

So I get set up, and I have my headphones, and I'm sitting on the floor again, and I said, 'Hey Ronnie, can I try something? I've worked out a solo for this.' I played it, I look over, and I see in the control room, everybody's laughing. I'm thinking, 'I didn't think it was that bad.' He goes, 'Do one more.' I do it again, look over, and everybody's laughing. Did it again, look over, everybody's laughing. He goes, 'I want you to come in and take a listen.' So he played it, looks over at me, and says, 'What do you think?' And I go, 'Well, can I hear one of the other ones?' And he goes, 'No.' And I think, 'Uh oh, here we go,' because he liked to give me lessons and teach me stuff. And he goes, 'No, *because that's all three*! You're done kid!' Apparently, I'd worked out the solo so well that it was note-for-note, and three performances sounded like one performance. So they kept all three.

And then they kept inviting people in, like the guys from Mötley Crüe were there recording—'Have you heard this solo? You've got to check this out!' And then another late night, we were working in the studio together again, and Ronnie stops the tape, and he goes, 'Goldy, if Vivian [Campbell] ever doesn't work out, you'll be my first choice,' hits play again, then stops it again, and says, 'And I'm not just saying that to make you feel good.' And then that was it. Ronnie was a man of his word—Vivian was out and I was in. That's why there were no auditions for that spot.

JOE SATRIANI [Touring with Mick Jagger] was an unbelievable boost to my career, it goes without saying. I was nobody a few months earlier, and then all of a sudden, I had a full-page story in *Rolling Stone* magazine, and I was flying around with Mick Jagger and playing at the Tokyo Dome. It was a ridiculous change in fortune. The greatest part of it was that Mick turned out to be a cool guy, a very creative, natural musician. Fun to hang out with, generous, showed me that he was a guy that totally loved his audience and loved performing. Always gave 100 percent. And I was totally blown away, because sometimes you meet famous people, and they let you down. And he was just the opposite. So I got completely enthused by being with him for a year. I just thought, 'This is how you do it. This is how you always strive to be better, this is how you always give your best, and you can be nice to people, and you can do it all on the up and up, and do it right.' It was a great experience.

STU HAMM I met [Joe Satriani] through Steve. I had been doing some solo bass gigs and gigs with a trio—of my original material. And Cliff Cultreri—the guy who signed Steve and signed Joe—I invited him to a gig I did at a place called At My Place in Santa Monica, and they came down and liked what they heard, and they asked me if I would do a record for hardly any money. I said yes … and they gave me hardly any money. And I did the first record on like a budget of $3,000, which is ridiculous—*Radio Free Albemuth*.

I had Allan Holdsworth—who was on Relativity at the time—on the first track playing a solo, which was great. And I had a song on it that I had written, called 'Flow My Tears,' based on the Philip K. Dick novel,* and I had written the melody to be played by a trumpet—like a Miles Davis kind of thing. And the drummer, Mike Barsimanto, was playing with Mark Isham, who is a great trumpet player. So I was going to get Mark Isham to play, and I got him the track.

---

* *Flow My Tears, The Policeman Said*, published in 1974.

It turned out he wanted to record it in his own studio, and he wanted us to pay his engineer. And I didn't have fifty bucks. I don't mean I didn't have fifty bucks in the recording budget—*I didn't have fifty bucks to my name.*

So I called up Cliff at Relativity, and I said, 'I don't know what to do. I've run out of money and there are a couple of songs that need solos and melodies.' And said, 'Well, we just signed this new guy, he's a friend of Steve's. He's doing a gig at the NAMM show in Chicago. How about you go play with him and he'll play on your record?' So I flew up to San Francisco, when Joe was just finishing *Surfing With The Alien*, and he played on 'Flow My Tears' and 'Sexually Active.' And the plan was for me to put fretless bass on 'Always with Me, Always with You,' but we ran out of time. So I had to fly back to LA.*

WARREN HAYNES I met Dickey Betts and Gregg Allman when I was twenty years old, and was fortunate enough to spend a few hours hanging out in a recording studio with them. Dickey and I—as guitar players—stayed in touch, and as I got older, we would continue to see each other from time to time, and play together from time to time. And then when I was twenty-six, I got a call from Dickey, saying that he wanted to put a band together, and wanted us to write some music together.

It was a huge opportunity for me—even though I didn't think or realize that it would lead to me joining The Allman Brothers. It was just an opportunity for me to work with Dickey Betts, who I was a huge fan of. Three years later, The Allman Brothers reformed and asked me to join. Which was a shock to me, because they had always maintained that they would never get back together. And I had no reason to disbelieve that. So it was as big a surprise to me as it was to anyone else when they reformed. And when they asked me to join, that was the biggest break of my career—for sure.

---

* However, Hamm would soon serve as Satch's touring bassist.

not just metal

There were also talented guitarists outside of heavy metal during the 80s and 90s—especially within the realm of alternative rock. However, when they started recording songs that featured guitar solos, they would often be met with resistance from the alternative-rock press, and looked down upon by shredders …

BILLY CORGAN Absolutely. From the get-go. [Corgan experienced criticism from the alt-rock scene for having guitar solos in Smashing Pumpkins songs.]

CHRIS HASKETT [Rollins Band guitarist] [I felt] pretty much an even mixture of complete boredom and intimidation! I could never play like that. Most of it just bored us. There were a couple of bands that I actually liked—up to *Master Of Puppets* Metallica, early Slayer. *Master Of Puppets* was in my little Walkman for a year—partially because of the sound of it. That was metal sounding 'good,' as opposed to metal sounding sludgy. But some of the other bands, after a while … especially speed metal—I liked Anthrax, but other than that, most speed metal, it's got no groove. There's very few drummers that can actually swing at those tempos. So most of it has no funk—it has no groove to it. We used to call it 'hamster fucking'—that's what it sounded like. It held no appeal for me. Because it was metal, but it wasn't heavy. Then again, I'm in the minority in this. It stopped being heavy and was showboating, rather than actual real meat and potatoes heavy music.

A lot of those guys, it was also a whole bunch of technical things where it's kind of like, the whole tapping thing, it was never going to ever fit with the style of music that we were playing, and I'll never be able to learn to do it well, so I'll just skip that whole step. I'm not a very fast player—this is not my thing. I was kind of relieved to not have to get into that kind of speed race of guitar playing that was going on that was very prevalent back then. But that said, there were a lot of people with amazing chops that I do like, but most of them tend to be the outside guy—guys like Steve Vai and Mike Keneally, and a lot of the Zappa guys. The guys that have this serious technique, but the technique isn't the be-all/end-all—it is just a means to the end.

DUANE DENISON [Jesus Lizard, Tomahawk guitarist] I wouldn't say complete disdain, but it was somewhat frowned upon. I think that due to just the excesses of the corporate-rock genre and this sort of guitar hero worship, to us, it seemed like it was unnecessary and kind of a frivolous afterthought—that just wasn't really necessary for the message of the music. And that if the song was interesting, I wanted the guitar parts and the riffs to be interesting enough that you didn't necessarily need the solos—though I did occasionally take some. But it wasn't on every song, which is what you get when you listen to a lot of classic rock or metal. Personally, I never looked down on solos or hated it, but it wasn't what it was about—it was more about textures and chord things and rhythmic power.

AL JOURGENSEN [Ministry singer-guitarist] If you look to all the great early punk-rock songs—Richard Hell, The Ramones, the Pistols, Buzzcocks, Magazine, Wire—there was no emphasis on lead guitar playing there. At all. It was all song-craft. So that really started in the late 70s/early 80s, as completely the antithesis of the Eric Claptons, Jimmy Pages, and Jimi Hendrixes. It's like, 'We don't need to be a technical master to write good tunes.' And I thought that's a very healthy attitude. And [Ministry guitarist] Mikey Scaccia embraced that later in his life, too. To a sense like, 'This song is awesome. It doesn't need me to go shred and rip on this section. It would sound forced.' So he acquired restraint and taste.

In the immortal words of B.B. King, it's like, 'The best note that's ever been played isn't played.' There's no need for it—the best one may be silence. Silence may be the best note that you will ever play. I think a lot of these other people realized too, you don't need a standard, forced guitar lead in every song to make that song. And if you do, it's forced. You do what you do for each individual song. Each individual song is a journey; each album is a journey. Each lead is a journey if you take it as that, instead of just forcing it on a song, just because you think,

'OK. We're going to leave a section for a guitar lead.' Well, what if it doesn't need a guitar lead? Can you think of something else that can be there? And they don't. They just force it. So I think that's a healthy thing for the state of music.

KIM THAYIL [Soundgarden guitarist] I think guitar solos were part of the overindulgence of popular music—according to the punk rockers and the indie underground. Occasionally, some hardcore guys would whip out a solo, because the guitarist knew how to play that. Often, guitarists would learn their craft without developing improvisational skills or leads skills—they would focus more on rhythmic things and chords. They would consciously avoid guitar solos, because it was seen as some kind of 'elitist indulgence,' from the stadium-rock era of the 70s—as well as the prog rock era of the 70s. Borrowing from classical music was kind of considered obnoxious—at least in the punk, hardcore, and post-punk scene. In the post-hardcore scene, though, you had a lot of guitar players who started borrowing and incorporating guitar leads.

CURT KIRKWOOD [Meat Puppets singer-guitarist] Some people thought it was unnecessary. It's like, if you're playing a lead, it's not punk rock. But I thought that was just more of a way to kind of push you to do something—either just forget it, swallow, and just do it, like, '*Here's a lead, anyway.*' One of the things I thought why people loathed to play any solos was sort of like, 'Oh, you're just masturbating.' But one thing that I never lost was what I was into was just playing guitar—playing punk rock was an excuse to play guitar … playing *any* music was an excuse to play guitar. I didn't really ever separate the leads from the other stuff. I wasn't that into playing leads, but my brother* would say, 'You're good at that. There should be a lead on there and there.' So I would do it anyway, and just kind of change the song up. But I didn't really care not to put them in there—I thought it was fun.

DUANE DENISON Usually the lyrics were the last thing to go on—I tried doing it that way [letting the lyrics influence the music], and it just never worked. Typically, a song would start off with just a pattern or a motif or a theme. And that could be a bass line or a short melodic figure on the guitar, and then I would try and develop it, harmonize it, put different intervals over it, transpose it, play it backward, build a part around that, and then try to have the other sections somewhat related to that, so there was some kind of cohesion and unity. So it was

---

* Meat Puppets bassist Cris Kirkwood.

actually a composition. I know that people will think like, '*What*?!' But we actually put a lot of time and thought into those arrangements. I'd like to think they've held up well as a result.

But as far as rhythm guitar, I tried to avoid the standard chord voicings and shapes. Obviously, there's times where only a power chord will do, and I was not shy about that. But trying to add notes and things where there was a certain amount of dissonance and angularity that you didn't typically hear in rock guitar players—at least up until that point. There were others, but I'd like to think I did it differently. And you had to have the right kind of sound to bring that out. If I had a more saturated 'metal sound,' those chords would have just turned to mush, and those riffs, there wouldn't have been any articulation to it. So it had to be a little cleaner and brighter to begin with. But it was all really about trying to not do the typical thing, and not just have it be barre chords and blues licks—which is what classic rock up to that point had been.

CHRIS HASKETT By the time Henry [Rollins] and I started doing a band together, it was an audience with a wider attention span, I suppose. There was space to put in a guitar solo if it was appropriate. But I came to solos pretty late. In almost every band I've been in, I'm the weak link. When I started playing with Henry, I was in a band with Andrew Weiss and Sim Cain, who are the rhythm section of Gone, and they had already been playing together like, ten years. And they were both amazing. And then combined, they were more than the sum of their parts.

When I started out, I'd just write riffs and hooks and play them to death, and my solos—if you go back and listen to *Hot Animal Machine*—tend to just be the main riff repeated without the vocals. [*Laughs*] But it was also a baptism by fire— if you want to be in a band with people that good, you're going to get better … or you're going to be out. And then when Andrew left and we replaced him with Melvin Gibbs, I mean, Christ … you'd *better* be on your game and find your voice!

DUANE DENISON There was a time in the 80s when there was a bunch of guitar players—mostly English—who did a lot of interesting chord and textural and effects stuff, and didn't do a lot of solos. Andy Gill from Gang Of Four, the late John McGeoch from Magazine and Siouxsie & The Banshees, and Geordie Walker from Killing Joke. Those were very influential.

KIM THAYIL I guess guitar solos in a way were taking away from the vocal, from the lyrics, from the riff, from the rhythm. And I think that was a way in which it was perceived—both as an indulgence and an inefficient way to convey a musical idea in song form. Of course, there were really great guitarists that came out of that period—guys like D. Boon from the Minutemen and Curt Kirkwood from the Meat Puppets. These guys, when they started off, their solos were kind of noisy or just a fast instrumental accent or dimension to the song. It just added energy to the song.

But in the post-hardcore thing in the mid to late 80s, these guys were incorporating their guitar chops more … obviously, D. Boon had passed away by then,* but he was definitely getting his little weird beatnik blues licks in on the Minutemen albums, up to the mid 80s. And the guitarists from Saccharine Trust, St. Vitus, and Black Flag definitely incorporated in guitar solos and doing it more.

But initially with punk rock, that was not really a thing. The Ramones didn't play any solos. The Sex Pistols played pretty sparse, their solo style was very much like Johnny Thunders from The New York Dolls—a few string bends here and there, a couple triplets, and that was about it. It fulfilled the function of accenting the song. Sort of like shifting gears—accelerating. But as far as exploring musical themes in a way that a lot of the late 70s bands may do—Crimson or Yes, or even to some extent Zeppelin or Sabbath—that was kind of frowned upon. The music was moving away from that and more song, riff, and vocal oriented.

But it's strange, because concurrent to this, you had Eddie Van Halen come out, who changed the idea of how a guitar could sound and how lead guitar can change the technique, but also how it was incorporated in the songs. And by the way, Eddie Van Halen—one of the greatest guitarists ever, one of the best soloists ever—was not overindulgent in his use of the guitar solo in a song. As a matter of fact, the first album has a lot of great leads, but there aren't really a whole lot of solos, per se—they're like quick flourishes and fills. And on *Van Halen II*, there are definitely some great guitar solo parts, but it's not lead heavy. It really isn't. Everything was more song-oriented—the songs were a lot tighter, oriented toward the lyric, the vocal, the pop arrangements.

CURT KIRKWOOD Eddie Van Halen in the late 70s started becoming unavoidable. I was in a band, and we were covering 'Ain't Talkin'' 'Bout Love' and 'Jamie's Cryin',' and the guys in the band wanted me to learn the solos like they were on the record. And that was impossible for me. It just wasn't my style. It was too technically advanced for me at the time—it probably *still* is. But it taught me a lesson right

---

* Boon died following an automobile accident on December 22 1985.

away—I realized there are a group of these guys, and I think Van Halen really influenced a lot of them. I was into Allan Holdsworth before that, and I saw some similarities there, but even there, that was a little bit more advanced than I was. So I realized, 'I'm not going to play like that. I don't think I can catch up.' And that just grew—Van Halen influenced a lot of people.

Van Halen definitely split a lot of things there. I think just because Eddie could play anything, and Alex is a great drummer, I've always heard similarities there, say, Van Halen preceded other LA stuff—the Chili Peppers and all that stuff. And probably at the time, the biggest band in LA was Van Halen, when punk rock started to happen over there. Van Halen were huge and still in the same city. You tend to think, 'Well, it's showbiz,' but I think LA has its thing where those people influence one another, or they have similar influences, being from the same city. It was a little more 'metal suburban' than your punk rock, but I'm sure they could have played really good punk rock!

KIM THAYIL Van Halen was definitely a pop-rock band with some metal attributes—a great guitarist and flashy pyrotechnic technique. But they did not indulge in it the way that the prog bands did or the 70s hard rock/metal bands did.

CURT KIRKWOOD I heard about Steve Vai through Frank Zappa—those albums back then when he was playing with Zappa. And I always liked it. It's amazing, some of that stuff. It almost doesn't sound like guitar, some of it—especially with Steve Vai. I think that became more of the standard—a cut above your average 70s-rock riffing, which was more I would say influenced by Ted Nugent sort of style.

KIM THAYIL When I first heard Steve Vai, I was just kind of learning how to play guitar. Steve Vai, as I understood it, was nineteen years old and was discovered by Frank Zappa. And my best friend had a Zappa album, and we would listen to it, and go, 'Good God. This fucking guitarist is like … nineteen or something!' And do you know what he did to get in Zappa's band? He took 'The Black Page'* and transcribed it! We thought, 'Holy shit, this guy must be a hotshot music reader, who knows a buttload of theory.' And that was way over my head. I was sixteen and probably learning how to play 'Wild Thing' or 'Louie Louie'—I just knew a few cowboy chords or power chords.

---

* An instrumental originally arranged for drums and known for its technical complexity.

My best friend played sax, clarinet, ukulele, keyboards … he plays all single-reed instruments, but he knew a lot about classical and he was a jazz-head. And my mom was a music teacher and she played piano and was classically trained, and did the Royal Academy in London, and went to school in Bombay, India. And I thought, 'Wow, this guy is nineteen and probably well-versed in all that, but also developed an incredible ear and is able to hang with the progressive rock and jazz wildness of Zappa.' That was really heady for me as a teenager to try to understand. So I'll have the utmost respect for Steve Vai for no other reason that he made my head spin by the idea that he was playing with Zappa at such a young age.

And like I said, I'm a Zappa fan, my best friend is the hugest Zappa fan, and a lot of our friends were Zappa fans. It was a real big deal. When I think of Steve Vai, I think of his work with Frank Zappa—not of his work with Whitesnake. I think Steve Vai playing with Whitesnake is 'slumming' for him. Which I think some people do for fun, but I would discourage people from slumming—if people are great players, they should really challenge themselves and do amazing things. They should go up and ahead of their abilities, not beneath their abilities. Unfortunately, because all the money to be made was in rock'n'roll in the 80s and in the 90s—and probably to some degree in this day—if you're a guitar player and you want to make money as a guitar player, the money was in rock music. Especially in the 80s through the early 90s—with MTV and the glam bands.

So if you were a great guitar player and you wanted to make a buck, you'd knock it down a few notches and go slumming, and play well beneath your abilities. I don't know if that's a little patronizing of the market or the genre, but when people challenge themselves and play slightly above their abilities, that's where cool stuff starts happening and inventive things start happening. So I'll always think of Steve Vai in terms of the work he did with Zappa, which is very impressive. And the same with Satriani. That's not necessarily what I listen to or listen for when I'm listening to guitar generally or most of the time, and it's certainly not in my skillset, but it is something that I definitely respect and regard well. And there are contexts in which that kind of playing is beautiful and blows me away.

DUANE DENISON I liked what Vai did on that Public Image album. And I think that a lot of people who like Vai don't even know about that album. But I thought that was interesting. It wasn't my thing, but I didn't hate it. I didn't feel any need to downgrade it every chance I got, because I practiced and worked at music, so I respected it. It just wasn't our thing. At that point, we were so caught up in our own world, a lot of that went right by me. I would hear things occasionally—what I would call 'the soundman music.' You would go to the club and the soundman … it doesn't matter who's playing there, they're going to play *their music*—and it was usually stuff like that.

KIM THAYIL I have *Surfing With The Alien.* My mom sent it to me! It's something my mom would dig, because it's so musical and well recorded, and I dig it for that aspect, as well. But of course, you can see it kind of conflicts with the aesthetic I had developed listening to Black Flag and The Meat Puppets. But there's room there. There's always room to listen to some great guitar player.

BILLY CORGAN I honestly didn't pay much attention [to guitarists such as Steve Vai and Joe Satriani]. I certainly respect them, [but] I wasn't a listener. I listened to Vai very early on, and then after that, I just didn't pay any attention. I didn't follow that 'train.' I got off right about then.

DUANE DENISON Jeff Beck is one guitarist that it seems everybody respects. He somehow has endured and evolved and manages to stay relevant and cool—in a way that the other guys just don't of that era. Like, compared to the other great English guys, it seems like they all just stopped developing. And he never did. He'll drop out of sight for a while, stay home, and come up with something. The next time you see him, he's got a new thing, and it's amazing. I totally respect that.

AL JOURGENSEN I laud their professionalism and their technique and their chops, but a lot of the music actually sounds forced. What I think people rebelled against for a while is … it's a circle jerk. These guys are just trying to out-riff each other or whatever on each song, and that becomes the focal point of the song, and I think it's a very limited narrative of your creativity. Just focusing everything on one thing—as opposed to the song itself.

CHRIS HASKETT It's interesting—there's a whole era of particularly American music, that it's almost like it never happened. There's this kind of gap between the beginning of Sonic Youth and the first Lollapalooza,* and it's like, nobody has any memory of Jesus Lizard, early Sonic Youth, Bullet LaVolta, us, fIREHOSE … remember, fIREHOSE was the biggest band on college radio for, like, a decade!

---

* The then-touring music festival organized by Perry Farrell of Jane's Addiction, first held in the summer of 1991.

Good luck finding anybody under the age of thirty who has ever heard of them. And I'm not saying people should only listen to old music, but it's really weird how much history disappeared. It's almost Orwellian, because there was so much richness—there was so much fantastically amazing creative stuff going on. To me, Jesus Lizard should be a stadium band. If I see somebody wearing one of their shirts I'm like, 'Hey! Cool!' And you can tell—they're going to be a slightly bigger, bald guy my age. Invariably, it's always that.

DUANE DENISON We all kind of liked some prog rock, to be honest. And we weren't ashamed to listen to it—we liked it. When punk rock came along, we were all excited and enthused. But we didn't throw our record collections away. And as much as I liked the Pistols, The Clash, The Ramones, and Motörhead, I didn't want to play just those kind of chords and riffs. None of us did. We had already been informed by other styles. [Jesus Lizard singer] David Yow was a fusion fan, for Christ's sake! His favorite bands of all time were Led Zeppelin and Pink Floyd. So we couldn't just pretend like we had never heard that stuff, and know what the really great bands sounded like. So it was informed by that. And 'subtle' is the right word—we didn't want to be overly nerdy or prog-y about it. We did a lot of stuff with unusual time signatures, but we wanted to make sure that it rocked. It wasn't just to be tricky or to be clever. There's a way to do it and a way that still rocks. I'd like to think we did that … *at least sometimes.*

BRUCE KULICK You've got the guy in Weezer [Rivers Cuomo] who can play great guitar, too. And Billy Corgan was always an amazing lead player, from the Smashing Pumpkins. Some of them had a tremendous amount of technical ability. He just channeled it in a unique, fresh way. I'm always looking for that, but I still think when I listen to the Muse guitar player [Matt Bellamy], he's not Brian May, he's not as unique as that, but he's still approaching his music and guitar playing to that, than he is to hiding the fact that he can play, or trying to make it weird.

the **end**
of shred?

With the emergence of such back-to-basics styles as grunge and alt-rock during the early/mid 90s, was shred dead?

MARK WOOD Boy, Billy Sheehan and Steve Vai in David Lee Roth's band … I think that maneuver was the end for anybody who played fast. It was like, 'Enough of these fast notes! We have to slow it down!' And then Kurt Cobain destroyed it for everybody.

JAS OBRECHT Yngwie and the dozens of other guitarists who specialized in precise, complex, high-energy, lightning-fast solos helped ring the death knell for heavy-metal guitar, in a way.

With some players, it almost became a gymnastic competition. This, in turn, opened the door for the more song-oriented bands of the 1990s, like Nirvana, where the guitar was not the dominant focus of the music. And the changing tastes that followed contributed to the decline in fortunes and fame for many of the big hair metal guys.

WOLF MARSHALL It was time for a change after so much great guitar in the 80s, and the very early 90s. Grunge came along, and everything was very over-simplified. It was actually like an 'anti-shred' movement. Which I feel bad for people who were really just starting to get their groove in the last bit of the 80s and the early 90s—suddenly, Kurt Cobain started winning the polls and I just didn't think he was the same kind of guitarist as say, Van Halen. But that's just the nature of pop music. It became underground and I think that in many ways, it slowly swings back and forth like a pendulum.

PHIL COLLEN Same thing as that happened in England in the 70s, when the punk thing happened, and then the new wave thing. Just a period in time. In a good way. It just got so boring—all these guys doing Olympic kind of scales. It's like missing the point completely. I was overjoyed when I first heard Nirvana. I was like, 'Oh, this is refreshing!' As I did when I first heard the Sex Pistols—it was the same deal out in England. I still think Steve Jones's guitar playing on that* is some of my favorite guitar playing I've ever heard. I can still really get off on that sound. And he's a great player—he does just wonderful stuff. It's so aggressive, and he really means it. It's wonderful.

DUANE DENISON There are a lot of factors. Socio-economic factors. I just think people associated it with that glam-y hair metal from the 80s, like Poison, Cinderella, and Ratt—the big hair, colorful kind of stuff. And I think people had had enough of that. The mood had shifted in the country. And when 'Smells Like Teen Spirit' came out, that was like the rallying call. Everything changed from that point on. And I think there was other metal—whether it was Motörhead or Venom—that was more aggressive, dirty, underground, and noisy, and that never went away. But it wasn't so silly and over-the-top and 'MTV-friendly.'

The mood of the country changed and people wanted to hear something else. And then that went away, and all the grunge/underground/90s ... like, for a while, the indie-rock scene—even separate from that—was fairly hard and aggressive. Whether it was Jesus Lizard of Shellac or Cop Shoot Cop. I have Satellite Radio in my car, and when I listen to the indie stations now, it's unrecognizable when I compare it. Like, what they call 'indie rock' now is nothing ... if you want to hear music like that, you have to listen to underground metal, like High On Fire or Mastodon or something like that, to get that same kind of grind. But I just think the mood changed and the atmosphere changed, and everything changed overnight.

PAUL GILBERT I love those [shredder] guys, but I must admit at that point, I started really not paying attention as much. During that era, I was much more into *Pet Sounds* by The Beach Boys, and I was listening to the Tears For Fears' 'Sowing The

---

* *Never Mind The Bollocks, Here's The Sex Pistols* (1977).

Seeds Of Love' single, because it was such a Beatle-y thing. I was getting back into my Beatles records, and really getting away from guitar. So those [shred] artists, I know an embarrassingly small amount of their music. And it has nothing to do with the quality of it—it just has to do with where I was at, at the time.

I know 'Satch Boogie' and 'The Attitude Song,' and *Ah Via Musicom* I really liked—I did listen to that a good bit. And Stevie Ray Vaughan I liked, but somehow, I just wasn't into blues at that time—I was into pop. I was really getting into songs that had minor seventh flat fives in them. So a song like 'My Love' by Wings was just extremely fascinating to me, whereas the whole guitar thing, I just needed a break from it. You'd be surprised with how little I know of that era in terms of guitar.

TY TABOR By the end of the 80s, you had nothing but hair bands being signed, with a wannabe Eddie Van Halen guitarist. And it was just because they were shoving it down everybody's throats, as 'This is what rock will be now.' That killed rock for me. Because in the 70s, rock radio would be David Bowie doing 'Ziggy Stardust' one song, Aerosmith the next song, then Jefferson Airplane the next song. And each thing you name is entirely different from the other. Nobody sounded alike. It was, you knew who the band was the second somebody played a note.

In the 80s, *all of that died.* There was a whole period of time where if you didn't know it was a new album by whoever, it took a while to even know who the heck it was, because it might have been the same band—for a while. And I know that sounds like an old grandpa, but that's what music in rock turned into in the 80s for me—it was the most depressing time in rock music in my whole life, to date. [*Laughs*] It's been much better since then.

BLUES SARACENO [Poison guitarist; solo artist] You've got to realize, I was never a guitar guy. I was a music guy. My strength was in my musicianship more than ever my guitar playing. But I was a kid from Middletown, Connecticut, living in his parents' garage, and somebody offered me a record deal, so, 'No problem man, let's do it!' I decided, 'If they want to make me a guitar guy, then I'll be a guitar guy,' because I didn't have a ton of other opportunities at that point. So I became a guitar guy. And the funny part is ... *I'm not really a guitar guy.* [*Laughs*] Which ended up working way better, as I got into the TV and film stuff.

MIKE VARNEY It's just sad, at any point in time, there's far less people with talent than people with talent, and when the bar gets raised so high—like it was raised by Shrapnel artists and Steve Vai, Joe Satriani, Eric Johnson, and all these other guys—it only makes sense that masses without talent would say, 'We need some new heroes, because we're never going to be as good as these guys. We need to support somebody who can be playing six months, and make punk rock.' And not that all punk records are like that, but I'm just saying that the musicianship got dummied-down in the early 90s, and a lot more people leveled the playing field for a lot of people that were out of work. Because they couldn't shred and they couldn't play at a super-level, and because there were more people that wanted to play music than there were positions open for them that demanded a much higher, refined skillset. They just started doing music that was kind of anti-musicianship.

And then you find guys on my label going for auditions and practically changing their names, and for sure, hiding any arpeggios or speed picking—they have to just go with right out power chords, if they want to work. Not the main artists on my label, but some of the guys that didn't make it with Shrapnel, and still wanted to stay in the game—some of them really reinvented themselves. And they had to dummy down their playing, because it was frowned upon to be great. Look at the Olympics or look at any other sport or anything like that—you're rewarded by getting better and better. And at a certain point, this became too much for the masses to handle, so they just sort of voted it out, and made it a lot cooler to not be able to do it. But I think that's all fine. That's all evolution.

BY THE MID 90S, GUITAR SOLOS WERE FEATURED LESS OFTEN IN ROCK TUNES. NOT EVERYBODY WAS HAPPY ABOUT THAT.

DAVE MENIKETTI Didn't really love it. It was one of those kinds of things that to me, to be the ultimate guitar player was all about expression. And where's your expression? Anybody can play those chords, but unless you're doing something unique with those chords, where can you make yourself unique as a guitar player? The expressiveness of the guitar playing to me was the soloing. And you're missing this whole thing about it that is very important.

Obviously, there is amazing rhythm-chop kind of guitar playing, and there's stuff that I can't do myself that other guys can do that is just truly amazing work—either with the picking technique or whether they're using their fingers or whatever the case may be. But I'd say for me, the expressiveness and uniqueness of being your own guitar player that people know who you are as soon as they hear something being played on a song, that comes from soloing. And the approach that you give—your vibrato, your expression, whatever. So to me, that was the blandest period for guitar players. The fact that I would look at these guys live onstage and they're looking at their shoes or they've got their back to the audience and they're not playing any solos, I just felt like, '*What's the point here?*'

DUANE DENISON I think it was just a natural thing, part of because of what we liked. When we looked at the bands that we had listened to, at least when we first met—whether it was The Birthday Party or Killing Joke—solos were not a big part of it. And also, for me, Jesus Lizard was like a three-piece band with a vocalist, so if I were to solo, there was just a fairly high-end bass and a very cymbal-heavy drum kit behind me. So there wasn't a whole lot of mid-range to anchor things. I kind of felt out in the open.

Like, you'd have some really driving, powerful, textured piece going, and the guitar goes to take a solo, all that mid-range information suddenly disappears, and you've got all these high notes flying out at you, typically. It just didn't seem like a good idea. And we never voiced this, but it kind of felt like, 'Well, let's not do that. Let's be different and try to make the parts as interesting as possible, and have different variations of chord voicings and riffs, so that you don't miss that … in fact, solos would sound silly or out of place on a lot of that music.'

WOLF MARSHALL Alice In Chains and Pearl Jam did have a little bit more guitar intensity. Jerry Cantrell is a great guitar player, and I also really like Pearl Jam—they had some good stuff. Their grooves were different. They were funkier—they almost crossed over to the Red Hot Chili Peppers' territory, which is another band from that period that I think didn't really fall into the grunge thing, and they got popular because of *Blood Sugar Sex Magik*. That was a good album. It felt like a Beatles album—good songs all the way through, and the playing all matched. It was like listening to *Revolver*, and when you hear the solo in 'Taxman,' that's cool—it goes with the song.

My point is that you would have that kind of magic inside some of the bands that were really the grunge scene. So they kind of lasted a little bit longer, whereas I don't know if a lot of the grunge bands had the same following, but I think the Red Hot Chili Peppers still do. They lasted through that. And the same with Slash's band. He kept going through all that stuff—he didn't feel like he had to address that movement. Admittedly, he was at the tail end of past Van Halen and past Yngwie. He was the next guitar hero and he was already more classic than shred—he was thinking more about the great classic rock players of the 70s. Those were his favorite guys. I mean, he could do shred, but it wasn't his focus. He was more into the melodic blues-rock players.

GEORGE LYNCH I think guitar technique and guitar playing is like any other human endeavor—it's subject to boom and bust. It's like action and thinking. You seem to gravitate toward something, and then everybody latches onto it. It just falls under its own weight, eventually. It becomes a parody of itself and it becomes too much—it becomes excessive. With technique and guitar in the 80s, where rock'n'roll started out as a message-driven thing, and it's about the songs in the late 70s and 80s, and then the hair period/the metal period, and the image thing. The guitar/flamboyant/histrionic/shred-a-varius guitar playing sort of became 'the thing.'

And then it just got away from itself. It was like a runaway freight train. You get guys growing up on Yngwie, and they start with *that* and take it to the next level. It's like, 'OK. Normal people can't appreciate this. It's so far away from actually saying anything. You're not "talking guitar" anymore—it's not lyrical, it's not "Stairway To Heaven," it's not "Hotel California," it's not anything like that. It's like you're in the Olympics and you're trying to compete.' And that's not what music is about.

It reached a point of saturation … and entropy, I guess. It just can't go forward anymore—you've reached a wall. What are you going to [do], play 128th notes? I mean, it's not humanly possible to technically play that fast or listen to it … so what are you going to do? And you have this huge backlash, and everybody drops way back down toward the complete opposite end of the spectrum, and it starts evolving again, and then we repeat ourselves. We sometime make the same mistake again.

modern day

Which modern day shredders are carrying the torch for their fleet-fingered forefathers?

JEFF WATERS Personally, as a metal fan, I was worried in the 90s, when traditional metal and thrash mostly went right out. Labels started getting rid of all the metal bands, and no agents wanted to book them, and there were no places for metal bands to play. Bands like Maiden and Priest kind of stayed out of North America for years, because there was nowhere really to play. And when Priest made it back with Ripper [Owens], they were playing clubs in Vancouver, whereas a few years earlier, they were playing stadiums and arenas. So when that 'decline' of that music in North America went down, I kind of got out, too, and said, 'Nobody wants us.' It was kind of depressing, as a metal fan, for me.

And then I started hearing these bands, in 2005/2006—Michael Amott from Arch Enemy, Alexi Laiho from Children Of Bodom, and Matt Heafy and Corey Beaulieu from Trivium. We toured with Trivium for a few months in Europe in 2007, and I remember coming out of the dressing room, going sightseeing every day. And as I'd be leaving at one in the afternoon every day, you would hear these one or two kids—Matt and Corey—downloading stuff off of the internet. Scales and tab and things like that, and they'd be yelling, 'Hey Waters, come in here for a minute! Can you show us this Chris Holmes solo in this "Blind In Texas" song by W.A.S.P.? Or can you show us your "Never Neverland" solo?'

I was just smiling, because guitar players were finally realizing that it's not about the 90s where … remember, Metallica even gave up on solos. They said,

'Eh, let's not do solos.' And bands were coming out and not playing solos—kids were in high schools starting bands and not even knowing what a solo was.

And finally, people started realizing with the Internet, 'Holy crap. Randy Rhoads … listen to that guitar! Listen to Van Halen back then!' And now, kids were going, 'Oh, but to be that good and play that stuff, you've got to practice your guitar four hours a day for five years.' That's when the hope came back to me personally as a metal and metal guitar fan, when I would see these kids learning this stuff, and Alexi Laiho did not just pick that up over a couple of years—he must have been eight hours a day in his room practicing this stuff. And the same with Matt and Corey. There's lots of guitar players now that have really learned it—it's just that the business is so different, so you're not going to really hear as much about a lot of these players. It's a totally different business now.

MIKE VARNEY There's a lot of young guys between eighteen and twenty-five that are knee deep in all this stuff. I just had a meeting with a manager yesterday, he's managing a guy named Christian Robinson—this guy is like Vinnie Moore, Joey Tafolla, Tony MacAlpine, and he's eighteen years old. I put out a record two years ago with Dario Lorina,[*] and within four months of putting the record out, Zakk Wylde picked him to be in Black Label Society. So he and Zakk are out there doing acoustic gigs—the guy's playing piano and singing with Zakk, playing guitar with Zakk. This guy was twenty-three when I signed him. And I did a record with a guy named Jacky Vincent two years ago.[†] That year, in *Guitar World*, Jacky won 'Best Shred Album' and 'Best Shredder.' Jacky Vincent is a great player. And the guys in Avenged Sevenfold have done some cool stuff. There are guys in England that are just tearing it up right now. There's a whole army of young guitar players that are great out there.

MICHAEL ANGELO BATIO There's a whole movement of this whole kinda 'glam thing' going on. For example, Black Veil Brides and Falling In Reverse. Jacky Vincent, I played on his album and so did Paul Gilbert—he's on Shrapnel. He's twenty-three or twenty-four, and he's in Falling In Reverse—they're a pretty boy band, but he's a great guitarist. One of the things that I tried to do—and this is my legacy, that I feel—if you look at every other genre of music, if you look at jazz, country, orchestral music, the music is at a highest level it can be. And so is the musicianship. Where I felt that rock songwriting was at the highest level it can

* *Dario Lorina* (2013).
† *Star X Speed Story* (2013).

be. I don't think you can write much better rock songs than AC/DC or Hendrix or Zeppelin. You can write equally as good, but that's the A-list. But I felt the musicianship really wasn't there in the early days of rock. So I wanted to elevate it. I wanted to say, 'Why not have guitar playing as good as a first chair violinist in a symphony orchestra? What is wrong with that?' It doesn't change the quality of the music, but the players can be better.

In every other established genre of music, you have the best of the best—playing and writing. But rock I felt, it was more stylistic. I love Hendrix, but I wasn't really influenced by Hendrix. And here's how I'm going to answer your question—this day, metal is really alive and well. It's in the form of death metal and all these other genres. These young guitar players are the best that have ever been in rock. So when you look at the Jacky Vincents, what about Jeff Loomis from Arch Enemy? And then you can name fifty other bands—Trivium, Corey Beaulieu is a great guitarist. Who did he study? My stuff. You see these great young players today, and there are a lot of them. And what they do is they still have taken the fundamentals that we started in rock in the 80s. And you can safely say 70s, too, but I think the LA 80s scene just blew up: Vai, myself, Paul Gilbert, Tony MacAlpine; even Yngwie back then lived in LA. The LA scene was where it was at.

JOE STUMP I think it's having a bigger resurgence in the last few years, whether it's YouTube or *Guitar Hero* and all those different types of things. Or just younger players getting turned on to old school players, through their parents' records.

RON JARZOMBEK Who's totally carrying the progressive metal torch I would say is Animals As Leaders. Protest The Hero, I like what those guys are doing. Those guys don't really even solo, though—their songs are just so busy and they've got so many cool things going on. There's a lot of the YouTube guys that are getting pretty popular these days, but that's one thing that I don't like about what's happening currently with guitar—they're just playing solos over backing tracks. When I was a kid, Mike Varney discovered guitar players, and they didn't just play a solo over something—they came out with a full album, where they wrote everything, got players together, constructed parts, and did the arrangement. They did everything—they didn't just solo over something. And right now, the way a lot of guitar players are, you'll see the coming up on Facebook or YouTube, and they're just soloing.

JEFF WATSON There's some amazing players. There's a guy online named Damien

[Salazar], who plays in Brazil on the street—you can find him on YouTube—and he outplays everybody we've been talking about, to the degree that *we're* sharing his videos. I was talking to Steve Morse a couple of months ago—he was coming back from Brazil—and he said, 'I just finished this huge concert with Deep Purple. We come out and there's one way out of this stadium. All the windows are open because it's blazing hot. And there's this guy sitting on the side of the road just blazing solos over all the Deep Purple songs. I was intimidated by the guy's ability!' So if you want to look up a player that probably should get some recognition, [it's] this guy named Damien. You'll be blown away.

CHRIS CAFFERY The guys in DragonForce and the guys in Avenged Sevenfold are a couple of the best players that are actually part of bands. The same way I said for Priest and Maiden, I think they hold the torch over.

BRIAN TATLER I think Joe Bonamassa is a brilliant player. He comes from blues, but I really like what he does with the blues. It's almost like he's stolen bits from some of the greatest guitarists that have ever been, and beautifully combined them into his style. I just think it's a fabulous style he's got.

COREY BEAULIEU [Trivium guitarist] A newer player that comes to mind is Chuck Wepfer, who plays in the band The Bloodline—he's definitely an old-schooler as well, as far as the 80s kind of style of guitar playing. People looking for a new band or a new guitar player that carries the torch of that style of guitar playing, they should definitely check out The Bloodline—they have a lot of that influence of the old school way of shredding.

STEVE LYNCH Chris Broderick, I think he's a great player. Both the guys from Avenged Sevenfold* are really good players.

GARY HOEY Avenged Sevenfold, when they came out sounded like they were doing that a little bit, but now they're more 'Metallica' than that. That's a hard question, because I'm not hearing a lot of that sound when I listen to the radio. There's a new sound to the way rock sounds now, that it's not really going back to the 80s. I hear the 80s more in country music than I hear anywhere else!

---

* Zacky Vengeance and Synyster Gates.

DAVID T. CHASTAIN I don't really listen to much modern day music, but I would say Gus G. has a lot of the same attributes as the 80s players. Great vibrato, and can shred when called upon to do so.

BILLY CORGAN I don't listen to anybody. Honestly, I have no idea. I couldn't even tell you who's good anymore.

BRUCE KULICK If everybody wanted to hear the guy who is a talented shredder and it's all about shredding, I'd be scratching my head all the time. And there are a lot of new bands that have a lot of talented people in it, but I just don't get it. It goes right over my head, and they might have a singer in the band that is screaming instead of singing, and that goes over my head, too. Believe it or not, my dinner music is more Frank Sinatra, so I don't think I want to listen to a 'screaming shredder' in my free time. [*Laughs*]

JIM MATHEOS [Fates Warning, OSI guitarist; solo artist] I definitely don't listen to metal. And music in general that I listen to is not guitar-centric at all. One person I can think of that I really like as a guitar player right now is a guy named David Rawlings, who is a bluegrass player and plays with Gillian Welch and some solo stuff. He's amazing—he does some really odd stuff, some weird note choices. I like him a lot. As far as metal goes, I can't really say that there's anybody new that I listen to.

GUTHRIE GOVAN I don't really know. At this point, I'm mostly trying to avoid listening to guitar players all the time. And, in particular, if there's a guitar player who's playing a million notes and they're using a lot of overdrive, I don't really want to listen to it. Partially because it might color what I'm trying to do, and I want to keep whatever it is that I'm doing fresh, and not informed by whatever anybody else is doing in the same genre. But also, I find it harder to listen to that stuff and just derive honest enjoyment from it, because to some extent, it reminds me of work. And I sometimes find it hard to listen to modern—dare I say—'advanced' guitar players, without hearing the lineage in what they're doing, without trying to guess where they borrowed a lick from. Sometimes, it's more fun for me to listen to a sax player or to listen to electronic music, where I don't know how it's done.

STEVE LYNCH Another guitarist is Guthrie Govan—he's a brilliant player. I don't know if you've ever seen him play fretless guitar, but it's pretty amazing to watch him. He's just a really tasty player. He's one of those that is up-and-coming—he's more known in Europe right now than he is in the States. But I think it's just a matter of time before people are really going to recognize him.

GUTHRIE GOVAN I started playing when I was three, and I grew up in a rock'n'roll house—I was listening to a lot of pre-army Elvis, Chuck Berry, and stuff like that. And going through my parents' record collection—Hendrix, Cream, and stuff of that nature. So my background as a kid thirsty for more knowledge was more coming from the guitar tradition of my parents' generation. So when I discovered at the age of thirteen or fourteen that there was this world of hard rock and heavy metal guys doing preposterous new things on the guitar, my main interest was in trying to absorb some of this new vocabulary. To learn different things that were possible to do on the instrument, that I wouldn't have learned about from my parents' record collection.

So I was never that crazy about a lot of the heavy metal stuff that the older kids at school would play for me. In many cases, I was wading through the heavy metal to get to the guitar solo and work out what the soloist was doing. The people who were notably exempt from that would be Yngwie. I know it's fashionable to challenge Yngwie these days—in some ways, you can argue he's become an easy target—but I remember hearing him for the first time and not only hearing preposterous loads of technique but also hearing the real passion. Just the way he was digging into notes and the vibrato he had, seemed very expressive and very fiery. To me, it sounded like someone who really had something to say. So he stood out from the crowd for me, instantly—'This guy's the real deal. He means what he's playing.' In the same way that 60s Clapton meant what he was playing—he's an angry young man, he's showing off, but it's not technique for technique's sake. There's some genuine, fire-breathing energy that he's trying to convey here.

Van Halen, obviously, you have to love what Eddie did. In retrospect, I think the stuff that was most exciting about Eddie was his tone and his rhythm playing. He figured out a way to make a one-guitar rock lineup sound completely self-contained, and the guitar was this versatile creature that could go from outlining the harmony to doing the pyrotechnics and then going back to the rhythm part. And it was all part of the same, inter-connected fabric of guitar playing. So with Van Halen, I was never listening to the song and waiting for the guitar solo, because he was doing the right thing for the song all the way through. And that made an impact on me.

I also have to say Steve Vai. The way I would normally explain it in an interview is: Steve Vai found all these horrible noises on the guitar, and if anyone else made them, it would be a mistake. But Steve found a way to welcome all of these outrageous noises into the official dictionary of guitar player language. So he made the dictionary of what we were allowed to do as guitar players a whole lot bigger. And I love that there was a sense of humor there. I love the fact that you could hear he was coming from the world of Zappa. Zappa is a huge deal in my musical cosmos.

HERMAN LI Alexi Laiho, I guess, is our generation—he's definitely one of the guitar heroes now. Tosin Abasi from Animals As Leaders. Guthrie Govan is really good. I saw Angel Vivaldi recently—he was awesome. He played well and looked great onstage—his stage presence. Jacky Vincent, he was playing in Falling In Reverse— he brought shredding into that kind of genre that they usually don't do it. He even had a Shrapnel instrumental album!

COREY BEAULIEU Alexi from Children Of Bodom—he's definitely got the 80s flair in his playing. A lot of the newer bands are into more of the 'djent' stuff. The guitar playing in that doesn't remind me of the 80s era of guitar solos, but it's great that there are so many technically proficient guitar players out nowadays— definitely a lot more than there were ten years ago. People playing solos and having musicianship in metal again is definitely welcomed.

CARRYING THE TORCH?

ALEXI LAIHO I wouldn't name myself as somebody who carries anything, but I've been told by a lot of pretty amazing dudes that I am definitely one of those guys who carries the torch. It's nice to get a compliment like that from guys like Zakk Wylde. It was amazing how guitar players—especially lead guitar players—had such a huge role [in the 80s]. They were there with the singer of the band. *They were that important.* And it was essential to have an awesome lead guitar player in a band, if you were going to make it. To me, it's something that was very appealing. Those are the sort of bands that I grew up with. Basically, anybody that was involved with Ozzy Osbourne, like Randy Rhoads, Jake E. Lee, and Zakk Wylde. And of course Steve Vai. It's just the fact that I think the 80s guitar players, they were so extreme. And it just seemed to be very competitive.

COREY BEAULIEU I can't really say if we're 'carrying the torch.' I guess other people can say that. But we definitely carry the influence from that era. Growing up, that was the era of bands that we grew up on—cut our teeth on—playing guitar. I got into hard rock/heavy metal by hearing Guns N' Roses, and I wanted to pick up a guitar from hearing Metallica for the first time. And pretty much grew up on the 80s thrash movement, Iron Maiden, Judas Priest, Yngwie Malmsteen, and even some of the hair-metal stuff—George Lynch from Dokken was a huge influence. Even having Joe Satriani's *Surfing With The Alien* and Steve Vai's *Passion And Warfare*, growing up as a teenager in the 90s, when it was more stripped back—there was grunge and nu-metal.

There weren't really the guitar heroes of the 80s when I was growing up. So I went back to an era to find the music that as a guitar player and music fan, I wanted to hear. I loved big riffs and guitar solos. That was the era that had the quintessential guitar hero era. Even from when we started, that sound and what those bands did laid the blueprint for what we loved as musicians and we would incorporate that into our music. When we first came out on *Ascendancy*,[*] that was right around the time that guitar solos came back into fashion, and we were doing that, and that was just from what we love about heavy metal and what the bands we listened to did. That's what we wanted to do.

HERMAN LI I have heard that from even some of the guys that I look up to. It's a cool thing. When we first came out, no one was really doing solos. And now, it's cool again, apparently—you see people doing it again in so many bands. We're honored if they give us that mention.

ADAM DUTKIEWICZ [Killswitch Engage guitarist] I never claimed to be a shredder, that's for sure. I'm more of a jack of all trades/master of none kind of guy. But I like playing metal and rock guitar. It's fun. Solos can be pretty fun to play.

RON 'BUMBLEFOOT' THAL I think there's a whole bunch of us carrying the torch, and there will be more after us. There are so many young dudes that will have very long stretches making music; that will inspire a whole generation after them. I am a singer-songwriter who plays guitar, that is just trying to make as many people happy as possible—that's really ultimately what it is. That's really the truth with how I see myself. I think others see it differently, but that's how I see it all.

---

[*] Trivium's second album, released in 2005.

GUTHRIE GOVAN I like being able to defend the idea of having technique, or playing lots of notes—as long as it's sincere. Because when anything gets as involved and crazy as technical guitar playing did in 80s/90s rock, there is always going to be a backlash. You might even argue that grunge saved the day, and somebody had to intervene, before anything caught fire! Something needed to be 'reset' there. But there's been this lasting stigma ever since, that if you're a rock guitar player, and you try too hard or you play too many notes or you're in some way over-achieving, that's supposed to be an offensive thing.

And I think it's a shame that there's so many music critics out there who will dismiss all technical playing in the same fell swoop. Because I don't think it should be like that. I think everyone had a certain kind of music they hear in their head, and their role is to express that as honestly as possible. Some of us hear a million notes a second and some of us hear one note a minute. I don't want to hear B.B. King shredding, neither do I want to hear Yngwie trying not to shred. It's all about being true to yourself. So I'll try and carry a little bit or a torch for that, I guess. Try to preserve the credibility of having some headroom in your technique in a rock guitar context.

MIKE VARNEY To me, the instrumental thing is great, but ultimately, it gets down to a guy probably singing and having some songs, because it seems like the fan base is there for all this stuff, but for whatever reason, the demographic or the times, people are getting into music in different ways other than buying it. That's what makes it difficult. I go to meet this manager who's got a great young guitar player, but now, it's like, 'People love it, but who's willing to pay for it?' When you can go listen to a Joe Satriani song on Pandora and get a lot of this stuff for free, or go on YouTube and get everything you want for free.

The real challenge will be, going forward—how will people make money and justify investing in records from label standpoints, when the record seems to be nothing more than a calling card to help the artist to tour and sell merchandise? Maybe when Spotify gets enough subscribers they will be able to pay enough money back to the various artists that are still going strong but are not household names, but people are listening to them every day. I've got artists whose records are out of print, and they get played more on some of these sites than the records I put out yesterday! There seems to be some longevity, but where will the money come to support these artists that are out there giving their heart and soul to it? That's the question. I have some degree of faith that it will work itself out. But in the meantime, it's hard on everybody.

STEVE LYNCH I'm glad to see it's really coming back. And you can see now, a lot of these players—these young kids, sitting in their bedrooms in Japan—are just ripping it up. Or anywhere in the world—it could be Norway, anywhere in Europe or America. Where they're ripping up Steve Vai stuff like there's nothing to it. Or Joe Satriani, or Yngwie, or any of these guys. It's like the previous players put it out there into the ether, and these other kids now are picking up on it, because it's already out there. I'm a true believer in that—that you put it out there, and other people pick up on it. And that's been proven, time and time again.

standout
players, A–M

What made certain guitarists special?
Part 1

REB BEACH [WINGER]

STEVE LYNCH Reb Beach had that real melodic/legato sound, [like] Allan Holdsworth had. I thought he was a brilliant player. Some of the songs where he just cut loose at the end of the song really showed what a good player he really was. I think that they probably weren't as big of an influence as Eric Johnson, Joe Satriani, and Steve Vai, but they had their own core of people that really appreciated their playing and were a big influence on them.

ADRIAN BELEW [KING CRIMSON]

STEVE STEVENS I actually saw them at the Savoy Theatre in New York on that first tour that they did.* When I've met Adrian Belew and Tony Levin, I mentioned I was at that show, and they both said, 'That was probably the best show that we played on that entire tour.' They were astounding. I always loved Fripp and I was aware of Adrian from Frank Zappa, as well. And, once again, two really innovative guys, making great music. Fripp kind of reinvented himself for that version of King Crimson, in that kind of mathematical/arpeggio style.

It's very 'math' guitar, which I thought was amazing for a guitar player to

---

* The first tour by the *Discipline*-era lineup of King Crimson—Fripp, Belew, Bruford, and Levin—in 1981.

totally reinvent himself based on inviting another guitar player to come into the band, with a very unique style with Adrian. I saw Adrian's very first solo tour, and he's one of those guitar players—certainly at that time … I saw him at the Bottom Line, and I was maybe ten feet away from him, and couldn't figure out how he was doing any of the sounds that he was doing. So off from what you'd normally expect from a guitar player. But also what's great about Adrian is, he still maintains when he goes to his clean guitar style, he's got one foot in that Hendrix door, that kind of Strat, beautiful, single-coil sound, as well. He's as unorthodox and orthodox as you can be at the same time.

CHRIS HASKETT When *Discipline* came out, that just blew everybody's mind. Because at that point, that was the third incarnation of King Crimson, and I was a huge fan of the first, and especially the second one. Because in The Rollins Band, that trio—*Larks' Tongues In Aspic*, *Starless And Bible Black*, and *Red*—that's the aesthetic, that's the underlying background against what I was writing all those riffs. It's dark, it's evil, it's fast, and it's heavy. I can so easily hear Henry [Rollins] singing on *Starless*—you can take John Wetton off and put Henry on it, and it would sound completely natural.

But *Discipline*, also, because Belew was already a hero from the Zappa days, and he's already been with Talking Heads by then, and Bowie. It's an amazing combination. And *Discipline* was the first of three of those [80s-era Crimson] records—*Discipline*, *Beat*, and *Three Of A Perfect Pair*. It's interesting because, going from that kind of sludgy, dark, heavy, thickness of *Red*, to that crystalline, purity … because they were both using Roland JC-120s, which were new at that point, and it's really clean and very crisp playing. But again, it's one of those things that I went, 'That's amazing … *I can't do that.*' [*Laughs*] But they stayed on the turntable for a long time.

STEVE HACKETT Adrian was very good with King Crimson. I enjoyed his work very much. I thought perhaps he was probably the most innovative. I think of him really coming to the forefront during that time, whereas I think for me, the 1970s was when I first arrived on the scene. In a way, I think Adrian's playing was something that would often stray over into his sense of humor. Very innovative, but in a sense, there was something quirky about it, that raised a smile. Almost at times as if it was a caricature of what the guitar could do, and I thought it was a very good approach.

NUNO BETTENCOURT [EXTREME]

GUTHRIE GOVAN For the same reason I enjoyed Eddie Van Halen, Nuno was one of the most tight, in-time, funky, in-the-pocket players of that whole generation. He was the tightest player in Extreme. There was just something about his timing that had total conviction. I guess that band had found a cool way to crystalize certain heavy metal/grandstanding chops based things with an understanding of hard rock meets funk grooviness. They found a good blend. It was a different way to present some of the circus tricks that guitar players were expected to do between the 80s and 90s. I liked the funkiness of it, I liked Nuno's tone— there was something very honest about it. He wasn't hiding behind anything. It was very dry. It was like, 'Here's what it sounds like when you're standing in a room with my amp. *There's nothing between the guitar and the amp.*' That kind of honesty sonically is always a good thing for me. I enjoy hearing what a player really sounds like.

CASPAR BRÖTZMANN [CASPAR BRÖTZMANN MASSAKER]

DUANE DENISON A guy who disappeared, who I thought was going to take over the world in the 90s, was Caspar Brötzmann. He's from Berlin, and his father was a famous free-jazz saxophonist—Peter Brötzmann. He comes from a music family, and they used to call him 'Adolf Hendrix,' because he's German and played a Strat through Marshalls. Really noisy. He had a couple of albums out, and everybody was influenced by him, whether it was Sonic Youth … everybody would go see him. And I don't know what happened to him. He just disappeared. He got some coverage in the guitar mags back in the day.

BUCKETHEAD [GUNS N' ROSES, PRAXIS, SOLO ARTIST]

JAS OBRECHT Buckethead is an extraordinary player, one of the best natural guitarists on the planet. When I began seeing him play around San Francisco with The Deli Creeps in the late 1980s, I thought he was taking shred to a new level. He's also an extremely sensitive player, capable of composing such achingly beautiful songs as 'I Love My Parents.' His choice to perform in a mask is brilliant—to his fans, he hasn't aged a day since 1989.

RON 'BUMBLEFOOT' THAL There were a bunch of guys that grew up on the same kind of stuff. There was me, Buckethead, Mattias Eklundh, Christophe Godin, Guthrie Govan. We were all from the same generation, and I think we all probably drew from the same inspirations and influences.

I met Buckethead in the late 90s at a NAMM show, and I saw him the next year, and he had a copy of my album, *Hands*, and asked me if I would sing on some of his stuff. And I was like, 'Yeah! That would be fun.' So I remember I tried calling him, no answer. Tried again later, no answer. It seemed like he just went off the grid. And then I found out that he had joined Guns N' Roses. I was like, 'Ah, OK. *That explains it.*' I guess we would have worked together in the late 90s, if life took a different turn. But he's phenomenal. Very identifiable. Of course, the chromatic tapping riffs, the use of the whammy pedal, and the killswitch. Those three things, you put those together, and you have all the main ingredients right there. From there, you take Paul Gilbert–style picking riffs, and put those in there. But he's a guy who's capable of playing any style of music and doing anything with anyone and making it sound right.

MICHAEL 'WÜRZEL' BURSTON, PHIL 'WIZZÖ' CAMPBELL, 'FAST' EDDIE CLARKE, BRIAN 'ROBBO' ROBERTSON [MOTÖRHEAD]

DUANE DENISON ['Fast' Eddie Clarke] could play with finesse and some technique, but at the same time, would grind it out and wasn't afraid to just play rhythm. And actually, even the guys who came after him, like Würzel … there was a time where they were a four-piece, with two guitars,* and that was awesome. The other night, I listened to a lot of Motörhead in honor of Phil Taylor passing away†—much to my wife and daughter's dismay—really loud in the basement, while drinking. And I was like, 'Man … *that stuff sounds good.*' There's no one really like them.

VIVIAN CAMPBELL [DIO, WHITESNAKE, DEF LEPPARD]

CRAIG GOLDY Regardless of the war that him and Ronnie had together … I know the background of how it started and why it began, and I wish it didn't get as heated. But Vivian Campbell is a great guitar player. He was part of that sound, because *Holy Diver*, and *The Last In Line* had a different sound. He was part of a band that created its own sound and he had his own way. And a lot of it was also help from Ronnie, because I know that Ronnie made most of the decision-making

---

* Würzel and Wizzö, who played together in the four-piece lineup of Motörhead during the 80s and 90s.

† Motörhead's drummer, also known as 'Philthy Animal,' died on November 11 2015.

in that band. But at the same time, he also wanted people to shine. And he shined. He shined above many.

STEVE CLARK, PHIL COLLEN, PETE WILLIS [DEF LEPPARD]

BRIAN TATLER I liked Def Leppard when they appeared. I probably first heard them on Radio One—they did some session for somebody. I remember thinking, 'They've got some great riffs.' There was a track called 'Answer To The Master,' and thinking, 'Oh, that's good,' and I taped it. And then there was the EP,* and I bought a copy of that somewhere, and liked 'Getcha Rocks Off.' I thought both guitarists were good—good solos, good riffs. I was always into *riffs*—a band like Black Sabbath or Led Zeppelin could come up with great riffs. And I felt Def Leppard had great riffs. I remember trying to figure out how to play 'Wasted' and 'Getcha Rocks Off.'

I thought Phil Collen was a superior player to Pete Willis, to be honest.† I'd seen them with Pete Willis, and then I'd seen Girl,‡ and I thought he was a good player. And we'd done some gigs with Girl, and we'd met Phil Collen backstage. I remember we had a little jam in a dressing room in London or somewhere, and showed each other a few licks. He was a really, really nice guy. So when he got the job in Def Leppard, I thought, 'They've obviously picked this guy because (a) he's really good, and (b) he's really nice. And now they're going to get on with him and he's not going to turn into a monster six months later.' It made perfect sense—that decision to choose him.

PHIL COLLEN Steve's playing was very underrated. And I think Steve had a very similar thing to Jimmy Page, where it was more about the kind of stuff he would do—it wasn't stock, it wasn't standard by any stretch. He played this stuff, and you'd go, 'Wow. I've never heard that before. I've never heard that progression, I've never heard that signature of whatever you're playing.' And that was great. There are so many guitar players who can play guitar, and it's kind of boring. It's like listening to someone who can sing all these scales, and you'd rather hear Aretha Franklin or someone who's just got this soul and vibe. And that's what Steve had. He had a real uniqueness to his style.

He'd come in with these ideas and it would blow me away. I'd go, 'Wow!

---

* *The Def Leppard EP* (1979).
† Collen replaced Willis in 1982.
‡ Collen's earlier band.

Where did you get that from?' 'Oh, I don't know. I just thought of it last night.' So that was the thing. And again, Jimmy Page. Everyone goes, 'Yeah, guitar playing.' But Jimmy's genius was *the songs*—the structure, the production, the measures, the signatures, what he's actually playing melodically and rhythmically. It's not standard by a long shot. It comes from everything—it's blues, jazz, rock, folk music. It's everything incorporated. It's so open-minded. I do find there is a closed-mindedness, especially to rock music. A lot of people are close-minded in their lives and their lifestyles, as well. I think if you look at it from that point of view, then the music is never open to other stuff. And Jimmy Page—as with Steve—the more you let in, the more you put out.

KURT COBAIN [NIRVANA]

KIM THAYIL I think he definitely is underrated. In many cases, he's underrated amongst certainly musicians and guitarists who perhaps think that his soloing doesn't show proficiency. But I'd want them to understand that context of our scene and our genre, and to know where Nirvana came from, or where Soundgarden came from, or Mudhoney, and understand that context. And within that context, you cannot imagine those solos being anywhere different to fit those songs and to fit Kurt's voice. You can play a nice melodic solo if you want to that's coherent, and repeatable. But it's not going to have that tension and that angularity and the emotiveness that is present in Kurt's voice. And it makes entire sense that the guitar is approached and performed in a similar fashion.

I know that a lot of metal dudes who are more oriented toward proficiency see him as kind of crude and rudimentary—at least as a soloist, and perhaps as a guitarist. But that's just not the case. And I think there are journalists who can flow between various genres and understand how the genres, subcultures, and subgenres in rock all relate and where they come in terms of history. Really good rock journalists understand this—they understand the lineage and how things are connected. And there's the art aesthetic: that totally embraces Kurt's soloing, because it's emotive or it's impressionistic—similar to what many of our solos are.

Soundgarden probably have a greater spectrum, compositionally, than Nirvana does, and we have a greater variety of songs stylistically and compositionally that grabs the function of proficiency or our style of writing—the fact that we have four different writers. But given that spectrum, we come from and understand the general aesthetic, which was popularized by Nirvana. We certainly were part of the scene that initiated that.

I think he's underrated amongst musicians who perhaps may not see the proficiency in the way he played and perhaps may not appreciate the technique of his guitar playing, and may not see a challenge in it over the course of the learning and experimentation of an established or developing guitarist, even. But certainly from the artist's perspective of applying it to popular culture, it is definitely great, and in terms of rock history and interconnectedness of the various subgenres, it's very important. So, overrated in some fields and underrated in others—but definitely great, regardless.

CURT KIRKWOOD I thought he was great. I still do. It's something where he didn't step out of what he did. You never feel uncomfortable, you never feel like he missed it. He didn't shoot too high. And it still blows my mind how well worked out the stuff is—and a big part of it is the guitar sound. I think he had a really good left hand*—getting down to the rhythm. He was one of the best guitar players around, and I wouldn't say he played a lot of leads or anything, but his right hand was like a clamp for doing chords. I saw similarities there—I always thought James Hetfield was a great guitar player that way, too, with the chords. Just an assuredness and just grabbing it real hard there, and the hand locking on to where it's just an amazing sound. Like a machine—but not mechanical. 'No holes' is what I always saw with Cobain. Because it's pretty simple, a lot of it. I don't know if he's underrated, but people don't talk about it much—they don't say, 'Oh, what a great guitar player.' That's a big part of it. The guitar was badass in that stuff. Johnny Ramone, too—no holes there, just about perfect every time.

HARRY CODY [SHOTGUN MESSIAH]

STU HAMM Harry had a really cool sound and great attitude. Everything I'd throw at him, he'd bounce back. On the song 'If You're Scared, Stay Home!' from *The Urge*, he plays some great stuff on. Really melodic. He was in that band Shotgun Messiah, that Relativity Records put a lot of money into, thinking they were going to be the next Guns N' Roses or something. And he was a really cool guy—he didn't have any of that rock-star vibe of some of the other guys that I worked with. You listen back to him, and he's got a really unique sound and style. The last time I saw him, he was in Florida—years and years ago—and he was working for a record company.

---

* Cobain played guitar left-handed.

BILLY CORGAN [SMASHING PUMPKINS]

BRUCE KULICK You think of him because of the way his voice and those songs and all the controversy around the Smashing Pumpkins. But the more I've read about the guy, the more I realized he is quite an accomplished guitar player. You had plenty of these guys in these alternative bands that are actually accomplished on their instrument. And they're not featured in the way that Eddie Van Halen is, but they can hold their own if their music was to showcase it. But they choose to write different kinds of styles. So that's why we don't we talk about them the same way.

DEAN DELEO [STONE TEMPLE PILOTS]

CURT KIRKWOOD He has a classical tonal beauty. A sense of composition that's super simple—he never takes it too far. It's perfect. Something like the song 'Vasoline' off of *Purple* is a great example of a cool little snatch of solo that he does in there, that is just himself. I've talked to him about it, and he said one time, 'Guitar has to have a little bit of the blues in it. If you're going to play rock guitar, it still has to have some of it in it.' But it's a little more exotic—really kind of understated. Like I said, he never really dicks around too much, but has an amazing tone. He's one of those people that figured it out and was born with that in his hands. He's got a really bluesy approach to rhythm—it's like a little behind the beat, it's not pushing it. Which makes it a big part of the groove.

WARREN DEMARTINI [RATT]

ROSS THE BOSS I think his tone was really pretty brilliant. I think he didn't overplay, he had a very nice taste—a nice use of notes and patterns. A very unique sound, and a sound that you knew it was him playing. I liked Ratt—when Ratt songs came over the radio, they were really good.

VERNON REID [Living Colour guitarist; solo artist] Lyrical. Just very lyrical. I thought he told a story. Him and Randy Rhoads, they told a story in their playing.

GARY HOEY Warren DeMartini was a great player—he was in the George Lynch era, but what separated Warren from so many others was his vibrato, and his tone was unique. He took his time with solos, great phrasing. I always felt his solos were mixed too low and the drums were too loud on Ratt albums … but maybe that's because I'm a guitar player! [*Laughs*]

MICHAEL DENNER, HANK SHERMANN [MERCYFUL FATE]

JIM MATHEOS I guess it was a combination really of the lead playing, which, to me, was extremely melodic, which I always look for. And probably more important was the writing—the way they wrote the songs, structured them; the guitar players were almost always doing two different things. A lot of counterpoint going on, which was really new at that time in metal. So that was just a huge influence on us. Those guys weren't by any mean shredders—they were more melodic. That's always the stuff that I lean toward.

HANK SHERMANN The cool thing about it is, Michael and I have this natural chemistry, and we compliment each other very well. He is like the super natural born talent. I rate him up there with Michael Schenker—in terms of what he is able to do with the tone and the way he played the melodies. Whereas, myself, I'm more aggressive and I need to fight more for it, I have to rehearse more for it. I have to do everything much more in order to at least keep up.

Michael is just a natural-born talent—very tasteful. Even though it's very aggressive, he's very calm when he plays the solos. So in that respect, we really fit each other well—he takes care of all the melodic parts and I can go a little more nuts. And also, when we play two harmony guitars, in more of a Thin Lizzy approach, that is something that has been composed that way. We're having a lot of fun. A lot of bands these days play kind of the same style, and you can't tell the difference. Me and Michael have different tones, different background, and different talents.

DUANE DENISON [JESUS LIZARD, TOMAHAWK]

CHRIS HASKETT He's fantastic. I have happy envy, because he can play anything—he went off and played with Hank Williams III. I love Jesus Lizard. He's got the whole thing—he's got the chops, he's got the timber, and he's got the taste. Those riffs are fantastic. 'Then Comes Dudley' is amazing. Jesus Lizard are one of my favorite American bands of all time. And if you go off and listen to the stuff he was playing with Hank Williams III, you go, 'He can't be good at both these things … that's not fair to the rest of us!' I remember seeing the Jesus Lizard at the old 9:30

Club in DC, and just being blown away. The first time I saw them, I was like, 'I hope they're good.' And they were as good as you'd hope they'd be.

AL DI MEOLA [RETURN TO FOREVER, SOLO ARTIST]

JOE STUMP That's why I went to Berklee, because Al went there—and all I wanted to do was play guitar. At the time, I remember being in my friend's basement, and my friend's older brother had Al Di Meola's *Elegant Gypsy*, and he put on 'Race With The Devil,' and at the time, you had UFO-era Schenker and Rainbow-era Blackmore. I loved those guys, but when you heard Al play, he was one of the first guys I ever heard playing on a whole other level of blazing fast technique—with the distorted guitar tone. I was knocked out.

STEVE LYNCH When I first heard Al Di Meola, you didn't hear very many people that picked that fast, and I really liked the sound that he got, because he played out of the Phrygian mode, and he used the harmonic minor more, so it had more of a Spanish sound. And that really appealed to me. There weren't very many people—there was Alvin Lee from Ten Years After, who was a really fast picker, there was John McLaughlin, who could hit really fast, and Robert Fripp, and Adrian Belew. But he really made that whole Spanish style of guitar—with the really quick picking—real popular.

DIMEBAG DARRELL [PANTERA, DAMAGEPLAN]

CHRIS CAFFERY He was one of those people that had a particular sound that you knew it was him. He took heavy metal and the essence of thrash metal, and turned it into this really cool power metal. I don't really consider Pantera thrash or speed metal. I just consider them really aggressive power metal. His playing and his brother's drumming and the voice and that whole vibe of Pantera, it was a big, giant middle finger from the state of Texas. They just went out and they out-heavied everybody. He didn't really have to play lead in his music to get his reputation, but he was a badass lead player. He didn't feature himself as a lead player, but when he did, it was anything he wanted. He was a lightning fast player. He was very fluid, but he was more into laying back and writing these riffs from hell with his brother, and just having this really super heavy band, that onstage would destroy anybody.

TY TABOR I think Dime was unbelievable. Dime was a friend of mine. We knew

Who says bassists can't tap?
Billy Sheehan with two hands
on the neck.

OPPOSITE George Lynch shredding on a Les Paul alongside Lynch Mob singer Oni Logan. ABOVE Racer X and Mr. Big's Paul Gilbert. LEFT TNT's Ronni Le Tekrø.

One of the few alt-rockers not opposed to good old fashioned shredding, Smashing Pumpkins' Billy Corgan.

ABOVE One of Dimebag Darrell's favorite guitarists, Ty Tabor of King's X. **RIGHT** The world's first heavy metal violinist, Mark Wood.

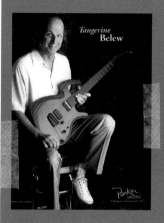

CLOCKWISE FROM LEFT More ads, this time featuring Lita Ford, Adrian Belew, Children of Bodom's Alexi Laiho, and DragonForce's Herman Li.

RIGHT The man who single handedly kept shred alive during the lean '90s, Pantera's Dimebag Darrell. **BELOW** Even more vintage ads! Jennifer Batten, Greg Howe, and Living Colour's Vernon Reid.

Jennifer Batten and Friends
Ibanez 540S

Ibanez

I love hot is hot.

HAMER USA

each other for many, many years. Our bands started back around 1980 or so. I remember seeing Pantera at a little club in Houston in the mid 80s, doing [songs by] Loverboy and stuff like that—in spandex! They were doing the same stuff we were doing, when I first met those guys, which was cover tunes and occasionally throw something in if you can get away with it. When *Cowboys From Hell* came out, all I know is the next time I saw Dime, I was just like, 'Man, where did that come from?! What the heck happened to you guys? This is unbelievable!' We were friends through all the albums. Dime came to several shows, hung out with us; we shut down clubs and closed the doors, and just hung out for hours. But I had huge respect for him. He had incredible feeling. He was the real deal. He knew what was important about guitar. He didn't just get up there and try to show off. He had the ability to, but he played with purpose. And that's why I admire what he did in that genre. He was a true artist in that genre.

KARL SANDERS You cannot deny his influence on modern guitar playing. I saw him play several times with Pantera, and it always seemed like he was taking what was on the record and somehow exploding it into much, much more. It was almost like he was more than one guitar player—contained within one human being. Mind-blowing to see live. It's undeniable—Dimebag brought a wave of popularity back to Dean Guitars. But that's not why I played them—I played them because when I went to Thoroughbred Music in Tampa, and picked up a Dean guitar, it could do what I needed it to do. It was a *metal guitar*. So I started playing it, Dimebag be damned—I didn't care what he played. I'm not that kind of guy to necessarily get sucked up or caught up in emulating my heroes. I played them because they were great guitars and I loved them and I grew to love the company.

MARK WOOD His whammy bar and Whammy Pedal, he was doing violin-like techniques. I don't know if you've read the bass player's book,[*] in that period of time, it's astounding how much they did under the influence of drugs and alcohol! Unbelievable how Dimebag was able to comprehend and get around that instrument so brilliantly. That's the prodigy that he was.

K.K. DOWNING, GLENN TIPTON [JUDAS PRIEST]

RON JARZOMBEK Mostly, it was Glenn Tipton. Just his writing and his playing—

---

[*] Rex Brown with Mark Eglinton, *Official Truth, 101 Proof: The Inside Story Of Pantera* (2013).

that was my big hero. I still have his haircut, too! [*Laughs*] I think him and K.K., I don't know who was responsible for specific tunes, but if you take a song like 'Sinner' or 'Tyrant,' or any of the early Priest, before they went through their 'commercial' phase, they just took everything up a notch. Black Sabbath set it all up, and then Priest came out and took things up to a higher level. Tipton's solos were always awesome, and just the writing.

And then *Stained Class* came out and every song on that album was just totally bitching. With *British Steel* and all that, then things kind of got a little too normal. But mainly the albums *Sin After Sin* and *Stained Class* were favorites of mine. Then they had some really cool songs, like 'Delivering The Goods.' But a lot of the guitar solo stuff that they did on 'Tyrant' was awesome. Just good songs—'Victim Of Changes,' 'Ripper,' 'Island Of Domination.' And of course, their playing was also part of that. The collective everything they were doing had a really big influence on me. You can't really put Glenn Tipton up against Yngwie or somebody like that. But when you take everything that he's done—including all the songs—then the weight gets kind of shifted.

CHRIS CAFFERY Actually, in the 80s as well, there were a couple of guitar duos that really inspired people—that being Glenn Tipton–K.K. Downing and Adrian Smith–Dave Murray. Priest and Maiden were playing a huge influence on a lot of different metal players at that time, as well. Judas Priest, in essence, invented thrash metal. That song 'Exciter' was really one of the first—other than 'Fast As A Shark' by Accept—of the first so-called speed-metal songs. I don't consider Queen a speed-metal band, but 'Stone Cold Crazy' kind of had that little thrash stutter to it. But Judas Priest, when I saw them open up for Kiss at the first concert I ever saw, looking at K.K. Downing, with the leather and the Flying V, *Priest was really cool.* More so than even just the playing. Tipton and Downing, they were just badass stage performers.

K.K. DOWNING For the most part, I remembered Glenn saying he fancied this and this solo, and I was just relaxed and laid back, and thought, 'Fine, as long as we play more or less an equal amount of time.' I was never that bothered about it. I realize now that Glenn picked up on the stuff that was more maybe commercial or melodic to solo over. But there were exceptions—'Painkiller' being one of them. But it was fairly obvious that I had the task of playing the solos that were more difficult to play over, because a two-note structure, it's pretty tough to play over, because there's a lot less to harmonize with.

Where, for example, something like 'Sinner'—which is just basically E and D, going backward and forward—it was a much more difficult task. But I kind of liked that, thinking, 'How do I make this work? How can I keep people's interest? What can I do over this solo that's going to add something to the song?' And that's kind of what happened, really. There are lots of solos that I did that were more of a task I think really—which was fine, because I liked to take on that challenge.

DR. KNOW [BAD BRAINS]

VERNON REID Dr. Know, he is special because the Bad Brains, they were influenced by … and this is really important—hardcore owes a great debt to jazz-fusion. Hardcore owes a great debt to Mahavishnu Orchestra. If you listen to *The Inner Mounting Flame*, that's really like, *punk-jazz*. And I think he was very influenced by that and Return To Forever. They play very different music, but Dr. Know brought those influences into the mix.

THE EDGE [U2]

JOE SATRIANI You'd have to say that The Edge from U2 really had a super effect on guitar playing. And this is not that small group of players, let's say, that I would say I was a part of just as a fan. I was really thinking about playing a lot, and I wanted to be focused on the greatest kind of accomplishments in electric guitar. And then along comes a new sensation that really appeals to every man and woman—not just the guitar crazies. And I think that The Edge had a lot to do with that.

That guitar sound was something that normal people really loved. They loved the way he weaved his guitar sound into a song, and it was still a rock band. It was still four guys in a band, just playing. I think that had a very big, big impact on guitar in the 80s. Certainly on the sales of the instruments that The Edge was playing, certainly on the amplifiers—just what it did for resurrecting the [Vox] AC30. He kind of did to that what Brian May did to the AC30. So yeah, I would say when you look at guitarists in the 80s, it's very easy to say, Randy and Eddie and Yngwie and Vai and George Lynch and guys like that. But you can't discount Stevie Ray Vaughan and The Edge—they almost just *owned* that decade.

TY TABOR He wasn't an influence on me, but I recognized him as being an influence, and having a huge impact on a change in guitar style, and where music went. He certainly changed music in a major way, because after he got popular, there were a whole group of bands with 'The Edge sound' all of a sudden. And nobody had played guitar like that before. I love any of the guitarists that come along and express themselves in their own way. The ones that everyone else copies, there's a reason why we love them—they're the ones that brought us a new thing when they did it. Eddie Van Halen was certainly one of those people. Yngwie is, too—there was nothing like him when I heard him. I think that Phil Keaggy is one of those guitarists, also, but most definitely Allan Holdsworth, who I think influenced every one of the guys you'll probably talk to.

JAS OBRECHT The Edge of U2 and Andy Summers of The Police deserve credit for not only inventing unique guitar sounds, but for also helping to usher in an era where the principle of 'less is more' was on full display. The Edge was especially good at this—he made simplicity an attractive quality during an era when most rock guitarists were focusing on spewing out fast, knuckle-busting solos. The Edge was expert at turning his limitations into a style, so much so that soon after U2's 'Sunday Bloody Sunday' and 'New Year's Day' hit the radio airwaves and MTV, British music publications were running ads for 'Wanted: U2-style guitarist.' The Edge was very important to the development of 1980s rock guitar. He's one of those rare transitional musicians.

HERMAN FRANK, WOLF HOFFMANN [ACCEPT]

JIM MATHEOS The melody always stuck out. Great sounds. I'm a huge Schenker fan, and to me, Wolf was another … I hesitate to say 'another version,' but you could tell he was very influenced by Schenker, so you can hear a lot of melody coming through his solos. Kind of pentatonic-based more so than classically influenced, than someone like Uli Jon Roth. And that's also something else I lean toward. The melody, the sound, and again, the writing. I think that whole record* was a huge influence on the metal scene in general, and Fates Warning. It's one of the handful of records I can say were one of my favorite records of the 80s. It's just so original. And 'Fast As A Shark,' these days you listen to it and it doesn't sound like anything special as far as speed. But when that first came out, it was just *unbelievable*. I couldn't believe what they were doing. We were trying to learn that as a band, and we couldn't cop it. Groundbreaking.

---

* *Restless And Wild* (1982).

ACE FREHLEY [KISS, SOLO ARTIST]

HANK SHERMANN Even though it was kind of standard phrasing that he did, I think he did them pretty thematic—you can always follow or hum them. Even though it's a fairly simple style, he certainly had a unique way of doing that simple, ordinary style. Also, his attitude in live performance. I saw them in 1976 in Copenhagen—it was like, 'Whoa!' And also, his tone. Like I said, the style is very simple, but the way he plays it is what it's all about, it's what made him famous and also made him 'Ace Frehley,' and unique to everyone else. Even if other guys played the same style, Ace just had that something extra. And also, his solos on the early Kiss albums were really phenomenal. He has some really classic solos from the *Hotter Than Hell* album—it's really well composed. He can be very proud of that.

JOHN FRUSCIANTE [RED HOT CHILI PEPPERS, SOLO ARTIST]

CHRIS HASKETT John Frusciante, it goes without saying, is fantastic. Some guys seem to have Strats growing out of them, and he's one. In DC, we seem to have guys that have Teles growing out of them—Danny Gatton, Roy Buchanan, Pedro Sera-Leyva, Bill Kirchen, etc.—but anyway, Frusciante knows how to wring the wood out of a Strat. He's almost got a kind of zen-like tastefulness in his solos. I've never heard him overplay. Being in that band, you're bound to touch on both *Band Of Gypsys** and Funkadelic/Eddie Hazel territory, and, when he did, it never sounded like a cop—it was always clearly *him* paying a subtle tribute to those musics. It's hard to pick a favorite, but because we toured together on *Blood Sugar Sex Magik*, I'm quite partial to it—it's branded into my head. So if I have to pick a favorite Frusciante moment on it, it might be the beautiful *Ladyland*-ness of 'Sir Psycho Sexy.'

RORY GALLAGHER [SOLO ARTIST]

VIVIAN CAMPBELL Rory was my first guitar hero. Marc Bolan and T. Rex was the first thing that made me want to own a guitar, but Rory Gallagher was the first person that made me want to actually *learn how to play it*. The first album I had of his was the *Live In Europe* album. Rory was the first concert I saw—at the Ulster Hall in Belfast, the following year, 1973. He was really in his element as a

---

* Jimi Hendrix's live album from 1970.

live performer—that's when he was at his best. I saw him many times, because I grew up in Belfast during the 1970s, and very few acts played there because of the political troubles. And Rory would always play every Christmas—he would play a series of shows at the Ulster Hall.

So he was the first guitarist where I actually dropped the needle on the record and learned to play parts. Like, his version of 'Messin' With The Kid' was one of the very first songs of his I tried to disseminate. And again, I picked up a lot of my heavy-handed habits starting with him, because he played a lot of pinch harmonics, which have become part of my sound, as well. So we kind of had a heavy right hand. And then when I moved from there to studying Gary Moore's playing, I became even more heavy-handed, and that's where I got a lot of the palm-muting—from Gary. So I think to me, it's very evident who my influences are. If you're familiar with Gary Moore and you're familiar with Rory Gallagher, I think there is a lot of that in my playing that is very evident.

BILLY GIBBONS [ZZ TOP]

CURT KIRKWOOD I think the sound changed mostly with the guitar sound, and they brought in what sounded like new-wave drumming.* It seemed a little more linear. They shifted from the honky-tonk sort of rock-blues thing—which seemed like more big blocks of stuff—to a more streamlined thing. I think to go along with how drum machines started to come around, and you started to have things that were perfect rhythm-wise, and synthesizer in there probably, doing something. Definitely the guitar thing became a little bit new—it seemed to have something that stayed for a number of albums. And it went from a traditional Les Paul sound to a little more space-aged. It was reflected in the titles, when you had *Eliminator* and *Afterburner*. That's somebody who I think knows more of what they're doing and has an idea of where they're going, rather than getting up there and throwing down.

I've seen ZZ Top a number of times. I think they probably jammed out a lot earlier on, but when the 80s came around, they started to be this sort of space aged, big band, three-piece sound—where the guitar started to sound like saxophone sections, cool 80s sounding drums. Coming from if you look back at three-pieces like Cream, it was a big departure. A lot of people were into it obviously—when they did 'Sharp Dressed Man' and that stuff. I think [Gibbons's solos] have always

---

* On ZZ Top's 80s recordings, such as *Eliminator* (1983).

been deeply rooted in that oceanic knowledge and sense of the blues—which is what I really respect. I listen to quite a bit of it, but I never learned how to play it. I never got the basics. It seems like that guy's encyclopedic in a way, yet without sounding derivative. I read one time he said that it was 'abstract blues,' and it made me think, 'Well … *all blues is pretty abstract.*' But, somehow, it still sounds like blues guitar at its base.

BRAD GILLIS [NIGHT RANGER, OZZY OSBOURNE]

JEFF WATSON Brad came into the band from a funk kind of thing. He was in a band called Rubicon and was a funk player. Whereas my strength was soloing, his strength was more rhythmic. He was a real strong rhythm player. We utilized our strengths, and that was intentional. That was done by Fitz. He had heard us both, and goes, 'I'm going to start this band, and we're going to put these two guys together, because the two of them have such individual strengths and they can also do harmony stuff.'

He was also well equipped to do that Ozzy gig. At the time, I was thinking, 'Oh man, I would be perfect for that band.' But in retrospect, he was a better choice. I never played in cover bands—ever. I started out in an original band as a writer, and never played much in cover bands—except for sitting in once in a while. Where Brad *lived* in cover bands, so he knew those songs before he went out to do those shows, and that really helped him. I wish I had played in cover bands, because I would be able to go out and jam with people. But he had, and was well equipped for that gig.

I worked with him—he had to get his chops up to go out and do that. I was showing him lots of approaches and different licks, and he used a lot of them in his stand-alone solo when he was out there. He'd call me from the road and go, 'Hey, there's a radio show on tonight. You're going to hear this part, I kind of ripped you off on it—you showed me a couple of weeks ago!' But it's all fine in that regard. I was standing on the side of the stage when they played Oakland Arena here.

GREG GINN [BLACK FLAG, GONE]

CURT KIRKWOOD Black Flag is amazing—back in the mid 80s, [we] did a lot of shows with them. I always thought it was a big influence across the board. Even when I first heard Nirvana, and the little guitar bends that would go along with the voice—not so much the extended leads—but that's the kind of thing Greg would do. He didn't do a lot of extended leads back then, but what he did was crazy and definitely non-traditional. Really compelling. I loved it.

SCOTT GORHAM, GARY MOORE, BRIAN ROBERTSON [THIN LIZZY]

PHIL COLLEN It's funny—I just got Scott Gorham to start using metal guitar picks. And I got the idea off of Brian May, because he used to use a sixpence. We'd just done a tour in England, and Black Star Riders—which is basically the remnants of Thin Lizzy—were out there. I loved what they did—it was very melodic. The big thing that everyone misses about Thin Lizzy was Phil Lynott's voice and how he expressed himself—that made them really special. So you've got this really cool groove band, but I think people miss that point.

Not everyone can sing this stuff—you need someone who is an absolute character. It's like, Stone Temple Pilots with Scott Weiland. Or Axl Rose. You need *a character* who is absolutely essential to these bands. That's what you're listening to. And then on top of that, you've got this amazing music going on underneath. That's really what Thin Lizzy had. It was more than just the dual guitar thing. And they complimented Phil Lynott—he was very much an artist. And that was what Scott and Brian Robertson absolutely did.

I saw Gary Moore with Thin Lizzy—it was him and Scott—and it was really good. But I preferred the band with Brian Robertson. That was a chemistry and that was a dynamic that was able to push that stuff forward. There's only a certain amount of time with bands and inspiration—it's alive for only a certain amount of time, and then it disappears. It just goes away. People get families; people get distracted, and different things going on in their lives. That dynamic is very fragile.

Some of those early Lizzy albums, the stuff with Robertson and Gorham, especially, that to me is when that stuff shined. So it's going to influence a lot. Like Queen, they had that amazing chemistry or dynamic. Theirs was a big time period, Queen. But Thin Lizzy, it was just a few albums. It was *Jailbreak*, that's when it really came into its stride. And *Black Rose*—that was actually Gary Moore. But there was a time period, and that influenced everyone. And that's what's so attractive about that chemistry and that dynamic.

STEVE HACKETT, STEVE HOWE [GTR]

STEVE STEVENS I am absolutely a fan of both Steve Howe and Steve Hackett. I will say that once the 80s hit, I did not keep up with the works of many of my early heroes all that much—I was finally making my own records, etc. On paper, Asia looked like a prog-rock dream band. I loved all the players, and John Wetton's work on the first U.K. record* was incredible. What many people don't realize was that many of the prog guys never really made real money during the 70s. Who would have thought Genesis were in debt around the time of *Lamb Lies Down On Broadway*? I think they were tired of working their asses off for a decade, and wanted to make real big money, and create something that would be accepted by the general record buying public. I certainly don't fault them for that one bit. I was an old school fan and did lose interest, however. I guess I'm just an early-70s prog-rock snob, when those guys were making truly adventurous music.

STEVE HACKETT I heard Steve Howe before he was with Yes—let alone Asia. So I was aware of him when he played with a band called Tomorrow. I think [for] all of those albums that he made, he came up with iconic stuff. He was very confident, he was very competent, and he brought a lot to Yes, and he brought a lot to all the projects that he played on. He's something of a country player at heart. There's something there—that he absolutely loves country stuff. He would be playing a Gretsch sometimes, which was foreign to me. I remember that stuff way back I think in the Beatles days, and it wasn't really what I was going for myself.

KIRK HAMMETT, JEFF HANNEMAN, KERRY KING, DAVE
MUSTAINE [METALLICA, SLAYER, MEGADETH]

JEFF WATERS When the shredders were getting hailed—the Malmsteens and the Vais and the Van Halens—for their soloing, you could see a lot of guitar players slamming Kirk Hammett. And I was one right from the beginning who was like, '*What is wrong with you people*?!' On the *Kill 'Em All* album, they doubled the volume of the lead guitar solos more than they ever should have been. They should have never been that loud on a normal record. And somehow, Kirk comes in with this screaming wah sound that blows your head off, and is way too loud in a proper mix, but that's what made it stand out as being amazing. There was so much feel in that guy's playing.

And it's like Hanneman and King—some would say, 'The Slayer guys, what are they doing? They're playing out of key.' And you've got to laugh, because those guys have their own style, and that's more important than doing an awesome,

---

* *U.K.* (1978), the eponymous debut album by the British prog-rock group.

fast scale, and doing this diminished scale, and doing it really fast and clear, and doing it like a teacher would do or the guitar shredding guys would do. *This is style.* They had their own style and they stuck with it. And Hanneman, King, and Hammett had that style. Hammett influenced so many guitar players—beginner players—who would grab a Flying V and a wah pedal, and shred away and have a good time. If you [try to] put him in a technical category, you can't. You can't put Hanneman, King, and Hammett in there. But to me, that technical category is so not important—compared to, 'Is it their own style?' and 'Is it amazing?' That's so much more important than just technically being a good player. I mean, there's a million good players out there—that's not what it's about.

Mustaine, besides his riffing ability, if you listen to *Rust In Peace*, you don't even need to have a vocal track on there—you can just listen to the rhythms and go, 'Oh my God. He could have actually done an instrumental album!' But the thing that blows me away about him is someone like Glenn Tipton, for me, I opened my eyes to something when I listen to Priest in the early 80s, and I noticed Tipton would write songs where the guitar would play one note or strum one chord … and then just do nothing—when Rob Halford was singing. And the second Halford finished the sentence, bang, here comes the guitar riff. So what that does is the listener listens to it and their attention is completely focused on the singer, and then the second the singer is done singing, you completely focus on the guitar riff.

And I know Hetfield—for sure—subconsciously or consciously does the same thing. In his case, because he plays the guitar and sings, he has to simplify a little bit of the riff when he's singing, and as soon as he's done the vocals, he goes into the more complex/awesome Metallica riff. Mustaine is a freak of nature—he somehow completely defies that strategy, and can play these crazy rhythms like a Hetfield, but he can sing over them. He doesn't have to stop and play one note or one chord to be able to sing over top of the riff. It's like two hands on the piano— one hand is playing a completely different time than the other. And that's what Mustaine does with his voice and guitar—they're two separate things completely. They're not one.

BRIAN TATLER James is outrageous as a rhythm player—he's absolutely so tight. What he does with his right hand is phenomenal. I think it almost keeps the whole thing together. It's very difficult to play. I've copied some of their songs, I mean, I teach guitar, and people want to learn their songs sometimes, so they've asked me how to play 'Battery,' 'Master Of Puppets,' or 'Creeping Death,' and what he's doing with his right hand—fast down-picking—is extremely difficult to do without tensing up. I admire that they can go onstage and do those songs night after night, and keep the energy up. They're one of the greatest rock bands of all-time. I've listened to a lot of Megadeth albums over the years, and Dave Mustaine is a very good player. I like the way he writes—he comes up with some brilliant riffs. Another very talented guy. At one point, there was a lot of talent in Metallica, wasn't there? It was almost too much—I think something had to give. [*Laughs*]

JEFF HEALEY [SOLO ARTIST]

ROGER COSTA There's all kind of things you can point to with Jeff that were unique. His style of playing, where he lay the guitar flat on his lap and he used the whole strength of his arm to do these amazing bends and had a wicked tremolo. But it really boils down to the fact that he was—as a player—a genius-level musician. People throw that word around a lot, but I think in Jeff's case, it was *really* true. He could hear something once and play it back for you, and tell you what the notes were. He had perfect pitch. And he loved to play. I think that came through in his playing. He had chops like no one else.

In the last years of his life, he never practiced anymore—he would play maybe fifteen minutes a week if he didn't have any gigs, just to keep his calluses.* But his practices were going out to jam. It didn't matter what gear, you could always tell that it was Jeff playing. It had to do with the note choices and the way he attacked the guitar. And there was something unique about the way he played. It wasn't so much to do with the fact that he was holding his guitar in a different way than other people—it had to do with what was coming from inside through his fingers.

WARREN HAYNES Jeff used to open for The Allman Brothers. I remember always being a fan of what he did. But one night, I gained a whole new admiration for Jeff. We were in Canada, and the Allman Brothers and Little Feat were touring together, and myself and some of the guys in Little Feat went out to hear Jeff Healey play in his Dixieland band [The Jazz Wizards], where he was playing trumpet or cornet or something. And hearing him play that music—in an equally adept way, with all this history that came along with it—really opened my mind to what a serious musician he was.

---

* Jeff passed away in 2008 from cancer, at the age of forty-one.

ALLAN HOLDSWORTH [U.K., SOLO ARTIST]

STU HAMM I remember the stuff I really liked of Allan's was his work with Bill Bruford on *Feels Good To Me* and *One Of A Kind*—because I was a huge Jeff Berlin fan. I loved his playing on that; I loved his playing on the first U.K. album. There's a record by a band called Gong, called *Gazeuse!*—'Percolations (Part I & II)' and 'Expresso' is just the greatest tone he had. *Fantastic.* I've known Allan a little bit. I've known a lot of people who have played with him. Man, I'd love to play with him someday. I'm just such a fan of his playing. I was so pleased and happy to get him on the record.* I went to his house in Torrance and played it back, and he was the usual Allan—'Oh, it's terrible! It sucks! You don't have to pay me. I apologize for being such a terrible musician.' And of course I listened to it, and was just amazed with how wonderful he sounds on it. I was blessed to have him on there.

GREG HOWE Allan Holdsworth was another humongous influence on me. He kind of redefined the legato approach to guitar. Today, you hear people say, 'This guy's got a great technique. He's got a great left hand—it's very *Holdsworth-ian*.' Just like Stevie Ray Vaughan almost redefined blues, when you think about it, when people say things like, 'This guy's a great blues player, you should hear him. And his tone is great—this guy can do *Stevie Ray Vaughan* all day.' Stevie Ray Vaughan has become almost the new standard for the sound of blues. 'Can you play blues?' Somebody rips out a Stevie Ray Vaughan lick, and that means blues. Holdsworth I think set that new standard for legato. Legato is almost synonymous with Allan Holdsworth. And I don't think—even to this day—anybody does it better than that. I don't think there's anyone that even comes close, actually. So to me, he was huge.

STEVE LYNCH Allan Holdsworth, just the legato and the scales that he used, he sounded so fluid in everything that he did. A totally different kind of player—not using the pick very much at all, he usually did a lot of hammer-ons and slides. That's what gave him that real fluid legato sound, and I loved that sound. It was one of the coolest things I'd ever heard.

RICHIE KOTZEN Back then, when I heard Allan play, it was very much like Eddie Van Halen—it sounded like another instrument. Like, when Eddie played the guitar, it doesn't even sound sometimes like a guitar. It sounds like something

---

* Hamm's solo debut, *Radio Free Albemuth* (1988).

else. And Allan had that same thing happening but in a different way, because he's more of a jazz guy. So it was pretty crazy to hear that, like, 'What is that? A violin?' Again, it comes down to something I talked about earlier—when I mentioned Stevie Ray Vaughan, it's something in the hands. It's how you finger the note and phrasing. It's the way you speak, y'know? It's very personal. And the great guitar players—the ones that we all talk about—when you hear them play, you can tell it's them, because you hear their personality. And that's coming through their hands. It wouldn't matter if they're playing through a Tweed Deluxe or a Soldano amplifier. It doesn't matter—they're going to sound the way they sound.

JEFF WATSON I brought Holdsworth in to play with me on my first album,[*] on a song called 'Forest Of Feeling,' and he stayed at the house. We were drinking buddies in LA back then—I don't drink now. But it was really monstrously influential to see this guy and his legato—his left hand was insanely good. That also changed my world. Y'know, Holdsworth and I did a song on an album for *Guitar For The Practicing Musician*, in the late 80s, early 90s, we did 'Play That Funky Music'—if you've never heard it, it's sick fun!

He's a sweetheart and really smart. But I wasn't listening to him before we starting talking and having a beer. I was getting ready to do the album, and I actually brought him in to do a solo on the last Night Ranger record of the 80s, when we were still with MCA. He played on it, and it was such unbelievable guitar playing, but the band said, 'What are you thinking, having this guy play on our album?!' It was *so* outside of what Night Ranger was—we were a pop band, and he was playing just this monster stuff. So that didn't work.

But right after that, I went in and started getting ready for *Lone Ranger*, and Allan flew up and stayed here. I was listening to him practice—he played through a little Boogie 50 caliber. And the intro to the song 'Forest Of Feeling' is Allan playing through an old ADA Stereo Tapped Delay—I have all this gear in my studio, I never get rid of anything—and he picked that and he played the intro through that. It's the oddest note choice. It's very clean, unusual tones. And I wasn't here—I was out getting lunch! I came back, and he goes, 'I've got an intro.' Steve Smith played drums on that, and trading with Allan Holdsworth, I have to tell you, I didn't just trade off with Allan, I tried to keep up and play my remedial riff over and over, basically. And Allan got to be Allan. And he really hates the mix of the album, too! But he's out of this world.

---

[*] *Lone Ranger* (1992).

This was on sixteen-track two-inch, which I still have. It's a twenty-four-track machine, with two-inch heads on it, with sixteen tracks, so it sounds fatter. Anyway, I was downstairs eating, and he was just upstairs by himself, warming up, taking solos, and then erasing them! It wasn't like Pro Tools where you keep everything and pick and choose—he would just erase right over it. We were losing our minds, going, '*What are you doing?!*'

TY TABOR Holdsworth comes from someplace that I just sat there and scratched my head, and was like, 'I don't even know what his foundation is to be thinking like this. It is just so incredibly different, and not of the usual thought patterns of how you develop runs and licks and everything about guitar that existed.' Everything he did was a surprise, with a different kind of expression that I'd ever heard someone do—including his vibrato on the string, was totally his own.

Because back in the 80s, everybody had Eddie Van Halen's vibrato and sound and pick-attack and style, and everybody pretty much was developing off of him. And there was this huge rash of guitarists that came along in the 80s that were Van Halen clones, to me. Most of them. Holdsworth just had nothing to do whatsoever with that way of thinking. Nothing to do with it. Just another universe of coming from somewhere else that just blew my mind. I don't know where he's coming from—I just know it's his own thing. Nobody else on this Earth plays like him.

Allan Holdsworth had a big impact during the 80s on all of the guitarists you've probably heard. *A huge impact.* Nobody was speaking his name on the street, but everybody that everybody was listening to was listening to him. So he had a huge impact. I know he totally changed my life—when I first heard him in UK, it was mind-altering. It was mind-expanding. It taught me the rules that I had known about guitar before that moment no longer applied. It was just a breakthrough for me when I heard him.

CURT KIRKWOOD [MEAT PUPPETS]

CHRIS HASKETT The first time I saw the Meat Puppets, I noticed he played almost the entire set on the neck pickup of his Les Paul. I always associate neck pickups with being slightly more muddy, or a nice, clean jazz tone. What's really interesting about those Meat Puppet records—my favorites are *Mirage* and *Monsters*—is, aurally, they sound like Nugent records! The quality and the sound of the drums, and the way the mix is set ... or even Steve Miller. I'm not saying the music sounds like Steve Miller, but the production aesthetic was ... everything's dry. He's another one of these guys where, I just give up. I can't do that. And they can sing! Just a fantastic guitar player. Makes me wonder, 'How did I keep going?'

KIM THAYIL When I first heard that first Meat Puppets album,[*] I thought, 'What is this crap? It's like very sloppy, generic hardcore.' And then the more I listened to it, put it on the second side, I was like, 'Wait a minute ... *there's something kind of acid-drenched and psychedelic doing on here.*' And the next thing you know, it became one of my favorite hardcore albums ever at the time. And then the second album came out.[†] Just spanning that wild, super-sonic, falling apart guitar playing, to this kick-backed, stoned, tripped out, psychedelic guitar playing. And then you start getting these proficient elements on *Up On The Sun*, which was like, you were able to turn to your friends, and say, 'I told you this guy can play—check it out!' To this day, they're so influential with Soundgarden—and me, specifically.

SHAWN LANE [JONAS HELBORG, BLACK OAK ARKANSAS; SOLO ARTIST]

WARREN HAYNES I met him briefly, and after he passed, I realized we have a lot of friends in common. He was a tremendous talent. Shawn really had technique for days. His chops were pretty outstanding. He also was a unique voice on the guitar—I think that's one of the most important things. He played a lot with Jeff Sipe—the drummer who I'm playing with a lot these days. And I hear a lot of Shawn Lane stories. I need to hear more of his playing, because everything I've heard is pretty outstanding.

JAKE E. LEE [OZZY OSBOURNE, BADLANDS, RED DRAGON CARTEL]

ALEXI LAIHO He did have his own unique sound and way of playing. His sound was very inspirational for me—just that sort of unforgiving mid-rangey type of sound. And he was insane when you think about it—he did all this crazy shit *without* a whammy bar. He was definitely a type of a circus character—what I mean by that is not a clown, I mean like crazy, insane. I think he's definitely an underrated guitar player.

---

[*] *Meat Puppets* (1982).
[†] *Meat Puppets II* (1984).

ALEX LIFESON [RUSH]

RON JARZOMBEK I think overall, the guitarist who influenced me the most from a progressive point of view is undoubtedly Alex Lifeson. Well, Rush actually. Fantastic individual players, but even more special when they work together … concepts, songwriting, their use of timing figures, working with musical themes— *everything.* Alex has unbelievable speed—as showcased in solos like 'Freewill,' 'Natural Science,' and 'La Villa Strangiato.' And his use of layered guitars is nothing short of brilliant.

JIM MATHEOS I always go back to the writing—for me, it's always the writing first. And when I say 'writing,' not just the songs—the solos, the construction. He's got a really unique way of expressing himself in solos. His chord choices opened me up to a lot of stuff. Before Rush, I was a Black Sabbath guy, so it was all power chords. But when Rush came along, he opened it up to these fuller chords— suspended chords which I'd never heard before. It really opened up my playing a lot. Very unique and innovative.

RIK EMMETT Alex and I have a lot in common. We came from the same time period, so when I hear Alex play, I hear a fair amount of Jeff Beck and Jimmy Page in what he does—that 'Yardbirds school' that influenced me, he's definitely got that, too. But I do think being a Toronto boy and coming up during that period and in that era, the English progressive bands had a lot to do with forming and shaping the way we heard things. So Steve Howe of Yes was a huge influence on me, I would say David Gilmour of Pink Floyd was an influence on me, but was probably a bigger influence on Alex.

Alex has this ability to really 'bite' into music. He's a very physical kind of guy when he plays, and he plays hard when he's getting excited. I can't think of it in any other way except you know the way he makes that face, like his teeth are gritted and his eyes are squeezing closed? He just looks like he's using every fiber of his body to squeeze notes out. Whereas Clapton always has this very calm, placid, 'British gentleman' kind of approach to playing. Whereas Alex looks like, '*This hurts*'—which I love, because I totally come from that school, where you make all the stupid faces, that you're not even aware that you're making.

The thing I like about Alex is that in many ways, he humanized what Rush was doing. He made it so that the punters were going, 'Oh yeah, that's rock.' Which is not to say that Geddy doesn't have bass lines that are fantastic lines, but I think

Alex was kind of the guy that would say to the band, 'Yeah, but let's make this *heavier.* Let's not keep it so esoteric, let's have a moment where all hell breaks loose and I'll turn my amp up to eleven and we'll see what happens.' I always liked that about his playing. He's a sweetheart of a guy. He's an extremely talented person—I don't think people know how talented he actually is. Because when you're in a band like Rush, you tend to be sublimating what you do to the collective, because it's all about the ensemble. I don't know if you've ever seen his paintings, but he's gifted on a lot of levels. He's a connoisseur when it comes to wine and he's got a pretty good golf game. I think Lifeson is the kind of guy that whatever he tried, he would bring a lot of 'natural gift' to it. I admire that in him a great deal.

STEVE MORSE Alex really has that gift of finding great voicings and a really competent way of soloing. His voicings are like Pete Townshend—his chord parts alone are enough reason to study what he does. You listen to any of their songs, listen to how he supports it with the guitar, and generally, with one guitar. So I always loved the inventive way he could put riffs in just the right places, and then put beautiful chord voicings for contrast, and had I think a pretty wide variety of approaches to soloing. And good use of effects, and more importantly, a super nice guy who was a pilot. And me being a pilot, we got along great. And I love the fact that they were so successful, but very straightforward, easy to talk to people.

That was one of the greatest things about the tour for me.* We would play early enough that there was almost empty seats—almost completely empty. Then, by the last few songs, it was full, or nearly so. So we started changing the setlist around—I put what I thought was the strongest stuff near the end, where people would remember it. But I hired another singer-guitarist, Terry Brock, to go on that tour, because we had done some vocals on that album†—we did the Eric Johnson song 'Distant Star,' Spencer Davis's 'Gimme Some Lovin'' as an encore, and 'Book Of Dreams.' That was my experimental, 'Let's try some vocals' album. So Terry was a big help—he'd just stay out of the way on some of the trio stuff we were doing, but was great at backup with his guitar. He could play some of the parts that we harmonized on the album, that don't get harmonized on the live performance with only one guitar. So that was nice.

And I remember during the very beginning of the tour, I was very ambitious— we had lots of crew and there was lots of traveling. The money was very minimal— less than what we would make at a club. Because Rush—unlike some bands, who

---

* The Steve Morse Band opened for Rush in 1985.
† *Stand Up* (1985).

actually require bands to pay to play as an opening group for exposure—were paying something, but just not very much. And they didn't need to, because most bands would do it for free. The record company had pledged some tour support, so it could break even, and very early in the tour, decided that they weren't going to. And they also decided they weren't going to release that album as a CD. For some reason, they were doing a huge cutback on this kind of funny music on their label, and that branch of the label* was getting ready to be closed.

So here I was, I had hired everybody, made this commitment for the tour, and now, I was a guy who lived in a single-wide trailer, looking at a $25,000 shortfall for the tour. So I decided to just go ahead and go for it. But I got a signature loan from my bank in my little town in Georgia, and was able to do the tour, and then after that, a few years paying that back. It was very much the thing to do. It exposed the music to a lot of different fans who had never heard us, and like I said, the guys in Rush were just so cool. They took the whole band out to dinner one time near the end of the tour, just to express their thanks, and were always super respectful. They were the model of what a band should be like to the opening band.

JEFF LOOMIS [ARCH ENEMY, NEVERMORE]

ADAM DUTKIEWICZ I've always thought Jeff Loomis—above and beyond—is one of the greatest guitar players of our time. He's absolutely a virtuoso. He's incredible. You don't really need to do anything but listen to him to understand how special he is. His speed, his intricacy, the notes he plays—he's a monster. There are not many people around who can play like that guy. And if you go see him live, he sounds like that right in front of you, too. I found out about him when he was in Nevermore, and was like, 'Who the hell is this guy? He's incredible!' He's something else.

STEVE LUKATHER [TOTO]

DAVE MENIKETTI He's one of my favorite players. To me, he's one of the consummate players as far as guitar players go. How can you say anything bad about Lukather, except 'I wish I were him.' He's got the chops from hell, and for me, just one of those guys that if you were to put all of these guys in a room, I think Lukather could do whatever any of those other guys can do, and would also do it with great passion and emotion, as well.

---

* Elektra/Musician, a jazz-oriented subsidiary of Elektra Records, launched in 1982.

GEORGE LYNCH [DOKKEN, LYNCH MOB]

STEVE LYNCH I think George's finesse on the guitar is superb. I look at his vibrato and his attack—he's a very tasty player and he's a technical wizard. They'd always ask me and they always asked him [if we were related]. So one time, when I saw him at a NAMM show—this is back in the 80s—we were talking about that, and I said, 'You know what I tell them now if they ask if we're related? I just say, "No. We're divorced now."'

GARY HOEY When I heard Dokken, when I heard George Lynch, I loved his vibrato and his feel—what he would squeeze out of the notes. And the way that he chose his notes. That was what a lot of guitar players loved about George—he's got a vibrato and a sound that is so uniquely his, and it's very emotional and powerful, and his harmonics. Everything about his approach was something that I really enjoyed.

ADAM DUTKIEWICZ Just tasty licks. He's not one of those over-analytical guitar players. He plays some really thoughtful licks, but he also plays with balls. Good stuff.

TONY MACALPINE [SOLO ARTIST]

JEFF WATSON Tony MacAlpine was over here a lot, playing my grand piano mostly, actually. He was brilliant at it. Mozart, Beethoven—the whole realm. We'd just sit around going, 'This is great!' Serve tea, put out some hors d'oeuvres, and Tony's just cranking on the grand piano. But he was an early shredder—his facility was outstanding.

MICK MARS [MÖTLEY CRÜE]

LITA FORD I think Mick is fucking brilliant. I think because his personality is very low-key, he's just such a mellow dude—he's not one to want to be the first to speak, like, 'Hey! Look at me!' He's just laid back—he just follows the Crüe, does his thing, and keep his mouth shut. Kind of like a Joe Perry. Joe Perry does the same—he's just quiet and doesn't seem like a rock star. They don't fit into those rock star shoes—they're just musicians. But I loved Mick Mars's playing in the early 80s. I thought he was great—with slide guitar, it just sounded wicked. I don't know who his influences are, but if I had to choose, I would probably say Billy Gibbons.

BRIAN MAY [QUEEN, SOLO ARTIST]

STEVE STEVENS A huge fan. When the first Queen record came out,* I remember the first time I heard 'Keep Yourself Alive'—it was played on a radio station in New York, that had a Friday night show called *Things From England*, and they had gotten the first Queen record before it was released in the States, and played 'Keep Yourself Alive.' I just thought, '*Who is this guitar player?*' So I bought the first record as an English import. And he was just hinting at what he was capable of doing later on with all his guitar orchestrations. But it was obvious that here was a new guy on the scene, and also, there's some beautiful acoustic guitar on that record as well, and I've always been a fan of guys who can play all styles of guitar.

My first guitar hero might be Steve Howe from Yes, and I loved the fact that he played every different style of guitar, and I thought Brian May was definitely in that English school of using all his guitar styles and sounds for guitar orchestration. That concept is still near and dear to me. The first Queen album came out in 1973, so here's a band that's looking to evolve [in the 80s], and that's really important. You certainly don't want to just repeat the record that you did five years before. And I love the fact that 'Another One Bites The Dust' has that Chic/Nile Rodgers guitar on it. He was delving into different areas, and once again, utilizing some incredible guitar orchestration on those records.

STEVE HACKETT He credits me as an influence, and he cites the very track that I talked about, which is 'The Musical Box'—the first track on the *Nursery Cryme* album, which has a harmony guitar solo at the end. It has a three-part harmony guitar solo. I think Brian is immensely good, and he and I worked together on a couple of different projects—we worked on an album called *Feedback 86* of mine, and we also worked on Rock Against Repatriation† together as well—we did a version of 'Sailing,' both a vocal version and an instrumental version of the tune.

THURSTON MOORE, LEE RANALDO [SONIC YOUTH]

CHRIS HASKETT Thurston and Lee? I knew about Glenn Branca through *The Ascension*, so when I first heard *about* Sonic Youth, I thought I knew what to expect. And boy was I wrong. They had moved away from Branca's—and Rhys

---

* *Queen* (1973).
† A charity project instigated by Hackett, with the aim of helping to stop the repatriation of Vietnamese 'boat people' in Hong Kong.

Chatham's—powerful unisons and into something with much more space in it. Sure, people had been doing stuff with 'prepared' instruments before—Fred Frith comes to mind. But that was always tweaky avant-garde, whereas Sonic Youth were an undeniable great *rock* band. I, probably like most guitar players, have usually approached the guitar with a pretty conventional template of sounds an electric guitar 'ought' to make. And thus stay pretty much within the bounds of the techniques which produce *those* sounds—i.e. 'playing' a guitar is a pretty delineated set of techniques and actions. When you consider that runs the gamut of Hendrix to Adrian Belew, it's a pretty broad spectrum.

But when you listen to Sonic Youth, the horizon has been pushed way, way back, because they were approaching the instrument without that conventional limitation on what 'playing' means. I mean, *all* those billions of guitars, each in its own tuning, the drumsticks under the strings, etc. The approach was a purer aural aesthetic: not simply 'What are the possible sounds a guitar can make if I *play* it?' But rather, 'What are *all* the sounds a guitar can make?' It's an aesthetic you find in Elliott Sharp, Arto Lindsay, and Einstürzende Neubauten, too: the simple question 'What does it sound like?' Unfettered by, 'How did we make that sound?' Groundbreaking. And nobody's come near it since.

VINNIE MOORE [UFO, SOLO ARTIST]

JOE STUMP I first heard Vinnie Moore on a very early Vicious Rumors record.* There was this unaccompanied guitar solo on the record, called 'Invader,' that was *ripping.* I also really liked his first two neoclassical releases, *Mind's Eye* and *Time Odyssey*—some great stuff playing and composition-wise on both those records. His rock stuff is cool as well—he's always had a nice balance of technique and melody throughout all his releases.

STEVE MORSE [DIXIE DREGS, DEEP PURPLE, SOLO ARTIST]

JAS OBRECHT Steve Morse is one of the first people I ever interviewed. He was touring with the Dixie Dregs. I went to see them in San Francisco in '78, and I interviewed Steve and [bassist] Andy West. I liked Steve instantly. First of all, he had this hybrid guitar that was a Telecaster body with a Stratocaster neck, and five—count 'em, five—pickups. Unheard of. He also had a very complex

---

* *Soldiers Of The Night* (1985).

setup. His shows were thrilling. And it was extremely daring to do an instrumental band—especially when the Dixie Dregs were being promoted as a Southern rock band. Steve himself called his music 'electronic chamber music.'

With the exception of some drum parts, he pretty much wrote every note everybody played in the band. When I asked Andy West, 'Is it hard being in a band where someone else writes almost every note you play?,' Andy responded by saying something like, 'It would be, except that what Steve shows me is exactly the right notes to play.' Steve is extraordinarily focused on the music. He has a real genius for putting it together. My favorite of Steve's records are the ones he did with the Dixie Dregs and The Dregs between 1977 and 1981.*

RIK EMMETT Steve is a monster. He just has this ability to burn on a level that is so intense. He reinvented his right hand at a certain point—I think when he was in college at Miami, he decided he was going to become a pick guy. Both he and Eddie Van Halen have a kind of a thing where the pick is being driven by the middle finger, not the first finger. But I think Steve keeps two fingers on the pick almost all the time. So his picking is really, really precise. He's a left-handed guy who plays right-handed, and his left hand has tons and tons of endurance, and he's made it so his right hand now has the same level of endurance.

But we did some sessions together, and he came and played on a Triumph record when he was in town for a week.† And he pushes himself hard. He's a guy that could play a solo on something, and I was sitting in the control room with [producer] Thom Trumbo, and our jaws would be on the floor. And he would then say to us, 'I'm so sorry. I apologize. I just don't seem to have it today.' And we'd go, '*Are you kidding me?!*'

He's got a really nice approach. When I play chords, I tend to think of them as a grouping of notes and then I move from chord to chord, and the harmonic structure of the song is kind of a harmonic landscape that's moving in chord voicings. And I don't think Steve thinks like that. I think he really thinks in a very kind of counterpoint kind of way, that each note in a chord is part of his own sort of line, moving through the music. And so he tends to have an almost Bach-work kind of approach, as to how notes interact and how harmony gets created by lines that are being played—in the bass, in the mid-range, on the top end.

Whereas I think a lot of guitar players, we learn how to play a C and a G in

---

* *Free Fall* (1977), *What If* (1978), *Night Of The Living Dregs* (1979), *Dregs Of The Earth* (1980), and *Unsung Heroes* (1981).
† He appears on 'All The King's Horses' and 'Head For Nowhere' from *Surveillance* (1987).

the first position, we strum those chords, and we think of them as, 'Well, there's a block of notes I'm playing together.' And I don't think Steve tends to think that way. He tends to think of lines that run and how 'that note will reach this point, it will be then spelling the third of the chord, whereas this other thing is creating the minor seventh on the top, and the root is coming from this guy on the neck, but then on the very next thing, we're going to have a bassline pick up the root.' I would say pre-Romantic period kind of theory/harmony of the way things work. Even when he's roaring around playing those lines at the speed of light, those notes matter to him—like every single one of them is leading somewhere, and is going to hit a harmonic moment that is going to pay off for the piece of music. He's not just playing a million notes at blinding speed that don't relate. They all have a purpose for him—so, a very purposeful player.

Finally, I'll say this—he's got a fairly strong Southern boy/country kind of streak in him, but he's very much a fusion guy in the sense that he likes to rock. He's been in Deep Purple a long time, and I don't think he would have survived that experience if he wasn't a guy that really liked to rock.* But he's a pretty high-minded kind of musician as well. So, in the truest sense, he's a very 'American' kind of fusion player. He doesn't have a lot of blues in what he does—it's more of a country thing than it is a blues thing. But there's a reason why they probably had to retire him out of every guitar poll ever—because he would just win year after year after year! He was that good.

JEFF WATSON Interestingly enough, I never listened to Steve before I met him and we started palling around. We became friends before I realized how good he was, and then we'd be hanging out and he'd be practicing all the time, and I'd think, 'Shit, man, I've got to get on my game. He's insanely good!' That was very motivational. But Steve and I argue a lot about the world and politics and things, and we do a lot of mechanical work—we fix engines, we put in my well system together, we built a fence, he put in my trash compactor when I was on my road and he was staying here, we fly in his airplanes. It's mostly just fun other things than guitar stuff. He's really brilliant.

This is how crazy Steve is—there is a thunderstorm, and he's out in his hangar, dodging lightning, re-packing the parachute on his Ultralight airplane! He's a brilliant pilot. I landed on his backyard in Georgia one time, and also on a landing strip in Placerville, when he moved out here. He used to fly for Delta—

---

* In 1994, Steve replaced Ritchie Blackmore in Deep Purple.

did you know he used to be a commercial pilot? I don't have an older brother, but he would be the closest thing to an older brother I have in the world. But he was out re-packing a parachute in a thunderstorm on his Ultralight. I'm like, 'You fucking idiot … *get inside!*' He's like, 'I can get this done, and it's going to pass. I think I'm going to go up … '

DAVE MURRAY, ADRIAN SMITH [IRON MAIDEN]

JIM MATHEOS It was probably one of the first bands that I ever really got into that had that harmony/dual-guitar playing. I know there were lots before that, but for me, that really stuck out. Again, songwriting and the harmony guitar playing, which was really the first I heard taking it to that level—and something that Fates tried to emulate early on, for sure.

RICHIE KOTZEN The music, the songs, the sound of the band—the guitar playing was a part of it, but Bruce Dickinson's voice, the way Steve Harris played the bass. And being a young adolescent boy, the lyrics resonated with me—I loved all the 'devil talk.' It was all-encompassing. That's why that band was so great—the guitar playing is fantastic and fits the song. And their solos elevate the songs to another level. But it's the whole picture. You can have a great guitar player play an amazing solo in a shitty song, and it doesn't mean anything. Who cares? You're not going to listen to it. So Iron Maiden, you've got great songs, a great singer, a great bass player, and great guitar players playing really cool solos that really fit the songs.

CHRIS CAFFERY The Maiden guitarists, they really were the first to incorporate those dual harmony leads that were specific written lead parts for the two players to have melodies that became actual parts of the songs. That was something that I don't think was done much before Maiden had come around doing that—*at all.* A lot of the bands in the 70s were primarily single lead guitar players. Even if they had two guitarists, it was sort of in the AC/DC formula, where one of them was a rhythm player. Priest and Maiden were the first two bands to kind of have two specific lead players.

standout players, N–Z

What made certain guitarists special?
Part 2

DAVE NAVARRO [JANE'S ADDICTION, RED
HOT CHILI PEPPERS, SOLO ARTIST]

CHRIS HASKETT Dave, along with Earl Slick,* he's perhaps the most 'rock star' rock star I've ever met. Not in a bad way at all; more like, being around guys like that is really like what you imagine meeting a rock star is like when you're a kid. They've just got that … THING. I'm sure there's lots of other people like that out there, but I don't get invited to their parties. I first met Dave in 1990 or 1991, when Rollins Band was opening for Jane's Addiction. Dave's got it all—an amazing technical fluidity, a distinctive voice and tone, and he's a super nice and smart guy to hang out with (makes ya sick, don't it?). Anyway, one of the things I was immediately struck with when I first saw them was his use of really long delays in his solos (like I was using at the time, only he did it better). He really implemented the delay time to either add an almost bowed-like sustain or juxtapose the notes in really interesting ways. The high point for me was always watching them do 'Pigs In Zen.'

CRISS OLIVA [SAVATAGE]

CHRIS CAFFERY He always played something that sounded like it was the way

---

* New York–based guitarist best known for his work with David Bowie.

it was supposed to be. Even if he took a wrong note, he would bend it so it sounded right. And Criss actually influenced way more people than you realize. He unfortunately passed away in the early 90s,[*] but he could have been somebody that his name could have been mentioned a heck of a lot more if he hadn't have passed away, because the transition from Savatage to Trans-Siberian Orchestra would probably have happened with him involved. He was a special player. He had a really unique style that was kind of like a mixture between the classic metal players—along with Eddie Van Halen and Michael Schenker.

One of those people you listen to, and you can tell it was him, just by hearing the guitar—kind of what you would get out of a Dimebag or an Yngwie, where there is a particular style that goes along with that person's name. There's not a lot of guitar players who have that, where you say, '*That is an Yngwie style.*' There are people who play like Yngwie, there are a lot of people that play like Dimebag … but those are the ones that coined their own particular style.

Criss was just a really laid back kind of person. He was a very confident player. He did something different than most guitarists do, because he would always run completely clean guitar amps—which is kind of funny that everyone is using these processers now, that basically run through clean amps that have this world of sounds that come outside of it. Criss was using even sometimes bass amps … he would use a couple of different distortions and combinations of them, to get his sound. He also used—which I still use when I play with Savatage—a steel pick that had a very sharp tip to it. That was something that really helped him pick his fast speed and really had his aggressive sound. A lot of his tone came out of that pick.

JOHN PETRUCCI [DREAM THEATER]

STEVE MORSE I heard their demo and said, 'Wow. This guy's got it figured out. He knows what he's doing.' And they had yet recorded that album; it was just a demo.[†] I was like, 'If you need a producer, let me know!' I missed out on that, because they needed to go then and there, and we were still touring, and they got a bigger name. But they sounded so good. It was sort of like The Cars' first demo—the demo was so good, all the producer really needed to do was record it.

John, as a player, surprised me, because he was always so good, but he keeps getting better. I don't know how it's possible, because he's one of those guys, like Eric Johnson, who's particular about everything, and works really hard on

---

[*] Criss died on October 13 1993 when his vehicle was struck by a drunk driver.
[†] *When Dream And Day Unite* (1989)

details. Over the years, I can't believe how he keeps getting better. He's pretty much taken the right-hand picking ability to the next level—that I always tried to, but never could.

RON JARZOMBEK I loved just about everything that they were doing. Mike Portnoy and I were kind of 'phone buddies' at the time—along with Jason,[*] who knew Portnoy pretty good back then. I remember when they were going through their name change. They had the name 'Majesty' as their band, and Portnoy was telling me what other possible band names they were coming up with, and I remember 'Dream Theater' came up, and I said, 'Man, whenever anybody uses the word *dream*, it's just too vague.' And then the album came out, and it said Dream Theater. But musically, they were doing everything—they were taking Rush up quite a few notches. It was heavier. Of course Petrucci still is at the top of his game. And everything they were doing individually was great, as a band they were great, they had great songs, and every album, they just kept pushing it out, and being at the top of their genre.

GARY HOEY When Dream Theater came out, they were a band that had this progressive-rock sound, but yet it had more of a commercial appeal. And, for me, it was John Petrucci that gave it a thread that made it more digestible for me, because I wasn't the biggest progressive rock fan—even though I appreciate that technique and how many parts they can memorize in one song. I don't have that good of a memory! His sound in particular, I know he used Boogie amps and Ibanez guitars—Music Man now. I loved his tone and the way he used effects, and then again, his technique and the way he played, it was very precise, but he also has a feel in his playing that I think goes back to the blues and that emotional kind of connection. And you cannot deny his technique is awesome.

MARK WOOD John Petrucci is one the finest guitar players out there! His approach to composition and guitar artistry is *astounding*. I had a chance to see him perform with Steve Morse and The Dregs years ago … blew everyone away. At my music camp/festival this past summer[†] one of my orchestras performed 'Stream Of Consciousness' for our concert. The melodic content utilizing the Phrygian scale was eye opening, and a great lesson in scale application to composition.

---

[*] Jason McMaster, Watchtower's singer.
[†] MWROC: Mark Wood Rock Orchestra Camp.

RON 'BUMBLEFOOT' THAL Few guitar players ever achieve the level of flawless technique and incredible synchronization of their hands as John Petrucci has. And without any sacrifice of emotion, melody, or musicality. This barely scratches the surface of what makes John Petrucci one of the most respected guitarists of modern times. His writing and playing span the full spectrum from primal to intellectual, with undeniable conviction. Suggested listening (to name just a few): 'Home,' 'Glasgow Kiss,' 'Under A Glass Moon,' 'The Best Of Times,' 'Fatal Tragedy,' and 'Stream Of Consciousness.'

JIM MATHEOS Just his massive technique. He's incredible. Untouchable as far as his playing goes. I think he's one of the best out there right now.

PRINCE [SOLO ARTIST]

BRUCE KULICK Prince channeled some intense, funky version of Jimi Hendrix. There's no doubt. Prince was his own animal—he was another alien of many talents. He was completely unique. Yeah, he had some odd-looking instruments— that white instrument that looked like it came down from Zeus or the angels. He definitely played as if his whole diet of riff vocabulary would be Jimi Hendrix. *But done his way.* I think he was very talented, because he was a hell of a performer, and the songwriting and all the different versions of styles that he put out, the guitar work is almost secondary … or not secondary, but even further down the line. That is a shame.

VERNON REID [LIVING COLOUR]

CHRIS HASKETT Vernon Reid is one of my favorite musicians. I never come away from hanging out with him without learning something. To me, he's one of the consummate musicians, and he's one of the few people that's got that kind of technique that I'm usually not interested in, but he actually plays stuff that I'm interested in. He's got that technique, but he's informed by an entirely different tradition. Because a lot of the other guitarists that I was listening to back in the 80s weren't my contemporaries.

You don't necessarily play like a lot of the things you listen to. A lot of the things that inform your music and inform your ear and your aesthetic horizon as an artist, aren't exactly things that you emulate or come out. So I was listening a lot to James 'Blood' Ulmer—'Layout' on *Are You Glad To Be In America?* That changed my life when I heard that. I don't play like that, you won't hear that in any of the music I was making back then, but in terms of my mental map of the geography of music and the sounds that are in my head, that was massive. Sonny Sharrock, and Rowland Howard from The Birthday Party, were huge, but again, you won't hear that in the way I played then. But you do hear that tradition of that kind of Downtown, avant-garde thing in Vernon's playing. He's one of the few people I know that can actually integrate these two different things.

RICHIE SAMBORA [BON JOVI, SOLO ARTIST]

BRUCE KULICK Richie always did a great job in that band. He always approached his solos with melody—which I like. He was flashy enough without being over-the-top. But he wasn't Eddie Van Halen, either—I don't think that would have worked in Bon Jovi, to be quite honest. And how can you not give Richie credit for [taking] an amazing song and bringing it up a notch with the talk box thing? 'Livin' On A Prayer' having that in there certainly was an amazing element. Yeah, Peter Frampton used it years ago before that, but Richie added that element to such a great song and made it even better. I had to cover that song, so I know when you don't have the gimmicky thing, it doesn't sound quite as good! I have to admit, for Richie, he's a good guitar player, but he's an amazing singer. I remember his first solo record* and being blown away by it.

MIKE SCACCIA [MINISTRY, RIGOR MORTIS]

AL JOURGENSEN That's what Mikey was put on this world to do—*play guitar.* There was no doubt. There are very few people that you see that were just gifted from a very early age; that is what they were meant to be doing. Like, for instance, me: I've had peaks and valleys in my career. And there are times when I'm on top of the world and selling a gabillion records, and then there are other times when nobody could give a shit. You just have to know, 'OK. I like what I'm doing, so it doesn't matter what the sales are or what public perception is. Are you happy with what you're doing?' And I have been. But you have those reflective moments, where you think, 'Well, if I wasn't doing this, what would I be doing?' And I came to the conclusion that the only things I am qualified for on this planet, I would have to apply for a Walmart greeter or a dishwasher at Denny's. I mean, that's

---

* *Stranger In This Town* (1991).

about it—that's the extent of what I'm capable of! Whereas somebody like Mikey was put on this planet specifically for the purpose of playing guitar.

The guy spent his high school years locked in a room, growing his hair out, and learning every riff possible. Literally, eight hours a day—because he loved it. And that translated later, when he got away from being 'perfunctory proficiency' … say that real fast five times. In other words, to be good, you have to copy the best and do it well, and get as good as them at what they did. But still, it's not your ideas. Later in his life, as a guitar player, he was good enough to keep up with anyone—technically, he was proficient—but some of the tasteful licks he did at the end … my favorite leads that he did that were the most soul-felt were on my Buck Satan record.* The country record. We had the concept like, twenty-five, thirty years ago—me and him—and we kind of piddled around and picked around in the back of the bus, backstage, in between takes. Over the years, we accumulated riffs. And by the time we got to doing the album, the leads that he ripped on that were just epic. They're legendary.

Amongst the last two or three Ministry records he did with us were just incredible, because that was Mike Scaccia. The other stuff that he does on earlier Ministry and also with Rigor Mortis, really awesome stuff. Great technically. But it wasn't from his soul. So the last five or six years of his life, I really think he was playing from a different place he was playing in previous years.† I mean, just [a] consummate musician, and the most missed person in my life—including actual relatives. I miss him every day, still. He was my best friend and my little brother. It was great to at least see him reach the pinnacle of mastering something so well, that it came secondary. There was no thought into it anymore. Anything that he played came right from the gut—and nothing having to do with his head.

MICHAEL SCHENKER [UFO, MSG, TEMPLE OF ROCK]

TREY AZAGTHOTH Hey, I grew up on bands such as UFO, and it's really great stuff. I loved the UFO *Strangers In The Night* live record. That was one of my faves. The live versions of the songs 'Mother Mary,' 'This Kids,' 'Lights Out,' and 'Rock Bottom' are so fantastic on that record, and really inspired me. I also had the Scorpions' *Lonesome Crow* and *Lovedrive* records, both featuring Michael Schenker. Then, later, the MSG stuff came out, one of the singers being Graham Bonnet. All great stuff, no doubt. Schenker looked totally cool in UFO with the

---

* *Bikers Welcome Ladies Drink Free* (2011).
† Scaccia died in 2012 after suffering a heart attack at the age of forty-seven.

Gibson Flying V, and the playing combined with the band name resulted in some really way out feeling and flows.

I also bought a Gibson Flying V in around 1990, mainly because he and also K.K. Downing from Judas Priest made that guitar so amazingly badass. Even though they are twenty-two frets, I later had Hamer build me a custom Flying V, modeled after a Gibson—but with twenty-four frets and a Floyd Rose tremolo. When I think of the Flying V, I see Schenker in the old UFO days, tearing it up. Also, UFO had amazing rhythms and song arrangements in the mid-to-late 70s. As for me and Morbid Angel, rhythms and songwriting arrangements come first, and guitar solos are secondary. I learned this because of the bands and records I would listen to growing up, and UFO was certainly one of them.

JOE STUMP I had a bunch of the UFO records when I was growing up in high school and loved Schenker's playing in that. I really liked the way on the early Michael Schenker Group records, he was much more classical and although he did still play bluesy, he had a much stronger classical and European influence. The European end of his playing was much more prominent. So that's why I like those so much—it kind of combined two schools. *Assault Attack* was awesome—the sound of the record and killer tracks. You had the instrumental on there, 'Ulcer'; 'Desert Song' of course is awesome.

BRIAN TATLER I think it's just the taste of the licks—there's such feel and touch under Michael's fingers. All his solos—even from the first UFO album [with Schenker], *Phenomenon*, right up to his solo work, I just think he's a brilliant player. I don't know how he does it. I've watched him and I've listened to him and I've studied him—I still can't play like him. It's really strange. He can move a mode and off he goes—he'll analyze what key a song is and off he goes. But when I tried to do it, it doesn't quite work the same. And it's really frustrating—I've tried it and I've taped myself, and it just doesn't sound like Schenker. You can get the odd lick that's a bit Schenker-esque, but when you just watch him jam in say, the key of E, the way he moves across the neck, it's so incredible. So fluid. He's got a great style. One of the greatest rock guitarists of all-time.

MICHAEL SCHENKER, ULI JON ROTH, MATTHIAS JABS [SCORPIONS]

RON JARZOMBEK Uli Jon Roth had that whole harmonic minor thing going. He also had a lot of the Jimi Hendrix/bluesy stuff, which I'm not a big fan of. But then Yngwie comes along, and he's Mr. Harmonic Minor, too. That sound was just real distinctive, and I think even a lot of current guitar players, it's something they go into—like Jeff Loomis does a lot of diminished seventh kind of stuff, that's got that unique Egyptian sound. That sound of harmonic minor. Like Ritchie Blackmore's solo in … or even the full song, 'Gates Of Babylon,' the whole harmonic minor thing, it just sets up this very cool eerie kind of tonality. You put that up against just regular major and minor and bluesy stuff, and it stands out. It just fits better—the whole evil/metal kind of vibe. Now, of course, I do a lot of different kinds of scales, but when that harmonic minor comes up—especially for back then—it just stood out, and I liked that sound. And Uli had a lot of that.

JEFF WATERS I find it so incredible that a guitar player like Matthias Jabs can step into a band that's been around, had a couple of other legendary guitar players in the band already, comes in, and you would assume it would be, 'OK, we need a lead guitarist. We'll hire this guy.' And this guy, Matthias, steps in and with the songwriting legacy of Klaus Meine and Rudolf Schenker, and literally 'solo' a complete song around and during vocals—and then do a solo of course, and maybe an intro and an outro—I don't know where he got that idea from and how and why the Scorpions guys let him do this, but it turned out to be one of the most amazing things in music, that you could have huge choruses going on with all this vocal stuff and this guy soloing and shredding through this stuff. And he did it in a way that it wasn't him hitting the record button and just wailing. He was 'singing' around the vocals. He was literally another vocalist complimenting the singing. And I know it sounds really deep and all that shit, but it really is something. It's a really unique thing in history—especially in hard rock and metal.

JOE STUMP If you took a holy trinity of European hard-rock/metal masters, like Blackmore, Uli, and Schenker, you can take just about any guitar player of my generation, and you could point to [how] one of those guys—if not all of them—had an impact. Whether it's Kirk Hammett, Marty Friedman, or Yngwie. And especially to anybody that plays with any kind of European sensibility. Because a lot of American players really like a lot of other American players, where if you were interviewing all of these European guys, they would immediately cite some of those guys as influences—whether it's Hank Shermann and Michael Denner from Mercyful Fate, or Wolf Hoffman from Accept, you can immediately hear Schenker and Blackmore in their playing. Just anybody I can think of whose playing I like, almost always traces back to those guys.

NEAL SCHON [JOURNEY]

RONNI LE TEKRØ Fantastic guitar player. Journey, and his guitar playing, is one of the great American inventions—next to Coca Cola! Steve Perry … the combination of his voice and the guitar playing I think did it.

SLASH [GUNS N' ROSES, VELVET REVOLVER, SOLO ARTIST]

VERNON REID Slash is this great storyteller on the guitar.

MICHAEL ANGELO BATIO Back then, if you think about it, Gibson didn't know who they were. They couldn't give a Les Paul away, because nobody cared about Gibson. They wanted to play the BC Richs, the Ibanezs, the Charvels, the Jacksons. It took Guns N' Roses to bring back a Les Paul. Because I was with Gibson—they were doing Strat-style, locking-trem guitars. They had hired Wayne Charvel to make different kinds of shapes. Gibson had lost their identity, because they got caught up in the whole LA scene; that had nothing to do with a Les Paul or a Strat. They wanted 'super-Strats.' And then when Slash came along and played that Les Paul, Gibson found their identity again.

BRUCE KULICK For me, Slash certainly has his roots in the right place. I really think he probably grew up on a diet of many of the British guitarists—I know Hendrix is actually American, but he made it first in Britain. And he took it to another level—not so much with the tricks that Eddie did, but a little more fluid speed, a little more scale, but very much based in the kind of phrasing that I prefer. I know he's addicted to guitar, I've seen him live, I'm friends with some of the guys in his band—I don't know Slash, I've met him a few times and we always had a polite exchange, and I admire him. But his kind of playing is totally pure and powerful—it's a Les Paul through a loud amp, he doesn't get crazy with the pedals.

There couldn't have been a Guns N' Roses without him. And I know that Axl with the onward career of Guns N' Roses without Slash probably sounds fine—I never saw them and I know he's had some very talented guitar players—but I really feel in many ways that Slash is so much the heart and soul of how the tone of that band was created. Which is why there is so much mythology. It's not just his hat—it's Slash with a guitar. We all know the original guitar he [used on] *Appetite For Destruction* wasn't really a Gibson, but it was a damn good copy of one, right?

I use Slash as a comparison a lot when I do a clinic, and even though I might be representing ESP Guitars or Duncan pickups, I make sure that the people understand that, 'Look, the things that artists endorse, like Slash's guitar or a guitar pick or wah-wah pedal, these are tools that he can use and admires and likes. But it doesn't mean that you're going to sound like Slash. The guitar is too unique—it's about your hands.' Steve Lukather is a monster, who performed on *BK3*[*] with me. He didn't bring a guitar in the right key for the song—I was cutting an instrumental in E flat. And his guitar was in 440, and it wasn't going to work. To set it up would have been a nightmare. I said, 'Do you mind playing this ESP? I have this killer-sounding three-pickup Vintage Plus.' He grabbed it, kept it always on the bass pickup, *and it's pure Steve Lukather.* Even though I filled in some riffs from his performance and gaps with the same guitar, you know it's somebody else playing it. Same amp, same guitar. And that's what I love about guitar playing, and Slash, getting back to him, I think his tone and his style was definitive of Guns N' Roses, which was just such a hugely important band.

ROSS THE BOSS I thank God [for Slash's guitar playing]. The hair-metal thing, every guitar player looking the same, having the same equipment, using the same techniques—the whole thing kind of imploded at the same time. And then grunge came in, and it was over. But Guns N' Roses had taken it to the next level. Slash was like a breath of fresh air—that whole *Appetite* record, to this day it's still great.

CHRIS CAFFERY Of course, you can't deny the fact that Slash was probably one of the most important guitar players coming out of the 80s. He brought that mixture between the grunge and Alice Cooper–ish stage-like appearance together, and really created an identity that is undeniable. The fact that he can go out and headline festivals and big shows as just Slash, that's a testament—there's not a lot of people who have been able to do that as guitar players.

JOHN SYKES [WHITESNAKE, THIN LIZZY, BLUE MURDER]

BRUCE KULICK What John Sykes did, between the writing and that incredibly wonderful, wide vibrato and speed and tone that he created—especially on those Whitesnake songs that I know and enjoyed—that was magic. Another instance that I'm like, 'Why can't they [David Coverdale and Sykes] work together?' I know that Coverdale has gone on and worked with a lot of really good guitar

---

[*] Bruce's solo album from 2010.

players. But what Sykes did defines an era of Whitesnake that everybody is kind of looking for. 'Still Of The Night' deserves to be a classic solo—it's brilliant. He was doing kind of … Randy Rhoads died at a young age, and he did iconic stuff with Ozzy Osbourne, but I feel like Sykes also did that for Coverdale in Whitesnake. They're solos that were super, super-melodic and technically difficult to play—with amazing tone and phrasing. Not that long ago, I heard ['Still Of The Night'] on the radio, and I was like, 'Man, this song is unbelievable!' I don't care if it's your more modern version of a Led Zeppelin kind of thing—*it sounds amazing.* But I'm glad that Sykes got a chance to showcase his talents on that—because that everybody will always remember.

AKIRA TAKASAKI [LOUDNESS]

JEFF WATERS Akira had this Rhoads, Van Halen, Schenker, Blackmore, Van Halen … he must have been a huge Van Halen fan, because he tapped into this sound that a lot of guitar players have, and a lot of people don't understand how they get it. And I know how they get it—*it's cheap guitars and cheap necks.* Not the $3,000 Gibson model, but the $600 Epiphone model. Not the DV8-R from ESP that costs $3,000, but the cheapy one from Dave Mustaine. Back in the day, in 2003, I remember I had the expensive one and the cheap one, and the cheaper necks, sometimes they're horrible and the intonation is out, but those are the necks that have the life, the sounds, the squeals, the noise, the mess, the character. He seemed to capture that real twangy neck original thing like Van Halen had, but with some Blackmore and some real rock'n'roll stuff. And a lot of those pinch harmonics—things that Zakk Wylde got famous for, were really done by Jake E. Lee, that he got from inheriting the Jake E. Lee legacy. And that of course came from Van Halen and guys before him.

But Akira was one of those rare freaks that had that this ability to do the fast technical stuff and scales and move all over the place, but had this feel that you just couldn't copy it. It's like Angus Young, Gary Moore, and Matthias Jabs—who was my favorite at this—taking one single note, putting one finger on it, bending it, and making it sing. Making it *feel.* And that's something I can't do. I can't take one note and make it sing—I've got to play a couple of notes and do a scale or a little lick or something. I don't really focus on trying to get one note and make it sing, because it's something inside you, and those guys are the best at that. Matthias is great—he just hits one note, and you go, '*How do you do that?*' It's in the blood. You can't learn that stuff. Akira was like that—he was just such a 'feel' guitar player.

RON 'BUMBLEFOOT' THAL [GUNS N' ROSES, SOLO ARTIST]

GUTHRIE GOVAN This was 'Spotlight' doing its job. I would read about these players, and there was something about the little write-up on Ron that had spoke to me. It was like, 'I like this guy. I haven't heard a note that he's played, but I know I'm going to enjoy what he does.' So I just wrote to him, and said, 'I would like to buy your demo … and here's mine, in case you're curious.' And he sent his back. He was like, 'You don't need to buy it. I want you to have this, and I like your demo,' and we just stayed in touch. We carried on sending cassette tapes to each other.

But Ron was—and still is—way ahead of his time. The stuff he was doing back then, before his first album came out, he was kind of a turning point for me. He was the first player in the field of complicated rock guitar playing, where I had absolutely no idea how he was doing the stuff he was doing. All the other people you would read about in guitar magazines or see on MTV, you could kind of trace the lineage of what they were doing. You could spot something that maybe used to be a Jimmy Page lick or used to be a Van Halen lick or used to be a Nuno lick. And everything seemed to be connected to everything else. With Ron, he somehow seemed to be thinking so far outside the box that it was impossible to tell what was making him tick or where he was coming from. It was really exciting. Just really grateful that someone that eccentric existed, and technically, it just was beyond.

KIM THAYIL [SOUNDGARDEN]

CHRIS HASKETT Kim's awesome. With Kim, it's a very subtle thing—he's never showy about technical prowess. A lot of the Soundgarden stuff, they keep it very 'meat and potatoes.' And what's interesting about it are the melodic lines—not the technique. It's the melody of the solos. There's not a lot of speedy runs in Soundgarden. But what he does play is almost perfect for the song. And it's nice, because it was also quite refreshing to hear somebody who wasn't trying to just show off. Who doesn't need to.

That's the thing—they say 'Little dogs bark, big dogs don't have to.' If you're playing the right thing, you don't need to add twenty more notes to it. And with Soundgarden, also, they had two guitarists,* which I always said, 'I was the only guitarist in a two-guitar band,' when I was with Rollins. But again, there are so many aspects to being a really interesting and really good guitarist, and then in the broader

---

* Singer Chris Cornell sometimes plays guitar as well.

spectrum, being a really good musician. Because there are a lot of good guitarists who are terrible musicians. But Kim is both—good guitarist and good musician.

DEREK TRUCKS [THE ALLMAN BROTHERS BAND, THE DEREK TRUCKS BAND, TEDESCHI TRUCKS BAND]

KIM THAYIL Here's a guitar player who is absolutely one of my favorite guitar players—and I share zero amount of his skillset—and that is Derek Trucks. I can honestly say the way that guy improvises and the way he plays slide is just fucking beautiful. He captures it, it's emotive, it's just amazing.

WARREN HAYNES Derek and I have known each other since he was eleven. He was playing great even then. And I've watched him somehow continue to get better and better through the years. I think Derek discovered early on how important it was that he find his own voice. And he did that at a much younger age than most people do—partially by exposing himself to a lot of influences that aren't typical rock guitar influences. Y'know, Middle Eastern music and steel-guitar sounds and melodies. And taking jazz music and incorporating it to slide guitar—which had not been done to that extent. Derek is just an extremely talented musician, and always had the right philosophy and approach to remaining a student of music.

VINNIE VINCENT [KISS, VINNIE VINCENT INVASION]

BRUCE KULICK The only things I'm familiar about with that album* is I knew some of the drama around it, because I would hear things from people that worked with him. Obviously, why wouldn't you get some gossip on someone that was that controversial in the history of Kiss! But the two things that stood out for me was first of all, in many ways, The Vinnie Vincent Invasion was pretty damn cool for the time. You look at it now, and you go, 'Oh my God—look at his hair!' You look at the clothes, right? But the other thing that was pretty outrageous that I remember was his lead guitar, he mixed it *so loud*—that was pretty extreme for back then. But it was about him, and he had some fierce guitar work.

It wasn't completely my cup of tea, but I thought it fit better for what would be a Vinnie Vincent Invasion band, than what would be Kiss. I was not impressed with him overplaying—I've heard some versions of 'Cold Gin,'† and whatever he's

---

* The Vinnie Vincent Invasion's self-titled debut, released in 1986.
† Recorded when Vinnie toured with Kiss from 1982 to '84.

doing, it's too leftfield of what 'Cold Gin' should be about. And even though I didn't have to do every Ace riff and was never given that kind of direction by Gene and Paul, I still feel like my go-to riffs are in the right vein.

So Vinnie, I've got to give him credit—a talented guitar player and a talented songwriter—but I think his work in Kiss, as much as they might have been popular in that era, to be that flashy, I don't think that they were really that appropriate for Kiss. But probably very appropriate for Vinnie Vincent Invasion. And as you know, that imploded, and that became Slaughter—a very successful band that we toured with, later on.

ZAKK WYLDE [OZZY OSBOURNE, BLACK LABEL SOCIETY]

CHRIS CAFFERY I think that Zakk—in a lot of ways—he's got maximum exposure as a personality, but I think that a lot of times had, for some reason, a lack of respect from the guitar-playing world. And I think that just comes out of jealousy. Because he got so big, and there might be players out there that might be technically better than him in some ways, but if you watched him, Zakk can do the chicken-pickin' stuff like Jerry Reed did. He can play great blues. He kind of focused on being 'Zakk Wylde,' and that is another thing—when you listen to him with the squeals that he did, he made a sound. I think certain guitar players wish they were that much of a household name. Regardless of how much they might practice or how many *Guitar Player* magazines they're going to be in, Black Label Society is alongside Motörhead on the Hot Topic T-shirt wall. And I think that separates Zakk from everybody else.

ANGUS YOUNG [AC/DC]

PAUL GILBERT I totally love Angus. First of all, AC/DC is just such an exciting band. I remember the first AC/DC song I ever heard was maybe 'Let There Be Rock' or 'Whole Lotta Rosie'—one of those songs off the first live album*—and it was just so exciting. I was glued to the radio when it came on, like, '*What is this?!*' And Angus, it was funny, at the time in the late 70s, early 80s, the virtuoso thing was just starting to take off. In a way, if you were into the virtuoso culture at the time, Angus, people would put him down. Like, 'Oh, that's so simple,' or 'All they play are blues licks.' And I don't think I ever fell into that.

---

* *If You Want Blood* (1978).

I remember as a guitar player, I was more into Van Halen, but I still loved what AC/DC did, and I still spent time with that music. I learned all the songs—'Riff Raff'—and played those songs a ton when I was in a band. Just loved them. And when you listen to Angus, you wouldn't want to put an Yngwie solo in an AC/DC song. It would just be wrong. Angus is playing the perfect guitar for the style, and you wouldn't want to change a note.

DWEEZIL ZAPPA [ZAPPA PLAYS ZAPPA, SOLO ARTIST]

BLUES SARACENO He's outstanding. He and I have always gotten along, because it's almost like totally opposing guitar styles. What makes him unique is his sense of timing. He has such an avant-garde sense of timing. We would jam and I would watch his foot, and his foot was never on the one or the three, or the two or the four—it was on some random pattern. Yet, it would repeat. So it was some random pattern that repeated … that I guess isn't random. He had the ability to mimic stuff—especially when it came to his dad's type of stuff, he could hear things and could play all these harmonies. It was a very different approach. I would just show up and punch it, and he would take his time and methodically approach it differently.

He had the record with the green Charvel on the cover.* I remember driving to New York City with my dad for the day, and he said, 'I'll get you anything you want.' And I said, 'I want the Dweezil Zappa record!' The interesting thing about him was at one point, he went to me and said, 'I'm going to go out on the road and start playing my dad's stuff—I really want to get it to a different generation. The problem is there is some stuff that is not even meant to be played on guitar … *but I'm going to do it.*'

So at one point, he took a year out and re-taught himself how to play guitar—with different techniques, like sweep-picking and alternate picking. I remember thinking, 'You're crazy. Why would you take a year out of your life? You already know how to play guitar!' He literally just woodshedded for a year. And the stuff he can do now is just ridiculous. He can do stuff on the guitar that I didn't even think could be done. Now, what makes him stand out even more than just his guitar prowess is his musicianship—it's on a whole other level. Think about it—he's doing the Zappa Plays Zappa tour.† What other guitar player on the planet can pull that off? It's a short list … I'm not one of them. [*Laughs*]

---

* *Havin' A Bad Day* (1986).
† In which Dweezil plays Frank's music.

crucial shred

Here, many of the guitarists interviewed for this book discuss the songs or albums that feature some of their best playing or soloing.

ALCATRAZZ, *DISTURBING THE PEACE* (1985)

STEVE VAI After I had heard Edward and Yngwie, I realized that you could create tone where the notes are really clear. Because I wasn't doing that. I had this very fast kind of picking style, and I could play all these very bizarre type melodies and stuff, but it didn't sound great. When somebody comes along and does something that wakes you up, it inspires you to focus on things. So I knew I didn't want to sound like those guys—I knew it wasn't possible—but I knew that it gave me a leg up to redefine my playing. So, virtually overnight, I changed my style so the notes would come out clearer and cleaner, with more presence and tone. It was all about the tone in my fingers. It's when I realized that tone isn't necessarily in your amp—it's in your head.

The Alcatrazz record was my opportunity to record music with this new style of playing, and, also, the band was turning to be one of the major contributors of the music, so it gave me the opportunity to do the music that was kind of important to me in a rock format. And they trusted the music that I was writing and enjoyed it … we all worked on it, and Graham wrote lyrics and all, but I knew I was totally uninterested in writing or playing music like the previous Alcatrazz with Yngwie. I mean, I thought it was great—it was fascinating and cool. But it wasn't me. And I never really was capable of conforming because I just never thought I was good enough to try and sound like somebody else. It never made sense.

What I didn't realize is, accidentally, I was developing my own style as a result. So, the Alcatrazz record was a great opportunity to first of all, be with some really cool guys—I really liked the guys in the band. They were funny, they were smart, we had a great time. And they gave me an opportunity to make my first record— basically in a rock band like that. And I got to work with Eddie Kramer. I will say that I was a little bit of a self-centered prick at the time … maybe a lot! Because I always felt that I needed to do it my way, my way, my way. As a result, *poor Eddie Kramer*—I was a big pain in his ass. But having said that, we got something out of it that I thought was pretty cool. I still like that record.

THE ALLMAN BROTHERS BAND, 'SOULSHINE'
(FROM *WHERE IT ALL BEGINS*, 1994)

WARREN HAYNES The guitar solo doesn't change that much from night to night. I tend to play it somewhat similarly. I try to approach it as different as possible, but within the same sort of parameters. And I've kind of been looking at that song that way since I wrote it, which was a long time ago. Some songs I tend to change the solos more drastically, and others stay a little more close to the bone. 'Soulshine' seems like one of those songs that is very melodic, and the approach to the solo is very much within the melody and structure of the song. When I first wrote it, it was so simple—I kept looking for ways to make it more complicated. And nothing seemed to work. I took that as a sign to leave it alone. But it was just a simple little song that I really had no idea that so many people would identify with it.

ANNIHILATOR, 'ALISON HELL' (FROM *ALICE IN HELL*, 1989)

JEFF WATERS The actual solo is kind of blur, because that was written in '85, in my parents' basement. I don't know where it came from. But then when I moved to Vancouver, and the song 'Alison Hell,' we'd just done a video for and signed to Roadrunner Records, and it was released on our version of MTV's *Headbangers Ball*, called the *MuchMusic Power Hour*. I had a girlfriend who knew this guitar player, Brian MacLeod, and Brian was the guitar player in a Canadian band called The Headpins. He was an amazing guitar player—he died of cancer [in 1992]. Just before he died, I ended up on his boat in Vancouver Harbor, and my girlfriend took me because she knew him.

She wanted to play my song, 'Alison Hell,' for Brian MacLeod—I don't know why, but she wanted to play it for him. And he played it and rewound the solo three times, and he looks at me, and goes, 'Holy shit, dude. That's amazing. That is complete start-to-finish Michael Schenker.' And I went, 'Oh, whoa!' And then I listened to the solo and I realized, 'Oh my God … it's Michael Schenker!' [*Laughs*] You can tell that is where I got the whole feel from. No notes were copied or it wasn't a copy of a solo—it just was that was the best I could do as not Michael Schenker. That was kind of a revelation, because I never really heard that again in any of my solos. That was just a special, weird time.

AUTOGRAPH, 'TURN UP THE RADIO' (FROM *SIGN IN PLEASE*, 1984)

STEVE LYNCH We were at Victory Studios in North Hollywood. We weren't even a band—we just rehearsed there on weekends. And all of us were in different paid bands. I was in a group with the keyboard player [Steven Isham] called Holly Penfield, on Dreamland Records. The singer [Steve Plunkett] was playing with Earl Slick in a group called Silver Condor, on Columbia Records. Our drummer [Keni Richards] was playing with a band called The Coup, on A&M Records, and the bass player [Randy Rand] was playing with Lita Ford. So we got together on weekends. We jammed out and had a good time drinking beer. We all knew each other, so we got together in Victory Studios, and jammed out on a Saturday or Sunday. We started throwing together some tunes, and Andy Johns came down— the producer—and he listened to some of our songs, and said, 'Hey, I really like your songs. Why don't we go into the studio and cut a demo?'

And the way 'Turn Up The Radio' came about, I was standing onstage, everybody was taking a break. I started playing this riff, and they said, 'What is that? That's kind of cool.' So everybody got up onstage, and we started jamming around with it. Within a half-hour, we had the music to the whole thing going— we had the groove going and everything. Everybody said, 'We should put that on the demo. Let's come up with some words.' At first, it was like, 'Turn up the cassette machine.' In fact, we put that on the first demo, and then we changed it—when we went into the studio with Andy—to 'radio.' Because we thought that cassette machines may not be around for long … and we were right!

Then we went out and toured with Van Halen after that, which was kind of weird. Keni, the drummer, played the demo that we did with Andy for David Lee Roth one morning when he was jogging with him—they used to jog on Sunset Boulevard every morning at 8:30. And David Lee Roth really liked it. A lot. He said, 'Why don't you guys come out and open for us on the *1984* tour? Just for a few months—however long you want to do it.' Keni said, 'That's great ... *but we're not really a band.* We only have these five songs, and we're all playing in different bands right now.' So Keni came to rehearsal next weekend and threw that at us, and we were like, 'Y'know, we're all done recording with these other bands that we're involved with. We really could go out and do a few months. It would be kind of fun. We'll just write some more songs. Let's go and do it.' So we did it.

At rehearsal, we passed the hat, so we collected enough money to rent an RV and drive from Los Angeles to Florida, for the first gig. We did it, and then the next thing you know, RCA, Warner Bros, Geffen, A&M—all of them were saying, 'Are you guys signed?' And we go, 'No. We're not really even a band. We just thought of the name Autograph on the way here, actually, in the RV.' They said, 'Well, we like your sound,' and they were throwing offers at us. RCA made us an offer at Madison Square Garden that we couldn't refuse, and we took it. We decided to quit our other bands and go with this.

Basically, what I did [in the solo] was, I went in and thought, 'I would like the solo to transpose into another key, and just like a bridge, take it somewhere else for a little while.' So that's what we did with it—we took it up to the key of A major, and I started out playing A Mixolydian on top of it, and that seemed to work really well in that key. I tried out different things over and over again—it was an odd key and an odd mode for me to play in, and I hadn't done anything with the Mixolydian mode before. So I played around with it for quite a bit, and I wanted it to sound really melodic, so I tried a lot of different things. I probably worked on it for a whole week, for several hours, trying stuff, and going, 'Nah.' I did that with a lot of my solos. I would try different things and go, 'No. That's not it. It didn't start out right, it's not ending right, the middle part is very weak.'

But I tried enough things where I eventually got to the point where I thought, 'This is actually working out for me.' And when I brought it in, everybody thought, 'Wow. That really is a good solo.' And I doubled it. In fact, I doubled all my solos on the first three records—which was difficult to do, to match up some of the bends and vibrato stuff. But even though they're sometimes slightly out, it kind of sounds cool like that. They're not perfectly in pitch. So I just doubled all of them, because I liked the way they sounded. I put one at ten and one at two, and that's the way it was panned. Sometimes, I'd pan it hard left and hard right. But I liked the sound of doubling the solos.

JASON BECKER, *PERPETUAL BURN* (1988)

JASON BECKER After Marty Friedman and I finished recording *Speed Metal Symphony*, I was very happy with it, but I had so many ideas that I wanted to get out. I spent tons of time writing at my four-track. I would play stuff for Mike Varney and Marty. It became obvious that this had to become a solo album. There wasn't any room for vocals. Varney suggested that Marty put together a solo album, too. I wasn't thinking about my age. Playing with and learning from Friedman added years of experience, creativity, and confidence to my whole outlook. He was the catapult for everything for me. I recorded at the same studio that we did *Speed Metal Symphony* in, and with the same engineer, Steve Fontano, so I was comfortable in that way, but this time, I had to run the show. Marty wasn't there when we recorded Atma Anur's drums. That made me a little nervous, but Fontano complimented me on how I was bobbing my head to keep Atma in time. That felt really good.

I remember when I had Fontano lay the click track down for 'Air,' he didn't know what the hell I was doing. Six minutes of click track is pretty funny to hear in a professional studio. When recording the first licks in 'Perpetual Burn,' I had to use a bar in between them, instead of stopping like I wanted, because there was too much feedback when I stopped, and the gate wouldn't respond quick enough.

I did my first take of the blues solo in 'Eleven Blue Egyptians' late at night. It sounded stiff but I couldn't figure out why. Fontano suggested I get sleep and try again tomorrow. I usually hate to leave something hanging, but I took his advice. The next day it just flowed out of me easily.

Marty, of course, was recording *Dragon's Kiss* at the same time. He was working extra long hours. He was giving Fontano a break from hitting record during 'Air.' During recording, Marty and I both nodded off in the middle of a lick. We woke up and cracked up. One day, Marty called me to do my part on 'Jewel.' His dad was visiting in the studio. I have no idea why, but I was being argumentative. As always, Marty was calm and understanding. I still feel bad about that. I was a butthole to my mentor in front of his dad. I love his parents. On another day, Marty called me in to play a part for him because the drummer, Deen Castronovo, had played it too fast. He knew I could play the part fast enough. That felt so nice, being able to help the person who had constantly helped me.

I met Greg Howe at this time. We got along great. He had me play a harmony to a lick that he had always wanted to play with another guitarist. We had a blast hanging and jamming. Greg was working with Billy Sheehan, so I got to spend a little time with him. I was stoked when he compared 'Air' to Van Halen's 'Eruption,' for its uniqueness and innovation. 'Opus Pocus,' 'Air,' and 'Altitudes' stand out for me. They are totally uniquely me. No one else did stuff like that. 'Dweller In The Cellar,' too. Actually, every song stands out. In a way, I sort of created a new style of guitar music with these songs.

ADRIAN BELEW, 'BIG ELECTRIC CAT' (FROM *LONE RHINO*, 1982)

ADRIAN BELEW Seymour Duncan was an old friend of mine, and at this point, he started to become famous for his pickups—which he's now world famous for. And I had a little Music Master Fender with one pickup. A very cheap, little guitar—a blue one. I still have it. And I thought, 'Well, I'm just going to send this to Seymour and have it made fretless.' I don't know why, I just thought, 'I wonder what you could do if you have a guitar with no frets on it?'

He sent it back to me, and when he did, I got it out of the case, I tuned it up, I plugged it into our little recording board—my friend had a recording studio with an eight-track recorder. And I plugged it through a box that I really liked, it was called the Foxx Tone Machine—it was an octave divider, and if you dialed it in correctly, you could get a tone very reminiscent of 'Purple Haze.' The very high, screamy kind of sound. So we plugged it in, I just started playing, and that's what I played. Later, I recorded some more of it, so that's not the first take, but honestly, that song was 'in the guitar' when it arrived.

BUMBLEFOOT, *THE ADVENTURES OF BUMBLEFOOT* (1995)

RON 'BUMBLEFOOT' THAL There were a few songs that I had on my Fostex eight-track reel-to-reel, and at this point, for that album, I picked up two ADATs and a Mackie 24x8 board. I still was living at home, in mom and dad's basement; I had gear in the corner, and a pair of headphones so I wouldn't disturb them, and did all recording and mixing with headphones, and a blanket over a Marshall half-stack and a little SM57 under it, that I would keep checking, to make sure the blanket didn't move the mic.

During the summer, the air conditioner would go on—the big air conditioner unit—and it would make too much noise, so I would have to wait for it to stop running, [then] hit record. And have just a little punch-in/punch-out footswitch that I would step on—it had a slight delay to it, and I got a feel for exactly how much latency it was on this little RadioShack, ten-dollar on/off stomp switch. It was about two thirds of a second, and I had it down where I could just punch in and get it right. And then every once in a while, I would sneak upstairs and turn the thermostat up to ninety, so the air conditioner wouldn't go on, and about two hours later, my mother would start screaming, '*Who turned off the thermostat? RONALD!*'

But yeah, I would just bust out songs and I started off talking about the concept for the album. I had the one song, 'Bumblefoot,' which is an animal disease, so I said, 'How about every song is named after a different animal disease? I'll come up with a song that matches those diseases.' And I got to work—'Strawberry Footrot,' 'Fistulous Withers,' 'Ick,' 'Blue Tongue,' 'Limberneck.' I would just record, and there was no editing—it all just had to be done the old-fashioned way. I had an Alesis drum machine that had a sequencer in it, so that I would just write all the sequences and everything for it, and would record that, and layer everything on top of it.

After it was all done, I went back and I transcribed the whole album. It took about six months, and was two hundred pages. I never released it—until we did the fifteen-year anniversary five years go, and at that point, I spent another six months just getting the typesetting and everything nice and adding a little introduction to it, and put out the book. It was two hundred pages of every single note, and picking, fingers, musical notation, tab, and any additional instructions, like, 'Wipe hand across strings here.'

[I have] very good memories of making that album. And even the artwork, staring at my foot in my little apartment—my first apartment that I had rented, that I ended up moving back home afterward—with Windows 3.11 … I don't think it was Windows 95 yet. Just an old PC and CorelDRAW 4, and staring at my foot and drawing lines and nudging and rounding the edges of lines and vector imaging, and spending two weeks just making the album art. And then uploaded this huge 1.4MB file overnight to California—which now, it would happen in 1.4 seconds, back then, it was an all-night thing—hoping that the connection didn't break. I remember it all well.

CACOPHONY, *SPEED METAL SYMPHONY* (1987) AND *GO OFF!* (1988)

MARTY FRIEDMAN Well, most of *Speed Metal Symphony* was going to be my solo album. But I met Jason, and tried to force in little spots for him to write on, although most of the record was written. I wanted to give him some showcases on there, so I kind of postponed my solo record and added some Jason stuff in there, and that's how *Speed Metal Symphony* came about. And then *Go Off!* was more of a band effort—with Jason contributing just as much as I did.

JASON BECKER I was seventeen years old and I just followed Marty's lead. We had so much fun writing and creating together. The first thing I recorded was a little bass part at the end of the track 'Speed Metal Symphony.' I was really nervous. I remember doing background vocals on 'Burn The Ground.' I kept ruining takes because I kept laughing. Yelling 'Burn the ground!' was funny to me. I really like the title track. I wrote a lot of cool parts for it. It was innovative for two guitars to be doing so much counterpoint, weird harmonies, and complex interplay. I also like 'Desert Island.' I played a nice clean part.

I had a lot more to do with *Go Off!*, but I felt like we weren't quite ready to record when we went into the studio. Once we started, I could see we were fine. It was so much fun. It was very loose and creative. I am partial to 'Images,' which is the one I wrote by myself, influenced by Debussy. I had lyrics for it, but they were lame, so we made it an instrumental. I think the last melody on the title track is some of my best playing and writing. I played the acoustic guitar at the end of 'Black Cat.' Marty did an off-the-cuff solo over that. He didn't think it was very good, but I talked him into using it.

DEF LEPPARD, 'PHOTOGRAPH' AND 'ROCK OF AGES' (FROM *PYROMANIA*, 1983)

PHIL COLLEN I remember using my Ibanez Destroyer—the one that is actually in the ['Photograph'] video. A three-pickup Ibanez Destroyer that had DiMarzios on. I plugged into my fifty-watt Girl head—not a master volume one. I loved this amp—it got stolen at some point. I literally just plugged it in and it sounds like it is on the album. Me and Mutt figured out how the solo should go, and we wanted it to be melodic and not step over the lead vocal—and still have a melodic relief from the rest of the stuff. So we double-tracked it. I did that on a lot of those solos. 'Foolin'' I think was the same thing—I double-tracked the solo and it gave it an edge. At the end, I was just kind of improvising on the outro. It is always amazing to work with Mutt Lange—he's an absolute genius. It's always so inspiring, because he'll get so much out of you and draw stuff out of you that you didn't realize you even had.

'Rock Of Ages' is the same guitar—Ibanez Destroyer. Thomas Dolby had played keyboards on this track, and there was a lot of space in it. It was a different type of solo—bending the strings and just making the single notes work. A lot of people struggle to sustain a note, because they're not confident in their own vibrato. So that solo, it was more about that. I always think solos, you have to be part of the song—you can't go too far out on a tangent that you fuck the song up. You have to be within context, and hopefully, you stick with it—groove and melody. That's the thing. And if you do get an option to shine with a bit of shredding and it fits in, great. But if it's out of context, don't do it.

DIAMOND HEAD, 'AM I EVIL?' (FROM *LIGHTNING TO THE NATIONS*, 1980)

BRIAN TATLER We'd been working on that song for a long time, and I always felt it wasn't actually finished until we got in the studio. So we were in the studio recording that song for our album, *Lightning To The Nations*, and I got about 90 percent of the solo done, but the tapping bit, I seemed to be just tapping in the same key, and the recording engineer, Paul Robbins, suggested changing the chords underneath it. So I did the tapping bit, and he played a keyboard and suggested, 'Why don't you play an A and then a F and then an A sharp and then a F sharp, and then go up to B?' It sounded great, so that was it—a great idea, very musical, very dramatic. So once that little last bit was done, the whole song felt complete to me. That felt like the final piece of the jigsaw, and the epic was completed.

DIO, 'RAINBOW IN THE DARK' (FROM *HOLY DIVER*, 1983) AND
'THE LAST IN LINE' (FROM *THE LAST IN LINE*, 1984)

VIVIAN CAMPBELL ['Rainbow In The Dark'] was actually the very first solo we recorded for the *Holy Diver* album. And as usual, I've never ever—certainly in my early days—prepared for recording a solo. I always relied on inspiration. In the studio, I was just playing guitar all day—drinking coffee, smoking Marlboros, playing guitar … and playing in A, because the song is in A. So I knew I was going to be doing a solo in A, but I still didn't actually sit down and work it out. And then, that evening, Ronnie says, 'OK, let's get a guitar sound. Let's do this.' So I went in, got a guitar sound, they rolled the tape, and the solo on the record is the very first take. I have no idea where or how that came from, but it came out. Afterward, Ronnie went, 'Wow, that's great! Do you want to try another?' And I said, 'Yeah, OK.'

And here's the problem—because I'm doing a second one, I'm thinking, 'Oh shit. I can't do what I did on that.' So now, I'm really starting to put up mental blocks in front of myself. And I'm thinking, 'Well, I can't start there, because that's where I started the other one.' So I'm thinking about it too much. I do the second one, and Ronnie says, 'OK … *we'll just keep the first one.*' [*Laughs*] That was a great example of how that method worked for me. But I think it's fair to say—more often than not—it didn't work. I'd go into the studio ready to cut a guitar solo, and hope for that inspiration to strike, and if it didn't, I'd think, 'Oh shit. I've really got to sit down and think about this.'

I prefer not to have an audience. I've never liked having a lot of people around the studio when I'm cutting a solo—because it's a creative thing for me, it's not a performance. It's not like I have it in my back pocket and I'm ready to go. I'm very much 'fishing for it,' and the more people are around me, the more I find it distracting. I'm a little bit more at ease with that nowadays. I have gotten to the stage, like even with this Last In Line record,* where nine times out of ten, I would sit down and try and map out something before going to the studio. But I never did that in my twenties.

['The Last In Line'] was more pieced together. By the second Dio album, I had gotten to the stage where I kicked everyone out of the studio. And by everyone, it was really just Ronnie and Angelo [Arcuri], our engineer. So I'd ask them to go play pinball or have a coffee, and Angelo would set me up with a couple tracks, and he would show me on the machine, 'OK. Record, play'—so I knew how to punch myself in and how to stop, and how to change tracks. I'd just start fishing, and it came together. The actual end result was a composite track between … I can't remember if I did two or three passes at it, but Ronnie and Angelo came back in and they started hacking it together. That was a much more 'composed' solo. It was one of those instances where I started playing, and I thought, 'Fuck, just blowing away in A is not going to cut it here.' So I got the first thing [*sings first lines of the solo*] and said, 'OK, that's cool.' I literally was building it as I went.

DIO, 'I COULD HAVE BEEN A DREAMER' AND 'ALL THE FOOLS SAILED AWAY' (FROM *DREAM EVIL*, 1987)

CRAIG GOLDY I always like to compose a solo. And in my world, a solo is like a paragraph—it begins with an opening statement and it ends with a closing statement, and has supporting facts in between … always begins with 'Hello' and ends with 'Goodbye.' I would try to put that into the solos as I would compose

---

* *Holy Crown* (2016).

them. And also, that it should be some sort of a musical interpretation of what the song is about. In my world, when you're able to mix modes—so you can go in between major and minor and Dorian and things like that within the same solo—that makes it more 'dreamier,' or creates an atmosphere.

So that ['I Could Have Been A Dreamer'] was one of the first songs I was able to really utilize that method within the composing of the solo. And people seem to like that solo. That was one of my favorites that I was able to put together. Because Ronnie was one of those that he was from the era where guys would go in and they would just improvise, make a composite, and then make one solo out of several takes. But I would like to go in with an already worked-out solo that I thought fit the song best. So sometimes, he would go, 'Great, as is,' and sometimes, he wouldn't. That was one of them that he said, 'Great. Let's keep that one.'

[For 'All The Fools Sailed Away'] I tried to create a theme. That's why there's a portion of that song that is a melody that is interwoven throughout the song—I tried to create it and have a theme. In fact, my first composition of that solo, Ronnie was like, 'Nah. Let's try something else.' So I had a secondary one. That was the first song that actually had a 'backup' solo composed! So we used the second one instead. But it was our first of many that Simon Wright, the drummer, would call an epic. Something comedians do is they use a joke or a punch line three or four times throughout their performance, because it kind of makes things more memorable. So that solo, I wanted to make it more memorable.

DOKKEN, *UNDER LOCK AND KEY* (1985)

GEORGE LYNCH I think the *Under Lock And Key* record is the most satisfying to listen to. We really reached our apex as a band. The two records previous to that[*] were just leading up to that record. We'd taken enough baby steps, and, 'OK. We've arrived. Now we know what we want to do, and we have the resources to do it the way we want to, and the knowledge to get it done.' I felt we really had something to prove.

And from a guitar standpoint, Michael Wagener got a *phenomenal* guitar sound. We spent a lot of time getting those guitar sounds—a couple of days of mic testing and preamp testing and different amps and different amp combinations and speaker cabinet combinations and different rooms and different mics. It was a very unorthodox process we used to record that.

I did a side-chain into what I usually do for my demos when I'm writing

---

* *Breaking The Chains* (1981) and *Tooth And Nail* (1984).

songs at home, which is a Fostex cassette analog tape recorder—an X-15—and I ran my Tom Scholz Rockman X100 into that, with some pedals and an Echoplex. And that all went into a channel on the board. I remember Michael was very against doing that. He was like, 'It's very primitive. Why would you do that when you have a two-inch Studer tape machine sitting there, and you have your Fostex X-15?' And I said, 'Well, I don't know. I just think it has *a thing* that this thing doesn't have.'

And he ended up using it—not a lot, but it was in there. It was in the mix. But he even admitted it; he said, 'It kind of just makes everything bigger and glues it all together on its own. It's like a really small tone, but when you put it in with all the other amps, it kind of glues it all together. It fills in the blanks.' And I just remember it was one of the best recording experiences I have ever had. I loved working with Michael—we were in a big room, had lots of time to really dial everything in, and I took my time with it.

DRAGONFORCE, 'THROUGH THE FIRE AND THE FLAMES' (FROM *INHUMAN RAMPAGE*, 2005) AND 'HEROES OF OUR TIME' (FROM *ULTRA BEATDOWN*, 2008)

HERMAN LI That song … how many solos are there? About three or four—I can't remember. The way we approached that solo is just like any DragonForce song—we try to split even between Sam [Totman] and myself, and make sure that we've got the right parts for each other, that fit our style. Certain parts and the backing music fits Sam, and certain times, the way it's written, it fits me. So we divide it up based on the music. And to be honest, when we were doing that, we approach it like every single solo—we try to make the best we can and I would say most over-the-top, but try to fit the song.

The song is fast—200bpm—you've got to keep up with it. And at the same time, we didn't know if it was going to be the first song on the album or not. We never look at it that way. Not just the solo, but the whole song, we have a string breaking on the song that we left on it—the whammy bar does a high-pitched squeal, the string broke, and we left it. We thought that those things are interesting and different, so a lot of the solo has a whammy pedal, and I guess the most famous thing is the 'Pac-Man' sound!

The 'Heroes Of Our Time' solo—my solo—to give it an 'x-factor,' I introduced the Hot Hand, which is made by this company, Source Audio, which is a remote control that detects the hand motion to cause the wah-wah sound. So

I used that device—I guess the first time people really saw it in a music video was for that song.

LITA FORD, 'OUT FOR BLOOD' (FROM *OUT FOR BLOOD*, 1983)

LITA FORD I wanted people *to see* that I was playing that guitar solo. I remember doing the video, and attaching a ten-pound camera onto my guitar, because I wanted a close-up of my fingers on the fretboard. I wanted for people to see that I'm doing the guitar playing—that it's not a guy. I've heard so many different stories about who's playing the guitar on that song. It's Lita playing the guitar on that song! 'No it's not, there's some guy behind the curtain.' Are you kidding me? And they can be standing there looking at you, and it still doesn't register.

I was definitely discriminated upon for being a chick, no doubt. I still am—I still get it today. You get some silly comments or some kind of hurdle you have to jump to prove that you did the solos. People would make up any excuse they could just to say that it wasn't me playing the guitar. So I put together this three-piece band, sort of à la Jimi Hendrix—where he had a guitar player, bass player, and a drummer.

And that's what I did with the *Out For Blood* album—it was myself, Neil Merryweather, and Dusty Watson, and there was nobody else to look at on guitar. I was trying to shove myself in people's face, to say to them, 'It is *me* playing guitar.' If you listen to a record, you really don't know who is on the record—even if you read the credits, still people were in denial. So, it's been a fight.

MARTY FREIDMAN, *DRAGON'S KISS* (1988)

MARTY FRIEDMAN We were both in the same studio.[*] I was days and he was nights, so we were both basically there for both of our records, twenty-four hours a day. It was *insane*. It was just a whirlwind of work. It was a lot of work in, like, two weeks. I think the content was great and very fresh—especially at the time. Recording was slightly haphazard—sonically, it suffered. But for two weeks, I think it was damn good. I haven't heard any of that stuff in so long. I really like 'Forbidden City'—that's the only one that I really … well, that's not true, I do play a lot of stuff from *Dragon's Kiss* live. But 'Forbidden City' is probably the most exciting on all that stuff.

---

[*] At the same time that Marty was recording *Dragon's Kiss*, Jason Becker was recording *Perpetual Burn*.

JASON BECKER I remember writing the first couple bars of 'Jewel' and playing it for Marty. We then wrote the rest of the main melody together. He wrote the rest after that. We both really wanted it on our own albums. We made a bet, on a football game, to get it. He won because the Redskins beat the 49ers. It made sense because it was a little more his than mine. I barely remember how we wrote 'Saturation Point.' Maybe he just used a few of my ideas. It was a fun song to play together. 'Thunder March,' 'Jewel,' and 'Dragon Mistress' stand out. 'Namida,' too. He is brilliant to me. I wouldn't be the musician I am without his influence and friendship.

GTR, *GTR* (1986)

STEVE HACKETT When we started out, we wanted to work with guitar manufacturers. We were hoping to do it all with guitar synths, so I think 99 percent is with guitar synth and with MIDI controllers, which provided a whole new set of problems, because you had MIDI delay factors. You have to remember, when we started out, we started in the mid 80s with this, and the technology was there, but it wasn't as reliable as it is now. So I think if we were doing that now, I dare say the triggering would be a lot more reliable. But then you've got regular guitar playing on it.

Having said that—and although the album was called *GTR*—it was more of a collection of songs than it was a guitarist prize-fighting competition. We decided not to work like that. I think most guitar pairings—whether they're duos or trios—there's an irresistible urge to turn it into a competition. And then, once it becomes a 'big willy' contest, I think it robs it of its musical potential and appeal, which reduces it to the level of sport. Which is absolutely fine, if that's your intention—if that's what galvanizes you. But for us, we were trying to make the kind of album that was digestible and not something that was impenetrable—either too clever or too fast. So the guitars were the vehicles that we used.

To be honest, I don't think it was really an album that was driven by the consideration of solos as such. I think there are interesting solos on it—for instance, on 'Jekyll And Hyde' there is some pretty interesting stuff from the two of us. But the thing that galvanizes me the most on it is the thing that became the hit single, which was 'When The Heart Rules The Mind,' which I think has got the best guitar hook on the entire album. To be honest, we were talking to Brian Lane, who was managing the project at the time, and he was saying, 'Getting a hit record in the States is a science. It's not an art.' And that's all very well from the business end, but you've still got to write the thing, and it's still got to press all the right buttons with people. So I was using my instincts, but I was also using my head with this, as well. It was a very 'considered' album and project.

FRANK GAMBALE, *A PRESENT FOR THE FUTURE* (1987) AND *LIVE!* (1989)

FRANK GAMBALE In the 80s, I had done my first three records, all of which were pretty cool. I think my second record, *A Present For The Future*, had some cool stuff on it—it was definitely a refinement from the first one.* And the one after that was my live record from the Baked Potato, which most people say is the quintessential 'sweep album.' Because I had just come off the road with Chick Corea—I think we were on the road for three or four months, and I was dying to play my music. All respect to Chick—I love him and playing his music—I was dying to play mine. So we did a live recording at the Baked Potato in Hollywood, and we were ripping. The whole band was absolutely *shredding* on that CD.

I remember being in India one time—a friend of mine, Sandeep Chowta, brought me over there, and he and one of his friends blew me completely away by singing the entire solo to 'Credit Reference Blues' from the live CD. Note for note! They were both singing it in unison together with the solo. That's a pretty heavy solo, and it's long, too. It had that kind of an impact on some people—that was a pretty special moment to me. So I would say both those records.

I even have a story of Jerry Garcia from the Grateful Dead. I was touring with The Elektric Band, and my second record was out—it was before the live album. And this is from Jerry's publicist at the time—I was told that Jerry was driving along the road somewhere up in the Bay Area, and nearly drove off the road when he heard a solo from a track of mine that was playing on the radio at the time. And he called his publicist to call the radio station to find out who the heck it was, found out it was me, and that I was in Chick's band.

Coincidentally, about two weeks later, I was playing at the Greek Theatre in Berkeley, up in San Francisco, and Jerry and Mickey Hart came to the show, and I got to hang out with them for about an hour or so after the show. It was awesome. We even talked about the possibility of doing something together, but it never happened, sadly. I think he died soon after that. And I heard from another fellow who was very close to Jerry that he would spend hours watching my *Monster Licks* and sweep-picking video, trying to get to sweep. So it had reached a lot of people, this technique.

---

* *Brave New Guitar* (1985).

GUTHRIE GOVAN, VARIOUS SELECTIONS

GUTHRIE GOVAN Honestly, it's not really the solos that I'm proud of. A solo for me is a thing that will change every time I play a song. There aren't many solos on *Erotic Cakes*, and there are no solos on the Aristocrats stuff. I spend most of the time trying to work out arrangements and trying to work out the melody, and just to come up with a piece of music that I'm proud of, and a piece of music that I'm able to listen to repeatedly, without growing weary of it. And then tracking the solo for me is just a little treat at the end. It's like, 'Oh, now you can just have fun. You can just blow over these chords and do a stream of consciousness kind of thing.' Which is why it's funny sometimes when I see people online want transcriptions of solos from those records. It's like, 'Why?' It's never going to be played the same way again.

In soloing terms, I really try to have more of a 'jazz mentality'—you just let things flow. And if anything's changed in my playing over the years, it's probably [that I've] become more comfortable with the idea of just letting things flow and exploring and not being scared of the idea that something might go wrong. Not being too uptight about the idea of while exploring or trying to find something new, some kind of unwelcomed note might pop in there. I've come to embrace— more than I used to—this idea of imperfection, and that it's OK to play something that's flawed but sounds sincere and has a good flow to it.

When I think about stuff I've recorded that I'm proud of, I think of the chords in 'Pig's Day Off,' or the bassline in 'And Finally,' or the funny sound-effect thing in 'Eric,' or the main melody in 'Waves'—because that's a thing that I wrote more than twenty years ago. I've met teenagers now who really want to learn how to play that melody, and that's kind of a nice feeling.

STU HAMM, *RADIO FREE ALBEMUTH* (1988)

STU HAMM It's one of those things when you're in the moment, you don't realize how wonderful the moment is. A friend of mine, Joe Battaglia, recorded it, and we did some of it at Steve Vai's house. The first song on the first record I ever did [the title track], I've got Tommy Mars, Joe Satriani, and Allan Holdsworth on it! Where can you go from there? Hopefully, I've gotten better. I know I've gotten better as a composer and as a band leader and as a musician and as a bass player. But it was fun. It was a great time to be a bass player.

I didn't invent tapping and I didn't invent solo bass playing, but there's still some stuff that I got on tape I think before anyone else. And it was genuinely stuff that I was coming up with and trying to be creative. I was talking to Victor Wooten about this—bass is only sixty-six years old. And I remember when I was about fourteen, seeing Larry Graham pull the strings of the bass and get this weird sound out of it. And driving twenty miles to the closest music store in Vermont, taking a bass off the wall, and trying to see how I could do that.

And now, when kids are twelve or thirteen years old, there's this whole vocabulary of bass—of popping and slapping and chords and harmonics—that just didn't exist when I was a teenager. So I was excited to be part of the zeitgeist that was pushing the bass into a new direction.

JEFF HEALEY, VARIOUS SELECTIONS

ROGER COSTA Definitely on the cover of 'When A Blind Man Cries' on the Ian Gillan album, *Gillan's Inn*—fantastic, fantastic solo. From *Heal My Soul*, 'Daze Of The Night'—the guitar solo in that, I can listen to that a thousand times in a row … and I think I have! The places that he takes the solo are phenomenal. It's just so well put together. 'Evil And Here To Stay' from *Feel This*, in which he was channeling some of his jazz influences. His favorite musician hands down of all-time was Louis Armstrong. And Louis pioneered the notion of improv and of a musician taking solos. So I believe the solo on 'Evil And Here To Stay' is a one-take solo. He had a couple ideas of where it might go, and then he just ran with it. And it's phenomenal.

And then there are other looser, jammy things, like 'Nice Problem To Have' off *See The Light*, which is him jamming with Robbie Blunt from Robert Plant's band. It was completely unrehearsed—just a straight-up jam. On an album that came out after his passing, called *Live At Grossman's 1994*, there is a song called 'Coming Home Baby,' and it's mis-credited on the record as 'I'm Going Home.' It's an instrumental, and he and Pat Rush—who was on-again and off-again in Jeff's band—play really well together. That was the first gig that they actually did together in that band. And that song in particular, it's high energy and it's a great solo.

HEAR 'N AID, 'STARS' (1985)[*]

CRAIG GOLDY Definitely, Yngwie Malmsteen [was a standout soloist on *Stars*]. A lot of times, he says everything and nothing all at the same time—because he's

---

[*] A song written by members of Dio (but performed by a host of different singers and guitarists) to raise money for famine relief in Africa, issued as a single and as part of a compilation album of the same name.

always on 'ten.' But he does have a way of being melodic and he does know how to get feel and incorporate inflection and stuff like that. And boy, he did it. He was just on ten that day. Everything that came out of that guy was just perfect. And George Lynch. I've said this to people before, but I can understand why they call him 'Mr. Scary'—he *was* scary!

Because me and Ronnie were friends from the Rough Cutt days, we'd already worked in the studio together. So he flew me in while I was on tour with Giuffria, and he actually had me go first. He said, 'I knew you would start with a theme. I knew you'd set it up that way, instead of just coming in and blowing chunks.' That made me feel good. I really wasn't even near the talent set that George Lynch and Yngwie Malmsteen had. There were a couple of good takes in there, but boy, did that really show what a really great guitar player is made of.

Neal Schon, dear Lord, he was such a humble guy—we were listening back to one of our takes, and Neal comes over and says, 'Is that you? Is that all left-hand, or are you doing that thing'—where Eddie does the pull-offs with his right finger and his left. And he goes, 'How do you do that?' I couldn't accept that, because I thought he was just being nice, but I just laughed and said, 'Thanks.' That's why they chose him for the outro, because he's just a master of that—the melody and the single note type deal. I think Neal Schon is one of the most underrated guitar players in the world. That guy can smoke. And he can sing with this guitar. Wow. I tried doing stuff at the end, and it just didn't happen—no wonder they chose him for that. I did my thing and I still really wasn't 'in my own' yet—I was beginning to be in my own.

But George Lynch was playing, and I heard what I thought sounded like a wah-wah pedal. I looked down, fully expecting to see his foot on a wah-wah pedal, and there was nothing—it was just the way he was picking. And it scared me. It was like, 'Wow. How do you do that?' That's when I went back and tried to figure out how you get what I call 'vowel sounds.' Because you can have the generic note, which I call the 'consonants,' just the dah-dah-dah. But what about the *ahhh* and *oooo* and *waaah*? How do you make your guitar go *waaah* without a wah-wah pedal? And Ritchie had done that, and Eddie was able to. And I thought, 'How are they doing it?' So he actually scared me into doing vowel sounds. So it was really those guys who I thought stood out the most.

GARY HOEY, 'HOCUS POCUS' (FROM *ANIMAL INSTINCT*, 1993)

GARY HOEY I'd just come out of the band Heavy Bones on Warner Bros Records, and we made this big, huge record. Grunge came out, and the record didn't take off. So 'Hocus Pocus' was part of a solo record that I was recording for a very small amount of money—maybe $15,000 is all we had for the budget—and we talked about doing one cover song. My manager said, 'What was the riff you used to play in the garage when you were fifteen?' And I said, 'Well, I remember "Hocus Pocus" in the 70s.' I played the riff, and he was like, 'Wow, that's a really cool riff!' So we did it for that reason—we felt it was a cool song and we wanted to put the wah-wah instead of the yodeling.

So we recorded the song, but I remember the whole time I was making the record, he kept saying, 'Did you record "Hocus Pocus" today?' And I was like, 'No. I'll get to it.' Because it was a cover song, I wasn't that worried about it. He's like, 'No, man, *you'd better record it and get it done.*' So we recorded it very much toward the end of the record, and in the middle of the song, I quoted 'Stranglehold' by Ted Nugent, which, while we were recording the song, I did it spontaneously, without telling the guys I was going to do it. It was just a funny little joke when I did it. Just doing that riff added a little bit more excitement to the song.

We were very, very shocked when we had a hit—we didn't expect it at all. It was like the 80s had passed, grunge had come out, guitar solos were kind of dead … yet I snuck through with that song. I don't really know why—if it's because the DJ's liked it, I know radio got response when it got played. But yeah, the steel gauntlet was coming down, and luckily, I was really skinny and got under it before it caught me!

GREG HOWE, *GREG HOWE* (1988)

GREG HOWE I like the album, it's just that the production of the album is so raw and … bad, to be blunt, that it's very difficult for me to listen to it, on a sonic level. But I do like the songs. I think the songs are catchy. It was strange, because when I got signed, I was coming after the initial wave of these new guys, so Tony MacAlpine was already out there, Vinnie Moore was already out there, Paul Gilbert was already out there. And these guys were all amazing players. However, there was a similar approach stylistically—or at least genre-wise—with them. It was mainly coming from the neoclassical thing. It was all rooted in sort of metal/ neoclassical sounding stuff. Prog neoclassical. And they were very good at it.

So, the very first few songs that I sent to Mike, Mike got my demo and my demo was not anything like that. He said to me, 'I like your playing, but it sounds a little jazzy. *My label is a heavy metal label.* I need you to rock out somewhere,

I need you to write some songs that sound like they belong on my label.' The first two or three songs I sent him actually were sort of in that same genre, of neoclassical. And Mike said to me that, 'I think we have enough of this already.' Joey Tafolla had already been signed by then, as well. Joey was another guy that was coming from that same approach—which were songs rooted primarily in a Bach-esque format. Mike and I both agreed that we don't need another guy doing that.

So my approach became a little more on the blues side. Which is where I lived anyway—I was listening to Stevie Ray Vaughan, Van Halen, Hendrix. I was never really a big fan of the neoclassical sound. I just loved some of the guitar techniques that I would hear with the players. So, I was developing that level of skill and I was really happy to find that Mike wanted me to apply to a sort of more down-home-bluesy approach. A sort of prog-blues thing. That's really where it came from. That was the concept for the first album—we would keep the same level of technical proficiency, and the sort of fretboard gymnastics that Shrapnel was now developing their reputation for, but apply it in a slightly different genre of music.

BILLY IDOL, 'REBEL YELL' (FROM *REBEL YELL*, 1983)

STEVE STEVENS The solos were usually one of the last things to go on the record or sort of toward the end of the record. In Idol, we always joked he'd be like the 'punk police,' where he never wanted guitar solos to just be a gymnastic event. So if you were going to put a guitar solo on a song, there had to be a reason for it. And by the time we had gotten the backing track and some of the early guitar overdubs on 'Rebel Yell,' we just knew, '*This thing is a monster.*' It just sounded so good on every level—this was everything we were striving for. And I brought in a copy of the Billy Cobham record with Tommy Bolin on it, *Spectrum*, and I played them 'Quadrant 4,' and it's the solo where Tommy lets the feedback run wild on the Echoplex, and then varies the speed of it. I played it for Keith Forsey, Billy's producer, and I said, 'If we can capture something like that ... ' And they both agreed what we needed was this 'sonic blast.'

I kept coming back to 'Rebel Yell' for the solo—I didn't get it the first day. And at that time, there was a store in New York that sold cheap Chinese robots and ray guns. I was laying in bed, I was watching TV, had my guitar, and I had a tiny little Peavey amp. And I'm playing and I turn on the ray gun, and lo and behold, the ray-gun went through the pickups of the guitar. I went, 'Wow! If I can vary the speed of the ray-gun, I'd be able to do my own version of what Tommy Bolin was doing.'

So I opened the thing up, mucked around with it, and found the point where there's a resistor, and hooked up a guitar potentiometer to it, replaced the resistor, and that's exactly what it did—it varied the speed. So I got out my dad's drill, I drilled a hole in the ray gun, but a knob on it, and brought it into the studio. I played most of the solo, and said, 'Punch me in at this point,' and I ran it through a Lexicon PCM—so it would have delay to it. Those were the days when guitar players didn't record in the control room—I walked back in the control room, and everybody was just laughing. Like, 'You've got to be fucking kidding me! *This is amazing!*' So I knew I had hit on something, and that became the solo that's on the record.

JESUS LIZARD, VARIOUS SELECTIONS

DUANE DENISON There was kind of a jazzy, noir kind of thing that came on the song 'The Associate'; there was a slide solo on the song 'Nub' that was atmospheric and had a little bit of blues to it, but it was a little more atmospheric and evocative, as well. And on one of the later albums, it was maybe the best solo I ever did—on a song that not many people heard, 'Too Bad About The Fire,' from the album *Shot*. But there were chord solos—like on the song 'Monkey Trick' had this break where it was all chordal things. They weren't so much solos as they were breaks—the vocals would stop, and then the guitar would move to a different register and play a variation of the pre-existing riff.

Like the song 'If You Had Lips' had a noir-ish, Birthday Party sort of 'lurch' to it—I was trying to be Chet Atkins and failing, but coming up with something else as a result. 'Puss' was like a rotating arpeggio thing that came in and out of time. It's funny, I don't think David Yow ever liked it—he thought it was prissy or something, and wanted something more noisy and chaotic, which I can see. But it was different—once again, it wasn't the expected thing.

With a song like 'Thumper,' we would always try to work things out with the guitar and the bass, so the bass was kind of snaking around and doing these lines around the chords. So it wasn't just the bass playing the same thing as the guitar, doing a simplified parallel shadowing of the guitar parts. We wanted it to be somewhat contrapuntal in a way, where it was moving through the chords. And other people do that, too—it's nothing new. But we focused on it maybe a little more.

JUDAS PRIEST, 'THE RAGE' (FROM *BRITISH STEEL*, 1980),
'ROCK HARD, ROCK FREE' (FROM *DEFENDERS OF THE FAITH*,
1984), AND 'BLOOD RED SKIES' (FROM *RAM IT DOWN*, 1988)

K.K. DOWNING 'The Rage' was totally ad-libbed in the studio and ad-libbed onstage, really. There was a solo in the middle and one at the end, and I could have gone all night long really … and I think the guys should have let me! But I guess it was back in the day when we were still trying to put songs on vinyl, and we were restricted to seventeen or eighteen minutes a side.

I've been playing [*Defenders Of The Faith*] quite a lot lately, since it became the 'anniversary' of it. I just loved the record, I really liked the album. And I think with 'Rock Hard, Ride Free,' I really loved the sound and the vibe of it. It's great to play that solo, because it's not particularly difficult to play, but it's a really well constructed solo and fits the song really well.

['Blood Red Skies'] was kind of the first time I was getting into really more precision alternate picking stuff—on that record. Obviously then on *Painkiller* I stepped that up a notch as well, with solos like 'One Shot At Glory.' It just seemed to be that period where I went into that mode, and then I transported that into live solos like 'Victim Of Changes' and some of the more classic songs, when I was ad-libbing. That was fun to mix the two ingredients with fast alternate picking and combine scales with the so-called K.K./Hendrix mode, if you'd like. [*Laughs*] But I think, if anything gives me the identity, really, [it's] having combined those ingredients.

KILLSWITCH ENGAGE, 'BREATHE LIFE' (FROM
THE END OF HEARTACHE, 2004)

ADAM DUTKIEWICZ It was a funny thing to think about the very first solo I ever recorded for Killswitch, which was kind of a mistake. On *The End Of Heartache*, there's a song called 'Breathe Life.' We didn't have a guitar solo on it when we made the record. I went to go mix it with Andy Sneap, and we got to that part of the song, and we were talking about it, and we were just like, 'Y'know, it kind of feels like something is missing here, doesn't it?' And Andy's like, 'Yeah, there's kind of a big, long space in the song. Why don't you try a guitar solo?' At that point, I wasn't really into the idea. But we tried it, and made it up on the spot. Then, I started playing more guitar solos!

KING CRIMSON, 'THELA HUN GINJEET' (FROM *DISCIPLINE*, 1981)

ADRIAN BELEW I don't think I take a 'guitar solo' in that as much as I just go crazy, making sounds and background things, to cause some sort of chaos behind the guy who is speaking—who is me. But the guy speaking is talking about being held up at gunpoint and molested on the streets of some city—in this case, everyone thinks it's New York, but it was actually London … where that did happen to me, while I was making the recording. And so my role I thought behind the scenes there was just to create a lot of hell and angst—sirens and stuff like that. Later in the song, there is a guitar solo that I believe is Robert Fripp, and there are also a couple of sections where we play things together that sound like they're more 'instrumental sections'—but they're not really guitar solos.

I was using a guitar synthesizer. 'Thela Hun Ginjeet' was one of the first things I wrote when I got the GR-300 Roland Guitar Synthesizer. I had gone previously in 1980 to Japan with the Talking Heads, and they took me through their factory there—Roland did—and they gave me the GR-300. It wasn't even out in the United States or really anywhere. So I'm pretty certain I have the very first one. Later, Robert got one too. And I remember one of the first things I did is I really liked the hexaphonic pickup that it had, and I combined that sound with the normal Strat sound, and got this … I don't know what sound you would call that. But to me, it meant that I wanted to strum it really hard and make something in 'seven.' So I started the riff that opens that song, and the song was built around that.

KING'S X, 'OVER MY HEAD' (FROM *GRETCHEN GOES TO NEBRASKA*, 1989), 'IT'S LOVE' AND 'MOANJAM' (FROM *FAITH HOPE LOVE*, 1990)

TY TABOR What I remember most about ['Over My Head'] is it was a song that almost wasn't even going to make it on the album. What happened is [singer-bassist] Doug Pinnick had this part of the song written, where it had this cool [*sings the song's main chord progression*]. So he had all that. But he didn't have a complete song, and he played just that part for us one time when we were hanging out over at his place. And I argued with him on the spot. I said, 'Man, that is the coolest riff you've ever come up with. We have to work this one into the record and make a song out of this.'

At that point, we all—which was me, Doug, Jerry [Gaskill, drummer], and our manager at the time, Sam [Taylor]—were doing like eight-hour practice sessions a day. Just like normal people who would go to work, we would take a lunch break, eat at this place right next to the rehearsal room, go right back to work, and that's how we worked on songs. 'Over My Head' was one of those that we took into the lab and didn't come out until it was a complete song.

And the solos were pretty much just spontaneous—whatever I felt at the moment. The large majority of solos I do on record are solos that were when the record button is hit, I don't know what the solo is going to be. There are some solos that I have worked out, like there's a song called 'Mississippi Moon,' where I worked it out—note for note—what I wanted it to be, because it was more of a melodic musical part than a 'solo solo.' But regular solos, like 'Over My Head,' they were just spontaneous/whatever happened.

'It's Love' just kind of came together in the studio. I don't remember there being a struggle or anything, because it was pretty uneventful, really, when it went down. We were just mainly worried about making sure we got the harmonies to sound good and to sound like a choir on the *ahhh* section. I think we were more concerned with vocals than anything, because the music just went down, and there it was. The solo was just a single pass. Just, 'Let it roll and play what you want, we'll fade it out.' So I played longer than I imagined there was any need to, and it kind of died—it just falls apart. We figured, 'We're way past the fade, no big deal.' And Sam just said, 'Hey, I think we should just let this play until it falls apart. I like the solo.' So that's what happened.

'Moanjam,' I actually wrote on a … I didn't even have a drum machine or anything. I had this Styrofoam cooler on the floor—I had just come back from camping or something—and I put a mic on it, and I was able to thump one part, and make it sound like a kick drum, and tap another part with my finger and make it sound like a snare, and I just did that [*sings drum rhythm of the song*] long enough to play something to it, and I came up with all of the music to 'Moanjam' like that, on a little demo.

I handed it to Doug, and said, 'Hey, we need to make this a song.' And he said, 'Let's not even have lyrics, man, let's just play it and I'll moan on it. That's all I'll do—I'll just moan the blues all over it, and you play a ten-minute solo!' So when we first started doing the song, there were no lyrics. He was just going, 'Mmm mmm mmm mmm' in the mic, and just humming. That's why it's called 'Moanjam.' It was later that Doug decided to add some lyrics to it.

The solo was just me stretching out for a long time in the studio. I think it was just one complete take. I think I ran through it twice, and we kept the second one. And that was it. It was just, 'Go for it, play as long as you want to, see where it takes you, and you'll know where to bring us out.' And that's how it happened.

KISS, 'ROCKET RIDE' (FROM *ALIVE II*, 1977)

ACE FREHLEY It was very fun working with Sean.* Sean was a real character—he was one of our first tour managers, when we first started out. Sean always had some good ideas and some radical ideas. He was really instrumental in helping us do choreography in the very beginning. A lot of the choreography that we did onstage was really from Sean. He never really gets enough credit as I think he should. But I remember we wrote 'Rocket Ride' and another song. We recorded that stuff up in my attic, when I was living in Irvington, New York, in a townhouse. I remember it was a hot day and we were sweating—the air conditioning wasn't working properly.

KISS, 'NO, NO, NO' (FROM *CRAZY NIGHTS*, 1987)

AND 'UNHOLY' (FROM *REVENGE*, 1992)

BRUCE KULICK 'No, No, No' was pretty exciting. On an album that was considered somewhat 'pop' and produced by Ron Nevison, to have a guitar start out and go all by itself, it was pretty unusual. Probably the best-sounding [ESP guitar]—and I still own this one, and it just kills, it's got this huge tone—is the yellow one I'm holding on the back of *Crazy Nights*. It's a yellow Strat body and ESP neck, and kicks ass. *And that's the guitar.* I can practically see myself in the studio here in LA, recording that intro.

The finger-tapping thing, obviously for an intro after I was done with all the leads, was stylistically correct for that era. What's remarkable about it is the fact that I once read a review of *Crazy Nights* that said, 'The synthesizer intro of "No, No, No"' and I was like, 'WHAT? The guy thinks this is a keyboard?! I don't know if I'm supposed to be flattered or extremely pissed.' But I think I was more pissed about that. Maybe the chorus threw the guy, but I guess I played it pretty cleanly. So that was really a big score.

'No, No, No' was certainly a labor of love, writing it—it was mostly an idea Eric Carr and Gene Simmons had, or Eric probably started it, and I helped on some things, and then we brought it to Gene. I don't remember exactly, but I'm just proud that I was involved with some of the riffs in the sections of the song. But it's pretty cool that this track on a more pop-y Kiss album could have so much focus on the lead guitar work. So I was quite proud of it. And we did it live a lot, too. There are plenty of YouTube clips out there—the Monsters of Rock Festivals

---

* Sean Delaney, who co-wrote the tune with Ace.

in Europe—and that being a big section of the concert, where we come out of the Eric Carr drum solo into my thing. We were able to use it a lot live. So that was pretty damn cool.

The 'Unholy' guitar solo, now you're talking about a whole other animal, in the sense that I'm being produced by someone that I have tremendous respect for—Bob Ezrin. Bob is like a mad professor who—is in some ways, musically, a genius—can hear things and tear things apart. There's no accident why he's been involved with so many amazing songs and records.* So I do remember that the whole approach for lead guitar on *Revenge*—and certainly for a song that was going to be called 'Unholy'—was that I had to play from my balls and act like I'm just trying to really *destroy* everybody. The intention had to be pure, macho, brutal guitar work.

And I remember when I was given some of the directions of, 'We want you to really get wild on this record,' me thinking, 'Hmmm, I may have some pedals that can bring that out of me. Maybe the tone is not going to be a pure blues tone. Maybe this isn't "Clapton tone," maybe this isn't "No, No, No" tone. This has got to be something else.' And that's when I started to fool around with an overdrive pedal into a wah-wah pedal, and then overdriving it more through a delay pedal. I remember using one of these Roland Space Echos—I had a rack mount one.

With Ezrin, we experimented a lot, and we could spend possibly a whole day on a solo—just making it right. And I was also given the tapes of the rough mixes of the tracks, to go home and fool around and come up with ideas for the solos in my own studio, because I had one of these simpler home studios at the time. This is pre–Pro Tools, of course. But I was still able to practice a little bit and come up with some ideas, so it wasn't completely, 'OK … what have you got?' I already did some homework.

But I think on 'Unholy,' the reason why I do love the solo so much is it starts out right away fiery and intense, and then there's this very odd, twisty/turny chromatic seventh picking chord thing that goes down the fingerboard, that I'd been looking on YouTube, I actually jammed that song not that long ago in Hollywood at one of the popular clubs that's been doing these 'jam nights.' And I wanted to be sure the other guitar player knew some of the parts, so instead of me laying it all out for him, I looked on YouTube and there were a lot of people that teach the song. And of course, some of them have the parts right, and some of them have none of it very right. But whenever any of them tried the solo,

---

* Ezrin has produced classic recordings for the likes of Kiss, Alice Cooper, and Pink Floyd, among others.

they didn't get that riff right. I thought it was really funny, because I'm not Steve Vai—why can't they hear that? But I see that as a big compliment, too. If they can't figure it out, it must be unique.

And I'll never forget this—it's one of my 'warm fuzzy moments' of people that might have spoken of me, because I always do feel a bit underrated—Steve Vai once made a comment in the press that there's a note toward the end of the solo … it's not in the solo, it's actually in between the outro parts that Gene's singing, where I hit this wailing note. I just *nailed it*—whatever that note is. And every time it comes up when I play it live, I go, 'I know I can hit this note. Can I make it sound like it came out on *Revenge*?' Maybe 80 percent. I can never nail it exactly. It's just this wailing high note that exactly embodied that evil, murderous tone—it was almost its own character in the song. That's something that I was real proud of, and the fact that Steve recognized it and mentioned it, I just felt amazing from that.

RICHIE KOTZEN, *RICHIE KOTZEN* (1989) AND *FEVER DREAM* (1990)

RICHIE KOTZEN The first record was an eye-opener for me, because I had never really done a *real* record. I did a recording and printed a record with my band with a couple of original songs. It was a good record, but it was an EP with only five songs. This was a full album of all songs that I wrote. So it was an interesting experience. I remember writing the song 'Squeeze Play,' and I think it has a 9/8 riff in it, and I remember Steve Smith really liking that and he did an amazing solo, where we looped that riff over and over, and he soloed around it. I guess one of my favorite pieces from that record was a song called 'Strut It'—all of the song is a solo. That's the one that I remember the most.

From the second record, I knew that I did not want to be an instrumentalist, so I immediately started singing. That's what I wanted to do. I wanted to be a guy that wrote the kind of music that I grew up listening to—which was The Who, Led Zeppelin, and that sort of thing. I had a pretty cool song on there called 'Fall Of A Leader,' and I remember I really enjoyed playing that one. And there was a song called 'She' that I really liked, and I thought the solo was really interesting—I was doing some fingerpicking things. And then we had another song on there called 'Off The Rails'—I wrote the lyrics with Mike Varney—which is a crazy kind of barn burner/fast/over-the-top tune. And there's one other one, called 'Dream Of A New Day,' that we ended up having included in the *Bill & Ted's Bogus Journey* soundtrack. I remember that song had a really cool, funky thing to it, and the solo was a little different than the typical Shrapnel solos—it was a little more rhythmic.

LIVING COLOUR, 'CULT OF PERSONALITY' AND
'FUNNY VIBE' (FROM *VIVID*, 1988)

VERNON REID What I recall is that we were laying down guitars all day. We were at the end of the night, and I was beat. And [producer] Ed Stasium said, 'So tomorrow, we'll do solos.' And I said, 'You know what? Let me do one right now.' So I did one, and he really liked it. He said, 'Man, that's great!' And I said, 'Let me do one more.' And that is the solo that's on 'Cult Of Personality'—the second run at it. And the other thing about it is it's improvised and all of the fills and all of that is one take, it's one piece. It was a great day in the studio. We just were having a great time and I said, 'Let's just give it a go.' Actually, Ed liked the first one.

I believe ['Funny Vibe'] was an overdubbed solo. I don't think that was pieced together, because that song had a lot of parts. That's one of the ones where I'm playing rhythm guitar and I'm soloing on top of it, so that was an overdubbed solo. And I believe that was like the third try or something like that. Ed really liked it—working with Ed was great. He had perspective, because I was 'in it'—that one step removed is really important, because a lot of times, you're too close to it.

TONY MACALPINE, *EDGE OF INSANITY* (1986)
AND *MAXIMUM SECURITY* (1987)

TONY MACALPINE I think the writing for *Edge Of Insanity* happened pretty quick, and the recording was something that happened even faster. It was really my first record, and I didn't really have a lot of experience with what it took to be in a studio or that environment. But we did the record in three days, so it was really, really fast—working right to two or three in the morning. Amazing contributions Billy Sheehan—a good friend of mine to this day—made to the record. And Steve Smith. Just monumental playing. It was really an intense trio action. We recorded everything at once, and I went back in and did some solos. So that was really a fun record.

Maximum Security was a bit different. We had a much bigger budget, and we were doing this thing with PolyGram, and we were able to take more time, do the record in different studios, and put it together in a different way. And worked a lot slower. So I thought the playing was more 'grounded,' and I made a lot of friends over the years that I was able to do some guitar work with—Jeff Watson and George Lynch. So that was a lot of fun. There was a huge growth pattern.

As I got into records like *Premonition* and *Evolution*, I was really able to spend more time on a compositional level in a different way. I wasn't really trying to break new ground; I was trying to emphasize different types of instrumentation, like I did with songs like 'Time Table,' 'Freedom To Fly,' and 'Stream Dream.' I did different things, and it was really a lot of fun employing those ideas, after having conversations with Steve Vai—and subsequently working with him years later—I was able to employ some of those things that he talked about. And that was really helpful for me.

MANOWAR, 'MANOWAR' (FROM *BATTLE HYMNS*, 1982)

ROSS THE BOSS The song 'Manowar,' which I wrote, the solo is two solos climbing up and down at the same time. It's all major stuff. It just keeps going and keeps going. And then it joins together and then it breaks off. In one speaker, you hear it going up, and in the other speaker, you hear it going down. And as the notes cross in the middle, they join each other. I listened to that the other day, and I was like, 'Wow … I like that!' It's definitely two solos in one.

MEAT PUPPETS, 'SAM' AND 'SIX GALLON PIE' (FROM *FORBIDDEN PLACES*, 1991)

CURT KIRKWOOD ['Sam' is] just typical busted out, blues-rock sort of thing, that's at my very roots of learning how to play solos—going to my Jerry Snyder blues solo book that I had, when I was a teenager. And playing along with Eagles records, or whatever it is I used to do early on. I didn't really think about it that much. It's just a pretty simple, straight-ahead, ripping thing. I know that at its heart it was off-the-cuff, but I can't really remember. I know this much—working with [producer] Pete Anderson, he's pretty meticulous, so when I listen to it, it doesn't sound like it got pieced together.

Pete, he's one of the best guitar players around.* He would always meticulously work out his parts when he would do solos. But it sounds to me like I just ripped it—it's not that complicated. I still play about the same thing on that song, so the part fits. It could have been pieced together a little bit, but I think Pete just tried to get me to do the thing through, and get one that worked.

I was really into Mahavishnu, and I still like John McLaughlin—especially

---

* In addition to producing other artists, Anderson also played guitar in Dwight Yoakam's band from 1984 to 2002.

from the 70s. As far as speed goes, I never could really play that fast, so it doesn't seem that fast to me. Some of the country stuff that I did back there, like 'Out My Way,' I can play kind of quick. But it's pretty moderate, I would say.

'Six Gallon Pie,' that's all thought out—there's nothing impromptu there. That's just all pretty much fingerpicking, and then it goes into a little bit of a muted sort of thing in there for a measure or two. But that's completely prearranged. Something like Leo Kottke, James Burton—kind of a mixture in there. Leo Kottke was always one of my big favs—especially a big influence with the fingerpicking stuff.

And in that song I'm changing off—I hold the pick between my fingers in the beginning, and then I kind of do some pick work in there, and then go back to the fingerpicking, so it's a little bit of a bastardization of just a regular fingerpicking thing. I definitely kind of faked it—in terms of Leo, I just came up with stuff, like, 'This is how I can fingerpick, making up for my early classical lessons, how to do some kind of country rock fingerpicking.' But that one definitely has some James Burton in it, who I've always loved when he was playing the paisley guitar with Elvis Presley. Something like with his big Las Vegas band—'Promised Land' and stuff like that.

MEGADETH, *RUST IN PEACE* (1990)

MARTY FRIEDMAN My main memory was the doctor telling me not to play guitar, and I said, 'Well, I'm about to make my first major label album, so I'm going to have to ignore your advice.' He said, 'I know you're going to ignore my advice, but just play as *absolutely little* as possible. Don't noodle around, don't jam around—just play when the red light's on, and don't play anything unnecessary.' So most of that stuff is done in one or two takes.

It's good to have my background, because my background is always play in front of people, always play live. It's a show, so when you have to do a very good performance and you only have one or two takes, you don't have leeway to be screwing around. And even more so, I really wanted to make a good impression on this record, so I really had to bundle all that shit up in a short period of time.

I think it came out pretty good, and fans still talk about the record. I haven't heard it in a while, but people still talk about it, so I think it must have come out OK. But I was a bit nervous about not having a little more time to really nitpick over things, and got done really quickly. But I was just trying to listen to my doctor's advice as much as I could.

MERCYFUL FATE, 'CURSE OF THE PHARAOHS' (FROM *MELISSA*, 1983)

HANK SHERMANN Most of the songs, we have at least one solo each. Especially in the 80s, Michael was certainly more tasteful, so just because of that, you should have a good feel of when Michael is playing. I'm a little more crazy and out-of-tune, because I was not so focused on the lead work, as I was on the rhythm and composing songs. Later, I was getting more into the lead thing. So on almost all of the Mercyful Fate songs, we played 'ping-pong'—I started off with a solo, Michael took over, or we split them in the beginning of a song or at the end of the song.

In 'Curse Of The Pharaohs' … does Michael even have a solo? Maybe he doesn't. I know I have a long one in the middle. And then I have all the fills. I think just after the first verse, there is a solo there and that's Michael, and the rest might be me. The way I did it was I tend to plan—I had kind of a structure to them. Whereas Michael is very good being spontaneous. He comes up with always cool melodic stuff. So Michael doesn't plan too much.

But at that time, I was very inspired by the Scorpions albums with Uli Jon Roth. I was impressed with his solos—I was like, 'Whoa man … this is fucking out of this world!' Even though none of us could match his performance, we were just impressed of how they were well composed, they were well performed. And obviously, Michael Schenker from UFO—those are our two biggest influences. There's no doubt about that. So I was always trying to do crazy stuff—pre-planned and tried to execute them. Sometimes it went OK, sometimes I was a little too overambitious in what I wanted to achieve—maybe having too many notes. But it was a fun time.

METALLICA, 'JUMP IN THE FIRE' AND 'METAL
MILITIA' (FROM *KILL 'EM ALL*, 1983)

KIRK HAMMETT The first solo was basically started off how Dave Mustaine started off.* But the second solo in that song was created pretty much on the spot in the studio. It was one of the only solos on *Kill 'Em All* that was created on the spot. I had kind of a vague idea of where I wanted it to go. The rhythm background goes into double-time and I knew I wanted to go into double-time, too, to kind of match what the drums were doing. But that was about it.

I've always had a great ability to come up with guitar solos on the spot—I

---

* The song was first recorded for the band's 1982 demo *No Life 'Til Leather*, on which Dave plays.

think I have pretty good improvisation skills. My accuracy sometimes is kind of shaky, but I come from a school and an attitude that is really old school, and that really, you don't hear much of today. But the school I come from is, 'You never played the same song the same way, and you never play a guitar solo the same way twice in a row.' I've hardly ever played solos exactly like the record. There will always be a little change somewhere—a little inflection, or I'll change the phrasing here or there. It's always still recognizable, but it's embedded into me. So things like accuracy—as far as guitar solos are to the album—is not a high priority to me. The highest priority is expressing myself and sounding decent.

I know that 'Metal Militia' starts off with a tritone, right before the rest of the band kicks in. I remember I couldn't have the Tube Screamer on for the tritones, because it would feedback in the hole where those tri-tones would go. So I remember Lars sitting there, with the Tube Screamer in his hand, and I asked him to turn the Tube Screamer on after the tritones, so I could just start ripping immediately, and I wouldn't have to worry about turning on the Tube Screamer with my foot.

MORBID ANGEL, *COVENANT* (1993)

TREY AZAGTHOTH When we got to doing *Covenant*, I added the use of the Ibanez seven-string Universe guitar for some songs, and that helped expand things greatly with songwriting. Also on *Covenant*, I was starting to explore more with polyrhythms. On the first record,* we had left and right guitar variations happening, but not so much actual polyrhythms, which was something cool to explore in how it added another dimension to songs and soundscapes. On *Covenant*, songs such as 'Rapture' use a backward-guitar riffing flow. A lot of that song came about by first making some ideas on a demo, then playing the demo backward, and then making that into the riffs and flows for the song, meaning I would see how the riffs flowed backward, noticing the characteristics, and then play the riffs that way off the beat. That's just one little cool thing about how I compose music.

Then there is the 'dragging eight-track tape' vibe. That is another freaky artistic way I developed in learning how to write music. Imagine in the 70s having a Black Sabbath eight-track tape that you play in your car, and when you finish listening, you just toss it up on the car's dashboard. Then imagine the sun baking it, and then later listening to it, and understanding how an eight-track tape is constructed and how it would get warped, and then play warped. Well, for me,

---

* *Altars Of Madness* (1989).

I experienced such things, then later I would call that a songwriting technique dynamic, or feeling dynamic—the dragging eight-track tape feel. The song 'God Of Emptiness' off *Covenant* is all about such things.

Covenant has also some cool swing happening, such as in 'Sworn To The Black.' Then other stuff that's in your face and lots of crazy soloing going on with all of the songs. It is so obvious that *Covenant* contains some different combinations, inspirations, and approaches, plus a nice record budget and a great person mixing it [Flemming Rasmussen]. Also, it was the first death-metal record on a major label, and [had] two nice vids that were on MTV's *Headbangers Ball*, and each song used was like day and night difference from one another. I would call *Covenant* a really cool thing, and I'm pretty damn happy about it. *Altars* and *Blessed** were really cool records that I'm also very proud of as well, and I think each record contains songs that present very unique approaches to metal, in general.

STEVE MORSE (WITH ALBERT LEE AND ERIC JOHNSON
ON SELECT TRACKS), *STAND UP* (1985)

STEVE MORSE Eric was somebody that I had seen playing with The Dregs—we had done shows together. Eric was just this immaculate player. Everything he did sounded like it was a little shinier and more perfect than I'd ever heard. He was a perfectionist with his execution and tone. So I asked him if he would come up with lyrics on a song and sing, and I gave him a cassette of the tune I had already recorded, 'Distant Star.' He agreed—probably something he later regretted because of all the work it took. [*Laughs*]

But he wanted his own speaker cabinet and amp—he lived in Austin, Texas, I was on a farm south of Atlanta, Georgia, in my studio. He drove 950 miles—each way—with his tech guy, with the amp and speaker cabinets, to do this. He told me he wrote the lyrics along the way. He came to the studio, set it up, I stuck a mic in front of it, and said, 'I want to put it up on some wood.' We lifted it up on some wood blocks, and carefully positioned the mics. He was really quiet about it. We did the vocals first—in case I had to do it in two sessions, because I've been known to burn out vocalists with, 'Oh, that was awesome … but try it one more time' or 'Can you sing it up a third?' or 'How about a scream?' His vocals were immaculate and very quick. I might have over-compressed him a little bit, but it just sounded so good to me.

---

* *Blessed Are The Sick* (1991).

We went to the guitar, and he did some of the solos, and I liked every take. I was like, 'This is it! This is great!' And he's like, 'No, no, no. I don't like it.' I didn't have many empty tracks, because I'd already done the tune. I think I maybe only had two. It was killing me—I had to erase these awesome solos. But by about the third one or so, I just said, 'Eric, I'm dying. I can't do this. *You've got to keep that one.*' And he's like, 'All right.' He's so much of a perfectionist, he wasn't really happy about it, but he was like, 'OK … I guess.' And me—as the producer—I'm like, 'That sounds good, put up the controls.' And he was more like, 'Let's shape the EQ a little bit.' And really had an exact idea of the way he wanted it to sound. And I don't think I ever got it to sound that way. [*Laughs*] I don't think he was in love with the final sound so much. But I said, 'I'm sorry, I love it. Everybody who hears it loves it. If you can live with it, I want to keep it.'

And Albert came in much the same way—we did the vocals [on 'Rockin' Guitars'] first and said, 'It's just a fun tune. It's not a serious thing … how about a scream there?' So when it came to the scream, he said, 'I refuse to scream right before the solos,' and I said, 'That's kind of cool. We'll just leave that in!' Him just talking, saying, 'I refuse to scream.' And some of the lyrics he changed, because, with his accent and everything, they sounded stupid, and he said, 'I'm not comfortable with this.' And I said, 'Change them. Do whatever you want, man!' And of course, when he did the solos, every take is perfect. Every take was a keeper. It was just a matter of it's not like he would take an idea and keep perfecting it—just every solo was different, and it was pretty neat. These two guys are real, real amazing soloists.

MR. BIG, 'ADDICTED TO THAT RUSH' (FROM *MR. BIG*, 1989) AND
'DADDY, BROTHER, LOVER, LITTLE BOY' (FROM *LEAN IN TO IT*, 1991)

PAUL GILBERT ['Addicted To That Rush'] was me trying to imitate Billy [Sheehan]. Because I had seen him so many times in Talas, that I'd go home right after the gig and I would try to imitate what I heard him play on the bass—on my guitar. It was funny, because when I wrote a lot of the parts, I showed them to Billy, and I said, 'I've got all these patterns from you,' and he said, 'I've never done these patterns before!' That's what happens when you go from memory—the telephone game. You hear something, but it changes a little in your mind. So of course, he could play it in a second, but it was sort of my version of what I had heard Billy doing in Talas, and then bringing it full circle to Billy.

And it went really quickly. If anything, that kind of stuff was the easiest for us to do—just because when you work on something, that's what you're good at.

And I remember doing acoustic ballads, and that was actually—believe it or not—technically more challenging. It wasn't 'To Be With You,' it was another ballad we did, and I remember spending like, a day in the studio with the producer, trying to get me to play a good-sounding G chord. To me it sounded fine, but he wasn't satisfied with it, and it was just like, hour after hour of trying to get this G chord right. And I think 'Addicted To That Rush' was first take. When people see technique or flash, really the secret to it is it has to be easy. And both Billy and I have done that stuff so much, where it might seem athletic or difficult, we worked on it enough where it really wasn't—it was second nature for us at that point.

['Daddy, Brother, Lover, Little Boy'] was very worked out. And I remember really enjoying working with our producer, Kevin Elson, because we would record the rhythm track of the song, and he would make me a cassette of that, and he'd say, 'Go home with this tonight, because we're going to do the solo tomorrow.' So I would have all night to plan something out and it would save us time in the studio. Otherwise, I would be there tinkering away as we paid big money for the studio. So I would come in the next day and have it all planned out. I think I may have even double tracked that one.

I remember the trick with it was I wanted to do sixteenth notes—it was a pretty fast tempo. But the solo started on a syncopated accent, so I had to figure out a way to get into it and still make that accent come out. I had to start with a melody, and I'm glad I was smart enough to do that, because it attaches the solo to the song, and if I could pat myself on the back, hopefully I've been able to do that a whole lot within the shred style and still have it be something that attaches to the song. And maybe with the exception of those early Racer X albums, where I'm just going crazy with my three fast licks, with Mr. Big, we had time to be able to sit down and spend enough time to compose something where it actually related to the tune.

NIGHT RANGER, 'ROCK IN AMERICA' (FROM *MIDNIGHT MADNESS*, 1983) AND 'DON'T TELL ME YOU LOVE ME' (FROM *DAWN PATROL*, 1982)

JEFF WATSON [The eight-finger tapping technique] was written to address 'Rock In America,' because I had that slot in there and I wanted to make it special. We knew it was going to be a highlight on the album, so I wanted something that stood out. I generally wrote my solos for the songs. In Ranger, in the early days, I would figure them out. And that's a very Randy Rhoads thing—I would write out the concept and then develop the solo, and have it down pat before I went into the studio. That's how that came to be, as it was written specifically for that, and just kept developing it, because people were going, 'That's wild! What are you doing?' I kept working on it and woodshed it some more, and that's how that all came about.

The solo I'm most recognized for is the flat-picking solo in 'Don't Tell Me You Love Me.' It was the same approach—I took something that seemed impossible to play, and because my guitar technique is kind of backward, the front of my pick comes up instead of pointing down, and I start my licks with an upstroke. It facilitates me to sweep a couple of notes at a time and it's just in my DNA to do that. And that made me able to play those licks, because it's really difficult if you don't pick that style. And that's how that came about. It was the same thing—I said, 'This is ridiculously hard,' and I just woodshedded it for a long time, and we got it down to where I could play it. And I really had to develop it to pull it off live.

NITRO, 'FREIGHT TRAIN' AND 'MACHINE GUNN EDDIE' (FROM *O.F.R.*, 1989)

MICHAEL ANGELO BATIO When people say, 'Oh, Michael Angelo Batio, all you do is play fast,' my retort is, 'I don't play too fast, you just can't *hear* fast enough!' That solo in 'Freight Train,' it starts in E flat, it goes to F, it goes to D, then it goes to B flat. In other words, there's modulations there. And then it starts off with chromatic scales. I worked out ninety-something percent of that solo. And I loved the song 'Freight Train.' If Nitro was guilty of anything, our label wanted us to sound so over-the-top. But when you heard our demos, they really weren't like that.

I mean, 'Freight Train,' I'm sorry, it's a great song. It's a catchy song—the verse is catchy, the pre-chorus. The label produced it like that. We did not. That's not my rhythm guitar sound—they scooped it. They did certain things, but it sold so well. They said they wanted to piss off parents, and they told me that they wanted me to overplay all the time. Because we were at the end of the 80s—bigger hair, wilder clothes, faster guitar. The highest, the fastest, the loudest.

So 'Freight Train,' the actual solo, it's blindingly fast—but there's a method to the madness. And I played it live in concert—we played it virtually the same way every night. I mean, there are a few little variances, a few spots because in my own warped thinking, I improvised a few seconds here and there. But the majority of that solo is worked out. We toured for six months for the first record. I remember playing that song after about the first month on the road, and I swear, it started to seem slow to me! [*Laughs*] I felt like Spider-Man, like you see things in slow motion. That solo was starting to feel … it was like my warm-up solo. I look back at that now, and I think, 'How did I do that?' If I have any thoughts about that solo, it was that it was worked out.

['Machine Gunn Eddie' was] completely improvised. And it was one take. See, that's another thing, too—it was tape. There's no cheating—you can't punch in. Those were real, in-your-face solos. Again, it's my practice regime—I worked really hard, practicing before I went into the studio. At one time, I think I did four or five solos in one day. I was just so 'on' that day. Like the solo to 'O.F.R.'—if you listen to that, that is just string-skipping, wide interval mania. I was like, one/four, two/five, three/six, six/one—it was just so ridiculous. If you listen to it, listen to the jumps—that was the last solo I did on one of the days. It was just so out there. Allan Holdsworth was in the studio next to us when we were recording—in Costa Mesa, at a place called Front Page Productions—and I remember thinking when I was doing that 'O.F.R.' solo, I just wanted it to sound really out there. And he came into the studio and listened to it, and was chuckling, like, '*Wow!*'

RACER X, *STREET LETHAL* (1986) AND *SECOND HEAT* (1987)

PAUL GILBERT Well, every solo is the same solo! Which was kind of what you did—it was the thing where you pick a key, and you play it as fast as you possibly can. You put all your licks into that key. Really, when I listen to *Street Lethal*, every solo is the same solo, because I had my three fast licks and I did it. And they're three pretty good fast licks, so that's all right. But it's very different than trying to come up with a melody. We just did it really quick, and I was really excited about it, because it sounded like a record. It had reverb. Now when I listen to it, it has too much reverb. But at the time, that was an exotic thing that sounded different than your demo tapes. So it was like, 'Wow—it's got reverb and the snare sounds like a canon!' All that stuff, you couldn't get it to happen in your bedroom, so it was amazing to go to a studio and get those sounds.

I also double-tracked all the rhythm-guitar parts, which I don't think I'd ever done that before. And it made it sound like a 'production.' But I remember doing the entire album's doubled tracked guitar parts in I think it was three or four hours. Basically, just played them, and maybe we stopped two or three times because of a clam, but we had rehearsed for a year. I think my most shocking memory was when I joined Mr. Big and we'd spend, like, a day on a song. And I was panicking, going, 'Aren't we going to run out of time?' I was used to doing *the whole album* in four hours! So that to me was normal, because that was the only thing I knew.

Second Heat, we had a little more time—but not much. And we had Bruce Bouillet in the band, which was great. It still had a lot of reverb. I remember we were all kind of starving, and after Juan finished his bass tracks, we were still working on guitars and vocals, and because he had some extra time, he went and got a job at a candy-packing factory. So he would come back every night where we were staying, with all this candy and cookies. We had run out of money, so all we had to eat was candy and Pepperidge Farm cookies. So I think we were just high from sugar—that may have contributed to the fast guitar solos. We were just jittery. Most bands were doing dangerous drugs, but we were high on Pepperidge Farm and jellybeans!

RANDY RHOADS, 'SUICIDE SOLUTION' (UNACCOMPANIED SOLO FROM OZZY OSBOURNE'S *TRIBUTE*, 1987)

RUDY SARZO Randy had been working on a similar solo from the Quiet Riot days. Now, I would say the biggest difference from the Quiet Riot solo to the one with Ozzy is he really relied a lot on the Echoplex—I'm talking the old tape Echoplex. It was kind of gimmicky, but he left the Echoplex on to get a thicker tone back in the day—this is before he started using the Marshalls. He had a Peavey cabinet with six twelves, and a Peavey head. And, of course, he had the pedals—Overdrive and all that stuff. And he didn't start playing the Marshalls with the Altec Lansing speakers … actually, he had Altecs way back then, too, but it wasn't until he went to a factory and had a modified Marshall, and they put the Altecs in the Marshall that he got rid of the tape Echoplex—because he did not need it anymore. Then, he started using another Echoplex—it was the Roland Space Echo, but not tape. He started getting more musical rather than special effects, because now, you could expand in your playing.

Now, he's got these incredible songs with really sophisticated chord changes. And now all of sudden, you're going to do your solo? No, you cannot do the same solo, because you are not playing for sixteen, seventeen-year-old girls anymore—you're playing for a more sophisticated audience, and within the framework of very sophisticated music. So he had to change his approach with his guitar solo for all the Ozzy tours. As a matter of fact, we expanded on his guitar solo—on the *Diary Of A Madman* tour, there was a section that was added, that I think you can hear that in bootlegs. That was added on because Randy just got bored and wanted to write something new, without having to write a whole composition with vocals. He said, 'Let me expand on the solo and put this section in there'—which I believe was a transition from the guitar solo to the drums. So he was changing it a bit always. I think he found that section where he could experiment. As the tour progressed, he would change—he would do little things here and there. He would keep some, one night he would try something and go, 'I really didn't like it,' and add something else. It was his little spot where he could break free.

DAVID LEE ROTH, 'SHY BOY' (FROM *EAT 'EM AND SMILE*, 1986)

BILLY SHEEHAN Dave heard the song,* liked it, and decided to do it, and I said, 'Great!' And he was kind enough to let me keep my publishing on it, which I did, and it was a wonderful success for me as a result. And we did a rearrangement of it—we changed keys of the solo, which is kind of a cool idea. And that was that— he just liked the song and wanted to do it, and I was glad he did.

DAVID LEE ROTH, *A LITTLE AIN'T ENOUGH* (1991)

JASON BECKER I was having a blast, but at the same time, I was trying to quietly deal with ALS and my body getting weaker. I was limping and tripping a lot. I had a lot of fun, but I remember recording my acoustic part for 'Drop In The Bucket,' and my hand wasn't doing it right. I finally got it and went into the Little Mountain Studios bathroom, and looked at my left hand. The muscle between my thumb and first finger was pretty much gone. I cried. My favorite songs were the ones I wrote: 'It's Showtime' and 'Drop In The Bucket.' To me, those had the energy and the playful, fun vibe like old David Lee Roth stuff.

BLUES SARACENO, *NEVER LOOK BACK* (1989)

BLUES SARACENO I'd never been in a studio. The first three songs as they are on the record†—we had to re-cut them, because I did them on a four-track, but that was in essence the first three songs that the person who was responsible for signing me heard. So that very first record was exactly the demo that I ended up doing for a guitar company. Rich Lasner sent me a guitar, and explained to me, 'The more popular you are, the easier it is to get you an endorsement.' So I said, 'Let me make a demonstration of what I can do on this guitar, and I'll send it to you. If you like it, maybe I'll get an endorsement.'

So I did song one, sent it in, and he said, 'That's great! Can I get another one?' So I did song two. But they were really a lot of work—I put a lot of time into them. By the time I did the third one, I was like, 'Damn, I'm really earning this guitar,

---

* Originally recorded by Talas for *Sink Your Teeth Into That* (1982).
† 'Remember When,' 'Never Look Back,' and 'Full Tank.'

with no free lunch!' So those three songs were the ones that a guy from a pickup company had gotten—it was floating around—and that's how I got signed.

But then we had to go back and re-cut them, I remember thinking, 'All the magic was in the demo.' When I did those demos, I really laid it all on the line. So when I had to go back and re-cut the record, I was thinking, 'Damn. This isn't as good as the demo tape.' Even though the recording quality was better. The first record was hard for me, to be honest. We were scheduled two weeks to make a record, and at the end of two weeks, we had three songs done and the rhythm tracks, but we didn't have the leads. I was living in my parents' garage at the time, so I used a TASCAM eight-track, and I would record the solos on I think it was quarter-inch eight-track, and then we would fly it back in and mix it elsewhere. It was a hard record—it was an interesting introduction into the music industry. I had to work with a producer. I knew how I could get the best result, and having to work with somebody else was definitely different than how I wanted to do it.

I remember thinking, 'I'll never do another one of these guitar records. *This is too much work.*' So I did the first record and I only signed a one-record deal. And I remember we had to use a different drummer and a different bass player, and I got to work with Joe Franco, who is great. That guy is an amazing drummer, and what a nice guy. Originally, it was just me and this guy, Tom Polce, who was going to play drums, and the producer said, 'We're going to use Joe Franco, because he's well-known and respected.' So I was disappointed I didn't get to do the record with Tom, because it would have been a great opportunity for both of us. But I did get to work with Joe Franco, and that was an amazing experience. It was kind of my introduction to the industry—you don't get what you want, you get what you get.

THE MICHAEL SCHENKER GROUP, 'INTO THE ARENA'
(FROM *THE MICHAEL SCHENKER GROUP*, 1980)

MICHAEL SCHENKER I was getting ready for my first album. And my first album actually took me through quite a few rhythm sections. By the way, the first rhythm section was Denny Carmassi and Billy Sheehan. And then the second one was Joey Kramer and Tom Hamilton from Aerosmith—but then Steven Tyler came back, and they carried on. And I almost did it with Geddy Lee and Neil Peart from Rush. Eventually, Peter Mensch found me Simon Phillips and Mo Foster.

So when I was getting ready to go to the studio with Simon Phillips and Mo Foster, that was the time when I went through an edit of more compositions to what I already had. I went into a rehearsal studio, I was playing around, and came up with it on the spot there. I had a complete vision that I wanted tempo changes and some drama in it and some excitement. It's funny, because I didn't even come up with the name—it was [producer] Roger Glover. That song spoke to him—it was something like getting ready for the big fight. 'Into The Arena' was quite interesting. Roger Glover comes up with some clever ideas—he also came up with the title for 'Bijou Pleasurette.'

BILLY SHEEHAN VS. **STEVE VAI**, 'BASS/GUITAR DUEL'

(FROM THE *EAT 'EM AND SMILE* TOUR, 1986/87)

BILLY SHEEHAN That was Dave's idea. We both did an individual solo, and Dave said, 'Yeah, that's good … but not all that entertaining. We should make it like a tractor pull, and make it an exciting carnival event.' So his idea was to have Steve start a solo, then the other guy would come up from behind and stop him, push him aside and then start his thing, and then the other guy would come back, and back and forth, back and forth. And it turned out to be entertaining—as opposed to just musical showmanship. It was fun, it was a good gag, and was meant to be comedy. Dave really excelled in making things entertaining—as opposed to just musicianship or great singing and great songs. There's more to it than that—to entertain people. And he was a grand master at that.

SOUNDGARDEN, 'SLAVES AND BULLDOZERS' (FROM

BADMOTORFINGER, 1991); 'SPOONMAN' AND 'BLACK

HOLE SUN' (FROM *SUPERUNKNOWN*, 1994)

KIM THAYIL Every solo of 'Slaves And Bulldozers' when we play it live can be of different length and incorporate different elements, and I've played it with different feels emotively, on different parts of the neck. I'm having a hard time recalling the studio version, because we've done so many dozens—if not hundreds—of different versions. The way the song has developed over the past twenty years, it's in a very different place now than where it was on the record. But it was the same thing there. The song was slow and creeping, and it creeped up on you. And the guitar solo, you want things to unravel and explode at the same time. And that was the goal there.

We were working with Terry Date, and as a producer, they orientate themselves with the drums and creating a really nice bed for the rest of the instruments to sit in. And part of doing that is making sure things are oriented toward the kick and snare. 'Slaves And Bulldozers,' when you get to that part of the song, it needs to blow up and unravel, and I think the orientation from the producer's standpoint ... but the tendency is to keep it under wraps and within the confines of the groove and the riff.

There may be more of the rhythmic coherence on the studio version, but as soon as I had the opportunity to throw that out the window live, I did. And the only time I have to reel it in is if Chris decides he's going to solo, too, and when he does, that kind of defines the line. It's like, 'Well ... I can't do all this. I can't go in all these different modes or rhythms if it's going to clash with this coherent line that Chris is playing, because if I do that, it's going to sound out of place.' So I'm going to have to reference what he's doing in order to have what I'm doing still be contained within the song. But if you don't have that other guitar there and Chris is concentrating on his vocals, then I can go all over the place.

[On 'Spoonman'], because that song is in seven and it's got a pretty straight, tight arrangement, and there's percussive orientation there, the intro to the solo was a couple of triplets that Chris had actually written as part of the song. And then you go into percussion solos. So that definitely set parameters. I would kind of play that solo a little bit more regulated—I fuck it up and vary it live all the time. I think of that as being a song and a solo that required a little bit more focus and organization, because it starts with that little solo intro riff that Chris came up with, and then it goes into the 'spoon solo.' Because of that, I am trying to have an idea of what the time considerations are of the solo—maybe in terms of length and where my location on the neck will be in terms of key.

'Black Hole Sun' was a great opportunity to play a little bit modally and a little bit chaotically, because that's definitely the type of song that boils up in the point, and the title of the song and the lyrics, it lends itself to a certain psychedelia. The video imagery is definitely thinking of things like novas and other stellar elements. Those are components of the song lyrically and they're not necessarily components of the guitar solo, but it allows the guitar solo to certainly burst ... ah, there you go—sunburst, there's a guitar reference! It's the finish on a Les Paul and it's a way to approach a guitar solo in a song called 'Black Hole Sun.'

So there's definitely a lot of chaos that I was able to introduce there. Otherwise, you definitely have a well-arranged, memorable, beautiful vocal melody and pop rock song. So you almost want the contrast there of the wildness and chaos, but at the same time, you play modally, because that just sounds trippy—veering in and out of keys, and that gives it that psychedelic, 'Astronomy Domine' weirdness. And the time and length, it's like, 'Here are the bars I can play in and I'm going to try and capture the fluid psychedelia and the chaos all at some point there.'

Fortunately, Michael Beinhorn our producer, he was definitely helpful when I laid down a number of different versions of the solo and multitracked that, and then I arranged it so the solo would develop in a way that has some degree of drama and resolution, with what the song and the riff were doing. And Beinhorn totally understood that, read it, and was helpful in helping me identify phrases that I really liked in the performance.

TNT, 'CAUGHT BETWEEN THE TIGERS' (FROM *INTUITION*, 1989)

RONNI LE TEKRØ That album, *Intuition*, was probably the longest production in hard rock, because I recorded the guitars for eight months on that album! When you had tracks like 'Wisdom' or 'Caught Between The Tigers,' you hear sixty electric guitars … that sound like one. [*Laughs*]

TALAS, 'NV43345' (FROM *SINK YOUR TEETH INTO THAT*, 1982)

BILLY SHEEHAN I wanted to do a distortion/screaming feedback/over-the-top/ blazing solo, but my amp head failed me that day, and we only had a little time to do anything. So I thought, 'Well, I'll just do a clean, chordal piece.' And I winged it, completely. I didn't have any plan. I think a couple of things I did, I had done in some of my live solos, but they were never really formalized or decided upon. So I just winged it and that's what we got. I didn't put that much thought in it at all—it wasn't until later that people seemed to respond positively to it that I thought, '*Well, maybe it wasn't so bad after all …*'

TESTAMENT, 'PRACTICE WHAT YOU PREACH' (FROM *PRACTICE WHAT YOU PREACH*, 1989)

ALEX SKOLNICK If I have a signature solo, it's probably 'Practice What You Preach,' the title track off the third record. I was just having a conversation about this with Jimmy Herring, a great guitar player from Aquarium Rescue Unit—he's somebody more people should know. People in the jam band world know him. And he also plays in Widespread Panic. We were talking about playing live, and that record was the one where we tried to record as much as we could live. And Jimmy was saying there are some tracks on the new Widespread Panic record that he wishes he could do over, but everybody played great and they loved the solos and it fits the song, and I was saying, '*That's part of being in a band.*' And sometimes, you get lucky.

'Practice What You Preach,' I got very lucky. It was the best I played the solo, and everybody else was happy with their parts. It doesn't always work that way—there's been examples where I would have liked to do it again. And I think as time went on and technology got better, it was easier to go back in and fix your solos. So I did do that on later records, but *Practice What You Preach*, all those solos were played live with the band, with that take, as they went down. And that one in particular, I knew we were having a good take—it just felt really good, and the solo just really came together.

It's funny, it's inspired by a couple of the guys we've been talking about. It had been a few years since I had studied with Satriani, but I was finally grasping the theory that he taught me. I always thought, 'OK, I'm never going to be able to understand this.' I just finally got fed up and pushed myself to learn it. And the 'Practice What You Preach' solo was like an exercise to run through all the modes, and it ended up working great with the song. And then the very end of it has this kind of sliding opening string blues lick, and that was inspired by Stevie Ray Vaughan. I had learned the tune 'Scuttle Buttin',' this real fast, open-string thing. So, 'I have this lick, it can easily fit in that tune.' Of course, I'm playing much more distorted, but that's exactly the feel I'm going for there.

TRANS-SIBERIAN ORCHESTRA, 'CHRISTMAS EVE/SARAJEVO 12/24' (FROM *CHRISTMAS EVE AND OTHER STORIES*, 1996)

CHRIS CAFFERY I played mostly rhythm guitars on that—Al Pitrelli was doing a lot of the leads. That song was something that Paul O'Neill, my producer, arranged for about a decade, before we recorded it with TSO. I think it was something that he had originally tried to submit to the Scorpions. It was just an idea that Paul had. He managed Joan Jett, and one of the things that really broke her in music was a cover she had of 'Little Drummer Boy.' She got a lot of radio play at Christmas time with that song. And all of a sudden, in January, they released 'I Love Rock 'n' Roll' as a single, and it exploded.

So Paul had this arrangement of that song, and his initial intentions of that song were not to have that be what started TSO. TSO was an idea he had for a long time, that we had recorded with Savatage in the same way that we would get picked up on radio, and it would bring the rest of our record to radio. But what wound up happening is it got so big on radio that Atlantic Records wanted to maximize what we could do with it, and that's when Paul decided to finish the story, and do *Christmas Eve And Other Stories*, and release the first TSO record as that one.

And that's what launched TSO and started that Christmas trilogy, although Paul's first TSO record he still hasn't even released yet—called *Romanov*. He had that record written before, but TSO's future and everybody else's involved got kind of rewritten, because of that song. A lot of those harmony parts and things that are on that song are things that Paul was literally singing to Al to play. But that song had been recorded before.

TRIUMPH, 'FIGHT THE GOOD FIGHT' (FROM *ALLIED FORCES*, 1981)
AND 'MIDSUMMER'S DAYDREAM' (FROM *THUNDER SEVEN*, 1984)

RIK EMMETT 'Fight The Good Fight,' that would have been one probably where I would have approached it knowing that it had that certain chord progression in it, and knowing that I was going to try and hit certain chord tones and use an arpeggiated approach—probably started improvising and spent maybe a couple of hours punching in and creating certain licks in certain places.

Now, I can't remember specifically if I did it on this solo, but I did this more than once, where I would get the solo into a certain shape, and know that's the story I wanted to tell, in terms of notes and licks in certain places. And then I would come back maybe the next day, and kind of glue it all into place and play it. And I probably wouldn't have done it in a single flowing take—it was probably done with a few punch-ins. But it was probably created with four-bar phrases, eight-bar phrases, that kind of got 'pastiched' together, pasted together, and then I would have said, 'I'm happy with that. That's what we're going to do.' In that sense, that solo to me is sort of a 'story' kind of solo.

Two examples I would cite are the classic Jimmy Page 'Stairway To Heaven' solo—which had all of the right kind of licks in the right places, and it was the right story for the song. And then a guy like Don Felder, when him and Joe Walsh did the 'Hotel California' solo. My suspicion is that one was created in the same way that 'Fight The Good Fight' was.

The fact that they're trading back and forth either sixteen-bar chunks or thirty-two-bar chunks or whatever it is, for sure, they were definitely thinking about four-bar phrases/eight-bar phrases, and 'How are we going to order these eight-bar phrase things?' With Jimmy, I'm not so sure that's how it went down. He might have played that all in one flowing thing. But when you hear something at the end of a solo, something like [*sings the ending guitar solo phrases of 'Stairway To Heaven'*], to me, that's almost like a composed thing. Those are chunks where you go, 'Did he arrive at that just by happenstance? I don't think so.'

['Midsummer's Daydream' was] definitely recorded in pieces that were then edited together, because there is absolutely no way I could play what I had written from stem to stern. [*Laughs*] The engineer that I was working with at the time had some experience doing Glenn Gould sessions, and Gould would record things and then have large pieces of tape where he would then say, 'I think I'm going to take from A to bar 136, and that will be from tape fourteen.' He was doing this incredibly high-minded, quality approach kind of thing. For me, it was more a question of, 'Can I just play the damn thing and get a twelve-bar chunk that was done OK?' And, 'Let's mark that one, and I'll pick it up from the second thing and go from there.' So it would get edited together, and then later on, I would learn how to play it, so I could play it live.

Because I would write over my head—I would be able to write things that I wouldn't necessarily be able to play one section, and then flow without mistakes into the next. There were a lot of clams. But in terms of how that worked, it was that it had become a traditional thing for there to be a 'guitar piece' on Triumph albums, so the other guys would expect me to write something and record it. And I would probably spend the better part of a day, or at least a half-day, chasing something like that.

What I remember about the actual composition of the piece, I pretty much knew I was going to bookend it with the harmonics with the dropped D. I knew that was going to be the bookends for the thing. There's probably a lot of inspiration from McCartney's 'Blackbird,' that informed a lot of the writing of that—the idea of those kinds of fingerings where it's bass notes with melody that's locking in relatively straightforward patterns on the top. And then the use of open strings and flamenco-y kind of stuff that happens from time to time. I'm not really a trained/schooled fingerstyle player. I really just make it up as I go along, and taught myself how to make that stuff happen.

But when I write things, I tend to think about the dynamic spread of what it is that I've got—'Where are my quiet moments and what's happening there, and where is my biggest stuff, and what am I doing in terms of making it get powerful and loud? Or when am I slowing the thing down to make it so that the melody really matters and when am I driving the rhythm, so it becomes much more of an energetic thing that's more of a physical thing for a listener?' So when I write guitar pieces like 'Midsummer's Daydream,' those were probably fairly conscientious kinds of things that push the composition. Because like I said earlier, I kind of want pieces to be telling a story—so what's the narrative, and when is the story making the blood rush, and when is it searching for a tender moment?

STEVE VAI, *FLEX-ABLE* (1984)

STEVE VAI When I made that record, I had absolutely no expectations of it being successful, of me being famous, or recognized. I was very happy to just be a teacher and just record and record and record. So that was my advantage—I had no expectations, there was nobody I was catering to, there was no audience that I thought, 'I have to create something for.' It was strictly and entirely for my own kind of enjoyment, and the people around me that I was living with at the time. Which was Pia, who was my girlfriend at the time—we've been together for like, thirty-seven years—and then in the house, it was like a wayward home for musician refugees! I had this cool house out in Somar, and we had all these friends living in it, and it was just a fantastic time. So I would make music to make us laugh.

And I was enamored—*absolutely enamored*—with the recording process. I loved the idea of engineering, editing, EQ'ing, mixing, recording—it was just every day, all day, morning, noon, and night. I turned out tremendous amounts of stuff, but then at one point I thought, 'Let me just make a record and see what happens.' I didn't think anybody would be interested in it. I mean, something like 'The Attitude Song' ... well, let me say, I didn't set out to create an instrumental guitar record, so to speak. I don't really see that record as a conventional, instrumental guitar record. I mean, I've got *Blow By Blow* and *Wired* and all that incredible Beck stuff—this didn't sound anything like that.

And I was very unknown at the time, so I didn't sit there and do 'The Attitude Song' and think, 'Wow ... wait until people hear this!' I did that song, it used to be called 'The Night Before' when I recorded it, because way back, even before I was with Frank, Alice Cooper was looking for a guitar player, and I was told I could send a demo tape to a particular address, but I needed something that displayed my guitar playing, and the submissions were the next day, so I improvised the bass part to 'The Attitude Song,' and then just in one night, basically laid all those guitars down and thought, 'Wow. This is really whacky.' And I loved every minute of it, but you can't really compare a song like that to something like 'Little Green Men,' which was just something funny for us to laugh at, y'know?

STU HAMM I mostly remember sleeping out there in the studio, and he had this friggin' snake in an aquarium, and it smelt like stale snake. And the thing would go around and try to push the top of the aquarium and get out. When I would go to sleep, I was sure the snake would get out and kill me! Working with Steve was great—he is very much a perfectionist, coming from the Zappa years. Rehearsals were very long, and he worked us pretty hard. It was great though. One thing that I carried from those rehearsals is that when we would learn 'The Attitude Song,' he had us play it at completely different tempos. Like, literally too fast, and literally too slow, to really get a handle on the music. And man, it was *amazing*.

What people don't realize—or what some of the younger generation doesn't—is he did all that stuff on a four-track. This is before they came out with the first Harmonizer and stuff. Now, it's like anybody can play a single note, and have it harmonized over whatever they want. But the amazing thing about what Steve did back there was he actually had to play that stuff correctly—there was no Pro Tools, there was no moving around stuff a quarter-inch. Everything actually had to be played at the time, and the execution that you wanted to hear it back. It was just an amazing display of musicality and technical ability.

STEVE VAI, *PASSION AND WARFARE* (1990)

STU HAMM The *Passion And Warfare* sessions, that was when Steve had moved to Hollywood, in the hills. Certainly, the technology had advanced quite a bit, and Steve had more leeway at that time—it's the same kind of thing where for that music is still coming from a Zappa kind of place, for me, where it's precision of execution. Where me, the stuff I was coming from is more jazz and fusion and sort of a dialogue. In my own records, I'd say I've gotten better in the studio by learning to record a tape that's a piece of music and a performance, and not just an exercise in not making a mistake—if that makes any sense.

Whereas back in those days, recording with Steve, not that it wasn't enjoyable—the guy is at the top of his game, can hear when you're rushing a sixteenth note or whatever. And maybe I was just younger and where my head was at the time, but it certainly was trying to play correctly under 'the scrutiny of the master.' But when I listen back to it, it's great. Stuff like 'The Animal,' he gave me more free reign to be myself, but it's like all of us, we know so many musicians that when you're writing a song, you can leave a part vacant and know you can ask this musician or that musician for that song, for them to play on it. Which is assumingly why they called me for the songs they did on their records.

WATCHTOWER, *CONTROL AND RESISTANCE* (1989)

RON JARZOMBEK 'Instruments Of Random Murder' was a song that we had on the 1987 demo, where we had recorded the full songs before they were done for

Control And Resistance. And that solo, there's two sections in there where I kind of improvised a little bit. I remember when we were in Berlin recording it for the album, I was trying to duplicate what I had improvised, and it wasn't coming out quite right. So I liked the demo version a lot better. And that's the same for the solo in 'The Fall Of Reason'—some of that was improvised. But the main part of that solo is where I do all the triple tracking, where I'm playing the same line, and then it's in 'stacked thirds,' where it's a descending kind of a climb. After I heard that back, I decided to do all of the solos on *Control And Resistance* on three tracks, where I had a left and a right, doing the harmonies. And then the solo that was panned in the middle was like 'the focus,' and then the left and the right harmony ones were kind of playing off of that. And probably 'Instruments Of Random Murder' was the first solo that I did that triggered that whole idea to do all of that.

'Life Cycles' was pretty interesting, because I didn't know what I was going to record at the time, and it was a real spacey, kind of spooky song. I wanted to do some backward type stuff, and I got that idea from Rush's *Caress Of Steel* album, where Alex did all of this … notes were fading in instead of fading out, and it had this real mysterious kind of sound. I think that one probably sticks out the most. And it was real spontaneous, trying to write parts around a backward part, that you didn't know how it was going to go before. 'The Fall Of Reason' was another solo that I wish I would have had the recording I did on the demo, because we had the instruments that we had rented out for it, they weren't quite giving me enough sustain, so I couldn't have these real high, harmonic notes. Oh, the 'Control And Resistance' solo is pretty ripping, too. I just liked doing all that kind of stuff, where you have harmonies coming in and out, and lead parts playing off of each other. I think the solo for 'Control And Resistance' captured that probably the best on that album.

MARK WOOD, *VOODOO VIOLINCE* (1991)

MARK WOOD *Voodoo Violince* came out, and I remember John Stix, the producer, saying, 'We don't want any clean violin—it's got to be all distortion. It's got to be *a rock record*, Mark.' And it was all original material. I'll never forget writing it and getting feedback from John, and any time it sounded a little too esoteric or a little new age-y, 'Forget it—delete!' So we really focused that record on balls-to-the-wall rock'n'roll, beginning to ending, and a virtuoso Van Halen–type approach. And I could easily do that—I've been doing that for years. But I'm still an 'esoteric musician,' who can jump from Stravinsky to Mozart to Slayer in thirty seconds, and it all makes sense to me.

But unfortunately, the general public can't digest that easily, and I learned a lot about digesting and producing music—that, on first listen, you could be pulled into it as a rock audience. And that's really what I wanted to develop—my rock audience. I didn't want a jazz audience, I didn't want a classical audience, God forbid. But the rock guys, I knew they would dig what I'm doing. And I was good friends with Steve Vai, being Long Islanders, and I would send them stuff to give me feedback on. So it was a really exciting time for me.

We then got a really big following in Canada, during one of the few times that the currency in Canada was far better, and was financially feasible for them to bring an artist up from New York to tour—from Quebec to Montreal to Toronto. That was a really fun thing—to get in a broken down van and drive five hundred miles to play in some crummy little hole-in-the-wall in Sudbury, Canada. But for me, as a violin player, every time I played, people would go, 'I've never seen this before. I've never heard this before. I've never experienced this before.' And for me, as a musician, how many times can you have that kind of reaction?

Because on guitar, it's all been done—Frank Zappa to Steve Vai, you can name hundreds of brilliant guitar players. Man, it's all been done, and you'll never get the reaction of, '*I've never heard this before, I've never seen this before.*' So I was experiencing that. I was on *The Tonight Show*, got a tremendous amount of coverage, the record sold really well, and then we went back into the second album, *Against The Grain*.

Y&T, 'MEAN STREAK' (FROM *MEAN STREAK*, 1983)

DAVE MENIKETTI I remember that at least the last half of the solo was a worked-out piece that came up while we were writing the song. The first half of the solo was whatever happened at the time when I was recording the album. That's just what I do a lot. It kind of bothers some people because they have to sit there while I'm playing it—I'll play something for the first time and I'll have no idea what I'm going to do and what's going to happen, and maybe it will be ten times later that I'm finally getting the feel for it. I'm sure some engineers are like, '*I wish you would have worked the solos out.*' But for me, it's always better because I truly am playing with a lot of emotion at the time. It's what's coming right now versus a planned out/trying-to-play-it-cleanly kind of thing.

tools of
the **trade**

**The stories behind how some of shred's most
renowned instruments were obtained.**

MICHAEL ANGELO BATIO The double came when I was a boy. In Chicago, there
is a public television show—and it's still on, it's on cable—the call letters were
WTTW, it was channel eleven. And every Sunday was kind of like an *Austin
City Limits* thing—they would have concerts. So one week, you would see Willie
Nelson, you might see The Allman Brothers; next week it may be the music of
Beethoven. It was all different genres. And I used to watch it every week. I loved
it. And every once in a while, they'd have jazz concerts. And they had a concert
with a blind black guy. His name was Rahsaan Roland Kirk, and he could do
something called 'circular breathing'—he could breath in and out at the same
time. Pretty wild. I'm watching this guy, just riff out on these different reed
instruments—not just saxophone, but he could play flute, he could play a lot
of things. But he's playing saxophone, and at the end of the show, he puts on
a second sax, and plays two at the same time. And then I heard that at other
concerts, he could actually do three. I said, 'I'm left-handed. I play guitar right-
handed, but my air-guitar playing when I was a little kid was lefty. I'm going to
do this on guitar.'

What I did is I started drawing designs in high school, and it wasn't until I got
close to being signed to Atlantic Records—now we're looking at around 1984—
that I was in a position to talk to a company. And I always loved Dean Guitars,
even though I didn't really endorse them … I endorsed them for about a year in
the 80s, but then the original owner sold the company and it didn't really exist. So

from the mid 80s to the mid 90s, there really was no Dean Guitars. That's when I used Charvel and BC Rich and Gibson. I saw a concert with Eddie Van Halen—it was the second Van Halen tour—and I remember watching him play, and his guitar was angled upwards. I said, '*That's* how a human plays guitar.' And I saw a picture in one of the rock mags of a full body shot of Eddie, and I took tracing paper, and I just did a quick trace outline, and I flipped it up side down, and saw, 'There is my double.' I took a protractor, measured the angles of the two necks. It came to about 115 degrees.

So at the end of '83, beginning of '84, I approached Dean Guitars here in Chicago—they were still here. I talked to the owner. I told him I wanted necks at about 115 degrees, we took a left-handed and right-handed guitar called the Baby—they're the ones that Nancy Wilson used to use in Heart. They're smaller bodies but with full-sized necks—they look like Explorers. So we had a lefty and a righty, both of them painted white. We kind of eyeballed the 115 degrees, sawed it, and I came up with the mechanism, put it together, and that was the first double.

People just tripped out when they saw it. They freaked when they saw me play it. [It took me] about six months [to get comfortable playing it]. And then the first time I ever played it, we were on tour with Aerosmith. I played it at Alpine Valley, in front of 24,000 people. One of the women worked for Alpine Valley came to our dressing room, knocked on the door, and goes, 'Joe Perry and Brad Whitford want to see you.' So I go in their dressing room, and Joe goes—I wish I could do a good Boston accent—'*Ya gonna do it?*' And he makes the motion of the double guitar. I said, 'Yeah, I'm gonna do it!' And I did it. It wasn't very good, but I did it for the first time—with Aerosmith watching. It was awesome.

The quad guitar was actually something that I said as a joke. Here's what happened—I'm friends with Steve Vai now, but the 80s was very competitive. I had my double guitar, I was really known for it, but it was only in LA and through my instructional video. And again, in the 80s, I didn't know how many countries my videos got circulated in. They were everywhere. It's incredible. So I had my double guitar, I met Steve Vai at a studio when he was in David Lee Roth—I watched them rehearse. And what happened was literally days after I was talking to Vai, MTV debuts David Lee Roth,[*] and here's Steve Vai with the heart guitar. I was in the band Nitro, and we were signed to Rhino/Warner Bros. So we had this billion-dollar company behind us. And the president of our label was pissed! And then Steve at the time kind of reluctantly gave me credit for it. He said, 'Well, I

---

[*] The channel began airing the 'Just Like Paradise' video in 1988.

got the idea from Michael Angelo, but I didn't mean to take the wind out of his sails.' Our label was livid at him, because they felt like he stole my idea.

Here's what happened—we have a meeting. It's myself, the singer, and our first record hasn't even come out yet. We had just signed the papers and were finishing demos. We were getting all the ducks in a row, but it was signed, sealed, and delivered. And they loved us—they knew we were going to hit the charts. We had the machine behind us. So we sit down, we're in Santa Monica, and the president of our label looks at me, and goes, 'Michael, you have two necks. Steve Vai has three. What can you do?' I go, 'How about four?' He goes, 'FOUR!' Everybody's sitting, all the suits—picture guys back then with kind of long hair with ponytails. That's how everybody looked. The executives, it's kind of the mullet-y thing, but they have them in ponytails. But I made a joke about four, but here's the difference—I have an engineering mind. I have patents, I have trademarks; I have invented a guitar. How many people have invented a guitar? And now it's in the Rock and Roll Hall of Fame.

And I just happened to be super close friends with Wayne Charvel, who was one of the greatest guitar builders on the planet, from the company Charvel. So anything I asked Wayne to build, that guy could build it. See, with the double guitar, the engineering is very different. The way the mechanism hooks together, I had the case designed, many things I did back then I didn't change, because I really thought about it. But with the quad, the engineering was slick. *Really slick.* It was completely different. So I worked out the design, and when the president of our label said, 'Can you do four?' I said, 'Yes, I can do it.' And guess who built it? Gibson. It was Charvel through Gibson.

What I did is, I looked at the Steinberger guitars—I made four really small guitars, and we had back plates made out of aluminum. The back plate, you had to screw each guitar together, whereas my double, you don't—it locks together, it takes seconds to put it together and take it apart. But the engineering was completely different. So I drew up designs for Wayne, and said, 'Wayne, this is the engineering of it. Do your magic.' And he made it work. All of a sudden, we had this kickass quad guitar. He would decide the pickups, he would say, 'Michael, I've got these pieces of alder that are really light. I think this would be good.' I had the best of the best working with me. So anything I could think of, Wayne could do. That's how the quad guitar came out—I had two ... Steve Vai had three ... I came up with four. [*Laughs*]

JASON BECKER Cacophony: either Hurricane or Carvin guitars; I used my black and white Strat on *Speed Metal Symphony*, though. A Boss Super Overdrive pedal and 100-watt Marshall amps.

Roth: many different guitars—Carvin, Ibanez, Fender, Valley Arts, ESP, Hamer, Peavey, Les Paul. Marshall and Mesa Boogie amps.

ADRIAN BELEW I had one guitar, and it was a Fender Stratocaster. It wasn't a vintage guitar, but myself and Seymour Duncan made it look like one. [*Laughs*] We lit it on fire and dragged it through the yard and smacked it with screwdrivers—to sort of 'relic' it. This is way before that term even existed. Those came later—those are actually Mustangs.* And when I did the second solo album, *Twang Bar King*, Fender gave me two Mustangs, and a friend of mine, Mike Getz, painted them. Sort of a [Piet] Mondrian sort of look. And those became the *Twang Bar* guitars. They matched the cover artwork, which he did.

In terms of pedals, I had about six different pedals, and the guys in David Bowie's crew—when I worked with him the first time, in 1979—they built me a little pedal board. It was simply eight on and off switches. So you could connect the pedals to that pedal board. Inside the case, there was a little patch bay. So you'd turn on '#1' and it would be a Big Muff, you click it again, it would go off. One of them was a mute button. There were several Electro-Harmonix effects in there—I was good friends with Mike Matthews, the owner of that company. I had something I really liked called an Echo Flanger, which would make some interesting sounds. I had a compressor that I put on everything—it was a Dyna Comp. And everything kind of went through it first—I've always done that. There was probably some sort of delay—I'm not sure exactly which one. There was maybe a chorus unit. I can't tell you exactly what all those pedals were, but it was a very simple setup, and it allowed me to make just a few combinations—I'd step on two pedals at the same time or turn two on if I wanted. I always liked it that way. It was pretty simple.

PHIL COLLEN When I was in Girl, Ibanez came to a show in Tokyo, and they said, 'We've got these things, would you be up for playing it?' I played a couple, and thought, 'Oh, these are great!' I've got an Ibanez Firebird home in London, and it's awesome—it's one of the original 70s knockoff ones. It's a copy of the Gibson. It's as good as any Gibson I've ever played. It's just a beautiful sounding thing. I knew they made really good guitars. So I said, 'Can you customize one of these

---

* Belew was photographed with one of them for the cover of the January 1984 issue of *Guitar Player*.

Destroyers? Have three pickups in it, and make them DiMarzios, and have it black with a binding?' A really sexy looking thing. And a whammy bar—it had a Kahler on it.

They did it, and it just had its own sound. It really did. I dig it out now and again … it's a bit of a struggle to play. These Jackson PC1's just sound phenomenal—I got them all hot-rodded up. They've got titanium and they have DiMarzios on them. You can do so much with them and I can get anything out of it. They're easier to play. Plus, I use fatter necks. I think I was using .09 gauge strings then, and I'm up to .013 to .056 now. All of that stuff has changed over the years. But back then, it was really cool—that through a Marshall was really good. That stuff still sounds great—the *Pyromania* stuff. I love it.

K.K. DOWNING We were doing really good and playing big venues, and all I had was two Flying Vs and two Strats. And that was it—going into about '82, '83. Then Paul Hamer came along, and brought a Flying V to the show. I got to check it out, and he said, 'You can have these and as many as you want.' Because I started to worry about my early Vs—a '67 and a '70. I was out on the road, and was starting to think about them broken or stolen or something happening to them. It seemed to make sense. And I think all professional guys do that in the end— play gear that can be easily replaced if something goes wrong. Because you never know with shipping out gear all over the place, and there have been accidents that happened—guitars have been smashed. So it made sense to have a readymade product that could be reproduced at any point. And that's what we did. We put the old and now pretty valuable stuff in mothballs safely at home, and didn't have to worry about it too much.

If you were going to go with anybody, Hamer bought all of the Gibson machinery from Kalamazoo, when it was being retired by Gibson, because it wasn't fast enough to produce. It was the older gear. Well, this is the story that Hamer told us, anyway, and I think it's true, because they did put out a quality product— there's no doubt in my mind. Because I went to the factory a few times, and I saw all the shelves and the racking where they would mature all of their timbers before they did anything with it. Much longer than most guitar companies, I'm sure.

I've just gone into the attic and brought out an old pedal board that I had. I got involved with the guy that went on to make all of the gear, Pete Cornish. He was building racks for Pink Floyd, and went on to build our racks through the 80s. But before that, it was very basic. This old pedal board is now all seized up and has got mold on it! And that's what I used before we came into some money and got somebody to build us an expensive pedal board, which was remote. The first one wasn't. But our second lot was totally remote. Pete used to wire cockpits on airplanes, so everything he did was hardwired—everything was really smart.

What we requested to be built was exactly the same as something you might buy now, like Axe-FX or POD. Everything that was built for me in about '84, '85 was remote, as well. So my guitar tech could do all the switching for me if I wasn't at the pedal board. And I was—as far as I know—the first guy to ever actually have a guitar tuner on my pedal board. My office has got Marshall stacks, Flying Vs, Strats—it's where I work, really. But I've got one of the old Korgs here. It just says 'Korg Autochromatic Tuner.' When this came out, I thought, 'I'm going to put this on my pedal board, and I'm going to have a switch that kills my sound, but I can still see the guitar tuner.'

I gaffer-taped this guitar tuner to my pedal board, but the problem is I couldn't see it when the lights came on, because it had a red needle. So I took it apart one day in the dressing room, and I got an ink marker, and made the needle black, and I could see it! I used it for ages and ages. And now, of course, everybody has got a guitar tuner on their pedal board. But that's how it used to work. That's how our effects were built—we used to have effects that we really liked, and this guy would take them apart and just put the insides into one unit—whether it was a Phase-100 MXR or a Treble Booster or whatever it was. Pete did everything that everybody went on to do years later—just condense everything down into one little box. But it was exactly the same. And the lead was wrapped up in a big thing—I probably had about fourteen cables running into my pedal board, because everything was still done with cables.

RIK EMMETT I was a guitar collector and I had a lot of guitars. And then I started having guitar endorsement deals, so I would be able to get guitars custom made for me, and I would use those in live performances. I think the thing that most people remember is I had a Framus Akkerman guitar—Jan Akkerman from Focus had designed a model for a German guitar company. And I did that because I didn't want to be just another 'Les Paul guy.' But what I liked was that kind of Gibson Les Paul/335 territory. So I used that Akkerman for many years, and I would play that through usually fifty-watt Marshalls, pre–master volume. If you wanted it to be clean, you put it around one, and as you got it above about three or four, there was a lot of air on it. And I've always liked having that kind of a situation, so the amps that I use are generally very Marshall Plexi in nature—that's the distortion kind of sound that I like.

And I had some Dean guitars—that would have been around 1980, '81, '82. I had a Flying V and a Baby Z. Then I made a Yamaha deal, and they made me the SG-2000—they were kind of like the ones that Santana had been an endorsee of for a while. But mine had body sculpting in the back, and they weren't chambered. They were heavy as tree trunks. But they had really wide fingerboards and an almost two-inch nut. That was one of the things about the Akkerman that I loved—it had a very wide fingerboard, so you had lots of nice string spacing, and it made fingerstyle a little bit easier to play. But I always had Les Pauls, Teles, and Strats, and would get in the studio and try different guitars for different things.

And of course, when I made records, my acoustic guitars were always as important for layering texture. For example, a song like 'Fight The Good Fight,' a stock Tele that's being played really clean through a Roland Cube is one of the tracks, and it also had the Akkerman through a Marshall playing the heavy tracks, and it probably also had an acoustic guitar—maybe a twelve-string. My recordings tended to have kind of a Jimmy Page approach to making recordings. And then when I played live, it was like, 'Uh oh, I have to try and figure it out with one guitar through a Marshall.'

And as the 80s went on, Yamaha made some amps that I would use instead of the Marshalls, and I would have a pedal board that would always have some sort of delay unit and chorus unit on it, and probably a volume pedal or a wah. We played a couple of shows with AC/DC, and Angus had a rig where it was pretty much the sound of his wireless unit driving a relatively clean Marshall—not a very dirty one—but it was his wireless unit that gave him a punchy, overdriven kind of sound. It was fantastic and it moved a lot air. So there were a couple of tours where I would just go 'guitar and amp,' and if I wanted it clean, I would turn the guitar down, and if I wanted it dirty, I'd turn the guitar up.

LITA FORD In the 80s, I transferred from playing the Hamer Explorer model—which is what I played in The Runaways. I started on a Gibson SG, then I went to a Hamer Explorer, and I loved my Explorers. But then when I went solo, I wanted to give myself a makeover, so I started playing BC Rich guitars. I met Bernie Rico Sr., and he was amazing—just a great guy. And he turned me on to all these guitars. I dropped the Explorer and put it away, and started playing BC Riches, and they started making different shapes—the Mockingbird, the Warlock, and the Rich Bitch.

I just started burying myself in these guitars. They were *ferocious*-sounding. They had DiMarzio pickups and I would also use a preamp that was built into the guitar, so I would flip a little switch, instead of using the pedal board. I didn't use any effects during The Runaways days or the early Lita days—I just plugged straight into the amplifier. So I used the guitar to add any effects, like preamp, and then I added a delay and a wah. I went through probably every amp you could possibly think of, and wound up with my favorite amp, which was a JCM-800.

ACE FREHLEY I modified it myself.[*] I was the one that added the center pickup, I changed all the hardware, I put in the pearl tuning pegs, cream back plates on the Les Paul, green brackets, speed knobs. I modified that, and after I did that, I did it to my black Les Paul Customs, and kind of became my trademark. They rereleased it as the Budokan model, and most recently, they released a version of my '59 Les Paul that I used on my '78 solo album. The AF40[†] didn't sound very good live. I thought it was a nice thing—that they wanted to make this 'lightning bolt' guitar for me, and I gave them feedback on the prototype. But when I plugged it in, compared to a Les Paul, it just didn't cut the mustard. It didn't last very long on the road.

FRANK GAMBALE My career was definitely taking off at that point [in the mid-to-late 80s], so naturally, the guitar companies came fishing around, too. I remember meeting a guy named Rich Lasner—he's still around and he's an amazing guy—who at the time, he and another fellow named Bill Cummiskey, designed this incredible Saber guitar through Ibanez. I have the very first prototype ever made—it was so thin and incredible. It was light as a feather, and it was the most incredible guitar and radical at the time—how thin the body was. We all thought, 'Is this thing going to break?' And he said, 'Actually, in the center, it's the same thickness as a Les Paul.' So it was just tapered off at the edges.

I liked the guitar, but I saw where it could be improved upon. On my model, the pickup surrounds are flush with the body. The pickups are virtually at the body right where the line of where the body is. It was really brought down—kind of like lowering a car. Getting better traction. So that is what I did to that model. I really thought, 'This is great. *Let's make it even slicker.*' And I still love those FG Sabers. We made four different models over the years, and I think I was with them for roughly thirteen years. We made FGM100, 200, 300, and 400. And each model is an improvement on the one before.

---

[*] Ace's 1974 Heritage Cherry Burst Les Paul Custom.
[†] Ace's shortlived signature guitar from Washburn, released in the 80s.

PAUL GILBERT The first Ibanez I played was my uncle's guitar—my uncle was another really profound influence on me. This was before I even had an electric; I was playing an acoustic guitar, and my uncle had an Ibanez Destroyer—one of the 70s ones, kind of like the one that Eddie chopped up. I think it was actually the first electric guitar I ever put my hands on—I was just amazed how much easier it was to play than the acoustic I had been playing. So I fell in love with it.

Years went by, and I just didn't have enough money, so I'd just buy whatever I could find that was used, because I couldn't afford a new guitar. I found a used Les Paul that I played for a long time, and then I would find junky used guitars and fix them up. When I moved out to LA, I was playing an old Epiphone that I had found in my drummer's closet, and put some parts on. And I'd gained enough notoriety that guitar companies were starting to contact me—which was amazing. I couldn't believe it—I couldn't even afford a new guitar, and now, I'm being offered to work with a company!

Ibanez was by far the most attractive company to me, because not only were their instruments great, but also their philosophy as people. Their philosophy was they were really willing to come up with new instruments based on what their endorsers wanted and needed. And at the same time, there was some other companies that had been nice enough to contact me, but when I asked them, 'Can you make it bright pink? Can you put a Kahler tremolo on it? Can you put giant frets on it?' 'No. This is what we make and you have to play that.' And especially in the 80s, when everybody had to have some custom, hotrod, crazy thing, Ibanez was really cooperative and enthusiastic about trying to do stuff, and other companies really weren't. So it was just an obvious choice to go with them. And they started making me anything that I could think of.

The funny thing is, the first couple of guitars were sort of semi-designed by me, but when I started doing clinics for them, I would go to the music stores and try the stock instruments as well, and I ended up liking their stock instruments better than my custom ones! It was an RG in the late 80s that they sent out, and I still have that guitar—I used it for a lot of Mr. Big stuff. It made me learn that I had a bit to learn about guitar design, and although I could throw in an idea here or there, I really began to trust them and what they would make as an instrument.

CRAIG GOLDY I had just left Rough Cutt and was starting to form a band with Gregg Giuffria—called Giuffria. It was right around maybe '83, and we needed to get a guitar. At the time, Gregg had gotten an investor interested in the band, so he said, 'Let's go pick out a guitar.' I went to Guitar Center in Hollywood, with all intents and purposes of getting a Strat, because I loved Strats. And I still do. But I looked up, and on the wall was this purple Warlock, and I thought, 'What the hell is that?' So we got me one, but they didn't sell me the purple one—for some reason.

That same year, we went to the NAMM show, and Bernie Rico the owner, he was still alive* … it was one of those days where you could sit down and play, and people would listen. It was cool. I just picked up the guitar and started playing and there was something about it that allowed me to have personality—just like a Strat.

After a while, I started to learn what it was—what type of wood, what the fretboard was made out of, what type of pickups, what type of amplification really served me best, so it would allow me to be me. Like all the other guitar players have figured out long before me. I was a slow learner when it came to that, I guess. But there was something about the BC Rich, the way it looked. Because everybody had a signature look, and I was trying to find mine. And that's why I chose the Warlock, because the way it sounded and the way I was able to play on it.

STEVE HACKETT Primarily in the 80s, I was playing a 1957 Gibson Les Paul. The Schecter was a newer model with a Bill Lawrence pickup in it. And also, it had the Roland pickup, which enabled it to function with both the 500 at the time and the 707 Roland, and we also even hooked it up to [producer] Geoff Downes's Fairlight.† It was providing quite a lot of functions. Beyond those two guitars, I was playing a nylon Yairi—it's a Japanese make. And I was playing my Tony Zemaitis twelve-string.

Occasionally, I used Roland MIDI controllers—I used the 500 and the 707, that had a strange shape. In the main, [guitar synths] were monophonic and the technology was not as reliable. The dream was everything, and it might do it one in every five goes, but you'd get a lot of misfires and mis-triggering. I think this was to change shortly after we did that album—the technology became a lot more reliable.

STU HAMM Man, those Kubicki basses were so great, and Phil Kubicki was a great designer and a great man—I miss him.‡ I remember the first NAMM show I did was with Jackson-Charvel, with Steve Vai, and then from there, I started going to NAMM shows. And *Bass Player* magazine used to be a ten-page insert inside *Guitar Player* magazine. And I opened up the insert one day, and there's a picture

---

* Rico passed away in 1999.
† One of the first synthesizers with sampling capabilities.
‡ Kubicki passed away in 2013.

of this bass, that just looked really cool. And it was called the Kubicki Ex Factor. And it had this weird headstock, with a D extender, like an acoustic bass. It was reversed like a Steinberger, but the headstock was functional, because on the E string, there were actually two extra frets, so you could flip the capo where the nut is, and you would have two extra frets, where you could still finger everything as octaves. Like classical bassists have C extensions.

What I did is I went to the NAMM show and found out where the booth was. Walked by a couple of times, and then finally got up the nerve to pick up the bass and started playing all this new stuff that I had been coming up with—the seeds of 'Terminal Beach' and the tapping in 'Sexually Active.' All that slap/tappy stuff that I did. I got their attention, and they signed me as an artist. I still have the #45 bass—0045, the blue/black one. They were great basses, and they were a really integral part of my sound. And very bright and aggressive sounding to the tapping kind of sounds.

I remember playing it on *The Aresenio Hall Show*, and the soundman said, 'That sounds pretty cool … but did you bring a bass with you?' And Joe was never a real big fan of the sound. So at a certain point, Fender was trying to manufacture Kubicki basses, and I met Dan Smith and the guys at Fender, and I had a third P Bass pickup put in one of my Factors, so I could get a more traditional rock sound that Joe was looking for. It's sort of like an Alembic—it had a nice, interesting sound to it, but it wasn't actually a 'bass' sound. And especially if you're a traditionalist, and you go and do a session or something and they want a poppy P or J Bass sound, an Alembic or a bass like that is just not going to cut the mustard. And then through that kind of gave birth to the concept that I had for the Urge bass, which was the first Fender signature bass.

KIRK HAMMETT I used my black [1979] Flying V through a Marshall half-stack, with a wah pedal and a Tube Screamer [on *Kill 'Em All*]. And that was it.

CURT KIRKWOOD I got a Gibson Les Paul in 1976. I got a nice one when I was seventeen, and that's the one I started the band with. It got stolen pretty quickly, around 1980. So I got my other one—that I still have and play the most—right around then, in '81. Then I got a Goldtop right about the same time … maybe even before the Sunburst—the Goldtop that I did *Meat Puppets II* with, which I still have and play now and again. I did Eyes Adrift with that one, as well. And I have a couple more—another Sunburst and a black Studio Les Paul.

A guy in Phoenix just made a copycat of my '81 Sunburst that I play all the time—it's incredibly badass. It's not a Gibson Les Paul, but it's definitely one of the nicest guitars I own now. It's kind of a straight-up copy—it's a guy named Jimmy Bernard, and he works at Roberto-Venn School. It's been around for a while in Phoenix and teaches guitar building. I just met him and he said he wanted to build this for me, so over the last year, he did that.

A Morley chorus echo, a chorus delay—it has a light sensitive diode on the side of it. A cool little space-age thing that I used on a lot of the stuff in the 80s. A Big Muff Pi, Marshalls that I still have. A 100-watt Marshall. A little combo MusicMan amp on *Meat Puppets II*. *Up On The Sun* is all direct through a Scholz Rockman, which we rigged up to plug straight into the board, so there's really no amps on that album at all. I had the Scholz Rockman for a while—I thought it was really bitchin'.

I loved Boston when they came out—once again, I was probably seventeen. Another one of the things I had to cover in my band when I was covering Van Halen. But that record,* nothing sounded like it. Besides being a fun record, it had cool singing and really cool guitar sounds. The sounds on it—especially the guitar—was leading its way to the ZZ Top stuff of the 80s. The more technologically advanced, fuzz-rock sort of guitar. I loved it. I used to sit and play through it all the time. I loved the clean sound a lot, too, and that's where I thought, 'How do you get that sound on a record, through an amplifier? Why bother—just hook the Rockman up!' So we hardwired it and plugged it straight into the board, and *Up On The Sun* is all that.

BRUCE KULICK When I did the *Animalize* session, I brought a put-together Strat.[†] Again, Eddie broke all the rules with that—that you can throw anything together and make it work. I remember there was a company called Kubicki, and they were kind of a custom shop—they made beautiful necks. There was a luthier/repair guy on Long Island, a guy named Joe Pitcher, and he put this thing together for me, and it was a burgundy/fuchsia body, with a Floyd Rose on it, with a beautiful birds eye maple neck, with a rosewood fingerboard. And that's what I actually used when I went down to *Animalize*. Now, I probably had a Les Paul, or I still might have had my Strat from the Meat Loaf days, and I remember with The Good Rats I used a Les Paul and a BC Rich sometimes, as well. But that wasn't the right guitar for the Kiss session.

But I know when Paul said, 'OK, you're going to Europe,' I had to get some

---

* Boston's self-titled debut from 1976.
† Kulick played lead guitar on two tracks on Kiss's 1984 album *Animalize*.

guitars. So I remember seeing a used, Lake Placid Blue–ish Charvel in the window of Sam Ash on 48th Street—those were the good old days, none of that exists anymore down there. All gone. And I bought that one. Now, I needed a spare, and that other guitar wasn't really going to work compared to the other Charvels, and I remember Kiss kindly bought me a gold metal-flake guitar. And those were the two guitars that I took to Europe for the first tour with Kiss. This is pre–ESP Guitars. Even though ESP existed, they weren't making a mark in America yet—for another year.

And I fooled around with EMG pickups, even though I would ultimately become more a fan of the Seymour Duncan pickups. I did also have a black Eagle BC Rich. Sadly, the blue Charvel and the Eagle—and one other later Charvel—got stolen from the Kiss warehouse a few years later, and none of these resurfaced. The one that Paul lost did wind up popping up somewhere, and he got it back. But I have to say, my guitar collection was not very large at all, but I knew that I needed guitars with Floyd Roses, that could do this style that we've been discussing. And they did.

I was grateful when some friends of mine in New York started to work with a company called ESP, and turned me on to what they were about. And that's when I started to get the flip-flop blue 'M-1,' they would call it—Floyd Rose, one pickup, Strat-style neck. And that guitar is proudly on display at the Hard Rock in London, right outside the vault. That was a real important guitar. And then I continued having ESP put together things like that.

I still had some of the Charvels and I even tried a few Jacksons, but I was not that comfortable on the Jacksons. I was more comfortable when ESP turned me on within a few years in the 80s to the Horizon models. And that was even more comfortable to me than one of the Jacksons. Even though they were similar somewhat in construction. I was on the price guide for I think it was the 1986 catalog of ESP, playing that flip-flop blue M-1. So I was playing them in '85, during the *Asylum* tour. But '84 was all the Charvel, and that BC Rich.

And then, amp-wise, I was smart playing it out [in] that I wasn't really loyal to any company prior to that. Generally, I had a Marshall that worked or didn't work, or I would fool around with Boogie amps and different things. You think of Kiss, you think of Marshalls—even though, years later, some of those guys got into other amp things for endorsement purposes. But I was pretty content—even though I don't think they were amazing heads. But whatever Kiss had is what I used. Fortunately, most of them were modified with a master volume, so that you could get more gain out of it. So I never used pedals or anything—I'd just crank it and get my sound. And I kept things pretty simple in the beginning. It was just kind of funny that they had these older wireless units that sounded good, but they weren't really reliable.

I remember on my first tour, Bon Jovi was opening up, and they had all brand new gear, and I got into a whole distasteful conversation with Gene about it, because he didn't like hearing that I was complaining about our equipment, and the 'young guns' have new gear. But again, with Kiss, I definitely had the tone that I needed from their Marshall heads, and in time, I was really happy before the end of the 90s that Marshall got into the 900 series, which gave you more gain without having to mod the amp. Prior to that, it was their Marshall heads, that a few of them I liked, a few I didn't, but they were all in some ways modified, so they could give a little more crunch.

GEORGE LYNCH Kramer was kind of an accident. We just kind of fell into that—and when I say we, I mean myself and my guitar tech at the time, Matt Masciandaro. I don't even know the motivation behind going to them initially … I think it was a red one, with a maple neck. I've seen it in pictures, but I just don't remember the guitar that well. But I dug it, and when we were playing New York, Matt and I went to the Kramer headquarters, with the idea of working with them. And found out that they couldn't really do much as far as doing anything other than a stock guitar, because they didn't really build anything. Everything was built for them by ESP. And they just bought the parts basically. So I thought, 'Ah … OK. *I'll just go right to the source.*'

When we were touring Japan, I had a meeting with ESP, and during our meeting, we came up with that afternoon—in an hour—the concept and specs for the 'kamikaze,' which they did obviously a great job translating my ideas in terms of a reality. It's a somewhat iconic guitar, and is still being produced. So Kramer was really just a transitional thing, of me being a non-endorsed guy and not really knowing the endorsement game, and just kind of playing what I had. And assembled things myself out of parts a lot of times—Charvel, I would spend a lot of time out in the San Dimas factory, with Randy Zacuto and the Mighty Mite shop out there in California. I would just spend *days* in there, picking up parts and putting things together. My 'tiger' guitar was basically a twenty-dollar body and a twenty-dollar neck that I just slapped together and my friend painted it, and I put some spare parts on it. The guitar cost me forty dollars to build! Kramer was sort of my first experiment in endorsement, although it wasn't truly an endorsement. And then I went from that to ESP—for at least thirty years.

A friend of mine, John Garcia—'J. Frog'—the idea, the 'skeleton' guitar, was born out of us just hanging out and doing a little partying, and sketching crazy ideas. We actually started putting it together and he did the lion's share of the work on it. But conceptually, it was both our ideas. And it took about a year to finally put it all together—finding out ways to tweak it and things to add to it. And the original guitar was not a really 'playable' guitar. It was playable, but it didn't sound very good—it was actually difficult to play. From a luthier standpoint, it was built more to just be aesthetically what it was.

DAVE MENIKETTI I bought that guitar [a 1968 Les Paul] because I was so into the whole thing going down in what we used to call the British Invasion bands—Led Zeppelin and those type of bands—coming into the forefront. I heard the first two Zeppelin records and I thought Page was great. I loved his tone and approach, and I had to have a sunburst Les Paul. That was just what I was going to go for next—after I went through a Hendrix phase with a Stratocaster. I found this guy who was selling a six-year-old used sunburst Les Paul. It looked fantastic, it played great, and he said he was going to sell it to me. I was ready with the money, and he goes, 'But can I have it for a week? I've got this gig that is coming up, and once I'm done with the gig, you can have it.' So I said OK. Well, he took it to the gig, and somebody knocked the thing over and busted the neck.

So now, I have to wait another three weeks until this repair shop in Oakland repairs the neck. He said, 'I'll reduce the price by twenty-five bucks—you can have it for $225 instead of $250.' I said, 'OK, as long as it comes back fine.' And the guy did a great job—it looked great and it played great. So I paid the $225 in 1974—I've kept that thing and it's become my primary guitar ever since. The neck has broken maybe seven or eight more times on it—again, almost every time because somebody knocked it over on a stand, or a guitar tech accidentally dropped it. I got it repaired every single time, and the last time was probably about eight years ago. I took it to a popular guitar tech over here in the Bay Area, and he said, 'Y'know Dave, I can fix this again, but it's just going to keep breaking. You ought to take it to Gibson and have them do a neck just like the one you've got on it. They're going to have to do a custom version of it.'

I was really paranoid about doing that, because I didn't want to change anything about the original thing about that guitar. But I thought, 'He's probably right. I'd better just do it.' I sent the guitar in, and I said, 'I want my old neck back.' And they did an amazing job, because that is a neck profile that is not one of Gibson's neck profiles that they've had available for the last ten, fifteen, twenty years. They had to do a custom job on it and make it the same as my old neck was, and they even went out of their way and made the binding the same color as the binding as the rest of the guitar, they checked the finish on the peg head, they stamped my original serial number into the back—they did an amazing job. When I got that thing back, the first couple of months it was weird, because it was still kind of tacky, but after that, it was like, 'Oh my God … I don't know how they did it, *but they did it right!*' It didn't feel like it was another guitar—it felt like my old guitar.

STEVE MORSE After '86, it was the Music Man guitar, and before then, I was alternating between my Frankenstein Tele—which had the Stratocaster neck and an assortment of pickups, that I kept changing. But the idea was a blend between humbucking and single coil. And that evolved into my Music Man Steve Morse model, which was basically everything I had in my Frankenstein Tele, but with some improvements, such as one extra fret, a more accessible truss rod adjustment—which is extremely important for someone who travels around a lot. You don't need to do it much, but when you do, you do it instantly. Just stick a nail or small screwdriver in the little wheel and rotate it very precisely.

[It has] a shorter headstock, with the straighter pull and shorter pull on some of the strings from the nut onward. And the shorter headstock I particularly like, because I carry my guitar with me, and on the overheads, several times I have not been able to … even with my Tele, I designed a garment bag back in the day, where I could drape it over my shoulder and there would be a guitar inside the garment bag. It wouldn't be able to fold it, but back in those days, it was possible to hang stuff up in the closet. But with this new design and a three-quarter-size guitar case, I can put it in the overhead of any commercial plane I've ever seen.

And it's lightweight—we were able to get the weight and the balance perfect, so when you're sitting down and practicing, you let go of the guitar, it's perfectly balanced. And a nice rounded—but not cutaway—section for my right arm to sit on, to be slightly supported. And a pickguard to bring out the flat surface that I use sort of as a reference—with my fifth finger, on my right hand. I move the controls of the volume and tone while I'm playing, and also use it as an anchor, to help mute the strings that I'm not playing. Throw all those things together, and that's why my guitar I think is unique.

VERNON REID By the time we got to the Stones tour in 1989, I was using Mesa Boogie amps, using the Dual Rectifier amps—that's when those were really introduced. Before that, I used VHT power amps, and I used to use an MP-1 tube mini-preamp, but I switched over to Mesa Boogies, and I had a small 'city' of effects. It was really quite elaborate. I used Flash signal splitters, and I used to use an H3000. I used to have to do this thing where I had to preselect, because the H3000 would drop off the audio in between presets, because you had to switch the algorithms. This was like, micro-processing circa the 80s. So I had to do this thing where I preselected an effect, then put in a loop, then opened the loop, and it would give me the effect. There were kind of crazy workarounds. [*Laughs*]

And the guitars, I was playing ESP guitars, and then I transitioned from ESP to Hamer. I had a yin-yang [design] guitar, a Malcolm X guitar, and a guitar that was variously called the Relativity or E=mc2—which is Einstein's equation for the theory of relativity—on the fingerboard. Relativity was also called the clock guitar, because it actually had a Swatch Watch embedded into the body. And I had a guitar called Gold Finger. Each guitar was co-designed by myself and Jol Dantzig, and I would come up with crazy stuff, and each one had different variations on their fretboard pattern.

So the yin-yang had mother of pearl inlays, and Gold Finger had a thing where all the frets, the traditional kind of *swoosh* fret markers looked like they were melting. I had a couple of graphic ones—one of them was called Miss Voodoo. And the graphics of Miss Voodoo were done by Tony Fitzpatrick, who's a fine artist—he's done album covers for The Neville Brothers, and he was collected by Lou Reed. He's a bona fide American dude as a painter. And he basically did the guitar as a painting. I loved that. And that was the only one of the Hamers that has a maple neck, but you wouldn't know it's a maple neck, because it's completely painted yellow. It's a beautiful thing.

BLUES SARACENO Yamaha put out my first model, and it was kind of a Strat-shaped one—a utilitarian, two-humbucker Strat.* Kind of like your basic Superstrat, real nice mid-sized neck on it. And I was painting the guitar plaid at that time, because I wanted something that nobody else had. Van Halen had that guitar that was instantly identifiable, and I would customize my guitars. I remember going to Japan and we'd show up on Monday, and by Wednesday, people would be at the show and I would be signing copies of the guitar I would be playing on Monday night! Their turnaround was great—they could knock them off really fast. So I remember thinking, 'All right, well if that's the game, that's fine. I can't really

---

* The Blues Saraceno Yamaha RGZ 820R Plaid model.

change it. But what I'll do is I'll make it as hard as possible for people to copy.' So I came up with painting the guitars plaid, because it was a really intricate paint job, and that became my thing. And then I grew tired of it, because I grew sick of looking at them!

JOE SATRIANI Working with Ibanez has been fantastic, because they approach it with the idea that they wanted to work with guitar players who had innovations in mind that reflected where forward-thinking guitar players were going. In other words, what's pissing you off about old Fender and Gibson designs from the 50s, which are holding you back from doing what you want to do. Or even the newer guitar companies that were Ibanez's main competition at the time. So I had a lot of things to say. And I didn't mince words. I thought, 'If you guys can do *this* to the body, and *this* to the pickups, and *this* to the electronics, and you can change the shape of the neck and change the fret wire, and get a better material for the vibrato bar … I'd play it.'

So they didn't balk, and that was really the beginning of it, because at that time, I was putting my own guitars together using bodies from Boogie Bodies, necks from ESP, and other companies that were beginning to sell parts. So I knew that the guitar I wanted to build was an assembly of parts—it was going to be a body and a bolt-on neck, and I liked DiMarzio pickups already. And at that time—the summer of '87, after I recorded *Surfing With The Alien* and before it was released—I got introduced to D'Addario for my strings, DiMarzio for my pickups, and Ibanez for my guitars. So it was a great time of synergy, where we could take some existing products, and tweak them. And that's how we came up with the FRED, and eventually the Mo' Joe, and PAF Joe pickups, and the Satch Track pickups. I was able to influence D'Addario and Planet Waves to create straps.

And the most important thing was the Ibanez guitar. I did get them to source out different wood. I did get them to change the pickups and the wiring design, and I did get them to focus in on the Edge system that I preferred and make subtle changes that you can't really see, but have a lot to do with how the systems perform. I had them change the shape of the neck—the popular shape was wide and flat. And I said, 'I want something that's more like an early-60s Fender Strat.' So they followed my design ideas, and we wound up with a guitar that turned out to be the perfect tool for me—in the studio and live.

Now, when I go out on tour on this *Shockwave Supernova* tour, I'll have my 2410 and 2450 guitars out—the orange and the purple ones—and I'll bring some of the older ones out, and I can play any song from any part of my very long catalogue at this point, over fifteen albums, and those guitars do it. And they do it really well. They sound great, they stay in tune. It's remarkable what a fantastic electric guitar they've been able to build for me. But it's been teamwork—it's pulling in a lot of talented people to bear down on the design and come up with great solutions.

MICHAEL SCHENKER Rudolf* is the one who picked that [Flying V] for himself, and was also the one who played it first—on *Lonesome Crow*. I was playing a Les Paul, and I broke a string and had to play lead guitar, so quickly swapped guitars with Rudolf, and I kept it, because it was a fantastic combination between my amplifier and that guitar. I found something that spoke to me. The Flying V just happened to be the guitar that once I started using it, because of its shape, when you sit and play, you get used to sitting a certain way and balancing it. You almost can't play any other guitar anymore, because you don't know how to balance it. If it works, don't fix it. And that's how it went—until 2004, when Dean approached me, and I switched from the Gibson V to the Dean V.

BILLY SHEEHAN My main bass was my original P Bass, a '68 or '69 with a Telecaster neck, EBO neck pickup, dual output, that I Frankenstein-ed all the parts and pieces together over the years. I still have it and refer to it as 'the wife'—because I spent so much time with that bass. That was played through Pearce preamps— Dan Pearce from Buffalo, New York, made these great preamps. Ashly Audio Compression and crossovers—all Pro-Audio stuff in the racks, other than the preamp. Just racks full of all Pro-Audio stuff. BGW Power Amps, all JBL Pro-Audio fifteen-inch cabinets, with all JBL speakers—there was no consumer gear in my amp for a long time. In the early days, I used Ampeg stuff, and went to Hartke.

I went to Yamaha in … they contacted me in 1984, and then I went to a NAMM show in January of '85 I think it was, and we had made a deal then for me to use the basses. I really liked their quality control and they wanted to make something that fit me. So the first bass they did was a BB series that they modified for me with a bigger neck. It was nice, but the body shape was a little odd to me, so I was using the P Bass. And then I went to one other version of a bass, an RBX series—they were small and lightweight. Not much meat to them. And then next year we designed the Attitude bass, and that came out in '89 or '90.

---

* Rudolf Schenker, Scorpions rhythm guitarist and Michael's older brother.

HANK SHERMANN We have always been playing Marshall amps. Everyone—Jimi Hendrix, Ritchie Blackmore, Judas Priest, AC/DC, Iron Maiden—was playing Marshall. So when I went to London to actually buy my first, it had to be a Marshall. And when we started, we had the 1959 model, which was with no master volume—that was introduced in maybe '81 or '82. So we had the old ones, and they were exceptionally loud. Since we were playing heavy metal, we needed a little more gain, a little more crunch for the solos.

At the very beginning, we had two devices, which were a treble booster—an Electro-Harmonix LPB-1—and then we found a secret to substitute the Electro-Harmonix, which was the Boss KM-2, which is also a little micro-amplifier. It had a much smoother sound. And then we went to a Boss OD-1, which was an overdrive, and eventually, we ended up with the Tube Screamer from Ibanez—it must have been TS9. And then if we wanted to spice it up, we had a Cry Baby. When we went on to the second Mercyful Fate album, *Don't Break The Oath*, I got more into pedals—'Wow, there's a flanger! There's a phaser!' So I got an MXR Phase 100, to create some of the intros to some of the songs.

We never had the money to have the 'real deal' [guitars]. Being a fan of Ace Frehley, he played a Gibson Les Paul, and Uli Roth played a Stratocaster, Ritchie Blackmore played a Stratocaster with a big headstock. We never had the money for that. So we had to settle for Japanese versions. But they were actually pretty excellent. So I ended up with a Japanese brand called Morris. It was a Deluxe Stratocaster that I got in 1983, and I hung on to that for ten years. I did *Don't Break The Oath*, with that. Michael had a Japanese brand called Cort—which was a copy of the Flying V. I started with the Flying V—also some nameless Japanese brand—then. But because I was suddenly a huge fan of Uli Roth and the Scorpions, I had to have a Stratocaster. And then when I got that Deluxe Morris Stratocaster, I was totally blown away.

STEVE STEVENS Hamer was the first company that signed me as an endorsee. Before I was with Billy Idol, my previous band got signed to Aucoin Management, which managed Kiss, and Paul Stanley had come to see us, and I didn't really own anything. I might have owned a crappy Les Paul—a really crappy one. And they arranged for Paul to recommend me for a Hamer guitar endorsement. So they sent me one of their standards and a mini-Explorer. I always respected the fact that they would give guitars to a guy who didn't own guitars, based on that I sent them my demo tape and they were supportive.

And we introduced a guitar that was essentially like a Les Paul Junior double cutaway. It was a really simple guitar to begin with. It was a Les Paul Junior with a Floyd Rose on it, and that was the guitar I played primarily. Then we did an SS2, that had a hum/single/single on it, and a little bit more ergonomic body style, because the thing about a Junior is it does tend to fall neck-heavy. So I wanted a guitar that would stay in place once I took the hands off the neck. I think oddly enough, they called [the double cutaway model] a Sunburst—I don't know why.

I used to build effects pedal boards for people living in the music building I was in—a lot of guitar players weren't really hip to that, but I was a fan of Steve Hackett, Steve Howe, and Robert Fripp. And I noticed all those guys had pedal boards—Pete Cornish made those. So I got hip to that idea of assembling all your pedals in an enclosure and having a power supply through them. One of the guys in the building traded me a late-60s 100-watt Marshall half-stack, to build him a pedal board. And that was the amp that's on 'Rebel Yell' and 'Top Gun Anthem.' I still have that amp, I still record with it. So that was primarily the amp I used for recording.

Touring-wise, with Idol, I used JCM-800s. I had two of them behind me, and one had a MXR Chorus go through one side, so I was a using a quasi-stereo setup. Most of the pedals I had were a MXR Flanger, a Boss Compressor, and a Crybaby Wah. I had met Roger Mayer, who was Hendrix's guitar guru, and he gave me one of his Octavias—I had that on there. And a volume pedal and a Maestro Echoplex.

TY TABOR Around 1985, I bought an '83 Strat Elite, from a place called Rockin' Robin, in Houston, Texas. And the reason I got it was I was doing some work with another artist, who wanted a really nice, clean Strat tone, similar to … there was a new album by Gino Vannelli that was out at that time,[*] and it had some really great, stellar Strat tones on it. He was really shooting for me trying to emulate that kind of tone, so I tried out this Elite. It was one of the best-sounding Strats I ever heard in my life. It played like a bulldozer—it was like the most unplayable piece of … something you have to fight to play, of any guitar I've ever touched in my life. I mean, it was *so non-playable*—it was just unbelievable.

But, it was the best-sounding guitar I ever heard in my life. So, I just made myself play it for a few years, until I got to where I could play it. But it was like playing with a hand tied behind your back—it had such horrible action, and the strings were so tight. I don't know if it was just because it had possibly a longer scale

---

[*] *Black Cars* (1985).

length neck or something, but a lot tighter than a regular Strat, and extremely hard to play. I let tone win over playability, and I did that for years and years.

The thing about the guitar that made it have such unbelievable tone—not what I plugged it into—was that its pickups were extremely hot. They were the Fender active electronic pickups, but they were only made for two years, and only put in those guitars—they don't exist anywhere else. There are no other active electronic pickups that sound anything like them. Very unique pickups. But the thing about them is because they were so hot, they were extremely microphonic—you could literally sing into the mic. Which we've done on King's X records—sing into the pickup, to get a distorted vocal through the amp. That's how microphonic they were. It became a problem of we would get into certain venues, and even in the studio, you would get interference from anything and everything—a lot of RF signal interference, a lot of buzz, a lot of noise.

There were times where we would get into certain venues, where it would be so loud—the noise that these pickups would pick up—that I couldn't even use the guitar. So it was crippling shows! Eventually, for that reason alone, I started using other guitars, so I could depend on something from show to show. But it was truly a special, one-of-a-kind guitar. I have never touched another Strat—including another Strat Elite—that sounded anything near as good as that guitar. I still have it. I retired it a while back, when it almost disappeared a couple of times. The guitar started becoming 'known'—I no longer take it on the road, because it will be stolen.

Some of that was a joke—I'll be honest with you.* Some of it was just us having fun with people, because I literally had pedals that would light up and do things that had nothing in them at all, that my techs would just have an idea—'Hey, throw this on the floor and I'll tell everybody this is the secret!' They would have a pedal out there for two nights, that everybody was like, '*What is that*?!' And taking pictures of it, and then it would disappear, and they would have something else out there. At one point, they were even putting tape over the 'Fender' on my guitar, just as a joke, like we're really trying to hide things. Because anybody that walked up to the stage and really paid attention could really see what I was playing through. But because it was a real unusual set of gear, a lot of people from a distance just didn't recognize what was going on.

I was simply just playing through a very inexpensive Lab Series L5—which is a transistor amp—and I was not using the power of the head itself. I was actually

---

* Ty kept the make and model of his amp a 'secret' for many years.

disconnecting the power, and just using it as a preamp. And then I would run that into something like a Crown Micro-Tech for power. It was a really crude setup, but a setup where I could run it through ten cabinets on a stage with AC/DC, and turn it up loud enough to be heard in a mega-arena. That's why I was powering it with separate power, instead of just using the Lab power. But that's really all it was—an L5 with a Crown Micro-Tech most of the time. It had the natural preamp inside the guitar itself. And when I quit using the Elite live, what I did is I took the preamps out of some other Elites, and had them rackmounted, and the new guitars I was playing, I would run them through the Elite preamps section. And they were just a rackmount. So a lot of people were wondering what that was, too. But when I was playing the Strat itself, I didn't have to do that—straight into a Lab, straight into a Crown Micro-Tech, straight into the speakers. The only thing that I had in loop was a MidiVerb, for chorus every once in a while, and a delay pedal. And that's it. That was the whole setup.

BRIAN TATLER I'm kind of famous for using the white Flying V—that was my main guitar. Before that, I had a Fender Stratocaster. First of all, I liked Ritchie Blackmore a lot, so of course, I bought a Fender Strat. And then as I got into Michael Schenker, I bought a Flying V—it kind of followed that idea. It's a 1979, and I bought it in 1979, brand new, from a guitar shop in London—I think it was called EFR Guitars. An out-of-the-way place—I found it probably in an advert in *Sounds* or *Melody Maker*. Phoned them up, went down, had a go, and bought it there and then. I took the money with me in cash—in case I liked it, I was going to buy it, and if I didn't, I suppose I was going to come home. But I liked it.

It felt a bit weird at first, because the first thing you do is you put it on your lap, and it slides off your lap, because you're not used to it. You have to put it between your legs; otherwise, as I said, it just slides off your lap. It's a weird thing. It's not a great guitar to practice on, really. I prefer to practice on a Les Paul or something that sits comfortably. A Flying V looks great onstage, but no fun sitting at home trying to practice on it. I've still got the guitar—I've kept it safe and I use it for live work now and again. People like to see it.

[Brian added the thunderbolt design to the headstock] probably not long after I had it. I just drew it on with a felt pen, and just thought it looked good. [*Laughs*] It was about 1980. And it was always going into a Marshall amp—I think it was a JMP1. Y'know, the first ones that had preamps, that came out around '75—I had one of those. And I think I had a Laney cab and then probably a Marshall cab. And the only effect I used to use was a Morley power-wah-boost pedal, that you could do distortion with a control, and it had a wah with another button, and you could push it backward and forward, and turn the volume up and down.

JEFF WATSON For the first record, we were borrowing gear from everybody we could get. Brad had his Boogie from the Ozzy tour—he had one of the first Boogies. It was a smaller type of head. And I had my Ampeg V4. I went up to Sammy Hagar's house—which is up the road here—and borrowed his red Marshall. It was a 2x12, but it was an all-in-one, combined amp and cabinet. We took that down to LA.

And I was using my '56 Les Paul on the record. I don't think I had my black Les Paul then, so my '56 Les Paul, and my Guild F-412 twelve-string, that we used on 'Goodbye,' 'Let Him Run,' and all the early acoustic songs I did. 'When You Close Your Eyes,' I think I borrowed [a Flying V] from Hamer, because I didn't have one down there for the video shoot. I don't think it was mine! It's hanging up on the Rainbow on Sunset Boulevard—above table 17. But I never used them on the records.

[Around 1977] I was running this music store in Sacramento called Sunrise Music, and an old guy came in, in a cowboy hat and cowboy boots, and he had this brown case. He goes, 'This has been sitting underneath our bed since 1957. Nobody plays the damn thing.' I said, 'Let me have a look,' and it's a '56 Goldtop Les Paul—*brand new*! I got it for three hundred dollars. And the Guild twelve-string was the same thing—the guy comes into the music store and says, 'We can't play this. It's really hard to play.' The neck was bowed. Three hundred dollars. And to this day, they're sitting right here, as I speak to you.

MARK WOOD I had a double-neck violin that I built, I built a violin with a human hand—an arm with a knife through it—that held the strings up, I had a glow violin, I had a violin with a barrel at the end that I would shoot bottle rockets out of. During that time in the late 80s, I would walk out in spandex and my double-neck violin, and that was pretty much all I needed to do to get the crowd around me. And then I ended up inventing and patenting a self-supporting system ... I don't know if you know, I own the premier, number-one electric violin manufacturer in the world, where everyone from Jean-Luc Ponty to Jerry Goodman and all these electric violin players play my instruments. And we're manufactured on Long Island, in Huntington. It's Wood Violins, and we just celebrated our twenty-fifth anniversary.

So while I was getting my career together, I was building instruments—it was like this weird combination of Stradivarius, Leo Fender, and Eddie Van Halen, all at the same point. Again, I never even thought about it until, in reflection, I would see what I was actually achieving at the time. In the musical world, inventing something pretty much nobody's ever done before really slowed down a little bit about twenty years ago. I mean, how much better can we play guitar anymore? How much better can we play saxophone than John Coltrane, or trumpet than Miles Davis? And the violin world and the guitar world hit a wall with that, and then Kurt Cobain flipped it on its head, played one chord, and that was pretty much all he needed. But the invention of an instrument in popular music is unheard of, and has never been done since. It was me in my little woodshop.

My father's side of the family were woodworkers, and they built religious furniture for temples and churches around the world. And when the workmen left at night, I would sneak in and saw and cut and sand. I had no clue how to do this—*I just did it.* Completely instinctually. There were no rules. I didn't even measure anything, and I almost cut my thumb off one time, too—that's how haphazard the inventions started. I would build something, go out, play a gig with my band, and go, 'Oh, I've got to sand this thing lower, because my bow is hitting it or my hand is hitting it.' So I would go back into the shop the next day. While I was reworking my playing and my career, I would be fine-tuning this new way of playing an instrument. So it was a real interesting time for me.

'shred'

Lastly, responses to the question, 'What are your thoughts on the term "shred"?'

MARTY FRIEDMAN Fucking hate it! I really hate it. But what are you going to do? You can't control what everybody says. I don't like being lumped into anything, but if you're a guy who likes 'shredding' or the word 'shred' and you put me in there, then I'm happy as can possibly be.

JASON BECKER I don't like the word 'shred.' It dismisses any musicality or tasty playing that you do. I am a guitar player and creative composer. 'Shredder' is an insult. With that said, I don't take the word too seriously. If someone calls me a shredder, I don't mind.

GEORGE LYNCH Well, one person's 'shred' is another person's 'slow hand.' People—not necessarily guitar people—will just think anything fast is kind of 'shred.' Somebody might think the guitar player in Metallica is a shredding guitar player, where a schooled, technical guitarist that plays modern heavy music with an eight-string guitar or something doesn't think that's shredding. Shred is when you're playing at hyper-speed and very accurately. And that's always a moving target, because as guitar evolves and devolves, that target moves, as well.

Right now, it's pretty much at its peak—there are guys out there in that myopic genre that do that exceedingly well. And then there's just kids sitting in their bedrooms—*whole legions of them*—that play that well. I've got a kid that lives right next door to me that plays like that. It's just phenomenal—I could never play the way this guy plays. It's just a thing that people do, but it's so limiting—it's such a small thing to be good at. I just don't understand why.

I guess when you're younger and you're focused on just that—young drummers, too—it's just about the speed. Foot-pedal speed. 'I play 260 beats per minute barefoot, and I can sustain ten seconds.' When you grow up, that doesn't matter anymore. Speed is a tool. It's exhilarating, it requires a lot of technical ability and skill, and I think it should be used to express something that needs to be expressed, when it needs to be expressed. But to be used all the time, *just because*, it sort of cancels itself out.

ALEX SKOLNICK I have mixed feelings about it. I don't use it, but I don't mind it—because I think it's meant well. It's meant as a term of endearment—like saying, 'Somebody who can really play.' But sometimes, it's not taken that way. Sometimes, somebody that is just so focused on speed and technique, that that's all the music is really about, and it's missing other elements of great music. But I think it's a word like 'fusion.' That was a great word. And it just represented this amazing coming together of different styles of music. From guys like Wayne Shorter, who had been this amazing Blue Note artist doing straight-ahead jazz and part of Miles Davis' group, suddenly doing funky ethnic grooves with Weather Report. It was a fusion. Or McLaughlin with Indian musicians.

But then fast forward ten years, and 'fusion' refers to artists like Kenny G.— who I'll point out is one of the nicest people I've met in the music industry. [*Laughs*] And actually has a son who plays guitar, who you would call a shredder. So it's interesting. But just the way his music is categorized or others—even David Sanborn. Great musician, and he has worked with The Brecker Brothers, but suddenly, this very accessible electric instrumental music—that was called 'fusion,' and had nothing to do with the original fusion.

So I think 'shred' is a bit of a word like that—where it initially meant somebody that had really good technique. Eddie Van Halen was a shredder. Randy Rhoads was a shredder. But then later on, it just got overdone. And I don't want to say names, but I'm picturing somebody with multiple guitar necks and huge hair, and there, I just think that image is sort of a negative connotation of the word. It's like, fusion is the same thing—it really depends on the context. It shouldn't be a bad word. I try to look at shred and shredding the same way.

ALEXI LAIHO Playing is playing. It's kind of like the same thing when people ask me, 'What is Children Of Bodom? Are you black metal or death metal or thrash metal or blah blah blah?' It's like, '*It's metal.*' Playing is playing. I don't know if shredding means playing fast or … I haven't really over-analyzed that word—I have no reason to.

ADAM DUTKIEWICZ It's fun to hear. It's kind of a nerdy thing, but I'm a music nerd. I love it. Think about it—it's part of what makes metal guitar fun, hearing shredding. It's exciting. It's like if you're a drummer and you hear a fast double-bass groove or something like that. If it's your thing, it's your thing—and it's really exciting to hear.

JOE SATRIANI I don't care. Some people say it with a smile on their face, and others say it with a grimace. I don't think you can control that. It means different things to different people. When they're using it with a negative connotation, they're saying, 'You're just playing mindlessly. You're displaying technique for self-promotion. You're not playing the song.' But sometimes, a song needs somebody to stand up and shred. It may not be the guitar player—it may be the drummer. You may look at the drummer and say, 'Look, you can't just groove here. You've got to give me some crazy fills.' So it's all about arrangement, I think. But the average person, what do they care? They just want music to be fun to listen to. They want the right music at the right time in their lives. So if they say something like, 'I don't like shredding,' you've just got to learn to accept it.

TY TABOR I think 'shred' can apply to almost any kind of playing. For me, shred is an aggressive attack involving speed. I think you can shred on an acoustic guitar if you do it right. To me, it's the attitude behind what you're playing. I love Michael Hedges, and I love Leo Kottke, too—he was a huge influence of mine. Although I can't play anything like him, I have listened to him my whole life, and tried to incorporate some of the basics of him into some things.

MIKE VARNEY I have to say that the term 'shred' sort of drums up in my mind somebody who picks fast and doesn't really take into consideration the musicality behind it. So, when they say, 'Hey, this guy shreds,' a lot of times it just means he plays fast. When people say, 'That guy totally shreds,' to me, a lot of times it means the guy has just got a lot of flash and fast chops. The shred genre has all these guys that have flash and chops, and have really great musicality. But I think since shred is sort of a mainstream term and it's used by even non-musicians—I mean, a lot of people are called shredders who have a minimal amount of musicality and a lot of 'right hand.' A lot of back-and-forth fast picking.

So I think, unfortunately, there are kids that think that they're shredding when they're just picking fast. To me, to be a good shredder, you've got to be somebody that's got tons of musicality. But one of my favorite guitar players is Greg Howe. He's great, he's still doing cool stuff. That's what I love about Richie and Greg and Jason and all these guys—they're pushing forward. They're engaged in their careers and doing all that they can to move forward. That goes back to one of the things I was looking at when deciding which artists to put on my label—those guys that will be out there as the ambassadors for the label and for themselves, constantly getting exposed to more people.

MICHAEL ANGELO BATIO I think it is a term that, again, history repeats itself. They said the same thing to Franz Liszt over a hundred years ago. Franz Liszt was one of the greatest technical keyboard players. He was like a Rachmaninoff—he was mind-blowing, but his critics used to say, 'Oh, he's a *virtuoso*.' And they use that term in a derogatory way, to say, 'All he can do is play fast with no feeling.' Well, Franz Liszt is still remembered as one of the greatest pianists and composers that has ever lived.

I think the term 'shred' started off with critics trying to cut down what is good. They're trying to say what is good is bad. They try to say, for example—'Michael Angelo Batio can only play fast. There's no feeling, there's no melody, there's no songs.' And I think to myself, 'I got signed to two major labels—not because I could play fast. Because I could write.' And I wrote every single song in both bands. Tom Werman produced our first album—he did 'Every Rose Has Its Thorn' [by Poison], and Mötley Crüe, Dokken, and Twisted Sister. He knows a little bit about songwriting. I mean, we wrote great songs.

I think the term started off derogatory, but here's what I think—it can't be stopped. Because now, it's become a whole genre in itself. Like, you see Steve Vai—'Oh, I don't want to be a shred guitarist.' Well, dude, you are! I'm sorry, you are. People don't like the term, but it is what it is, because it's a style of guitar, but really what it means to me is someone who wants to be the best they can be on their instrument. Other people want to say that, but these guitarists are not going away. And the reason is very simple—the average shred guitar player is good. And the best of them are phenomenal. And it started with, 'Dude, he shreds.' Totally California—'*Dude, he was shredding!*'

Every other style of music, every other instrument, it is OK to play really fast and technical. Somewhere along the line, they said, 'If you're really good and technical in rock guitar, you're shredding, and that's bad.' It's not bad. We're all here. It's great. My thinking is if they want to call me a shredder, I'll wear it proudly, because I want to be the best I can be, and I know so does Steve Vai, so does Joe Satriani, so does Paul Gilbert, so goes Vinnie Moore, and so do all the other great guitarists that came up in the 80s. And if they want to call it shredders, why not? I'm in good company.

MARK WOOD Perfect. Because remember, in my world—the classical violin world—we've been shredding for 150–200 years! Listen to Vivaldi. We defined and we were the first ones on the block … for the last 400 years, Vivaldi is 350 years ago, Paganini was about 150 years ago, Jascha Heifetz about 50 years ago. Violin string playing—Yo-Yo Ma, Itzhak Perlman—we have that and will always have that virtuoso shredding. The guitar players were not the original and were not the first instrument to showcase. What the guitar players did is they put distortion on fast notes, and wah-wah pedals and echo and technique and technology, and put the blues into it.

Eddie Van Halen, it was really easy to write him off with the critics—'Oh, this guy is just noodling.' No, no, no. Eddie Van Halen and Randy Rhoads, these guys had blues in their hearts. The classical virtuosos didn't have a touch of blues or funk or soulfulness in the American sensibility. There was soulfulness in the Baroque Classical realm, but man, when Hendrix played ['The Star Spangled Banner'] at Woodstock, we'd never heard a guitar sound like that. And it was not about imitating the violin. It was blues.

Hendrix wasn't really part of the shred, and as you remember, Jimmy Page was pushed aside. People would say, 'You're listening to Jimmy Page, man? He doesn't play fast at all!' When Van Halen came out, Van Halen had everybody turn their backs temporarily on these great, great rock guitar players who couldn't play fast. And with Van Halen, people were like, 'Oh, everyone's got to play like Eddie and Randy now.' And I was already up to speed with this virtuoso stuff—with arpeggios and fast technique. So I was like, 'Oh, I can fit into this really easily. This is my home.' And thank God—right place, right time.

COREY BEAULIEU I always think of shredding as really good guitar playing. It doesn't necessarily have to be speed. I'm not playing a hundred miles an hour, flying up scales, but it isn't always the important part. When I hear a great guitar solo, like, if I can sing along to it and remember it, that's shred to me. Steve

Vai and Joe Satriani, the shred guys, they don't always have to play a hundred miles an hour or 100 percent of their technical ability to make something that's amazing. Even Marty Friedman's 'Tornado Of Souls'—he's not playing as fast as shit the whole time, but it's an epic guitar solo that stands out and makes the song better and you can remember it. And it adds something to the song that wasn't there before.

Someone can wow you with difficult stuff and play a million miles an hour, but you can watch someone do that in a bar, and leave and go home, and you don't remember a thing. But if you play something that can stick in someone's brain, I think that's the highest compliment you can have as a guitar player and as a songwriter—just to master your instrument to a point where you can use it as a creative tool that can make something memorable. At least that's how I look at my favorite shredders or guitar players—someone who can create something that is memorable with the guitar. It's something that takes a long time creatively and physically as a guitar player to be able to pull off. I've always admired that about my favorite players.

STEVE MORSE It's good. Very descriptive, because when you think of shredding, you think of power and steel teeth, pulling in opposite directions. Sort of destroying—a powerful yet orderly destruction of whatever the normalcy of the song was. I like the word 'shred'—I've always thought that was good.

STEVE LYNCH I think it's appropriate. It came from 'wood-shredding'—that is basically the full term, when I first heard it back in the late 70s/early 80s. But shredding, I think it's an appropriate term, actually. Because a lot of these guys, they just pick incredibly fast. It's one of those things that I didn't really get into— the whole arpeggio sweep picking thing or the speed-picking thing. I can pick fast enough, but most everything that I did that was really quite fast was the two-handed stuff, because I liked that legato sound. I just liked the sound of the notes coming out like a flurry like that—without even hearing the pick. I think Allan Holdsworth was the one that really got me into that particular sound, where you hear a flurry of notes, but you don't really hear the pick hitting them.

GUTHRIE GOVAN I think they moved the goalposts. The meaning of the word 'shred' has changed. At least that's my understanding of it. Twenty-something year ago, when I first encountered the word 'shred,' it seemed to represent this idea of to boldly go where no man has gone before. It's like, 'Let's push the outer-boundaries of what you can do with the vocabulary of this instrument.' Which is a praiseworthy thing, I think. This kind of pioneer spirit—'Let's take the guitar somewhere more extreme. Let's take it to a more hostile climate and see how we can make it survive there. Let's just push the limits of things.' I think that should be encouraged, because that is how new stuff happens.

Somewhere along the way, that connotation seemed to disappear, and in its place what we have now is the word 'shred' meaning, 'Playing a million notes for no reason, just for the sake of playing a million notes.' So it's become an ugly word. I kind of shudder when I hear it now. In particular, I'm horrified when I see some of the YouTube generation, who post footage of themselves practicing in their dark room, and the title of the video will be 'Shredding In A Minor.' What does it mean? Why are you shredding? This becomes an end rather than a means to an end for a certain kind of player. You asked earlier about carrying the torch for something, that's the other thing that I really do get on a bit of a soapbox—you shouldn't practice technique for the sake of technique. *You should practice technique because you have something to say.* And without developing your technique to a certain level, you won't be able to say it.

RICHIE KOTZEN If you take a player like Guthrie Govan—one of my favorite guitar players—and you call him a shredder, it's almost undermining. It's almost like something someone who couldn't play like that would say to dismiss them. He can do so much and he's so versatile, and he can play anything. Some guys can only shred. Some guys can only play really fast, and they're like the guys I talked about earlier that when they play slow, they sound like a two-year student. Those guys, I guess you can call them shredders—they can't really do anything else.

RONNI LE TEKRØ A shredder can be many things. I would say Joe Walsh is the ultimate shredder—with those strings, he makes people want to cry. To me, *that's* a shredder—a guy who plays soulful guitar, with originality and conviction.

LITA FORD I listened a lot to David Gilmour, because of his feel, and Jeff Beck, because of the way he could bend the guitar strings and make them sing and cry. I picked up on the bending of the strings, whereas I know a lot of shredders … there's a lot of differences in playing styles—shredding and feel. If you can pull off both, that would be great.

FRANK GAMBALE I'm equally at home playing slow, medium, or shredding—if we have to use that term. If it's always just shredding, it drives me crazy. I can't listen to it. Just the same as listening to 'slow hand' stuff all the time. I like variety. It's like a car—you wouldn't want to always drive it in first gear or sixth gear. You need all the gradients as you go up. Speed has a kind of exhilaration you just can't get any other way. But like anything, it's like eating sugar all the time—if you're always eating candy, ultimately it's not going to be as satisfying as having a good meal with a dessert at the end. Shred … I think we need to think of some other term now, perhaps! [*Laughs*]

STEVE STEVENS I remember a quote that I still have in my wallet, and it's from Les Paul. He said he played a show once and he was aware that some famous jazz musician—I forgot who it was—was going to be in the audience. And he played his worst show of his entire life, because he was trying to show off. And here's Les Paul, who's the innovator and also a shit-hot guitar player, saying, 'Don't ever play for the other musicians that might be around. Play for people who absolutely couldn't care less about your technique. Play for the people you're trying to move emotionally. And if technique is part of moving them emotionally, more power to you.'

BILLY CORGAN I think when you get to the point when an eleven-year-old kid on YouTube can play 'Eruption,' now it's a technical exercise. And there are people who are really, really good at what they do, but to me, the journey is out of it. There was an arc there—starting with Jimmy Page and Tony Iommi, starting in the late 60s, up through Brian May and Randy Rhoads, and into Yngwie. There was a whole arc there, where there was this continued exploration.

And Yngwie, for me personally, it peaked it out [with him]. You couldn't play any faster; you couldn't play any better. I mean, I saw Yngwie play in '85, drunk off his ass, and it was *sick* how good he could play. And that was it for me. It wasn't going to get any faster, better, more interesting, and that's been the case. I just haven't heard anybody that advanced the guitar—at least not from a virtuosity/violin expressive point of view. People have advanced the guitar like Wes Borland playing super low, Tom Morello with the kind of clean riffing. But nobody advanced it in another way. To me, Yngwie was the apotheosis, and that was it.

KIM THAYIL When I first heard the term 'shredding' in the 80s, I thought it implied wildness. Shredding—tearing something apart. I saw it as chaotic. So I would think of Curt Kirkwood's playing on *Meat Puppets I* as being shredding. I think a lot of hardcore punk-rock stuff is shredding, and hearing stuff like Discharge is shredding. But I later came to understand it, maybe the word evolved and changed, as it bounced from various subcultures—from punk rock to metal and back, and then eventually the top proficient jazz and classical rock guitarists. Now, when I hear the term 'shredding,' I'll hear it applied to people like the guys in DragonForce or Steve Vai or Joe Satriani.

CURT KIRKWOOD That's fairly descriptive, I think. It does the trick. If you think of somebody just opening up a phonebook and tearing pages out as fast as you can and shredding it, with stuff flying everywhere. I guess it's as good as you can get with that stuff—shredding, ripping. It seems to be some overtone of destruction in there. I guess with saxophone, it was 'wailing,' and sometimes people would say, 'Oh, it wails'—on the guitar, too. Jams, shreds … I think the shredding thing kind of came because it became moving a little faster.

DUANE DENISON I think it's overused. It's one of those words like 'brutal' or 'awesome' or 'that rocks!' Shred … I like the idea of shredding. I think of a cheese grater. If you're picking hard enough and fast enough, then yeah, that pick will start to shred and come apart. But I like to think it means that it's fast and noisy and chaotic, but usually it's not. Yeah, it's fast, but it's fastidious and over-precise and clean. And it's like, 'Well, that's not shredding. Shredding implies mayhem and frayed edges, doesn't it?' *I get it*—when people say that, I know what they're saying. I think it's overused.

CHRIS HASKETT These things become an ouroboros—the snake that eats its tail. It becomes an apt description, then people start playing like that, so if it wasn't true to begin with, it becomes true. Shredding, there's different ways to interpret it. I always think of shredding as the real Malmsteen-esque speed playing, which mostly, I don't hear any soul in it. The exception is Vernon Reid.

VERNON REID I'm sure some people find it offensive, as people always find something to be offended about. It doesn't bother me. When people say, 'Man, you shred!,' they mean it as a high compliment. I only think that shred kind of obviates nuance, and actually, a lot of what's really happening inside, there's many ways to do that. It kind of precludes nuance, a little bit … but that's just how guys are. [*Laughs*]

TONY MACALPINE I think I like Paul Gilbert's term better: 'stun guitar.' [*Laughs*]

PAUL GILBERT Oh, it's depressing. [*Laughs*] It's *so* adolescent—and not in a good way. There's adolescent things that I like—to me, I love punk rock. And punk rock doesn't require sophisticated virtuosity. I love the Ramones and the Sex Pistols—I've done a lot of listening to that stuff. And I really think that if somebody's got a musical ear and they spend a couple of years with the guitar, they can play a Ramones song with some authority.

But shred, the visual that comes to mind is skateboard culture. And I've actually talked to a friend of mine that is really heavily into skateboard culture. He said the same thing happens with skateboarders—there are virtuosos in that sport, and there are people that think they can just jump on it and go crazy. It's the skateboard equivalent of shred. So I guess what it is, is I think what people see as virtuosity and athleticism, and those things require years of passionate work. And shred to me, it just stinks of shortcuts. [*Laughs*]

BILLY SHEEHAN There's a spot for it. For it to become the exclusive and only thing is like any other musical thing that there's a spot for—if it's only about groove and groove only, it becomes pretty boring. You might as well just set the drum loop up and go for a walk. You need something else in there.

A movie isn't just car chases and it isn't just love scenes and it isn't just dialogue, or character profiling—there's a lot of things that go into a movie. The same as music. So it certainly has its place. To focus on it exclusively I think is a massive, huge mistake.

But it should be part of everyone's vocabulary—to at least visit it and take a look at it. As it would be good for everyone's vocabulary to know what blues licks are all about, why pop songs are popular, why classical music has reoccurring themes and the structure that it does. Those are all things that are important. So, shred is a viable and important thing. To focus on it exclusively—like anything exclusively—in a subject like music, which has so many parts, would be a mistake.

PHIL COLLEN I love it—in the right context. I think you can really fuck a song up by doing that shit. Sometimes, you don't want to hear it. But in the right place, *it sounds amazing.*

AFTERWORD
by uli jon roth

I think the 80s as such didn't really bring as much to the table—in terms of guitar playing—as the earlier periods did. In terms of novelty, of actually creating a new approach and a new sound. It became more slick, and in some ways, more digestible, actually. And also less melodic. I think the guitar playing in the 70s tended to be more melodic, and the majority of that was influential. And this sense of melody, a certain sense of economy—dealing with that which is musically important—got sacrificed by a lot of players in the 80s, when it went into what you call 'shred.' The word shred says it all—you shred something which is wholesome, and you make it less wholesome. Of course, it's a California term—just like 'gnarly' or whatever—but if you really look at it, you can interpret it that way.

The 80s became more flashy. Substance was frequently sacrificed for flashy displays of pyrotechnics, which were designed to impress people—but not necessarily touch them deeply. That was a prevailing trend. It doesn't mean that all of the players were like that, but the general thrust of the journey went in that direction. It became in many ways a relatively empty display of virtuosity–like, 'look what I can do' kind of stuff. Like David Copperfield vanishing tricks—producing the next rabbit out of the hat. And I'm not saying that disparagingly, it's just the way things are.

The same thing happened in classical music at some point, when the first virtuosos appeared, and they started developing an ever more impressive arsenal of musical gimmickry, almost. Some of which had artistic merit, but a lot of which didn't. And we felt something similar in the 80s, when showmanship very often became the dominant force. That is exactly why, in the mid 80s, I quit the business for thirteen years—because I didn't want to be part of that anymore. It alienated me.

Today, very often, I see talented players. Very often I deplore the general apathy toward quality guitar tone—it's very rare that you hear somebody who is able to produce even a decent tone. Most—to my ears—sound almost amateurish in terms of sound production, because the sound is usually just produced by gadgets. To my ears, that sounds very cheap. So, I find that deplorable. Technically, the standard has gone up, although a lot of players are very weak when it comes to rhythmical playing and accompaniment. But I guess that's just the sign of the times.

I don't really know where the journey is heading at the moment. I'm certainly trying to pursue my own journey, which is also a journey of discovery. And I'm finding new things all the time. I find it very exciting for me that the guitar is not yet finished. On the contrary, it's quite exciting. And I can see a lot of potential still in that instrument to be explored, and that's great. Because there is a time for everything. Some people would say, 'The electric guitar is already finished. It's time for something new.' But in my book, it isn't. We've come a long way, but I can still see a potentially exciting future for that instrument— as long as guitar players manage to somehow resonate with other people and with the audience. That art form has been lost a little bit—it's rare now that the guitar really resonates with people's hearts and their emotions, when you hear something new. It's usually not guitar-based. The guitar has been pushed into the sideman kind of role—where it once originated from. But I think that the guitar still has enough potential to contribute something really meaningful toward the world of music.

ULI JON ROTH
DECEMBER 2016

other books by greg prato

MUSIC

A Devil On One Shoulder And An Angel On
  The Other: The Story Of Shannon Hoon
  And Blind Melon

Touched By Magic: The Tommy Bolin Story

Grunge Is Dead: The Oral History Of
  Seattle Rock Music

No Schlock … Just Rock! (A Journalistic
  Journey: 2003–2008)

MTV Ruled The World: The Early Years Of
  Music Video

The Eric Carr Story

Too High To Die: Meet The Meat Puppets

The Faith No More & Mr. Bungle
  Companion

Overlooked/Underappreciated: 354
  Recordings That Demand Your
  Attention

Over The Electric Grapevine: Insight Into
  Primus And The World Of Les Claypool

Punk! Hardcore! Reggae! PMA! Bad
  Brains!

Iron Maiden: '80 '81

Survival Of The Fittest: Heavy Metal In The
  1990s

Scott Weiland: Memories Of A Rock Star

German Metal Machine: Scorpions In The
  70s

The Other Side Of Rainbow

SPORTS

Sack Exchange: The Definitive Oral History
  Of The 1980s New York Jets

Dynasty: The Oral History Of The New York
  Islanders, 1972–1984

Just Out Of Reach: The 1980s New York
  Yankees

The Seventh Year Stretch: New York Mets,
  1977–1983